Becoming International

When and how did the modern world become an international one? Jens Bartelson, a leading scholar of the history of international thought, provides new answers to this question by analyzing how relations between polities have been conceptualized across different historical contexts from the sixteenth century to the present day. A global intellectual history of the international system, this book challenges the widespread assumption that this system emerged as a result of a transition from empires to states, instead proposing that the international realm is but a continuation of imperial relations by other means. Showing how the international system spread through the creative appropriation of European concepts of nation and state by non-Europeans, Bartelson argues that this system has taken on a life of its own, to the point of becoming an empire in its own right.

JENS BARTELSON is Professor of Political Science at Lund University. He is the author of *War in International Thought* (Cambridge University Press, 2017), *Visions of World Community* (Cambridge University Press, 2009), *The Critique of the State* (Cambridge University Press, 2001) and *A Genealogy of Sovereignty* (Cambridge University Press, 1995), as well as numerous articles in leading journals in international relations, international law, political theory, and sociology.

Becoming International

JENS BARTELSON
Lunds Universitet, Sweden

Shaftesbury Road, Cambridge CB2 8EA, United Kingdom

One Liberty Plaza, 20th Floor, New York, NY 10006, USA

477 Williamstown Road, Port Melbourne, VIC 3207, Australia

314–321, 3rd Floor, Plot 3, Splendor Forum, Jasola District Centre, New Delhi – 110025, India

103 Penang Road, #05–06/07, Visioncrest Commercial, Singapore 238467

Cambridge University Press is part of Cambridge University Press & Assessment, a department of the University of Cambridge.

We share the University's mission to contribute to society through the pursuit of education, learning and research at the highest international levels of excellence.

www.cambridge.org
Information on this title: www.cambridge.org/9781009400701

DOI: 10.1017/9781009400718

First published 2023

A catalogue record for this publication is available from the British Library

A Cataloging-in-Publication data record for this book is available from the Library of Congress

ISBN 978-1-009-40070-1 Hardback
ISBN 978-1-009-40074-9 Paperback

To Caspian

Contents

Preface

The modern world is international insofar as it characterized by the division of humankind into nation-states. Although there is no shortage of accounts – historical or otherwise – which have tried to understand the process through which the world became international in this sense, most of these have assumed that this took place as a result of a transition from a premodern world of empires and cities. By contrast, this book is an attempt to write an intellectual history of the very *belief* that the world we inhabit is an international one and how such beliefs were translated to facts on the ground. Inquiring into the making and spread of the *social fact* of internationality, this book tries to answer the question of how an international realm was conceptualized into existence and became taken for granted as a given frame of reference for the study of politics.

I have tried this before. In my first book, written some thirty years ago, I assumed that there was a simple and straightforward logic to the rise of the international realm. I assumed that this boiled down to the function of sovereignty, understood as a frame effectively separating what was inside the state from what was outside it, so that the modern state and the international system emerged in tandem. Since then that very frame has been crumbling into dust through encounters with sources that recognized no such separation and instead spoke of distant worlds before anything international and populated by diverse forms of political association. I then began to realize that the coming into being of the international world cannot be understood with reference to its component parts or the functions of sovereignty, but that the international is a *sui generis* category with its own trajectory and meanings, waiting to be excavated from sources many of which have been of marginal concern to historians of international thought. Above all, I began to suspect that existing accounts of the origins of the international system and its cognates were more about legitimizing that system rather than a matter of making good sense of its emergence from the multiplicity of political forms that antedated the European quest for global preponderance. So this book is another attempt to set the historical record straight and get our ontological commitments right, saving us from the belief that the international world is cast in stone at a moment when it needs to be consigned to history for the sake of human flourishing.

Many people have helped me to bring this project to completion. Thanks to generous funding from The Bank of Sweden Tercentenary Foundation for our research program "State-Making and the Origins of Global Order in the Long Nineteenth Century and Beyond," my colleagues at Lund University and I at Lund University spent six years exploring the rise of the modern state and its consequences for global order. This book is my contribution to this endeavor, and I am greatly indebted to my colleagues in Lund with whom I collaborated closely: Amanda Cheney, Agustín Goenaga, Martin Hall, Johannes Lindvall, Ted Svensson, and Jan Teorell. During these years, Astrid Hedin, Sara Kalm, Juliane Liebsch, Klas Nilsson, and Sindre Gade Viksand provided valuable feedback on individual chapters.

Although the pandemic put an effective brake on any global feedback-fishing, a short visit to London School of Economics and Political Science during a crucial phase of writing turned out to be very productive. Many thanks to Mathias-Koenig Archibugi for inviting me, and to Martin Bayly, Chris Brown, Cornelia Navari, Emma Saint, Peter Wilson, and Rachel Zhou for good company and constructive comments on my work. Similar things happened in Gothenburg, where Bo Rothstein and Ann Towns helped me to identify and resolve tensions in my argument. I am also very much indebted to my friend and colleague Mathias Albert in Bielefeld. Mathias has not only been part of endless and exciting conversations over the years but has also invited me to seminars and workshops from which I have benefited enormously. Special thanks go to Mustafa Aksakal, Barry Buzan, Christian Büger, Julian Go, George Lawson, Iver Neumann, Ole Jacob Sending, and James Stafford for engaging with my work. But as usual, the feedback-fishing tour ended at the Norwegian Institute of International Affairs, where my dear friends and colleagues Benjamin de Carvalho and Halvard Leira hosted me for a talk when the book had been completed. I am grateful to Kristin Haugevik and Stein Sundstøl Eriksen for their perceptive comments on my presentation. Also, parts of the research for this book have been made possible through support from two projects at the Norwegian Institute of International Affairs: "Empires, Privateering, and the Sea" (grant number 262657) and "A Conceptual History of International Relations" (grant number 288639).

But my greatest gratitude goes to my dear colleagues Peter Haldén, Nick Onuf, and Sindre Gade Viksand who read the entire manuscript at various stages of completion and provided incisive criticism and valuable suggestions for improvement. And finally, it goes without saying that the finished product owes its existence to the support and diligence of John Haslam at the Press.

J.B.
Lund, October 2022

1 *Making Sense of the International*

Introduction

Most students of international relations quite naturally assume that their inquiries are confined to an international domain distinct from its component parts as well as from other domains of inquiry. Although scholars have disputed the precise nature and composition of this domain, its existence has long been taken for granted to the point of being naturalized.[1] But when and how did such an international domain emerge, and how has its existence become so widely taken for granted?

This book tells a story how such an international realm has been conceptualized into existence and does so in sharp contrast to existing accounts. Although many accounts of the origin of the international realm have been proposed during the past decades, and although scholars have disagreed about *when* such a realm first emerged, they have been in broad agreement that it did so only by superseding imperial forms of rule which had previously been dominant in and out of Europe. Hence if we are to believe these accounts, the world was imperial before it became international. To start with the standard textbook example: to those who have located the origin of the international system to the Peace of Westphalia in 1648, a system of sovereign states then replaced the Holy Roman Empire as the main loci of political authority in Europe.[2] To those who

[1] Throughout this book, I will use the term "international realm" as a deliberately vague shorthand to encompass the specifications of that realm in terms of a system, society, or community.

[2] The literature is extensive. Classical statements include Hans J. Morgenthau, *Politics among Nations. The Struggle for Peace and Power* (New York: Knopf, 1948), 210; Leo Gross, "The Peace of Westphalia, 1648–1948." *American Journal of International Law* 42 no. 1 (1948): 20–41; John Herz, "Rise and Demise of the Territorial State." *World Politics* 9 no. 4 (1957): 473–493. For an analysis, see Sebastian Schmidt, "To Order the Minds of Scholars: The Discourse of the Peace of Westphalia in International Relations Literature." *International Studies Quarterly* 55 no. 3 (2011): 601–623.

have traced its emergence to the Vienna settlement of 1815, a modern international system rose out of the failed French quest for empire during the French Revolutionary Wars, its subsequent spread being the result of successful claims to independence in the Americas and elsewhere.[3] To still others, a recognizably modern international system emerged during the long nineteenth century with the rise and spread of the nation-state, culminating at the Paris Peace Conference in 1919.[4] Finally, according to those who argue that a genuinely global international system emerged only after the end of the Second World War, it did so as a consequence of the universalization of the right to self-determination and the process of decolonization that soon followed.[5]

The historical accuracy of the above narratives has been intensely contested in recent years. According to what has become a standard objection, the Peace of Westphalia did not bring an international system of sovereign states into being. Although it granted independence to the United Provinces and conferred new territorial rights to German princes, it did not produce any recognizably modern system of sovereign states, since practices of territorial demarcation and international recognition were still unknown at that point in time. Hence the Westphalian origin of modern international relations is

[3] See, for example, Francis Harry Hinsley, *Power and the Pursuit of Peace: Theory and Practice in the History of Relations between States* (Cambridge: Cambridge University Press, 1967); David Armitage and Sanjay Subrahmanyam, (eds.) *The Age of Revolutions in Global Context, c. 1760–1840* (Basingstoke: Palgrave Macmillan, 2009); David Armitage et al. "Interchange: Nationalism and Internationalism in the Era of the Civil War." *Journal of American History* 98 no. 2 (2011): 455–489.

[4] See, for example, Rodney Bruce Hall, *National Collective Identity: Social Constructs and International Systems* (New York: Columbia University Press, 1999); Christopher A. Bayly, *The Birth of the Modern World 1780–1914. Global Connections and Comparisons* (Oxford: Blackwell, 2004); Eric D. Weitz, "From the Vienna to the Paris system: International Politics and the Entangled Histories of Human Rights, Forced Deportations, and Civilizing Missions." *The American Historical Review* 113 no. 5 (2008): 1313–1343; Barry Buzan and George Lawson, *The Global Transformation. History, Modernity, and the Making of International Relations* (Cambridge: Cambridge University Press, 2015); Jürgen Osterhammel, *The Transformation of the World. A Global History of the Nineteenth Century* (Princeton: Princeton University Press, 2014).

[5] See, for example, Amitav Acharya and Barry Buzan, *The Making of Global International Relations* (Cambridge: Cambridge University Press, 2019); Jan C. Jansen and Jürgen Osterhammel, *Decolonization: A Short History* (Princeton: Princeton University Press, 2017).

but a myth, however important to disciplinary identity.[6] Against those who take Vienna 1815 as the benchmark date, it has been objected that even if the Napoleonic wars marked the end of imperial aspirations in Europe, European imperial expansion on other continents continued unabated.[7] By the same token, those who have located the emergence of a modern international system to the long nineteenth century have been met with the objection that this system did little but further entrench imperial relations between Europe and the non-European world as a result of its exclusion of colonial peoples and its unequal inclusion of peripheral polities.[8] Finally, those

[6] See, for example, Stephen D. Krasner, "Westphalia and All That." in Judith Goldstein and Robert O. Keohane (eds.) *Ideas and Foreign Policy.* (Ithaca, NY: Cornell University Press, 1993), 235–64; Andreas Osiander, "Sovereignty, International Relations, and the Westphalian myth." *International Organization* 55 no. 2 (2001): 251–287; Benno Teschke, *The Myth of 1648: Class, Geopolitics, and the Making of Modern International Relations* (London: Verso, 2003); Stéphane Beaulac, *The Power of Language in the Making of International Law: The Word Sovereignty in Bodin and Vattel and the Myth of Westphalia* (Leiden: Martinus Nijhoff, 2004); Derek Croxton, *Westphalia: The Last Christian Peace* (Houndmills, Basingstoke: Palgrave MacMillan 2013); Benjamin De Carvalho, Halvard Leira, and John M. Hobson, "The Big Bangs of IR: The Myths that Your Teachers Still Tell You About 1648 and 1919." *Millennium* 39 no. 3 (2011): 735–758; John M. Hobson, and Jason C. Sharman, "The Enduring Place of Hierarchy in World Politics: Tracing the Social Logics of Hierarchy and Political Change." *European Journal of International Relations* 11, no. 1 (2005): 63–98.

[7] See, for example, Jeremy Adelman, *Sovereignty and Revolution in the Iberian Atlantic* (Princeton: Princeton University Press, 2009); Jeremy Adelman, "An Age of Imperial Revolutions." *The American Historical Review* 113 no. 2 (2008): 319–340; Lauren Benton and Lisa Ford, *Rage for Order. The British Empire and the Origins of International Law 1800–1850* (Cambridge, MA.: Harvard University Press, 2016); Jennifer Pitts, *Boundaries of the International. Law and Empire* (Cambridge, MA.: Harvard University Press, 2018); Gabriel Paquette, *The European Seaborne Empires: From the Thirty Years War to the Age of Revolutions* (New Haven: Yale University Press, 2019).

[8] See, for example, Edward Keene, *Beyond the Anarchical Society: Grotius, colonialism and order in world politics* (Cambridge: Cambridge University Press, 2002); Erez Manela, *The Wilsonian Moment: Self-determination and the International Origins of Anticolonial Nationalism* (Oxford: Oxford University Press, 2007); Antony Anghie, *Imperialism, Sovereignty and the Making of International Law* (Cambridge: Cambridge University Press, 2007); Arnulf Becker Lorca, *Mestizo International Law. A Global Intellectual History 1842–1933* (Cambridge: Cambridge University Press, 2014); Susan Pedersen, *The Guardians: The League of Nations and the Crisis of Empire* (Oxford: Oxford University Press, 2015).

who have argued that a truly global international system had to wait until the right of self-determination had been enshrined in international law and decolonization had been completed have been met with the objection that this merely perpetuated existing inequalities between North and South, albeit now of a more informal and indirect kind than before.[9] On all of these accounts, however, becoming international presupposes a simultaneous transition from a world of empires to a world of states, leaving scholars to disagree about *when* this happened, *how* this happened, and with *what* consequences, but not *that* this has happened. Also, apart from assuming that the world of empires and the world of states can be arranged in a neat historical succession, these accounts have focused on the formation of the component parts of the international realm rather than on the emergence of that realm itself. From this point of view, the international realm emerged as a result of the rise of the sovereign state and is therefore understood to be epiphenomenal in relation to the modern state. This in turn implies that the historical validity of the above accounts depends on the ways in which the sovereign state has been conceptualized, so that the more detailed requirements that have been packed into definitions of the corresponding concept, the later an international system seems to have appeared on the scene, as well as conversely.[10]

Unsurprisingly, therefore, the above accounts of the making of an international realm have been criticized for being state-centric and for neglecting the role of non-state actors in the expansion of that realm into other continents. Since European states were initially unable to project their power far enough necessary to assert dominance over non-European polities, they outsourced imperial expansion by delegating sovereign prerogatives to a range of intermediaries. Foremost of

[9] See, for example, Quỳnh N Phạm and Robbie Shilliam, (eds.) *Meanings of Bandung: Postcolonial Orders and Decolonial Visions* (London: Rowman & Littlefield, 2016); Luis Eslava, Michael Fakhri, and Vasuki Nesiah, (eds.) *Bandung, Global History, and International Law: Critical Pasts and Pending Futures* (Cambridge: Cambridge University Press, 2017); Adom Getachew, *Worldmaking after Empire: The Rise and Fall of Self-determination* (Princeton: Princeton University Press, 2019).

[10] See Julia Costa Lopez, Benjamin De Carvalho, Andrew Latham, Ayşe Zarakol, Jens Bartelson, and Minda Holm, "In the Beginning There Was No Word (for it): Terms, concepts, and early sovereignty." *International Studies Review* 20 no. 3 (2018): 489–519.

these were trading companies and company states which would wage war on and conduct diplomacy with local rulers at the behest of their respective states, all while being allowed to profit from transcontinental trade and the exploitation of natural resources in the meantime. Hence the expansion of the international realm took place against the backdrop of cultural diversity and ongoing hybridization and did not result in any imposition of the state form on colonial polities until relatively late.[11]

The story I will tell in this book is different. First, I believe that trying to locate the historical origin of the international realm is a futile exercise that merely risks reifying that realm into an abstract thing and to perpetuate various historical myths of its origin in order to legitimize unequal relations of power within it. By contrast, this book is an inquiry into how the international realm has been *conceptualized into existence* and how such conceptualizations have taken hold of our political imagination. Pursuing this line of inquiry, I will focus on how relations between polities have been understood by different authors across a variety of cultural and historical contexts from the sixteenth century to the present day. To clear the ground for this kind of inquiry, I will critically engage what I call the *transitionist* view, according to which the emergence of an international realm is assumed to be coeval with a transition from a world of empires to a world of states, thereby rendering the international realm coextensive with the world of states while confining the world of empires to a premodern past. In contrast to this view, I will try to substantiate an *emergentist* account of the international realm by describing how it has emerged as a consequence of sustained efforts to make sense of relations between polities from the onset of European imperial expansion to the end of decolonization, arguing that the international realm is better understood as a continuation of the imperial world by

11 See, for example, Andrew Phillips and Jason C. Sharman. *International Order in Diversity: War, Trade and Rule in the Indian Ocean* (Cambridge: Cambridge University Press, 2015); Jason C. Sharman, *Empires of the Weak: The Real Story of European Expansion and the Creation of the New World Order* (Princeton: Princeton University Press, 2019); Kevin Blachford, "Revisiting the Expansion Thesis: International Society and the Role of the Dutch East India Company as a Merchant Empire." *European Journal of International Relations* 26 no. 4 (2020): 1230–1248; Jason C. Sharman and Andrew Phillips, *Outsourcing Empire: How Company-States Made the Modern World* (Princeton: Princeton University Press, 2020).

other means rather than as its historical successor.[12] As I will argue, the emergence of an international realm should be understood as a response to the global space opened up by the cartographical and geographical revolutions of the fifteenth and sixteenth centuries, which generated rival claims to universal sovereignty over that space.[13] As Peter Sloterdijk has remarked, "[t]he globe not only became the central medium of the new homogenizing approach to location ... in addition, through constant amendments to the maps, it documented the constant offensive of discoveries, conquests, openings and namings with which the advancing Europeans established themselves at sea and on land in the universal outside."[14] Third, and following from this global perspective, I will critically engage the *diffusionist* view according to which the international realm emerged and spread as a consequence of the imposition of European concepts such as sovereignty and nationhood on other peoples, eventually resulting in their inclusion into an international society of formally equal nation-states. As Hedley Bull and Adam Watson once formulated this view, "[t]he global international society of today is in large part the consequence of Europe's impact on the rest of the world over the last few centuries."[15] By contrast, I will emphasize the extent to which non-European peoples were actively involved in the shaping of the international realm by creatively appropriating European concepts and employing these for their own distinctive ideological and political ends.[16] Fourth, and in contrast to the often statist bias of conventional accounts of the international realm discussed above, I will show how the creation of

12 For the notion of interpolity relations, see Lauren Benton, "Possessing Empire. Iberian Claims and Interpolity Law." in Saliha Belmessous (ed.), *Native Claims. Indigenous Law against Empire, 1500–1920* (Oxford: Oxford University Press, 2011), 19–40; Lauren Benton and Adam Clulow, "Empire and Protection: Making Interpolity Law in the Early Modern World." *Journal of Global History* 12 no. 1 (2017): 74–92.

13 For the idea that a global realm antedated and conditioned the rise of an international realm, see Jens Bartelson, "The Social Construction of Globality." *International Political Sociology* 4 no. 3 (2010): 219–235.

14 Peter Sloterdijk, *Globes: Spheres II*. Trans. by Wieland Hoban (Cambridge, M.A.: MIT Press 2014), 785.

15 Hedley Bull and Adam Watson, "Introduction." in Hedley Bull and Adam Watson (eds), *The Expansion of International Society* (Oxford: Clarendon Press, 1984), 1–9, at 1.

16 See, for example, Marcos Tourinho, "The Co-Constitution of Order." *International Organization* 75 no. 2 (2021): 258–281.

an international realm has meant that this realm has taken on a life of its own, independent of its constituent parts sometimes even to the point of being viewed as constitutive of them.

There are compelling reasons for undertaking this kind of inquiry. First, with the purported starting point of the modern international system migrating ever closer to the present day, scholars of international relations have questioned the coherence and integrity of their entire enterprise and embarked on a search for more historically accurate ways to define their subject matter. Given the obvious difficulty of locating a clean break between imperial forms of rule on the one hand, and an international system of formally equal states on the other, an increasing number of scholars have argued that world politics is better understood in hierarchical rather than in squarely anarchical terms, all while suggesting that these forms of rule have coexisted and reinforced each other throughout early modern and modern history.[17] This renewed focus on hierarchy in world politics has been further reinforced by an increased interest in empire and imperialism among scholars of international relations and historians of political thought. Much of this scholarship suggests that empires and states have never been mutually exclusive forms of political association but has instead emphasized the extent to which empires and states have been co-constitutive and interdependent during the early modern and modern periods. For all their differences, many of these accounts converge on

[17] See, for example, David A. Lake, *Hierarchy in International Relations* (Ithaca: Cornell University Press, 2011); John M. Hobson, "The Twin Self-delusions of IR: Why 'hierarchy' and not 'anarchy' is the core concept of IR." *Millennium* 42 no. 3 (2014): 557–575; Janice Bially Mattern and Ayşe Zarakol, "Hierarchies in World Politics." *International Organization* 70 no. 3 (2016): 623–654; Ayşe Zarakol, (ed.) *Hierarchies in World Politics* (Cambridge: Cambridge University Press, 2017); Meghan McConaughey, Paul Musgrave, and Daniel H. Nexon. "Beyond Anarchy: Logics of political organization, hierarchy, and international structure." *International Theory* 10 no. 2 (2018): 181–218; Daniel H. Nexon and Iver B. Neumann, "Hegemonic-order theory: A field-theoretic account." *European Journal of International Relations* 24 no. 3 (2018): 662–686; Paul K. MacDonald, "Embedded Authority: a relational network approach to hierarchy in world politics." *Review of International Studies* 44 no.1 (2018): 128–150; Dani K. Nedal and Daniel H. Nexon, "Anarchy and Authority: International Structure, the Balance of Power, and Hierarchy." *Journal of Global Security Studies* 4 no. 2 (2019): 169–189; Lora Anne Viola, *The Closure of the International System: How Institutions Create Political Equalities and Hierarchies* (Cambridge: Cambridge University Press, 2020).

the assumption that the rise of an international system in Europe was premised on its hierarchical and imperial relations with the rest of the world.[18] Although these accounts have added much nuance and complexity to the understanding how hierarchical and anarchical features of world politics hang together, the implications for our understanding of the emergence of an international realm remain to be investigated. Second, an inquiry into how the international realm has been conceptualized will highlight the contingency of that realm, by showing how the political world might have looked radically different had other roads been taken at critical junctures. Although recent scholarship has broadened the scope of international relations to include polities and world orders outside Europe and prior to the rise of the West, these accounts have found it difficult to explain why the nation-state eventually was able to triumph over its competitors hence making the world international in this narrow sense.[19] While the emergence of an international realm has meant that many alternative forms of political association – real or imagined – fell by the wayside as the nation-state triumphed, there is nothing inevitable about this outcome. Third, and closely related to this point, an intellectual history of the international realm can help us understand the extent to which nationalism has

[18] See, for example, Tarak Barkawi and Mark Laffey, "Retrieving the Imperial: Empire and International relations." *Millennium* 31 no. 1 (2002): 109–127; Duncan Bell, (ed.) *Victorian Visions of Global Order: Empire and International Relations in Nineteenth-century Political Thought* (Cambridge: Cambridge University Press, 2007); Duncan Bell, *The Idea of Greater Britain: Empire and the Future of World Order, 1860–1900* (Princeton: Princeton University Press, 2009); Lauren Benton, *A Search for Sovereignty: Law and Geography in European Empires, 1400–1900* (Cambridge: Cambridge University Press, 2009); Julian Go, *Patterns of Empire: The British and American Empires, 1688 to the Present* (Cambridge: Cambridge University Press, 2011); John M. Hobson, *The Eurocentric Conception of World Politics* (Cambridge: Cambridge University Press, 2012); Andrew Fitzmaurice, *Sovereignty, Property and Empire, 1500–2000* (Cambridge: Cambridge University Press, 2014); Tarak Barkawi, *Soldiers of Empire* (Cambridge: Cambridge University Press, 2017); Lauren Benton, Adam Clulow, and Bain Attwood, (eds.) *Protection and Empire* (Cambridge: Cambridge University Press, 2018).

[19] Hendrik Spruyt, *The World Imagined: Collective Beliefs and Political Order in the Sinocentric, Islamic and Southeast Asian International Societies* (Cambridge: Cambridge University Press, 2020); Ayşe Zarakol, *Before the West: The Rise and Fall of Eastern World Orders* (Cambridge: Cambridge University Press, 2022).

been crucial to its rise and spread, and hence why nationalism is ready to be reactivated whenever the cohesion of the international realm or its component parts is challenged by inner or outer forces.[20] Finally, a related reason for embarking on this inquiry is to dissolve some of the normative problems that follow naturally when we uncritically accept transitionist accounts of the international realm. When we do this, we will face a false choice between the authoritarianism of empire and the democracy of the nation-state, since the latter presupposes the existence of a bounded and homogenous *demos*, characteristics that most conceptualizations of the former rule out almost by definition. This has given rise to the belief that supranational political authority necessarily must compromise democratic legitimacy and issue in a democratic deficit if left unchecked by constitutional rules or other arrangements.[21] But if there never was any clean break between empires and states other than in the nationalist imaginaries of the twentieth century, then we have no reason to assume that popular sovereignty necessarily must be thus confined but all the more reasons to explore old and new possibilities of widening its scope in a more cosmopolitan or planetary direction.[22]

As the title of this book indicates, this is not another attempt to locate the origin of notion of an international realm to a specific point

[20] See, for example, Jaakko Heiskanen, "Spectra of Sovereignty: Nationalism and International Relations." *International Political Sociology* 13 no. 3 (2019): 315–332; Moran Mandelbaum, *The Nation/State Fantasy. A Psychoanalytical Genealogy of Nationalism* (Houndsmills: Palgrave MacMillan, 2020); Siniša Malešević, *Grounded Nationalisms: A Sociological Analysis* (Cambridge: Cambridge University Press, 2019).

[21] See, for example, Jean L. Cohen, *Globalization and Sovereignty: Rethinking legality, legitimacy, and constitutionalism* (Cambridge: Cambridge University Press, 2012); James Tully, "Modern Constitutional Democracy and Imperialism." *Osgoode Hall Law Journal* 46, no. 3 (2008): 461–493; James Tully, "The Unfreedom of the Moderns in Comparison to their ideals of Constitutional Democracy." *The Modern Law Review* 65, no. 2 (2002): 204–228.

[22] For a survey of such possibilities prior to the nineteenth century, see Jens Bartelson, *Visions of World Community* (Cambridge: Cambridge University Press, 2009). For recent attempts in this direction, see Inés Valdez, *Transnational Cosmopolitanism: Kant, Du Bois, and Justice as a Political Craft* (Cambridge: Cambridge University Press, 2019); Paulina Ochoa Espejo, *On Borders: Territories, legitimacy, and the rights of place* (Oxford: Oxford University Press, 2020); Achille Mbembe, *Out of the Dark Night. Essays on Decolonization* (New York: Columbia University Press, 2021).

in time, but rather an inquiry into the process of *becoming international.* Here I am indebted to Nietzsche, when he held that while "Heraclitus will always be in the right for saying that being is an empty fiction", most other philosophers "kill and stuff whatever they worship, these gentlemen who idolize concepts – they endanger the life of whatever they worship ... Whatever is does not *become*; whatever becomes *is* not."[23] From this point of view, any attempt to locate the origin of the international realm by attributing the origin of its structure or meaning to a specific point in time and place is but a way of turning the international into a conceptual mummy, a stale artifice devoid of dynamism. By contrast, as Michel Foucault once remarked, "[t]he genealogist needs history to dispel the chimeras of the origin."[24] Instead of trying to locate the origins of things, Foucault proposes that we should focus on the conditions of their emergence, recognizing the fact that "[t]he isolation of different points of emergence does not conform to the successive configurations of an identical meaning; rather, they result from substitutions, displacements, disguised conquests, and systematic reversals."[25] Given my present concerns, I would like to suggest that the international realm is best understood as the cumulated consequences of attempts to make sense of intercourse among different polities by attributing temporality to these processes and structure to their outcomes at different points in time. From this point of view, the story of how the world became international is a story of how the social fact of *internationality* emerged and spread independently of its champions and detractors. Some people breathed life into the international realm because they believed that they stood to benefit from its coming into being. Others were sucked into the same realm despite, and sometimes because of, their resistance and protestations around their pending losses. Yet no one was able to tell how this vortex would affect their own destinies or that of the wider world in which the international realm was embedded. Yet once this process had gained sufficient momentum, becoming international was not an offer you could refuse, but a predicament you were likely to sleepwalk

23 Friedrich Nietzsche, "Reason." in Philosophy 1–2, in *Twilight of the Idols*, trans. by Richard Polt (Indianapolis: Hackett, 1997), 18–19.

24 Michel Foucault, "Nietzsche, Genealogy, History." in David Bouchard (ed.), *Language, Counter-Memory, Practice: Selected Essays and Interviews* (Ithaca, NY: Cornell University Press), 139–164, at 144.

25 Ibid., 151.

into in search of other desirables such as power, liberty, and equality. As such, this process was akin to what happens when spiritually inexperienced people play around with a Ouija board late at night: what they received was quite different from that for which they had bargained.

In this case it was an empire of states. As I will suggest, the habit of distinguishing between empires and states and placing them in historical succession has occluded the extent to which the modern international system itself displays characteristics of empire. Much like Roman and medieval conceptions of empire, the modern international system aspires to be *universal* insofar as it covers all the known world and is thus also *boundless* insofar as it recognizes no spatial limits or outside. Also, by virtue of dividing humankind into distinct polities, the modern international system comes with a commitment to *multiculturalism* and toleration characteristic of premodern conceptions of empire. But the modern international system seems to lack one essential characteristic of empire. Defined by the absence of centralized authority, there is no *emperor* there to rule the international system, only a multitude of states competing for security, power, and wealth. Yet arguably, the collective conviction that the international system is anarchic in character fulfills the same function of ruling humankind by keeping it divided in a state of war as well as any imaginable emperor of all the world would have been able to do. As I will suggest in Chapter 5, this makes it possible to interpret the final globalization of the international system not as the end of empire but rather as the fulfilment of ancient visions of empire.

The term "international" is used either in a generic sense to connote relations between distinct polities across time and space, or in a narrow sense to describe relations between *nation-states*. Although this book is intended as a genealogy of the international realm in the second sense, it starts from the assumption that a recognizably modern international realm was conceptualized to make sense of the practices of conquest and commerce brought about by the European expansion on other continents during the early modern period. As such, this book is self-consciously Eurocentric insofar as it argues that the Eurocentrism of international relations is *itself* European in origin. So when Jeremy Bentham famously coined the term "international" in 1780, this was not only to make sense of legal relations among European states, but part of an Enlightenment effort to expand the scope of legal categories to cover the fallout of intensified expansion and imperial rivalries in

Asia and the Atlantic world, as "it was calculated to express, in some significant way, the branch of law which goes commonly under the name of the *law of nations*."[26] Consequently, this book argues that the international realm was conceptualized to make sense of the causes and consequences of imperial rivalry during the early modern period before it was narrowed down to describe a multitude of territorially bounded sovereign states during the nineteenth and twentieth centuries.

Making sense of this process requires attention to changing meaning of the concepts of empire and state. Before political scientists and sociologists began to distinguish between empires and states during the twentieth century, such a distinction was mostly in the eyes of the beholder. During the early modern period, no categorical distinction was made between empires and states in legal and political thought, and whenever a distinction was being drawn, this was in order to legitimize or delegitimize particular instances of political rule in concrete contexts, and when some authors later started to conceive of an international realm in *sui generis* terms, this did not rule out that its parts could equally well be described as empires or states depending on the political context at hand. The modern categorical distinction between empires and states seems to have emerged only with the globalization of the international system in the twentieth century, and then in order to conceal the extent to which this system both depended on and perpetuated imperial forms of rule to the point of becoming an empire in its own right.

This book investigates the emergence of the international realm from the perspective of global intellectual history, a perspective from which "the global scale of the enterprise is established by the intention of the investigator and the terms of the investigation."[27] Yet by also being genealogical in outlook, the story to follow does not aim

[26] Jeremy Bentham, *An Introduction to the Principles of Morals and Legislation* (Oxford: Clarendon Press, 1907), 326n; Hidemi Suganami, "A Note on the Origin of the Word 'International'." *Review of International Studies* 4, no. 3 (1978): 226–232; David Armitage, "Globalizing Jeremy Bentham." *History of Political Thought* 32 no. 1 (2011): 63–82; Rochona Majumdar, "Postcolonial History." in Marek Tamm and Peter Burke (eds.), *Debating New Approaches to History* (London: Bloomsbury, 2019), 49–64, esp. 63.

[27] Samuel Moyn and Andrew Sartori, "Approaches to Global Intellectual History." in Samuel Moyn and Andrew Sartori, (eds.) *Global Intellectual History* (New York: Columbia University Press, 2013), 3–30, at 7; John Dunn, "Why We Need a Global History of Political Thought." in Béla Kapossy, (ed.) *Markets, Morals, Politics: Jealousy of Trade and the History of Political Thought* (Cambridge, M.A.: Harvard University Press, 2018), 285–309.

to provide an exhaustive account of the process through which the world became international. Instead, it aims to be a history of the present insofar as it directs attention to formative episodes in order to revise received accounts of these. By telling the story of how a wide range of authors – philosophers, lawyers, historians, publicists, diplomats, and statesmen – from across a variety of cultural and historical contexts have conceptualized relations between different polities, I will show how the international realm was assembled out of an array of disparate parts, and how the resulting worldview then was gradually naturalized to the point of excluding alternative accounts of world politics. This ambition to write a global genealogy of the international realm gives rise to some methodological challenges but also creates some opportunities for innovation. A first challenge stems from the absence of a pre-constituted object of inquiry characteristic of genealogical history. As Erez Manela has shown, even if the study of international society has become a hot topic in recent years, the *idea* of an international sphere has received relatively scant attention.[28] While making direct inferences about the existence of an international realm on the basis on occurrences of the corresponding term in the literature will confine the inquiry to the period after its coinage by Bentham, presupposing that anything international was present before that point will lead to anachronism. In this book, I handle this dilemma by focusing on the process of *becoming* international rather than on its outcomes. The inferences I make about this process are to a large extent indirect and based on how authors have conceptualized political authority and community in ways that imply the existence of something international. A second challenge concerns the difficulties of making inferences across different cultural and historical contexts. Just because authors separated by centuries and oceans conceptualize political authority in ways that permit us to make inferences about the presence of something international does not necessarily imply that these authors were invoking or appealing to the international in the same sense. In response to this problem, I have focused on how notions of authority, legitimacy and recognition have traveled across oceans and centuries and have taken on new meanings as

[28] Erez Manela, "International Society as a Historical Subject." *Diplomatic History* 44 no. 2 (2020): 184–209, referring to David Armitage, *Foundations of Modern International Thought* (Cambridge: Cambridge University Press, 2013).

a consequence of being reappropriated for different ideological and political purposes, all while assuming that conceptualizing an international realm as distinct from yet subsuming individual polities was made possible by the dissemination and uptake of these concepts.[29] Hence a third challenge has been to make sense of the contestations of meaning that have followed the appropriation and application of these concepts in concrete contexts. Here I will assume that these contestations follow the fault lines of underlying political conflicts over the proper locus and scope of political authority in which these concepts have been weaponized by stakeholders.[30] As Jeremy Adelman has pointed out, "[c]onceptions of sovereignty might be seen not as explanations of how old orders fell and new orders emerged, but as the consequences of struggles to sort out rival ideas and meanings."[31] Taken together, the above considerations imply that the making of an international realm is as a process of worldmaking through which actors have engaged in its construction by using a series of interrelated concepts that presuppose or imply its existence.[32]

In the next section, I will discuss some recent attempts account for the emergence of the international realm that have escaped the limitations of transitionism and diffusionism, arguing that whatever their merits, they leave crucial questions about the role of sovereignty, legitimacy, and recognition in this process unresolved. I end this chapter by outlining a plan for the rest of the book.

Becoming International

The idea that the modern international realm emerged in tandem with the modern state is not without historical support. There is no shortage

[29] See Christopher L. Hill, "Conceptual Universalization in the Transnational Nineteenth Century." in Samuel Moyn and Andrew Sartori, (eds.) *Global Intellectual History* (New York: Columbia University Press, 2013), 134–158; Richard Whatmore and Knud Haakonssen, "Global Possibilities in Intellectual History: A Note on Practice." *Global Intellectual History* 2 no. 1 (2017): 18–29.

[30] See Lauren Benton, "Beyond Anachronism: Histories of International Law and Global Legal Politics." *Journal of the History of International Law* 21 no. 1 (2019): 7–40.

[31] Jeremy Adelman, "Empires, Nations, and Revolutions." *Journal of the History of Ideas* 79 no. 1 (2018): 73–88, at 76.

[32] Compare Duncan Bell, "Making and Taking Worlds." in Samuel Moyn and Andrew Sartori, (eds.) *Global Intellectual History* (New York: Columbia University Press, 2013), 254–279.

of accounts that assume that empires and states can be ordered in historical succession, and that the international realm is the exclusive domain of the latter. Sometimes this is reflected in their periodization of the subject matter itself. For example, although some historians of political thought have focused on how Roman ideas of *imperium* were revived to justify of imperial rule during the early phases of European overseas expansion, they have had little to say about the meaning and usages of the concept of empire during the nineteenth and twentieth centuries.[33] Although more recent scholarship has focused on nineteenth century imperialism and its relationship to liberalism, the changing meaning of empire and its relationship to the state seem to have largely escaped attention.[34] Hence there has been a tendency among historians of legal and political thought to use the concept of empire in a generic sense to subsume very different kinds of polity with the only qualification that they must be somehow distinct from nation-states by virtue of their decentralized authority structures and multicultural composition. This tendency has been reinforced by some accounts of the concept of the state and its history, which by having had little to say about its relationship to conceptions of empire have come close to taking the triumph of the modern state for granted.[35]

[33] See, for example, Anthony Pagden, *Lords of All the World. Ideologies of Empire in Spain, Britain and France c.1500–c.1800* (New Haven: Yale University Press, 1995); Frances A. Yates, *Astraea: The Imperial Theme in the Sixteen Century* (London: Routledge & Kegan Paul, 1975): Anthony Pagden, *Burdens of Empire. 1539 to the present* (Cambridge: Cambridge University Press, 2015).

[34] See, for example, Uday Singh Mehta, *Liberalism and Empire. A Study in Nineteenth-Century British Liberal Thought* (Chicago: University of Chicago Press, 1999); David Armitage, *The Ideological Origins of the British Empire* (Cambridge: Cambridge University Press, 2001); Jennifer Pitts, *A Turn to Empire: The Rise of Imperial Liberalism in Britain and France* (Princeton: Princeton University Press, 2005); Jeanne Morefield, *Covenants without Swords: Liberal Idealism and the Spirit of Empire* (Princeton: Princeton University Press, 2005); Duncan Bell (ed.), *Victorian Visions of Global Order. Empire and International Relations in Nineteenth-Century Political Thought* (Cambridge: Cambridge University Press, 2007).

[35] See, for example, Quentin Skinner, *Foundations of Modern Political Thought, Vol II: The Reformation* (Cambridge: Cambridge University Press, 1978), 349; Quentin Skinner, "The Sovereign State: A Genealogy." in Hent Kalmo and Quentin Skinner (eds.) *Sovereignty in Fragments. The Past, Present, and Future of a Contested Concept* (Cambridge: Cambridge University Press, 2010), 26–46; James J. Sheehan, "The Problem of Sovereignty in European History." *The American Historical Review* 111 no.1 (2006): 1–15.

But as I would like to suggest, the idea that empires and states are categorically distinct forms of political rule is of a rather recent vintage, and so is its offspring, the doctrine I have labeled transitionism. Most modern definitions of the term "empire" assume that empires and nation states not only are categorically distinct forms of rule but that they can be ordered in historical sequence. This leaves theorists of empire with the difficulty of characterizing empires both as a variation of the state form *and* its historical negation. Either way empires are characterized less in *sui generis* terms, but more often in terms of their difference from the state. As Michael Doyle had it in his classical work, "[e]mpire, then, is a relationship, formal or informal, in which one state controls the effective political sovereignty of another political society. It can be achieved by force, by political collaboration, by economic, social, or cultural dependence."[36] As a consequence of this ambiguous view of what sovereignty is, "empires seem to combine aspects of both domestic and international politics ... with the domestic order, societies in an empire share the characteristic of individuals effectively subject to a single sovereign ... with the international order, societies in an empire share the characteristic of a less-than-full integration of social interaction and cultural values."[37] When understood in transhistorical terms, empires thus straddle the divide between the pre-modern and the modern worlds, since they "stand between what may be called the 'traditional' and the 'modern' political systems and regimes."[38] Hence empires are hard to make sense of without contrasting them with what supposedly appeared on the scene *after* their demise. Thus, there is a broad agreement that empires are distinct from territorially bounded states, and especially so from the modern nation-state. In a more recent version of this argument, we learn that "empires are large political units, expansionist or with a memory of power extended over space, polities that maintain distinction and hierarchy as they incorporate new people. The nation-state, by contrast, is based on the idea of a single people in a single territory constituting itself as a unique political community."[39] But as

[36] Michael Doyle, *Empires* (Ithaca: Cornell University Press, 1986), 45.
[37] Doyle, *Empires*, 35–6.
[38] Shmul N. Eisenstadt, *The Political Systems of Empires* (New York, the Free Press, 1963), 4.
[39] Jane Burbank and Frederick Cooper, *Empires in World History: Power and the politics of difference* (Princeton: Princeton University Press, 2010), 8.

Jennifer Pitts has remarked on this tendency to conceive of empires and states in historical succession, "if empires have often been analyzed in terms set by the nation-state, they have also too often been cast into a teleological history in which the imperial form precedes that of the nation state and grows increasingly atavistic with the triumph of the nation state-model."[40] Hence, for all their merits, the above accounts presuppose that the emergence of the modern international system occurred in tandem with a transition from empires to states. But if the distinction between empires and states does not really map onto the historical realities it is supposed to capture, this indicates that the meaning of these concepts should be contextualized and historicized to better understand what was at stake in making of the international realm.

Recent scholarship has done much to complicate the distinction between empires and states. For example, while it has been common to associate the emergence of the modern international system with the rise of territorially bounded states, Lauren Benton has shown that it was not until relatively late that sovereign authority became territorially bounded in Europe, and that it remained unbounded in the context of colonial empires for a long time thereafter. As she has argued, while international lawyers were busy articulating notions of territorial sovereignty, they were also "forced to recognize that imperial sovereignties preserved and created highly variegated legal geographies."[41] By the same token, as Jeremy Adelman has argued, "sovereignty did not have only one layer to it, radiating outward to territorial boundaries with concentric circles of authority; it had many layers, which rearranged according to shifting structures and circumstances."[42] If this is the case, people frequently tried to turn the polity in which they lived into something else – to claim autonomy from an overbearing emperor in the name of a people or to extend one people's power over others to make an empire, we should not

[40] Jennifer Pitts, "Political Theory of Empire and Imperialism." *Annual Review of Political Science* 13 (2010): 211–235, at 225.

[41] See, for example, Lauren Benton, *A Search for Sovereignty: Law and Geography in European Empires, 1400–1900* (Cambridge: Cambridge University Press, 2009), 36; Lauren Benton, *Law and Colonial Cultures: Legal Regimes in World History, 1400–1900* (Cambridge: Cambridge University Press, 2002).

[42] Jeremy Adelman, "An Age of Imperial Revolutions." *The American Historical Review* 113 no. 2 (2008): 319–340, at 330.

put "things into neatly defined boxes" but instead "look at ranges of political possibilities and tensions and conflicts among them."[43] Still others have pointed out that empires and nation-states never were mutually exclusive but rather overlapping forms of political association.[44] As Krishan Kumar has summarized the main upshot of this view, "empires have been part of the modern world as much as, and arguably more than, nation states. An 'age of nation-states' did not succeed an 'age of empire'; nationalism did not succeed imperialism. Nationalism was certainly the new thing, and nineteenth century imperialism showed the impress of the new thinking and the new forces."[45] As other scholars have pointed out, notions of nationhood remained entangled with those of empire with little or no contradiction between them being felt among the advocates and critics of empire alike.[46] Indeed, a closer look at the modern history of empires makes it possible to argue that the relationship between empires and states never was a matter of mere coexistence or succession. Instead, by the late eighteenth century, received understandings of empire were blended with the new languages of conquest, colonization, and commerce, which ushered in re-conceptualizations of empire and new practices of imperial governance.[47] By the same token, a series of recent studies have maintained that the difference between states and empires either is non-existent or overstated, and instead investigated

[43] Burbank and Cooper, *Empires in World History*, 8.

[44] See, for example, John Breuilly, "Modern Empires and Nation-States." *Thesis Eleven* 139 no. 1 (2017): 11–29; John A. Hall, "Taking Megalomanias Seriously: Rough Notes." *Thesis Eleven* 139 no. 1 (2017): 30–45.

[45] Krishan Kumar, *Visions of Empire. How Five Imperial Regimes Shaped the World* (Princeton: Princeton University Press, 2017), 35. Also Krishan Kumar, *Empires. A Historical and Political Sociology* (Oxford: Polity Press, 2021).

[46] See, for example, Pratap Bhanu Metha, "Liberalism, Nation, and Empire." in Sankar Muthu (ed.) *Empire in Modern Political Thought* (Cambridge: Cambridge University Press, 2012), 232–260; Uday Singh Metha, "Edmund Burke on Empire, Self-Understanding, and Sympathy." in Sankar Muthu (ed.) *Empire in Modern Political Thought* (Cambridge: Cambridge University Press, 2012), 155–183.

[47] See, for example, Sankar Muthu, "Introduction." in Sankar Muthu (ed.), *Empire in Modern Political Thought* (Cambridge: Cambridge University Press, 2012), 1–6; J. G. A. Pocock, *Barbarism and Religion: Volume 4, Barbarians, Savages and Empires* (Cambridge: Cambridge University Press, 2005), 229ff; Richard Koebner, *Empire* (Cambridge: Cambridge University Press, 1966), chs. 3–4.

the myriad of different ways in which claims to sovereignty and empire have been negotiated and reconciled in political and legal practice from the early modern period onwards.[48]

But to the extent that we are prepared to accept the above accounts, we ought to abandon or at least revise transitionist accounts of the international system within academic international relations, and instead focus on how the very idea of a distinct international sphere did emerge and spread in the first place. As David Armitage has argued, "the receptivity of large parts of the world to 'the contagion of sovereignty' which almost universally affected it still demands explanation, especially by attending to the determinants of its reception and domestication. Only then can we fully understand the energetic co-production of the national and the international around the globe in the nineteenth and twentieth centuries."[49] Some of these concerns are indeed reflected in recent attempts to explain how the modern international system was globalized. Legal historians who have studied the role of international recognition have emphasized how colonial and peripheral polities were compelled to conform to European standards of sovereignty and civilization in order to become recognizably as states, and how those which were eventually admitted into international society often were so on unequal terms and found themselves in positions of lasting inferiority.[50] Other historians have highlighted the extent to which violent contestations of sovereignty through revolutions and civil wars in the Americas paved the way for declarations

[48] See Dominic Lieven, "Dilemmas of Empire 1850–1918. Power, Territory, Identity." *Journal of Contemporary History* 34, no. 2 (1999): 163–200; Ken MacMillan, *Sovereignty and Possession in the English New World: The legal Foundations of Empire, 1576–1640* (Cambridge: Cambridge University Press, 2006); Krishan Kumar, "Nation-States as Empires, Empires as Nation-States: Two Principles, One Practice?." *Theory and Society* 39, no. 2 (2010): 119–143; Benton, *A Search for Sovereignty*; Saliha Belmessous (ed.), *Native Claims. Indigenous Law against Empire, 1500–1920* (Oxford: Oxford University Press, 2011); Saliha Belmessous (ed.), *Empire by Treaty: Negotiating European Expansion, 1600–1900* (Oxford: Oxford University Press, 2014).

[49] Armitage, *Foundations of Modern International Thought*, 28.

[50] Martti Koskenniemi, *The Gentle Civilizer of Nations: The Rise and Fall of International Law 1870–1960* (Cambridge: Cambridge University Press, 2001); Antony Anghie, *Imperialism, Sovereignty and the Making of International Law* (Cambridge: Cambridge University Press, 2007), 32–114; Ayşe Zarakol, *After Defeat. How the East Learned to Live with the West* (Cambridge: Cambridge University Press, 2010).

of independence during the late eighteenth and early nineteenth centuries.[51] Still others have described how intensified territorial competition among European empires towards the end of the nineteenth century generated widespread contestations of their sovereignty claims by anticolonial nationalists, some of which eventually issued in pleas for self-determination.[52]

Yet these explanations assume that the conceptual resources necessary for raising and staking claims to sovereignty were available across contexts characterized by imperial relations among those involved. They assume that the contagion of sovereignty somehow already had happened. For example, declarations of independence are meaningful and likely to be met with success only against the backdrop of shared norms of sovereignty, and such norms are meaningful only to the extent that actors already share the belief that political authority and territory ought to be congruent. Similarly, pleas for self-determination are meaningful only against the backdrop of shared notions of nationhood, and notions of nationhood are meaningful only to the extent that those involved also share a conviction that political authority and community ought to coincide within the same territory. Yet the explanations discussed above tell us little about how these assumptions necessary to contest imperial authority and raise claims to independence and self-determination became available to actors who were immersed in worlds defined by dense and long-standing imperial relations, and how these actors appropriated new conceptual resources for their own political ends. That most colonial and peripheral polities ended up as nation-states appear especially enigmatic considering that it took until the very end of the nineteenth century until the concept of the nation-state had found its way it into political science of the time, and then still with plenty of red flags attached.[53] Hence it is necessary to reconstruct the discursive

[51] See, for example, Bayly, *The Birth of the Modern World 1780–1914*, 140ff; Adelman, *Sovereignty and Revolution in the Iberian Atlantic*, 175–219.

[52] Bayly, *Birth of the Modern World*, 199–243; David Armitage and Sanjay Subrahmanyam, (eds.) *The Age of Revolutions in Global Context, c. 1760–1840* (Basingstoke: Palgrave Macmillan, 2009); David Armitage et al. "Interchange: Nationalism and Internationalism in the Era of the Civil War." *Journal of American History* 98 no. 2 (2011): 455–489.

[53] *OED*. For the first use of the term "nation-state" in English, see Charles Malcom Platt, "A Triad of Political Conceptions: State, Sovereign, Government." *Political Science Quarterly* 10 no. 2 (1895): 292–323.

antecedents through which the international realm became possible to conceptualize, rather than assuming that the necessary conceptual resources already were available to the interlocutors.

Outline of the Book

In the next chapter, I will describe how Roman and medieval of notions of *imperium* were re-appropriated during the sixteenth and seventeenth centuries to describe the sovereignty claims of nascent states as well as to legitimize their territorial aggrandizement in Europe and beyond. Since early modern conceptions of sovereignty came with few restrictions on the scope of rule in terms of peoples or places that could be legitimately subjected to its authority, early modern authors made no categorical distinction between empires and states. But even if these authors had no clear conception of a distinctive international realm, they nevertheless developed a rich vocabulary for describing relations between different polities in and out of Europe. Many of those who resisted imperial aggrandizement during this period maintained that the quest for universal sovereignty violated the natural liberty of both individuals and states and proposed that upholding the balance of power between European empires *cum* states was crucial to the preservation of natural liberty. From this Enlightenment historians and lawyers concluded that European powers constituted a system of sovereign and formally equal states held together by public law and balance of power in equal measures, relegating the quest for empire to the non-European world which from this point becomes a constitutive outside of the international realm.

Chapter 3 analyzes the many attempts to reconcile notions of empire with proliferating claims to independence during the Age of Revolutions, arguing that such claims and their relative success were precarious and contingent on the ideological context at hand, and rarely if ever translated into a demise of empires or imperial forms of rule. Claims to independence during this period are best understood in the context of emergent norms of international legal recognition, and against the backdrop of the competing visions of empire that animated global great power rivalries in the aftermath of the Napoleonic Wars. When seen from this perspective, the rise of independent states in the Americas looks less like a successful revolt against empire and an expansion of international society into a new continent and more like a continuation of empire with indirect means in a world defined by the interconnectedness of nominally sovereign states.

Chapter 4 deals with the rise of nationalism and pleas for self-determination during the latter half of the nineteenth century and describes some attempts to reconcile these with notions of empire and imperial rule. When the principle of nationality became constitutive of statehood towards the end of that century, this principle was used to justify wars of unification in Europe. But this principle also provided a new and potent justification of colonial rule at a moment when earlier standards of sovereignty and civilization were increasingly contested. Whereas European peoples were deemed ripe for self-government by virtue of constituting homogenous nations, non-European peoples were considered unfit for self-government on the grounds that they lacked the defining characteristics of nationhood and should therefore remain under European tutelage. Yet the idea of nationality was soon appropriated by anticolonial nationalists to debunk empire and imperial rule and to support claims to self-determination of non-European peoples. Although most of those claims were initially unsuccessful, the spread of anticolonial nationalism and the contestations of standards of legitimacy and recognition that ensued made membership of the international system the obvious escape route from imperial domination.

Chapter 5 describes how anti-imperialists of various stripes successfully raised clams to self-determination during the second half of the twentieth century, and how this issued in the final globalization of the international system and the universalization of the nation-state as the only *prima facie* legitimate form of rule to the exclusion of other forms of political association. Even if this spelled the end of formal imperial relations between the West and the rest of the world, critics were quick to point out how informal hierarchical relations were reproduced and further entrenched under conditions of sovereign equality. By amalgamating these seemingly incompatible forms of political association while marginalizing alternative forms in the process, a global international system was naturalized into brute fact of modern political life, with myths of origin invented in its support. Hence, rather than spelling the end of empire, it is possible to interpret the globalized international system not only as a continuation of imperial relations but as an empire in its own right.

In Chapter 6, I conclude this book by spelling out the implications of the preceding analysis for how we best should understand the coming into being of the international realm as the default setting of world politics, and how we best should understand the corresponding universalization of the nation-state as the predominant locus of political authority in the modern world. I end this chapter by discussing some contemporary proposals to overcome or reform the modern international system *cum* empire by invoking the concepts of globality and the planetary in search of viable alternatives and a normative ground from which to contest the many excesses of the modern international world.

2 Dividing the World

Introduction

According to what has long been a commonplace in the study of international relations, a modern international system emerged after the Peace of Westphalia in 1648, when sovereign states superseded the Holy Roman Empire as the predominant loci of political authority in Europe.[1] To some authors, the Peace marked the inauguration of an international legal order in Europe. As Hans Morgenthau once argued, "[a] core of rules of international law laying down the rights and duties of states in relation to each other developed in the fifteenth and sixteenth centuries. These rules of international law were securely established in 1648, when the treaty of Westphalia brought the religious wars to an end and made the territorial state the cornerstone of the modern state system."[2] To others, the true significance of Westphalia was not that it heralded a community of nations or a new international legal order, but rather that it "it led to the era of absolutist states, jealous of their territorial sovereignty to a point where the idea of an international community became an almost empty phrase and where international law came to depend upon the will of states more concerned with the preservation and expansion of their power than with the establishment of a rule of law."[3] Or, in a recent and more philosophical formulation of this view, "[d]ifferent but equal was the solution the European sovereigns arrived at with Treaty of Westphalia in 1648. It begat sovereignty as we know it and the state system. The state emerged as a solution to

1 For an overview, see Sebastian Schmidt, "To Order the Minds of Scholars: The Discourse of the Peace of Westphalia in International Relations Literature." *International Studies Quarterly* 55 no. 3 (2011): 601–623.

2 Hans J. Morgenthau, *Politics among Nations* (New York: Knopf, 1948), 210.

3 Leo Gross, "The Peace of Westphalia, 1648–1948." *American Journal of International Law* 42 no. 1 (1948): 20–41, at 39.

the problem of how to accommodate difference without collapsing it back onto sameness."[4]

Quite irrespective of whether the Peace of Westphalia is taken to mark the emergence of a new international legal order or the rise of an international system of sovereign states, these accounts rely on a contrast with what supposedly had existed before and now was being superseded. What had characterized Europe from the Middle Ages onwards was a hierarchical and imperial order based on claims to universal authority raised by either Pope or Emperor, claims legitimized with reference to universalist understandings of humankind as a whole or a *Respublica Christiana*. Whether in legal theory or in political practice, the main consequence of the Peace of Westphalia was that it brought a transition from a world of universal empire to a world of states, a transition from singularity to plurality.

The accuracy of this account has been thoroughly disputed in the past decades. First, it has been pointed out that the Holy Roman Empire did not aspire to universal monarchy in Europe, and hence posed no real threat to the independence of other states. Although the Empire still embodied claims to universal authority, these were mainly of symbolic significance at the time. Consequently, France and Sweden did not fight against the Empire proper, but against what they perceived as an unlawful bid for universal monarchy by the Habsburgs.[5] Second, the Peace of Westphalia did not contribute to the dismantling of the Holy Roman Empire but instead left it in a better working condition than before by clarifying its legal structure and the responsibilities of estates and princes within it, thereby contributing to its remarkable endurance.[6] Third, although the Peace of Westphalia granted considerable legal and political autonomy to these estates and princes, this autonomy had no resemblance to sovereignty in any recognizably modern sense of the term, since the conditions of their

[4] Charlotte Epstein, *Birth of the State: The Place of the Body in Crafting Modern Politics* (Oxford: Oxford University Press, 2021), 26.

[5] See, for example, Andreas Osiander, "Sovereignty, International Relations, and the Westphalian Myth." *International Organization* 55 no. 2 (2001): 251–287, esp. 252–264; Derek Croxton, "The Peace of Westphalia of 1648 and the Origins of Sovereignty." *The International History Review* 21 no. 3 (1999): 569–591, esp. 573, 583.

[6] Ibid., 574–580.

independence were defined and circumscribed by imperial law.[7] Thus, in sum, "[n]obody began or even ended the negotiations at Westphalia with the idea of creating an international system of sovereign, independent states."[8] What did happen roughly simultaneously, however, was that jurists like Herman Conring denied that that there was any continuity between the Roman Empire and claims to empire raised by the German king, and hence that the latter could legitimately claim sovereignty over smaller polities.[9]

Even if few scholars today believe that the Peace of Westphalia marked the true beginning of a modern international system, the view that the Reformation and the Thirty Years War were formative episodes is still widespread. For example, to Daniel Philpott, modern sovereign states emerged as a result of "prior revolutions in ideas about justice and political authority" which in turn "arose out of a crisis, often a major war, sometimes a major upheaval in the international system" of which the Thirty Years War was a paradigmatic instance.[10] Similarly, as Daniel Nexon has argued, the Reformation produced a crisis that upset the balance of power within as well as among the composite monarchies of the day, a crisis which had a destabilizing impact on the dynastic order and eventually issued in widespread religious warfare across the continent. Not only did composite states survive decades of religious discord, but "[s]hifts in the nature of warfare and economic relations ultimately contributed more to a Europe composed of sovereign-territorial and nation-states than did the introduction of new religious ideas."[11] Finally Andrew Phillips has explained how and

[7] Ibid., 575–590; Martti Koskenniemi, *To the Uttermost Parts of the Earth. Legal Imagination and International Power 1300–187* (Cambridge: Cambridge University Press, 2021), 811–815.

[8] Croxton, "The Peace of Westphalia of 1648 and the Origins of Sovereignty", 589. See also Stéphane Beualac, *The Power of Language in the Making of International Law. The word sovereignty in Bodin and Vattel and the Myth of Westphalia* (Leiden: Brill, 2004), 67–97.

[9] See Constantin Fasolt, *The Limits of History* (Chicago: University of Chicago Press, 2004), ch. 3; Koskenniemi, *To the Uttermost Parts of the Earth*, 814–815.

[10] Daniel Philpott, *Revolutions in Sovereignty* (Princeton: Princeton University Press, 2001), 4 & 44.

[11] Daniel H. Nexon, *The Struggle for Power in Early Modern Europe: Religious Conflict, Dynastic Empires, and International Change* (Princeton: Princeton University Press, 2009), 10.

why the universalist Christian order was transformed into an international order composed of sovereign states, by arguing that this process was driven by "a combination of institutional decay, the collapse of prevailing social imaginaries and the accompanying emergence of anti-systemic ideologies, and increases in violence interdependence both within and between political communities."[12]

But as James Muldoon has cautioned us, it would be a "mistake to assume a fundamental opposition between empire and state, identifying empire with medieval universalism and the state with modernity. To make this error is to overlook the roots of the idea of state sovereignty in the application of the concept of imperial jurisdiction to kings, the theory that the king in his kingdom possessed the powers of the emperor within the empire."[13] By implication, locating the origin of the modern international realm to the Peace of Westphalia and "rendering the state as the only subject of international law meant that the figures of the empire and the universal monarchy ... were no longer recognized in modern times as subjects of international law despite their continuing and thriving existence – largely to the detriment of the colonized Non-European peoples."[14] This implies that an exclusive focus on sovereign states is bound to be misleading if we want to understand how the world became international, but also that any talk of a modern international system at this point would be anachronistic. Hence, in this chapter, I shall suggest that early modern political thought was more preoccupied with rival claims to universal authority than with questions of political form. These claims to universal authority were raised not only on the European continent but also in the new global context created by the cartographical and geographical revolutions of the fifteenth and sixteenth centuries, and soon issued in intense competition for control over territories and trade by European powers. As I will argue, attempts by contemporary political and legal theorists to come to terms with what transpired in this new

[12] Andrew Phillips, *War, Religion and Empire: The Transformation of International Orders* (Cambridge: Cambridge University Press, 2010), 6.

[13] James Muldoon, *Empire and Order, 800–1800* (New York: St. Martins Press, 1999), 141.

[14] José Manuel Barreto, "Cerberus: Rethinking Grotius and the Westphalian System." in Martti Koskenniemi, Walter Rech, and Manuel Jiménez Fonseca (eds.) *International Law and Empire: Historical Explorations* (Oxford: Oxford University Press, 2017), 149–175, at 170.

domain ushered in the division of the known world into a European *inside* and a non-European *outside*, the former composed of sovereign states and the latter by a wide variety of polities, ranging from the great empires of the East to the tiniest tribes of the New World, some of which succumbed to the universal authority claims of the Europeans whereas others did not. That the European quest for world hegemony was eventually to become successful was far from obvious at that point in time, as the Europeans faced competition from non-European empires entertaining similar aspirations.[15] As Hendrik Spruyt and Ayşe Zarakol have shown in great detail, the Asian empires had successfully staked claims to boundless sovereignty and had created vast world orders long before European state-making and imperial expansion gained momentum. Indeed, the rise of the West was made possible by the largely simultaneous decline of the East during the early modern period.[16] This external arena of non-European empires operated as a constitutive outside against which rudimentary international relations could unfold inside Europe.

Hence it makes no sense of talking of a transition from a world of empires to a world of states during this period. This being so for three related reasons. First, early modern writers did not conceptualize empire and state as categorically distinct forms of political association or rule. As the Roman term *imperium* took on new connotations in this context, such a distinction was not meaningful. Once understood as the power of a magistrate or that of the Roman people over a given territory, the term gradually took on more abstract qualities and was believed to be capable of independent existence by early modern theorists of empire.[17] Furthermore, since some of those who articulated early modern notions of empire did so with explicit references to

[15] See, for example, Sanjay Subrahmanyam, "A Tale of Three Empires: Mughals, Ottomans, and Habsburgs in a Comparative Context." *Common Knowledge* 12 no. 1 (2006): 66–92.

[16] Hendrik Spruyt, *The World Imagined: Collective Beliefs and Political Order in the Sinocentric, Islamic and Southeast Asian International Societies* (Cambridge: Cambridge University Press, 2020); Ayşe Zarakol, *Before the West: The Rise and Fall of Eastern World Orders* (Cambridge: Cambridge University Press, 2022).

[17] John Richardson, "The Meaning of Imperium in the Last Century BC and the First AD." in Benedict Kingsbury and Benjamin Straumann (eds.) *The Roman Foundations of the Law of Nations: Alberico Gentili and the Justice of Empire* (Oxford: Oxford University Press, 2010), 21–29.

sovereignty understood in terms of indivisible authority, and since such indivisible authority was in the process of becoming a defining characteristic of the state, this made any distinction between empires and states difficult to imagine and maintain.[18] Consequently, since many of the authors conventionally credited with having conceptualized the state into existence did not recognize any fixed territorial limits on the scope of political rule, and made few if any assumptions to the effect that subject populations ought to be homogeneous or confined within the same territory, they could equally well be read, and indeed often were read by most of their contemporaries, as theorists of empire. To the extent that early modern authors distinguished between empires and states, they did so in terms of their geographical extension and the composition of their populations rather than in terms of principles of rule or standards of legitimacy.

Second, to political and legal theorists of the day, the important distinctions were not between empires and states in any recognizably modern sense of these terms, but between empires and an array of other equally complex amalgamations of political authority and community, such as composite monarchies, unions, and, most notably, *republics*.[19] When it comes to the former alternatives, they were hard to distinguish from empire with any precision, since composite monarchies and unions comprised a host of different peoples distributed across discontinuous spaces. Since neither empires nor composite monarchies were believed to be necessarily bounded or having homogenous populations, the difference between them was largely a matter

[18] Sometimes to the point of being the same thing, see, for example, Walter Ullmann, "This Realm of England Is an Empire." *The Journal of Ecclesiastical History* 30 no. 2 (1979): 175–203; Quentin Skinner, "A Genealogy of the Modern State." *Proceedings of the British Academy*. Vol. 162. (2009): 325–370.

[19] See, for example, John H. Elliott, "A Europe of Composite Monarchies." *Past & Present* 137 (1992): 48–71; Helmut Georg Koenigsberger, "*Dominium Regale or Dominium Politicum Et Regale: Monarchies and Parliaments in Early Modern Europe*." in Helmut G. Koenigsberger, *Politicians and Virtuosi: Essays on Early Modern History* (London: Hambledon Press, 1986), 1–26; Helmut G. Koenigsberger, "Composite States, Representative Institutions and the American Revolution." *Historical Research* 62 no. 148 (1989): 135–153; Peter Haldén, *Stability without Statehood: Lessons from Europe's History before the Sovereign State* (Basingstoke: Palgrave MacMillan, 2011); Ben Holland, *The Moral Person of the State: Pufendorf, Sovereignty and Composite Polities* (Cambridge: Cambridge University Press, 2017).

of rhetorical nuance and ideological preference. When it came to republics, however, the situation was slightly different. Since empires were believed to be ruled by a single ruler and were classified as monarchies, empires and republics were believed to be distinct forms of rule by early modern authors. Yet there was nothing in principle that kept republics from becoming or forming empires of their own, as Machiavelli would argue in his *Discorsi*.[20]

Third, those who were involved in the business of legitimizing empires and states capitalized on the same Roman symbolic legacy. The same metaphors, symbols, and rituals once used by the Romans were dusted off and recycled to bolster the legitimacy of European empires were routinely used for the purposes of justifying state making at home by all the major powers of the day.[21] This wide dissemination of Roman imperial values and symbols issued in a fierce competition for honor and liberty among European powers, bolstered by claims to uniqueness and superiority, thereby translating the Roman quest for universal empire into multiple quests for the aggrandizement of particular empires.[22] Taken together, this implies that these powers – notably Spain, France, and Britain – are best understood as *both* empires and states in the making, each raising claims if not to universal so at least to boundless political authority in Europe and elsewhere in the process.

Consequently, authors during this period did not conceptualize the intercourse among polities in any recognizably *international* terms. Since contemporary concepts were used to capture relations among a

20 Anthony Pagden, *Lords of All the World. Ideologies of Empire in Spain, Britain, and France c.1500–c.1800* (New Haven: Yale University Press, 1995), 16–17.

21 Pagden, *Lords of All the World*, 19–23.

22 On the legacy of Rome and the sources of early modern nationalism, see Caspar Hirschi, *The Origins of Nationalism. An Alternative History from Ancient Rome to Early Modern Germany* (Cambridge: Cambridge University Press, 2012); Jens Bartelson, *Visions of World Community* (Cambridge: Cambridge University Press, 2009), ch. 4; Eva Botella-Ordinas, "Exempt from Time and from Its Fatal Change: Spanish Imperial Ideology, 1450–1700." *Renaissance Studies* 26, no. 4 (2012): 580–604; Liah Greenfeld, *Nationalism: Five Roads to Modernity* (Cambridge, M.A.: Harvard University Press, 1992), 27–87; Guido Zernatto and Alfonso G. Mistretta, "Nation: The History of a Word." *The Review of Politics* 6 no. 3 (1944): 351–366; Ralph W. Mathisen, "Peregrini, Barbari, and Cives Romani: Concepts of Citizenship and the Legal Identity of Barbarians in the Later Roman Empire." *American Historical Review* 111 no. 4 (2006): 1011–1040.

much wider range of polities, I believe the term *interpolity* relations as suggested by Lauren Benton and others better describes how contemporary commentators understood the terms of their intercourse.[23] But during the second half of the eighteenth century, when clear references to a system of states begin to emerge in Enlightenment legal theory and historiography, the non-European world is refashioned from an undifferentiated outside into a world of empires – some European but others not – a world of variegated geographies and cultural differences, and governed according to different principles of rule and standards of legitimacy.[24]

Thus, in this chapter, I shall first describe how these empires *cum* states were understood and legitimized by some of those responsible for conceptualizing these entities into existence in the early modern period. I shall then proceed to discuss some important objections against empire and imperial rule raised during the same period to show how attempts to delegitimize claims to universal monarchy produced visions of a system of states based on the balance of power and the natural liberty of states. In the final section, I shall discuss attempts to conceptualize empires and states as distinct kinds of polity in eighteenth century legal and historical writing, showing how the division of the known world into distinct political spheres made the non-European outside constitutive of a system of states in Europe, with profound consequences for the subsequent spread of that system to other continents discussed in the following chapters.

In Defense of Empire

The Renaissance revival of Roman historiography and architecture provided attempts at aggrandizement by European powers during the early modern period with much of their impetus and legitimacy. Renaissance humanists such as Petrarch used the Roman emperors – most notably

[23] Lauren Benton, "Possessing Empire. Iberian Claims and Interpolity Law." in Saliha Belmessous (ed.), *Native Claims. Indigenous Law against Empire, 1500–1920* (Oxford: Oxford University Press, 2011), 19–40; Lauren Benton and Adam Clulow, "Empire and Protection: Making Interpolity Law in the Early Modern World." *Journal of Global History* 12 no. 1 (2017), 74–92.

[24] See Lauren Benton, *A Search for Sovereignty: Law and Geography in European* empires. 1400–1900 (Cambridge: Cambridge University Press, 2009), 1–38.

Julius Caesar – as examples of moral virtue and military valor to be emulated by contemporary princes and monarchs in Europe in their quest for power and glory.[25] Roman law also furnished the conceptual resources used by early modern authors to justify their acquisition of sovereignty and property rights overseas in the process of imperial expansion.[26] The election of Charles V as Holy Roman Emperor in 1519 gave these aspirations new significance, given the vast but disjointed territories thereby brought under his rule. As Thomas Dandelet has remarked, "[t]he previous two centuries had provided the literary blueprint and symbolic foundations for the revival, but it was the victories and conquests of Charles V and his armies that demonstrated the resurrection of real imperial power on a military and economic level."[27] But in early modern thought, empires were often imagined into existence before they could be claimed as possessions. This understanding gave the quest for empire its sometimes-surreal character. As Frances Yates observed about Charles V, "it is precisely as a phantom that Charles's empire was of importance, because it raised again the imperial idea and spread it through Europe in the symbolism of its propaganda."[28] In imperial rhetoric, the greatness of early modern empires was not only determined by their geographical extension or the valor of their rulers, but also by the diversity of beings brought under their sway: Poets like Ariosto interpreted the discovery of the Americas as a harbinger of a coming world monarchy and could thereby bring marvel at the unknown and the lust for power and glory to coincide.[29]

25 See Thomas James Dandelet, *The Renaissance of Empire in Early Modern Europe* (Cambridge: Cambridge University Press, 2014).

26 See Lauren Benton and Benjamin Straumann, "Acquiring Empire by Law: From Roman Doctrine to Early Modern European Practice." *Law & History Review* 28 no. 1 (2010): 1–38; Diego Panizza, "Alberico Gentili's *De Armis Romanis*: The Roman Model of the Just Empire." in Benedict Kingsbury and Benjamin Straumann (eds.) *The Roman Foundations of the Law of Nations: Alberico Gentili and the Justice of Empire* (Oxford: Oxford University Press, 2010), 53–84.

27 Dandelet, *Renaissance of Empire*, 111.

28 Frances A. Yates, *Astraea. The Imperial Theme in the Sixteenth Century* (London: Routledge & Kegan Paul, 1975), 1.

29 See, for example, Stephen Greenblatt, *Marvelous Possessions: The Wonder of the New World* (Chicago: University of Chicago Press, 1991); Tzvetan Todorov, *The Conquest of America: The Question of the Other* (New York: Harper& Row, 1984).

As Gabriel Paquette has argued in a recent book, Portuguese and Spanish overseas expansion was not due to any superiority on their behalf or of the wider civilization in which they partook, but rather the result of their systematic employment of violence which was "embedded in the institutions they established overseas"; to the "efficacious forms of governance and finance" which enabled them to "project and retain power across vast distances", and finally, to the collaboration of creole elites to maintain and extend control of conquered territories. Assisted by a mighty army of microbes, the creation of overseas empire was propelled by intense competition between European states yet compromised by rivalries among their elites.[30] But first you had to get to those distant shores. The creation of overseas empires presupposed that there was something out there to conquer in the first place, since expanding into what one believed to be an empty space would have made little or no sense. It further presupposed that there was a way of getting there, getting *over* the seas so that this "out there" quite literally becomes an *overseas*. And for this to be possible, the ocean must have been seen not as an unsurmountable abyss but as a navigable waterway, possible to master and traverse.

Yet many of the necessary intellectual resources were absent at the beginning of overseas expansion.[31] Medieval conceptions of empire had been fashioned out of Roman notions of *imperium* which mainly connoted *territorial* rule, and however discontinuous those territories and heterogenous their populations, no references were made to the possibility of extending such *imperium* to continents beyond the Euro-Asian landmass for the simple reason that their existence remained unknown or at least highly uncertain at the point when this conception of empire had been first fleshed out.[32] As Isidore of Seville had established in no uncertain terms back then, "the ocean is impassable to men, and those worlds which are beyond it are also unreachable."[33]

[30] Gabriel Paquette, *The European Seaborne Empires. From the Thirty Year's War to the Age of Revolutions* (New Haven: Yale University Press, 2019), 4.

[31] See, for example, Jorge Cañizares-Esguerra, *Nature, Empire, and Nation: Explorations of the History of Science in the Iberian World* (Stanford: Stanford University Press, 2006).

[32] See Anthony Pagden, *The Burdens of Empire. 1539 to the Present* (Cambridge: Cambridge University Press, 2015), 2–6.

[33] Isidore of Seville, *De Natura Rerum.* [612–615]. trans. by Calvin B. Kendall and Faith Wallis (Liverpool: Liverpool University Press, 2016), 40.III.168.

Thus the geographical and cartographical revolutions of the sixteenth century rendered earlier claims to have ruled the whole world void, but also opened a new global space to intense political and economic competition among European powers.[34]

At the time when Tommaso Campanella published his *Della Monarchia di Spagna* in 1600, the aspiration to universal monarchy had become of a truly planetary scope, stretching far beyond the geographical limits of the Roman and Christian worlds.[35] At this point, Iberian empires had become premised on the mastery of the transcontinental waterways connecting different parts of world in ways that transcended the territorial boundaries and geographical limits of the ancient world.[36] As the Spanish humanist Juan Vives noted in 1531, "[t]he whole globe is opened up to the human race, so that no one is so ignorant of events as to think that the wanderings of the ancients... are to be compared with the journeys of these travellers."[37] Hence the medieval notion of an *orbis terrarum* had been transcended in practice well before it was formally refuted by Copernicus in 1534, the impetus coming from the cartographical advances that followed upon the rediscovery Ptolemy's *Geography* in the late fifteenth century.[38] As Frank Lestringant has pointed out, the early modern dreams of universal empire "found the beginnings of its realization in the map or sphere that was dedicated to the monarch, framed by his arms and traversed by his ships, and that opened up to his dreams of empire a space of intervention stretching to the limits of the terraqueous

34 See Pagden, *Lords of all the World*, 29–62.

35 Tommaso Campanella, *A Discourse Touching the Spanish Monarchy* (London: Philemon Stephens, 1654). For interpretations, John M. Headley, *Tommaso Campanella and the Transformation of the World* (Princeton: Princeton University Press, 1997); Anthony Pagden, "Instruments of Empire: Tommaso Campanella and the Universal Monarchy of Spain." in Anthony Pagden, *Spanish Imperialism and the Political Imagination* (New Haven: Yale University Press, 1990), 37–64.

36 For this contrast, see David Armitage, "The Elephant and the Whale: Empires of Land and Sea." *Journal for Maritime Research* 9, no. 1 (2007): 23–36; Charles S. Maier, *Once within Borders: Territories of Power, Wealth and Belonging since* 1500 (Cambridge, MA.: Harvard University Press, 2016).

37 Juan Vives, *On Education.* [1531]. trans. by Foster Watson (Cambridge: Cambridge University Press, 1913), 3.

38 See Christian Jacob, *The Sovereign Map. Theoretical Approaches in Cartography Throughout History* (Chicago: University of Chicago Press, 2006), 61–64.

globe."[39] And as Peter Sloterdijk has remarked, "[d]iscovery aims for acquisition; this gave cartography its world-historical function."[40] Many early modern commentators were equally inclined to agree on the epochal significance of the discoveries. As Bodin argued in his *Methodus* (1566), whereas the ancients had lived within the confines of the Mediterranean basin, his contemporaries could "traverse the whole earth every year in frequent voyages and lead colonies into another world ... [n]ot only has this discovery developed an abundant and profitable commerce ... but also all men surprisingly work together in a world state, as if in one of the same city-state."[41] Similarly, both Abbé de Raynal and Adam Smith took the discovery of the Americas to mark the birth of the modern world. To Raynal, discovery and circumnavigation "gave rise to a revolution in the commerce, and in the power of nations, as well as in the manners, industry, and government of the whole world."[42] Similarly, to Smith, the "discovery of America, and that of a passage to the East Indies by the Cape of Good Hope, are the two greatest and most important events recorded in the history of mankind" insofar as they inaugurated a new age of trade and exchange on a planetary scale.[43]

Given this new global context of conquest and commerce, the concepts invoked to legitimize imperial expansion and claims to universal sovereignty had only vague resemblances to the notion of *imperium* in Roman law.[44] Rather many early modern conceptions of empire derived from medieval sources, with Dante's *De Monarchia* (1312–1313) being among the favorites. For example, Mercurio de Gattinara – grand chancellor to Charles V and the main architect of early Spanish

39 Frank Lestringant, *Mapping the Renaissance World: The Geographical Imagination in the Age of Discovery* (Cambridge: Polity Press, 1994), 23.

40 Peter Sloterdijk, *Globes: Spheres II*. Trans. by Wieland Hoban (Cambridge, M.A.: MIT Press 2014), 868.

41 Jean Bodin, *Method for the Easy Comprehension of History*. trans. by Beatrice Reynolds (New York: Columbia University Press, 1945), 301.

42 Abbé Guillaume-Thomas-François Raynal, *A Philosophical and Political History of the Settlements and Trade of the Europeans in the East and West Indies*. trans. by J. O. Justamond (London: W. Strahan and T. Cadell, 1783), I.I,1.

43 Adam Smith, *An Inquiry into the Nature and Causes of the Wealth of Nations* Vol. II, [1776–1778]. Ed. by Edwin Cannan (London: Methuen, 1904), VII. III, 91.

44 See John Richardson, *The Language of Empire: Rome and the Idea of Empire from the Third Century BC to the Second Century AD* (Cambridge: Cambridge University Press, 2008).

imperial ideology – justified his vision of universal monarchy with reference to this work and sought to persuade Erasmus to edit a new version of *De Monarchia* to bolster Spanish imperial claims.[45] As Dante defined the term in *De Monarchia*, "[t]emporal monarchy, then, which men call 'empire', is a single sovereign authority set over all others in time, that is to say over all authorities which operate in those things and over those things which are measured by time."[46] Such a pursuit of world monarchy was often legitimized with reference to the peace, justice and prosperity that world monarchy was supposed to bring, and the war, injustice, and poverty that would ensue from its absence, failure, or collapse. As Dante went on to explain, "it is apparent that the well-being of the world requires that there be a monarchy or empire", which also implies that if "[j]ustice is at its strongest only under a monarch; therefore for the best ordering of the world there must be a monarchy or empire."[47] This and similar justifications of empire in terms of its capacity to deliver security and justice to the world would continue to resonate throughout the early modern period, as would the corresponding claim that the Romans once had ruled the world by virtue of right rather than might.[48]

These dreams of boundless power found expression and partial justification in two different concepts. The first of these was based on revival of the Roman idea of *Dominus Mundi*, and was mainly used to describe relations between European powers on the one hand, and peoples and places in the non-European world on the other.[49] The other was the notion of *Monarchia Universalis*, which was used to describe similar aspirations to universal sovereignty but in the context

45 See John M. Headley, *The Emperor and His Chancellor: A Study of the Imperial Chancellery under Gattinara* (Cambridge: Cambridge University Press, 1983), 11, 95, 11; John M. Headley, "The Emperor and His Chancellor: Disputes over Empire, Administration and Pope (1519–1529)." in *Carlos V y la quiebra del humanismo político en Europa (1530–1558)* (Madrid: Sociedad Estatal para la Comemoración de los Centenarios de Felipe II y Carlos V, 2001), 21–35.

46 Dante Alighieri, *Monarchy,* edited by Prue Shaw. (Cambridge: Cambridge University Press, 1996), I.II.4.

47 Dante, *Monarchy*, I.V.11& I.XI.15.

48 John M. Headley, "The Habsburg World Empire and the Revival of Ghibellinism." [1978], in David Armitage (ed.), *Theories of Empire 1450–1800* (Farnham: Ashgate, 1998), 45–79.

49 See Anthony Pagden, *Lords of All the World. Ideologies of Empire in Spain, Britain and France c.1500–c.1800* (New Haven: Yale University Press, 1995).

of great power rivalry in Europe.[50] Although these concepts sometimes were used interchangeably by early modern authors, their usage followed different historical trajectories and gave rise to different ideological disputes. Whereas the former was met with the objection that the subjection of non-European peoples was illegal under natural law, the latter was met with resistance on the grounds that it threatened the interests and liberties of other European powers. While those who opposed the subjugation and dispossession of non-Europeans did so from within a scholastic legal framework that emphasized the natural rights and liberties of those peoples, those who opposed attempts to create a universal monarchy in Europe drew on a humanist legal framework that emphasized the right to wage preventive war to counteract and deter such attempts.

Legitimizing the authority claims of early modern empires was more a matter of historical rewriting than of rigorous philosophical or legal argument. Historical narratives supportive of Spanish claims to a world empire began to emerge already during the reigns of Charles V and Philip II. These narratives followed a predictable pattern. Chroniclers usually started by recounting the virtuous deeds and good examples of the Roman emperors, and then placed their patrons in neat succession to them by means of flattering comparisons centered on moral virtues, military valor, and glory. When doing so, they initially took the concept of empire and its cognates to signify the fact of possession rather than to describe an entity capable of existing independently of its component parts or even of the will of its ruler. None of this was very different from the way in which other authors during this period used to concept of the state to denote a mere extension of princely power rather than to describe an entity capable of existing independently of rulers as well as ruled.[51]

At the same time as medieval notions of empire were revived and recycled, others were in the process of articulating the foundations of what was to become a modern concept of the state. When seen in this context, the concept of empire looks like a ghost, as little but a

[50] See Franz Bosbach, "The European Debate on Universal Monarchy." in David Armitage (ed.) *Theories of Empire 1450–1800* (Farnham: Ashgate, 1998), 81–98.

[51] See, for example, Harvey C. Mansfield, "On the Impersonality of the Modern State: A Comment on Machiavelli's Use of Stato." *American Political Science Review* 77 no. 4 (1983): 849–857.

disturbing anachronism in a world in which the modern state was in the making. But even if Machiavelli has often been credited with taking the first steps towards the articulation of such a concept, it is equally possible to read *Discorsi sopra la prima deca di Tito Livio* (c. 1517) as a defense of a republican version of empire in which political liberty at home is a necessary condition of imperial aggrandizement abroad, as well as conversely.[52] But even so the concept of empire sometimes carried ontological commitments different from that of the state, insofar as claims to empire were often directed against a totality of political beings within a preordained universal order of things. As the confessor and courtier of Charles V – Antonio de Guevara – explained in his *Relox de Principes* (1529), just as there is but one God, "[a]ll superior and inferior things would bee well ordered, and many things much better by the arbitrement of one, then by the aduice of many."[53] From this divine order of things followed "that in one family there should bee but one Father, among one people there should be but one Citizen that should command, in one Prouince there should be Gourneour alone, and also that one King alone should gourne ... a Realme, and also that by one onely Captaine a puissant Army should be ledde."[54] Just as the elements of air, water and fire are subordinate to that of earth, the body to the soul, the beastly to the wise, woman to man, "it is very necessary, that in the Common-wealth many be governed by the one ... For in a common-wealth there can bee no greater enemie than hee that desireth than many should rule therein." But "furthermore and above all" God "willeth that there bee but one Monarchyall King and Lorde of the World."[55] Thus, all possible political associations are ordered according to the same principle of indivisible and supreme authority. On top of it all stands the virtuous prince: it is no coincidence that de Guevara

[52] For this argument, see Michael Hörnqvist, *Machiavelli and Empire* (Cambridge: Cambridge University Press, 2008); Michael Hörnqvist, "Machiavelli's Three Desires: Florentine Republicans on Liberty, Empire, and Justice." in Sankar Muthu (ed.) *Empire and Modern Political Thought* (Cambridge: Cambridge University Press, 2012), 7–29.

[53] Antonio de Guevara, *The Diall of Princes. Compiled by the reuerende father in God, Don Anthony of Gueuara, Bysshop of Guadix*. Trans. by Thomas North (London: 1557), I:x. Although his work is known to be a fabrication, this fact matters less in the present context. See Horacio Chiong Rivero, *The Rise of Pseudo-Historical Fiction. Fray Antonio de Guevara's Novelizations* (New York: Peter Lang, 2004).

[54] Guevara, *The Diall of Princes*, I.xxviii.

[55] Ibid.

devotes an entire book to the question of how the prince should govern himself and his household first and foremost before addressing the question of how his empire best should be governed.

Similar themes recur in *Historia Imperial y Cesárea* (1545) by the chronicler Pedro Mexia, in which he relates the "liues of the Roman Emperours, which held the Monarchie of the world."[56] Thus we learn of Ceasar that he came to be "the most mightie, the most redoubted, and most highly esteemed man that euer had been in the world, hauing subdued and conquered the greatest part thereof, with an Armie and by force, in as little time, as it might seeme that another man might be able to trauail those countries by reasonable iourneys."[57] As John Pocock has remarked about this curious work, it "is by definition a history of *translatio imperii*; the line of Caesars is unbroken to the moment of writing and the Roman Empire still exists."[58] Less burdened by cosmological references, the concept of empire is now simply used to describe the totality of Spanish possessions. Thus, for example, we learn that he, "hauing ruined the protestants, which made the greatest power of *Germany*, he would subiect the states of the Empire to his will, that he might keepe the Empire in his family, and make it hereditary."[59] As indicated by this more modern usage, Mexia thought of empire as an object that Charles and his successors could legitimately claim possession of, yet one which hardly could be said to exist independently of its components. But as Pocock has noted, Mexia traces the origin of those individual kingdoms that later were subjugated by Spain to the fall of the Roman Empire. Although he does not narrate the history of these provinces and kingdoms, he maintains that they had resulted from previous barbarian invasions, making the Spanish not only heirs to the Roman Empire, but equally also to that of the Goths. From this followed that the Spanish claim to universal monarchy was likely to be met with resistance from those kingdoms that were of barbarian origin.[60] Yet those in provinces

56 Pedro Mexia, *The Imperiall Historie: or the Liues of the Emperours, from Iulius Cæsar, the First Founder of the Roman Monarchy*. (London: Mathevv Lovvnes, 1623), 2

57 Mexia, *Imperiall Historie*, 14.

58 J. G. A. Pocock, *Barbarism and Religion* III. *The First Decline and Fall* (Cambridge: Cambridge University Press, 2003), 247.

59 Mexia, *Imperiall Historie*, 653.

60 Pocock, *Barbarism and Religion* III., 250–257.

that had been subjected to imperial rule, Charles "had alwaies endeuoured to maintaine the publike quiet; that he had vndertaken many paineful and dangerous voiages to come vnto them; that he had been carefull to gouerne them with iustice, to maintaine their rights and priuiledges, and to doe all other things whereunto a good Prince is bound."[61] Mexia here invokes a familiar defense of empire as the vanguard of liberty and justice, a defense that was to be singled out for target practice by those threatened by Spanish claims to universal monarchy more than a century later.

Being much more detailed and comprehensive than any of his predecessors, the last of the great Spanish imperial historians – Juan de Mariana – stands out from the rest by insisting that the Spanish empire had been founded *before* that of Rome and had then successfully resisted subordination to the latter thanks to the extraordinary virtue of its kings. Thus, from *De Rebus Hispaniae* (1592) we learn that Tubal, the first to occupy Spanish soil after the flood "founded the Spanish Monarchy, which continues to this time. This is that Empire which in all Ages has afforded Men Famous, both in Peace and War, which has been blessed with Plenty and Prosperity, and which has always furnished extraordinary matter to imploy the greatest Pens."[62] Here Mariana is explicitly invoking another unspoken but widespread justification of empire during this period, namely that it will bring prosperity to those who voluntarily subject themselves to its rule.

None of these historians distinguished sharply between empire and state, and most likely so because no such distinction was readily available to them. If we allow for the fact that their usage of the term *estado* still carried many of its medieval connotations since it was used to describe a *condition* in which a ruler or his possessions might find themselves in, and then also as a matter of the *standing* of the former and the *health* of the latter, they do occasionally use this term in a modern sense by implying that an *estado* is capable of existing independent of its ruler as well as ruled. As we have seen above, while Guevara does this by means of an analogy between macrocosm and microcosm, to the effect that a particular state is embedded within the empire as much as the empire is embedded within the whole of

61 Mexia, *Imperiall Historie*, 657.

62 Juan de Mariana, *The General History of Spain* (London: Richard Sare & Thomas Bennet, 1699), 1.

creation, Mexia uses the concepts of empire and state interchangeably. For example, "[a]mong all the glorius actions of Julius Caesar, the greatest in my opinion, ad which breeds most admiration, is, how he first project, then put it into practice, and lastly bring it to effect, to make himself Lord of the Roman State."[63] Finally, Mariana seems to have appropriated a new and trendy definition of sovereignty when he noted that "the irreconcilable Enmities betwixt near Relations, and even Brothers, may be a sufficient warning to Sovereigns not to divide their Dominions, especially when their Limits are but narrow. It is a certain Maxim, that Sovereignty admits of no Fellowship, and Ambition is not curbed by any ties, tho' never so Sacred."[64] Much the same goes for the concept of the nation, which is invoked in an archaic Roman sense by Mexia. For example, we learn that at the time of the Roman invasion, Britain "was inhabited by a fierce Nation."[65] The same usage of the concept of the nation can be found in Mariana, when he describes the coming of the Goths in the following way: "The coming of these Barbarous Nations was the ruin of *Spain,* for they seized indifferently as well what belonged to *Spaniards,* as *Romans,* and destroyed the Towns and open Country, whereupon ensued such a Famine, that the Natives fed upon human flesh, and the wild beasts ranged abroad to devour Men."[66]

If the Spanish had claimed, not without some success, to be the true vanguards of the Roman Empire during much of the sixteenth century, the French were trying hard to assume that role in the two following centuries. While drawing on the same symbolic legacy, the ideological underpinnings of French imperial ambitions were difficult to tell apart from those informing French state making during the same period. A perhaps less obvious but all the more revealing example in this regard is *Six Livres de la Republique* (1576) by Jean Bodin. Heavily relying on the same Roman sources that inspired his fellow imperial humanists at the time, *Six Livres* is famous for its definition of sovereignty in terms of indivisibility, and has therefore been taken to represent an important step towards the articulation

[63] Mexia, *The Imperiall Historie*, 2.

[64] Mariana, *The General History of Spain*, 137. Although there is no evidence that Mariana actually had read Bodin, his notion of sovereignty betrays strong affinities with that of the latter, see Harald E. Braun, *Juan de Mariana and Early Modern Spanish Political Thought.* (Aldershot: Ashgate, 2008), 74.

[65] Mexia, *Imperiall Historie*, 4.

[66] Mariana, *The General History of Spain*, 68.

of a recognizably modern concept of the state.[67] But it is also worth recalling that Bodin took the object of sovereign authority to be a multitude of families or households, made no reference to the proper scope of government, or implied that sovereignty had to be bounded in order to be effective or legitimate.[68] This implies that what Bodin had to say about the republic or commonwealth would apply equally to *any* polity regardless of its territorial scope or the number of families or households it happened to subsume. Indeed, given the imperial aspirations of Henry III and his patronage of Bodin's work, such a reading is perhaps less anachronistic than those that have read *Six Livres* squarely into the genealogy of the modern state. As Thomas Dandelet has shown, the *Six Livres* is sprinkled with references to the Roman Empire and the founding fathers of imperial humanism, which are used in support of far-ranging royal power and prerogatives.[69]

But apart from references to the symbolic legacy of the Romans, this reading could be further substantiated by looking into how Bodin uses the concept of *imperium* when discussing the prerogatives of the sovereign. When he raises the question "[w]hether the power of the sword (which the law calleth *merum imperium*, or meere power) be proper unto the soveraigne prince, and inseparable from the soveraignte; and that the Magistrats have not this *merum imperium* but onely the execution thereof", he does so only to confirm the view according to which the power of the sword was among the prerogatives that could not be delegated downwards.[70] By the same token, when he asks "[w]here the word, *imperium*, or power, signifieth not onely the power to command, or forbid, but even the magistrate himselfe", only to follow Cicero in concluding that the "greater power cannot by right be examined

67 See, for example, Quentin Skinner, "The State." in Terence Ball, James Farr, and Russell T. Hanson (eds.) *Political Innovation and Conceptual Change* (Cambridge: Cambridge University Press, 1989), 90–131; Julian H. Franklin, *Jean Bodin and the Rise of Absolutist Theory* (Cambridge: Cambridge University Press, 1973); Preston T. King, *The Ideology of Order: A Comparative Analysis of Jean Bodin and Thomas Hobbes* (London: Allen & Unwin, 1974).

68 See Stuart Elden, *The Birth of Territory* (Chicago: University of Chicago Press, 2013). 266–268.

69 Dandelet, *Renaissance of Empire*, 217–219.

70 Jean Bodin, *Six Bookes of a Commonwealth*. trans. by Knolles (London: 1606), Book III, 327.

by the lesse."[71] Given these usages of the term *imperium*, *Six Livres* marks the return to an older Roman legalist understanding of empire which had been largely absent in the predominantly historical defenses of imperial rule that accompanied the Spanish bid for universal empire.

Towards the end of the sixteenth century, conceptualizations of empire began to change. As we have seen above, humanist imperialism was a matter of legitimizing imperial ambitions in the present by constructing unbroken continuities with an imagined Roman past. While doing so, chroniclers and court historians rarely bothered to discuss the concept of empire in any detail but instead took some of its received meanings for granted and grafted them unto forever new geopolitical contexts. But these invocations of edifying examples drawn from the deeds of Roman emperors gave way to more abstract philosophical meditations on empire, all while earlier theological and mythological justifications of empire began to fade in favor of justifications derived from the precepts of secular statecraft. Rather than merely telling mythic histories supportive of this or that claim to empire, advocates of empire begin to tell us what empires *are*, what makes them different from other forms of political association, and, most importantly, how they ideally ought to be governed to preserve them in time and enlarge them in space.

Even if *De Monarchia Hispanica* (1600) by Tommaso Campanella never found favor with the Spanish crown, it was conceived at the crossroads between the Renaissance and the early modern world and tried to reconcile Christian and Neo-platonic theocratic ideas with those of emergent secular statecraft.[72] In the view of its author, all empires owed their existence to divine providence. While individual empires go through the cycles of rise, decline, and fall, the eternal idea of empire remains in search of new temporal instantiations.

[71] Bodin, *Six Bookes*, Book III, 347.

[72] For some important bakground accounts, see John M. Headley, *Tommaso Campanella and the Transformation of the World* (Princeton: Princeton University Press, 1997); Anthony Pagden, "Instruments of Empire: Tommaso Campanella and the Universal Monarchy of Spain." in Anthony Pagden, *Spanish Imperialism and the Political Imagination* (New Haven: Yale University Press, 1990), 37–64; Noel Malcolm, "The Crescent and the City of the Sun: Islam and the Renaissance Utopia of Tommaso Campanella." *Proceedings of the British Academy*. Vol. 125 (Oxford: Oxford University Press, 2004), 71–67, esp. 54–57.

Expanding on the Book of Daniel, he starts by noting that the "The Universal Monarchy of the World, beginning from the East, and so coming at length to the West, having passed through the Hands of the Assyrians, Medes, Persians, Greeks, and Romans ... it is a length coming to the Spaniard...and that with greater Splendour, than on any of his Predecessors."[73] Like all earlier instantiations of empire, the rise of Spain is conditioned by the confluence of providence, prudence, and opportunity. Since astrological observations tell us that the end of the world is imminent, "so before the end of the World, the Spaniard being joined in amity with the Pope, shall live in a more happy condition, and shall raign securely and peaceably ... neither yet shall he arrive to that height of Universal Monarchy he had aspired unto. But this is a businesse to be handled secretly, and not to be published openly to the World."[74] Such a universal monarchy was intended to put an end to all heresies and keep the Turks at bay. So, in apparent contrast to the more secular imperial schemes of the same period, Campanella envisaged a universal theocracy in which the Spanish king ruled with support from the Pope, because "how much it concerns the Interest of the King of Spain, that he endeavour the attaining to the Empire of the World by the means of the Pope."[75]

In order to achieve such a universal monarchy, the Spanish king must prudently capitalize on the opportunities for territorial expansion whenever they present themselves: "the King of Spain, following the order of things, and by observing the Rules of Prudence, together with Occasion, may bring all things under his Obedience."[76] To exercise such prudence, the king must harness religious beliefs, since "[a]ll Religions, as well the False, as the True, do prevail, and are Victorious, when they have once taken root in the Minds of men; upon which onely depend both their Tongue and Armes, which are the onely Instruments of attaining Dominion."[77] And the opportunities for such expansion "consists chiefly in this, that his Neighbouring Enemies are weak, and at discord among themselves touching both Points of Religion, and matters of State."[78] Yet to vanquish his

[73] Tommaso Campanella, *A Discourse Touching the Spanish Monarchy* (London: Philemon Stephens, 1654), Preface.
[74] Campanella, *Spanish Monarchy*, IV.10.
[75] Ibid., V.24. [76] Ibid., IV.15.
[77] Ibid., V.19. [78] Ibid., VII.30.

external enemies while overcoming internal discord, the king needs to embody those virtues that had made Roman emperors able to exercise imperial authority first and foremost over their own unruly passions:

> He cannot govern the World, that cannot govern an Empire, that cannot a Kingdom, that cannot a Province, nor he a Province, that cannot a City; nor he a City, that cannot a Village; nor he a Village, that cannot a Family; nor he a Family, that cannot a single House, nor he a single house that cannot govern himself.[79]

The foremost of those virtues was prudence. But in contrast to many of his contemporaries, Campanella discusses not only how universal monarchy is to be attained and what makes such an endeavor desirable and necessary, but also elaborates on the makeup of the world to be brought under imperial control. Doing this, he also tells us some important things about the limits and composition of an empire. Upon establishing a universal monarchy, the king needs to consider carefully the nature of the world to be conquered. He needs to know "the Division of the World into its parts, and of his own Dominions; the different manners and Customes of the several Nations of the Earth, and their Religions and Sects; as also the stories of all the former Kings."[80] The fact that different nations have different religions and different customs pose a very real challenge to imperial rule. Thus, the next step is to attain knowledge of its history and laws: "The King must also take care to have the General Histories and Annals of the Whole World, compiled in a compendious and succinct way...Let Him likewise cause a Brief Collection to be made of the Lawes of all the several Kingdomes and Principalities of the World."[81] But this knowledge is only of interest to the extent that it can be harnessed for the purpose of furthering imperial rule. And this is only achieved by means of arms, because "[w]hoever desires to become a great Monarch, it will behoove him to be continually in making War upon all his Neighbours that lye round about him."[82]

But the rush of power and glory will soon give way to despair at the many difficulties that come naturally with the imposition of new rule on foreign lands. The main challenge of that rule is to overcome or at least manage the cultural diversity that arises as a consequence

[79] Ibid., IX.32. [80] Ibid., IX.34. [81] Ibid., X.42.
[82] Ibid., XIX.116.

of constant conquests and the ceaseless incorporation of foreign lands into the empire. Campanella here embarks on a lengthy discussion of how to homogenize an empire for the sake of the cohesion necessary for its smooth and effective rule. Since any commonwealth stands to benefit from the presence of mutual love between subjects and the unity of religion among them, the Spanish empire would be well served if Spaniards would marry members of other nations: "for as much as the Spaniards are hated by all Nations, the best Course would be, that the King should endeavour to reconcile them to the Spaniard by intermarrying with them."[83] Thus, at the end of the day, the preservation of empires hinges on their successful homogenization: "[w]hosoever therefore is to Rule Several, and Different Nations, and would keep them all within the bounds of Obedience, let him endeavour to reduce them into a conformity, as far as he is able, and make them in all things like to each other."[84] Campanella here most clearly states what would remain a trade-off of imperial rule for centuries to come. One the one hand, to be perceived as legitimate by those on the receiving end, imperial rule must remain sensitive to the fact that an empire consists of a plurality of different peoples and communities, each with customs and laws of their own. On the other hand, to become effective, imperial rule must heed the precepts of secular statecraft and homogenize this plurality into a unity sufficiently cohesive to withstand external threats and internal discord.[85]

Despite its strange blend of philosophical influences, *De Monarchia Hispanica* is among the first works to use the concept of empire in a rather coherent and recognizably modern sense. This term is now used to describe not only a rule over a plurality of communities or peoples, but also to denote a polity capable of independent existence by virtue of being something more than the sum its component parts. While such an empire might be composed of many kingdoms and comprise several nations, these kingdoms and nations also exist independently of their rulers as well as of the larger empire of which they form part. Campanella also uses the concepts of state and nation in ways consonant with other early modern usages, in which states and nations are believed to exist independently of their rulers. Even if he does not attribute autonomous agency to any of these entities, they are understood

[83] Ibid., XVII.95–97. [84] Ibid., XIX.121
[85] Pagden, "Instruments of Empire", 58–64.

as being something more than mere possessions of the ruler and extensions of his will. Even if this recipe for imperial aggrandizement and consolidation was intended for the benefit of the Spanish crown, commentators quickly pointed out that it could equally well be applied to similar ends by any other state aspiring to great power status. As his English translator noted, "although this be designed wholly ... in reference to the Spanish Monarchy only, and the support of the Papacy; yet may all wise, Judicious men make very good use of the same, and apply what Counsells are here given ... to their own Affaires."[86] And eventually this conception of empire would find its way into the works of authors as diverse as Grotius and Richelieu.[87]

Similar understandings of empire and the paradoxes of its rule recur in a short treatise by Francis Bacon entitled *Of the True Greatness of Kingdoms and Estates* (1612/1625). Bacon is here adamant that the difference between empire and state is a matter of scale only. Thus, he informs us that "the greatness of an estate in bulk and territory doth fall under measure; and the greatness of finances and revenue doth fall under computation. The population may appear by musters; and the number and greatness of cities and towns by cards and maps."[88] He then goes on to elaborate on the means most appropriate for imperial aggrandizement, which he – like Campanella – identifies squarely with warfare, since "for empire and greatness, it importeth most, that a nation do profess arms as their principal honor, study, and occupation." But from the sweetness of many victories follows the challenges of rule. The successful manner of the Romans was to grant naturalization "not to singular persons alone, but likewise to whole families; yea to cities, and sometimes to nations." When in the latter case "putting both constitutions together, you will say that it was not the Romans that spread upon the world, but it was the world that spread upon the Romans; and that was the sure way of greatness."[89] Whereas Spain has not been that good at assimilating peoples brought

86 Campanella, *Spanish Monarchy*, translators note.

87 Pagden, "Instruments of Empire", 38.

88 Francis Bacon, "Of the True Greatness of Kingdoms and Estates." in Francis Bacon, *Essays, Civil and Moral*, Vol. II, Part I (New York: P. F. Collier & Son, 1909–1914), XXIX, 2. For a background, see Markku Peltonen, "Politics and Science: Francis Bacon and the True Greatness of States." *Historical Journal* 35, no. 2 (1992): 279–305.

89 Bacon, "Of the True Greatness of Kingdoms and Estates", 6.

under their control to their own culture and customs, "they have that which is next to it; that is, to employ almost indifferently all nations in their militia of ordinary soldiers; yea and sometimes in their highest commands."[90] But as a consequence of this relentless expansion into a world of marvelous diversity, those in charge of early modern empires had to face a peculiar paradox:

> To speak now of the true temper of empire, it is a thing rare and hard to keep; for both temper and distemper consist of contraries. But it is one thing to mingle contraries, another to interchange them. And certain it is that nothing destroyeth authority so much as the unequal and untimely interchange of power pressed too far, and relaxed too much.[91]

These were some of the important conceptualizations and justifications of *dominus mundi* and universal monarchy propagated and acted upon by the major powers of early modern Europe. Even if the outbreak of the Thirty Years War in 1618 in part was caused by quarrels over taxation and religious discord, its later phases are perhaps better understood as a contest of Spanish claims to universal monarchy in Europe by France, which soon was to raise similar claims. Whereas the treaties of Münster and Osnabrück were intended to curb such aspirations within Europe, they gave renewed sanction and further impetus to imperial pursuits *outside* Europe.[92] But the Westphalian settlement also brought new ways of justifying imperial expansion *inside* Europe, since territorial aggrandizement could now be legitimized with reference to the rights of conquest rather than by appealing to principles of dynastic succession, which had constituted the main basis for claims to empire in the past.[93]

In the next section, we shall see how Grotius provided important elements of such a theory of legitimate conquest. But let me conclude this section by pointing out that Hobbes furnished still others. Although he famously contributed to the articulation of a

[90] Ibid.

[91] Francis Bacon, "Of Empire." in Francis Bacon, *Essays, Civil and Moral*, Vol. II, Part I (New York: P. F. Collier & Son, 1909–1914), ch. XIX, 2.

[92] Barreto, "Cerberus", 164–166.

[93] See John Robertson, "Empire and Union: Two Concepts of the Early Modern European Political Order." in John Robertson (ed.), *A Union for Empire. Political Thought and the British Union of 1707* (Cambridge: Cambridge University Press, 1995), 3–36.

modern concept of the state, his understanding of sovereignty was in fact equally if not more compatible with ideas of imperial rule. This being so, since he conceived of no pre-constituted limits to sovereign authority, whether in terms of its territorial extent or the location of its subject populations. Thus we learn from *Leviathan* (1651) that "[w]hen in one Common-wealth there be divers Countries, that have their Lawes distinct from one another, or are farre distant in place, the Administration of Government being committed to divers persons, those Countries where the Sovereign is not resident, but governs by commission, are called Provinces."[94] Hobbes then goes on to exemplify this imperial arrangement with that of the "Romans, who had Soveraignty over many Provinces, yet governed them alwaies by Presidents and Praetors" and the "Colonies sent from England to Plant *Virginia*, and Sommer-Illands, through the Government of them there, were committed to Assemblies in *London*."[95] Formulations like this facilitated what was soon to become a bifurcation of the world into a European sphere of sovereign states and a non-European sphere of colonial empires in the coming centuries.

Against Empire

By the seventeenth century, Renaissance visions of empire had become difficult to realize and even more difficult to legitimize. The Spanish conquest of the Americas was judged illegal by many contemporary jurists while attempts at territorial aggrandizement in Europe were met with fierce resistance from rivaling powers. Claims to world dominion, which had first been raised in the context of overseas expansion, became difficult to justify with reference to legal principles. In the context of European interpolity relations, the most common way to oppose territorial expansion was by arguing that such schemes threatened the liberty of other states and disrupted the balance of power among them. Yet arguments dressed up as principled resistance to empire during the second half of the seventeenth century were often themselves little but clever justifications of aggrandizement, or at least likely to be perceived as such by others. The concept of

94 Thomas Hobbes, *Leviathan*. ed. by Richard Tuck (Cambridge: Cambridge University Press, 1991), XXII, 158–159.
95 Ibid., 159.

universal monarchy, for instance, which had been widely used to characterize quests for empire in the European context, was turned into a derogatory term and used to castigate those suspected of aspiring to boundless power and glory – often by actors themselves guilty of harboring similar aspirations – thereby trapping anti-imperial rhetoric in a game of mirrors, giving rise to self-fulfilling prophesies and cascading security dilemmas. In this section, I shall discuss some important arguments leveled against the idea of empire and practices of imperial aggrandizement. As I will argue, instead of taking arguments against empire as pointing towards a pending decline of empires, I think it would be more accurate to interpret these either as attempts to reconcile projects of overseas expansion with parallel claims to territorial sovereignty at home, or as attempts to reconcile aspirations to great power status in Europe with the need for legal and political order on that continent. As I will show, these different strands of criticism eventually converged in Enlightenment historiography, ushering in a vision of the world divided into a European sphere of states and a non-European sphere of empires.

A first wave of criticism was directed against the Spanish claims to sovereignty in the Americas concerned dominion both in the sense of political jurisdiction and in the sense of property rights, senses that were difficult to disentangle given the usages of this concept in legal thought.[96] As Anthony Pagden has noted, "claims to universal sovereignty were based upon a tacit assumption that each new society, as it came to light, would have to conform to a rule – the juridical concepts of Western Europe – which had been devised with no prior knowledge of its existence."[97] The legitimacy of such claims to universal sovereignty in the Americas was soon contested by members of the Salamanca School, culminating in the debate in Valladolid 1550–1551. The arguments of those contesting the legitimacy of Spanish

[96] See, for example, Anthony Pagden, "Dispossessing the Barbarian: The Language of Spanish Thomism and the Debate Over the Property Rights of the American Indians." in Anthony Pagden (ed.) *The Languages of Political Theory in Early-Modern Europe* (Cambridge: Cambridge University Press, 1987): 79–98; Antony Anghie, *Imperialism, Sovereignty and the Making of International Law* (Cambridge: Cambridge University Press, 2007); David A. Lupher, *Romans in a New World: Classical Models in Sixteenth-Century Spanish America* (Ann Arbor: University of Michigan Press, 2006).

[97] Pagden, *Lords of all the World*, 59.

rule shared certain characteristics in common. As David Lantigua has argued, these arguments "appealed to a universal juridical order and ecclesiastical forum transcending Spanish imperial power to protect non-Europeans from unjust political aggression and colonial oppression."[98] Although most of these arguments are well known, let me briefly recapitulate what they implied for the legitimacy of the Spanish claims to empire in the Americas, and by implication, for the coming into being of a realm of nominally equal political communities.

In 1539, Francisco de Vitoria delivered a series of lectures in which he disputed the rightfulness of Spanish dominion over the Indies and the dispossession and enslavement of their inhabitants that had ensued.[99] A couple of years later, Bartolomé de las Casas addressed the *Brevísima Relación de la Destrucción de las Indias* to Charles V, a short treatise that detailed the injustices perpetrated against the American Indians, which prompted Charles to assemble a *Junta* to assess the validity of its claims.[100] During the debates over the nature and extent of Christian jurisdiction over infidels that followed in Valladolid, the imperial humanist Juan Gines de Sepúlveda argued that wars of conquest and evangelization against the inhabitants of the New World were justified by virtue of the latter being sinful, irrational, and inferior. Las Casas retorted that however sinful and repulsive their customs may seem to the European observer, the American Indians were nevertheless rational and sociable enough to qualify as members of the great family of humankind, and were therefore entitled to the same set of rights as their conquerors.[101] As Vitoria had stated earlier, although apparently barbarous, this did in no way disqualified the American Indians from ownership (*dominium*) since

[98] David M. Lantigua, *Infidels and Empires in a New World Order. Early Modern Spanish Contributions to International Legal Thought* (Cambridge: Cambridge University Press, 2020), 5; Koskenniemi, *To the Uttermost Parts of the Earth*, 163–173.

[99] Francisco De Vitoria, *de Indis*. in Jeremy Lawrance and Anthony Pagden (eds.) *Vitoria: Political Writings* (Cambridge: Cambridge University Press, 1991).

[100] See Bartolomé de las Casas, *Brevísima Relación de la Destrucción de las Indias*. [1542] (Medellin: Imprenta Universidad de Antioquia, 2011). This issued in the Valladolid Debate (1550–1551), see Anthony Pagden, *The Fall of Natural Man: The American Indian and the Origins of Comparative Ethnology* (Cambridge: Cambridge University Press, 1986, 109–145.

[101] Anthony Pagden, *European Encounters with the New World. From Renaissance to Romanticism* (New Haven: Yale University Press, 1993), 51–87; Lantigua, *Infidels and Empires in a New World Order*, 141–186.

they "have some order in their affairs; they have properly organized cities, proper marriages, magistrates and overlords, laws, industries, and commerce, all of which require the use of reason."[102] Thus the natural rights enjoyed by the Indians implied that they could not be subjected to any external political authority or transfer their property without their consent.[103] Yet even if their communities were granted autonomous standing within the wider legal world order of which they were now considered part, the Spanish Crown had still ample grounds for waging war against them should they resist evangelization. Although missionary warfare was strongly condemned by Las Casas and Domingo de Soto on the grounds that it violated the natural rights of infidels, Vitoria had undercut that possibility by providing a new answer to the long-standing question of who had the legitimate authority to wage war. Only a prince who was the head of a "perfect community" could do so, the latter being "complete in itself: that is which is not part of another commonwealth."[104] But if only political communities that enjoyed such *de facto* independence could wage just war, this cast serious doubts on the Spanish right to do so against the infidels of America, while potentially bestowing the same right on the Indians in defense of their own communities.

Vitoria had been mostly concerned with questions of ownership and less with questions of political jurisdiction in the Americas. The validity of such claims to *dominium iurisdictionis* was contested by another prominent member of the Salamanca school, Domingo de Soto. Concerned equally with questions of ownership and jurisdiction, his *Relectio de Dominio* (1535) and *De Iustitia et Iure* (1553/1556) contested Spanish claims to universal jurisdiction by disputing those of the Roman Empire, so that to the extent that Spanish claims to universal jurisdiction were based on those of the Romans, a refutation of the latter would automatically spill over into a refutation of the former. De Soto began his lecture by distinguishing between *dominium* in the sense of ownership and *dominium* in the sense of jurisdiction, relegating the question whether "the emperor is lord of the whole

[102] Vitoria, *de Indis*, 250. For its contemporary reception, see José A. Fernández-Santamaría, *The State, War and Peace: Spanish Political Thought in the Renaissance 1516–1559* (Cambridge: Cambridge University Press, 1977).

[103] Lantigua, *Infidels and Empires in a New World Order*, 91, 110.

[104] Vitoria, *de Indis*, 301; compare Lantigua, *Infidels and Empires in a New World Order*, 124–125.

world" to the latter category. He then proceeded to refute such claims on the grounds that they were contrary to natural, divine, and positive law respectively. The idea of world dominion was contrary to the natural equality and liberty of men, and if somebody had indeed been intended for that role by God, then there would always have been a lord of all the world. Yet history provided no single example of such world lordship. Although it is true that the Romans had aspired to that position, the fact that they were unaware of the existence of other continents meant that they could not have ruled the whole world. Thus, the Roman claims to dominium appeared unfounded, since "[f]rom their own historians that their right was in force of arms (*ius erat in armis*), and they subjugated many unwilling nations through no other title than that they were more powerful."[105] But if the Roman claims to world dominium were invalid for that very reason, then the Spanish could not justify their dominion on such grounds either. Nor could their claims be substantiated in any other way, since whatever lordship the Romans had exercised had been based on the use of force rather than on consent on behalf of the conquered, and so were the claims to dominion raised by the Spanish over the New World and its inhabitants.[106] Vitoria and the Soto had thereby successfully delegitimized the claims to property rights and jurisdiction raised by the Spanish Crown in the Americas in favor of a pluralistic world order composed of distinct and independent communities that retained the rights of property and jurisdiction.

Many modern commentators have questioned the extent to which members of the Salamanca school actually recognized the Indians as moral and political equals in any genuine sense, and have instead held them responsible for legitimizing European imperialism and colonialism.[107] But as Martti Koskeniemmi has argued, the real

105 Quoted in Lupher, *Romans in a New World*, 65.

106 Lupher, *Romans in a New World*, 62–68; Lantigua, *Infidels and Empires in a New World Order*, 111–114; Koskenniemi, *To the Uttermost Parts of the Earth*, 174–181.

107 See, for example, Antony Anghie, "Francisco De Vitoria and the Colonial Origins of International Law." *Social & Legal Studies* 5, no. 3 (1996): 321–336; Brett Bowden, "The Colonial Origins of International Law. European Expansion and the Classical Standard of Civilization." *Journal of the History of International Law* 7, no. 1, (2005): 1–23; George Cavallar, "Vitoria, Grotius, Pufendorf, Wolff and Vattel: Accomplices of European Colonialism and Exploitation or True Cosmopolitans?" *Journal of the History of*

contribution of the Salamanca school was not so much their critique of empire as their articulation of a theory of universal property rights, of rights that were supposed to exist independently of *any* political authority. When the quest for territorial empires became economically harder to sustain during the seventeenth century, to be able to claim such property rights independently of political authority became crucial to the creation and justification of commercial empires in the following centuries.[108] The Salamanca school thereby unwittingly contributed to the bifurcation of the global space opened by the discoveries into two distinct spheres – one of overseas possessions and the other of European states – which now were able to coexist within the same legal framework, but with very different meanings attached to concept of *dominium* within each. In the former sphere, dominion understood as property rights could be claimed even in the absence of dominion understood as jurisdiction; in the latter property rights and sovereign authority were regarded as two sides of the same coin.[109]

Others disputed the legitimacy of the Spanish claims to universal empire on the grounds of its capacity to deliver benefits to those subjected to its authority. Starting from the Aristotelian premise that government is but a means to achieve the good life and the role of the legislator is to benefit the citizens, Diego de Covarrubias argued that since it is difficult enough to govern a large number of cities adequately given this objective, this implied that "by natural law and by nature ... the jurisdiction of the entire world has not been given to the Emperor."[110] Claims to universal empire were debunked on similar grounds by Fernando Vázquez de Menchaca, who maintained that if political communities exist only on authority of and for the good of their members, claims to political authority are historically contingent

International Law 10, no. 2 (2008):181–209; Andrew Fitzmaurice, "The Problem of Eurocentrism in the Thought of Francisco de Vitoria." in José Maria Beneyto and Justo Corti Varela (eds.), *At the Origins of Modernity: Francisco de Vitoria and the Discovery of International Law*. (Cham: Springer, 2017), 77–93.

108 Martti Koskenniemi, "Empire and International Law: The Real Spanish Contribution." *University of Toronto Law Journal* 61, no. 1 (2011): 1–36.

109 For a similar argument, see Andrew Fitzmaurice, *Sovereignty, Property and Empire, 1500–2000* (Cambridge: Cambridge University Press, 2014), 44–50.

110 Diego de Covarrubias y Leyva, *In Regulatem Peccatum* [1583]. Quoted and discussed in Pagden, *Lords of All the World*, 53.

and subject to change across time. Hence, to be legitimate, a ruler must be able to exercise his authority for the benefit of those subjected to his rule, a consideration that placed certain practical limits on the scope of political rule. Given these limits, universal empire represented a clear case of overextension, however, as it stands to reason it is "absolutely impossible that the sovereignty (*dominium*) over so many regions, peoples and provinces separated from each other by such enormous distances should reside with one man."[111] Thus, to Covarrubias and Vázquez de Menchaca, claims to universal empire were illegitimate not only because they violated the natural liberty of men, but because they transgressed the natural boundaries of political authority, these being defined with reference to the ability of a ruler to cater to the well-being of his subjects.

Some of the above arguments would continue to resonate during the seventeenth century, and notably in the work of Hugo Grotius.[112] Not unlike the members of the Salamanca School, much of what he said about empires and their legality indicate a critical stance. In *De Iure Belli ac Pacis Libri Tres* (1625), he uses the term *imperium* first and foremost with reference to the Roman Empire, and then to discuss what Roman historians and lawyers had said about its legal foundations. But he also uses this term to describe sovereign authority in general, which has been taken to indicate that he uses this concept to refer to sovereign states.[113] But as Annabel Brett has shown, Grotius did not possess a modern theory of sovereignty and did not distinguish

[111] Fernando Vázquez de Menchaca, *Controversiarum illustrium* [1564]. Quoted and discussed in Pagden, *Lords of all the World*, 59. For an analysis, see Annabel S. Brett, *Liberty, Right and Nature: Individual Rights in Later Scholastic Thought* (Cambridge: Cambridge University Press, 1997), 165–204.

[112] See, for example, Martin Van Gelderen, "From Domingo de Soto to Hugo Grotius: Theories of Monarchy and Civil Power in Spanish and Dutch Political Thought, 1555–1609." in Graham Darby (ed.) *Origins and Development of the Dutch Revolt* (Abingdon: Routledge 2001), 151–170; Edward Keene, *Beyond the Anarchical Society: Grotius, Colonialism and Order in World Politics* (Cambridge: Cambridge University Press, 2002); Arthur Weststeijn, "Provincializing Grotius: International Law and Empire in a Seventeenth-Century Malay Mirror." in Martti Koskenniemi, Walter Rech, and Manuel Jiménez Fonseca (eds.), *International Law and Empire: Historical Explorations* (Oxford: Oxford University Press, 2017), 21–38.

[113] Knud Haakonssen, "Hugo Grotius and the History of Political Thought." *Political Theory* 13, no. 2 (1985): 239–265.

sovereignty from *imperium*.[114] Although he takes *imperium* to extend over land spaces, he does not thereby imply that *imperium* has to be territorially bounded in order to be legitimate or effective, but seems rather to assume that subjects and populations constitute the primary objects of authority quite irrespective of where they happen to find themselves.[115] But the ambiguous usages of the term *imperium* should not be allowed to overshadow the fact that Grotius also used this term to describe empire in a more contemporary sense, and regarded the creation of such empires as *illegal* unless inflicted as punishment for wrongdoing.

The first sustained engagement with the notion of empire in this sense occurs in Book II when Grotius discusses unjust war. Using Dante's *De Monarchia* as a foil and echoing Vázquez de Menchaca, he first warns of the perils of overextension: "For as a Ship may be built to so vast a Bulk, as to be unwieldy, and not manageable, so an Empire may be extended over so great a Number of Men and Places so widely distant from each other, that the Government of it becomes a Task, to which no one Sovereign can be equal." Yet even if the creation of universal jurisdiction might seem desirable or expedient under certain circumstances, "the Right of Empire cannot be thence inferred. For Consent is the Original of all Right to Government, unless where Subjection is inflicted as a Punishment."[116] In Book III, Grotius proceeds to discuss the virtue of moderation in obtaining empire for the sole legitimate purposes of punishment or retribution. Ideally, conquerors should as far as possible intermix with the conquered, and the victorious should as far as possible "leave to the Conquered, either Kings or People, their own Government." The reasons for this lenient approach turn out to have more to do with imperatives of statecraft than with the rights of war, since "that their own Sovereignty should

[114] Annabel S. Brett, "The Subject of Sovereignty: Law, Politics and Moral Reasoning in Hugo Grotius." *Modern Intellectual History* 17 no. 3 (2020): 619–645.

[115] Annabel S. Brett, "The Space of Politics and the Space of War in Hugo Grotius's *De iure belli ac pacis*." *Global Intellectual History* 1 no. 1 (2018): 33–60; Elden, *Birth of Territory*, 259–268; Annabel S. Brett, *Changes of State: Nature and the Limits of the City in Early Modern Natural Law* (Princeton: Princeton University Press, 2011), 199, 210.

[116] Hugo Grotius, *De Iure Belli ac Pacis Libri Tres*. ed. by Richard Tuck (Indianapolis: Liberty Fund, 2005), II.XXII.XV, 1107–8.

be left to the Vanquished, is not only agreeable to Humanity, but often also to Policy."[117] Such compromises made it possible to divide sovereignty between polities without imposing overtly imperial and hierarchical relations between them with an eye to preserving what would otherwise likely be a precarious peace. Yet as John Robertson has pointed out, since Grotius granted those engaged in just war the right to conquer and punish their adversaries, Grotius thereby issued a generous license for territorial aggrandizement by means of conquest, a license soon to be cleverly used by Gustavus Adolphus during his German campaign.[118] Thus, although Grotius regarded universal empire as illegitimate, he, perhaps unwittingly, provided ample justifications for imperial expansion in Europe as well as elsewhere. In the former context, justifications of imperial expansion could be derived from his permissive view of the right to preventive war between sovereign states and the right of punishment. In the latter context, his view of sovereignty as inherently divisible and the fact that he acknowledged rights to wage private war gave states and trading companies free reign in search for profit wherever prior jurisdiction was deemed absent or weak. As José-Manuel Barreto has noted, "a new sovereign had been conjured into existence – a private company has become sovereign because it may go to war on its own volition, or without the express backing of any established holder of sovereignty."[119] In this way the division of the world into two distinct political spheres came to coincide with the distinction between the public and the private law in those commercial empires that superseded the quest for territorial aggrandizement on the European continent.

On that continent, and following the right of conquest, claims to universal monarchy could be challenged on the grounds that they furnished a recipe for constant warfare and violated the independence of individual states. Many of those who opposed universal monarchy on

[117] Grotius, *De Iure Belli ac Pacis*, III.XV.III–III.XV.VII, 1500–1504.

[118] Robertson, "Empire and Union", 18–19.

[119] Barreto, *Cerberus*, 158; Keene, *Beyond the Anarchical Society*. For commentaries, see Eric Wilson, "The VOC, Corporate Sovereignty and the Republican Sub-text of *De iure praedae*." in Hans W. Blom, *Property, Piracy and Punishment: Hugo Grotius on War and Booty in De iure praedae* – Concepts and Contexts (Leiden: Brill, 2009): 310–340. Also Philip J. Stern, *The Company-State: Corporate Sovereignty and the Early Modern Foundations of the British Empire in India* (Oxford: Oxford University Press, 2011).

such grounds held that balance of power was a better way of maintaining peace and international order even if that kind of argument itself sometimes carried imperialistic overtones.[120] Among the first attempts in this direction was the *Grand Design* (1638) of the Duc de Sully.[121] Written with the explicit aim to create the conditions of lasting peace in Europe, the *Design* outlined detailed plans for a federation of European states that would counteract hegemonic aspirations within Europe while keeping Turks and Russians at bay. According to Sully, the objective "was to divide Europe equally among a certain number of powers and in such a manner that none of them might have cause either of envy or fear from the possessions or power of the others."[122] Instead the states of Europe should be united in "an indissoluble bond of security and friendship."[123] Admittedly, therefore, the *Design* was a "general treaty of peace, wherein such methods would be projected as the public benefit and the general service of Europe might suggest as necessary to stop the progress of the excessive power of the house of Austria."[124] To realize this plan it was first necessary "to divest the house of Austria of the empire and of all the possessions in Germany, Italy, and the Low Countries; in a word, to reduce it to the sole kingdom of Spain."[125] Such dismembering of the Habsburg Empire would not only put a permanent end to its quest for hegemony, but also redistribute territories in such a way that a balance of power could be more easily maintained. To Sully, empires and states were of different size, but not necessarily governed according to different principles. While he identified the Habsburg Empire as illegitimate, the entities resulting from its breakup could be governed

[120] See Peter Schröder, "The Concepts of Universal Monarchy and Balance of Power in the First Half of the Seventeenth Century – A Case Study." in Martti Koskenniemi, Walter Rech, and Manuel Jiménez Fonseca (eds.) *International Law and Empire: Historical Explorations* (Oxford: Oxford University Press, 2017), 83–100; Martin van Gelderen, "Universal Monarchy, the Rights of War and Peace and the Balance of Power. Europe's Quest for Civil Order." in Hans-Åke Persson and Bo Stråth (eds.) *Reflections on Europe. Defining a Political Order in Time and Space* (Brussels: Peter Lang, 2007), 49–72.

[121] Maximilien de Béthune, Duc de Sully, *Grand Design of Henry IV, from Memoirs of Maximilian de Béthune duc de Sully* (London: Sweet and Maxwell, 1921). For a background, see Francis Harry Hinsley, *Power and the Pursuit of Peace: Theory and Practice in the History of Relations between States* (Cambridge: Cambridge University Press, 1963), 25ff.

[122] Ibid., 41. [123] Ibid., 30. [124] Ibid., 45–6. [125] Ibid., 35.

according to different principles – some being monarchies while others being republics – as long no one aspired to geopolitical preponderance. Yet it was obvious to his contemporaries that the upshot of the *Design* was not only to dismember the Habsburg Empire but to augment French power in the process, however much Sully tried to convince his readers that "[a]mong all these different dismemberings, we may observe that France reserved nothing for itself but the glory of distributing them with equity."[126] By insisting on such a massive redistribution of power in Europe, it was to provide a "new method for maintaining the equilibrium of Europe and for securing to each religion a more undisturbed peace than it had hitherto enjoyed."[127] But the *Design* also included a plan for compensating the Habsburgs for their territorial losses in Europe. This was "to increase its dominions in the three other parts of the world by assisting it to obtain and by declaring it the sole proprietor both of what we do know and what we may hereafter discover in those parts."[128] So, to Sully, the way to put an end to the relentless quest for universal monarchy in Europe was to channel the hunger for power and glory into territorial expansion on *other* continents.

Contrary to the view according to which the Peace of Westphalia in 1648 marked the end of empire in Europe and inaugurated a system of sovereign states, the Westphalian settlement merely served to *recalibrate* the parameters of imperial ambition in Europe. While the treaties of Münster and Osnabrück granted German princes more autonomy and turned what remained of the universalist aspirations of the Holy Roman Empire into more of a legal fiction, they also gave fresh impetus to the quest for imperial aggrandizement among European powers. Propelling this quest were the reciprocal and often self-fulfilling suspicions among the great powers that each in fact aspired to universal monarchy, as well as the shared conviction that such aspirations must be checked by means of alliances or preventive wars for the sake of peace and prosperity in Europe.[129] This makes it reasonable to describe the emergent balance of power in Europe less

[126] Ibid., 40. [127] Ibid., 46. [128] Ibid., 35–36.

[129] See Arno Strohmeyer, "Ideas of Peace in Early Modern Models of International Order: Universal Monarchy and Balance of Power in Comparison." in Jost Dülffer and Robert Frank (eds.), *Peace, War and Gender from Antiquity to the Present. Cross-cultural Perspectives* (Essen: Klartext Verlag, 2009), 65–80.

as a consequence of deliberate choices on behalf of the great powers, but more as an essential byproduct of their mutual suspicions and the ongoing competition for universal monarchy.[130]

Unsurprisingly, the quick rise of France after Westphalia provoked such suspicions among the Habsburgs, who were in the process of being dethroned from their position as the dominant dynasty in Europe. Those who wanted to challenge the power of the Habsburgs could now do so undeterred by their traditional dynastic claims to empire, and instead do this armed with the new and more versatile Grotian theory of conquest described earlier. As it turned out, the Habsburg suspicions were far from baseless. One of the boldest attempts to reassert French imperial ambition came from the historian and counsel to Louis XIV, Antoine d'Aubery. As he argued in his *Justes Pretentions du Roi sur l'Empire* (1667), since the French monarchy had remained essentially the same since the days of Clovis, and since Charlemagne had possessed Germany by virtue of being king of France and not in his capacity of Emperor, these lands now rightfully belonged to the French king. This being so, since any conquest undertaken for the right reasons and in the name of a sovereign state was fully legitimate.[131] Since the German kings only much later had been granted their titles by the Pope and the king of France, the latter was therefore the sole rightful and legitimate heir to the Holy Roman Empire: a looming dynastic union with Spain would eventually produce "an empire over all the sea and earth, and thus also a universal monarchy."[132]

These claims did not go down well in Vienna, where they provoked an almost immediate rebuttal from the Habsburg diplomat Franz von Lisola. His *Bouclier d'Estat et de Justice* (1667) sought to refute the French claims to German lands by exposing these as but a series of devious steps towards universal monarchy. According to Lisola, the French were operating on the assumption that "the Dominions of Sovereign Princes have always been the Dominions and Conquests of their Estates, and, That the Dominions and Conquests of Crowns

130 See Richard Devetak, "The Fear of Universal Monarchy: Balance of Power as an Ordering Practice of Liberty." *Proceedings of the British Academy* vol. 190 (2013):121–137.

131 Antoine d'Aubery, *Justes Pretentions du Roi sur l'Empire* (Paris: Antione Bertier, 1667), I.I & I.II.27.

132 Ibid., III.III, at 182.

can neither be alienated nor prescribed."[133] This implied that "their Design is to drive on their Conquests as far as ever the fortune of War will suffer them, and that those Overtures of Peace which they do make are but to amuse the neighbouring Princes."[134] By making any lasting peace impossible, the French actually aimed to destroy the Habsburg monarchy, which to Lisola was the only remaining bulwark against universal monarchy in Europe. Yet it is obvious from the ways in which both d'Aubery and Lisola used the concept of universal monarchy that it signified nothing but the undue preponderance of one state rather than an independent form of political association.

The invasion of the United Provinces by Louis XIV in 1672 incited fears in all of Europe that the French indeed aspired to universal monarchy, which produced another wave of proposals for restoring the balance of power in Europe.[135] As one anonymous author remarked in 1680, "[t]he great thing which has disturbed the Peace of Europe... and shaken the dismembered Kingdoms and States thereof, has been the huge designe of the Universal Monarchy, a designe which...has possessed the Genius of the Spanish and French Monarchies, which therefore...have been dangerous to all Europe."[136] The crisis of the Spanish succession did little to alleviate these fears among politicians and pamphleteers, who now believed that the joint ambitions of France and Spain would threaten English and Dutch overseas commerce. What set these authors apart from their predecessors was that they saw universal monarchy not as an unintended consequence of a will to power and glory, but as a natural outcome of mercantile competition. Thus, in a pamphlet entitled *A Discourse Concerning the Affairs of Spain* (1698), Andrew Fletcher started by arguing that governments were predisposed to pursue universal empire, his reason for writing being to put "all the other princes and states on their guard against whoever should pursue that ambition, to frustrate such a design, and spare

133 Franz von Lisola, *The Buckler of State and Justice against the Design Manifestly Discovered of the Universal Monarchy, under the Vain Pretext of the Queen of France, Her Pretensions Translated Out of French* (London: James Flesher for Richard Royson, 1667), 9.

134 von Lisola, *The Buckler of State and Justice*, 14.

135 For a background, see Steven Pincus, "The English Debate over Universal Monarchy." in John Robertson (ed.), *A Union for Empire: Political Thought and the British Union of 1707* (Cambridge: Cambridge University Press, 1995): 37–62.

136 Anon., *Discourses upon the Modern Affairs of Europe* (London: 1680), 1.

the world from so much ruin."[137] Fletcher then proceeded to describe the sources of Spanish decline, the causes of French ascendancy, and the possible outcomes of succession. Among the many sources of Spanish decline – which had kept its kings from attaining universal monarchy – were the failure to adopt modern practices of agriculture, industry, and commerce in the Indies, along with the intolerance of other religions that contributed to the depopulation and decay of Spanish dominions. Fletcher was worrying that France might rise to a position of preponderance in the event Louis should succeed in installing the Duke of Berry on the Spanish throne.[138] But if "the French were to become lords of Spain and of the Spanish Indies after renouncing the Spanish dominions in Italy to the Germans and Italians, they would do great damage to the commerce of the English and the Dutch."[139] Yet fortunately such a scheme was unlikely to succeed since "so formidable has the power of the Most Christian King become in our time, that should he have the desire to make himself master of any part of the Spanish Monarchy, he must expect to have the whole world allied against him."[140] To avert this tragic outcome, Fletcher proposed a redistribution of territories among all the contenders for the Spanish crown, and the restoration of the Spanish monarchy, whose imperial ambitions now had been bridled by a combination of commercial exchange, balance of power, and religious toleration.

Pamphleteers and political economists like Daniel Defoe and Charles Davenant were likewise inclined to regard the quest for universal monarchy as a natural if undesirable consequence of economic competition rather than of evil designs.[141] As Defoe stated, "if then

[137] Andrew Fletcher, "A Discourse Concerning the Affairs of Spain." in Andrew Fletcher, *Political Works* (Cambridge: Cambridge University Press, 1997), 84–117, at 84. For a background, see John Robertson, *The Case for the Enlightenment. Scotland and Naples 1680–1760* (Cambridge: Cambridge University Press, 2005), ch. 4.

[138] Fletcher was wrong here, since Louis ended up favoring his other grandson, the Duke of Anjou.

[139] Fletcher, "A Discourse Concerning the Affairs of Spain", 107.

[140] Ibid.

[141] For the context, see Steven Pincus, "The Making of a Great Power? Universal Monarchy, Political Economy, and the Transformation of English Political Culture." *European Legacy* 5, no. 4 (2000): 531–545; Steven Pincus, "Addison's Empire: Whig Conceptions of Empire in the Early 18th Century." *Parliamentary History* 31, no. 1 (2012): 99–117; Istvan Hont, *Jealousy of Trade. International Competition and the Nation State in Historical Perspective* (Cambridge, MA.: Harvard University Press, 2005), 210ff.

the French and Spaniard United, should make themselves in proportion too strong at Sea for the English and Dutch, they may bid very fair for a Universal Empire over this part of the World."[142] From this Defoe was able to conclude that "such a Union ... would be very pernicious to the Trade of England and Holland in general ... and absolutely inconsistent with the Ballance of Power in Europe."[143] To Davenant, the ongoing quest for universal monarchy was but a consequence of the fact the "forward parts" of humankind always had sought to accumulate as much wealth and power as possible. Peoples had "formed themselves into particular Principalities and Commonwealths ... finding they increased in Fame, and value with the World, as they increased in Wealth and Power ... proceeded forward still to fresh Conquests, till they had subdued all round about them; and from thence came what we call Universal Monarchy or Empire."[144] Even if nobody had ever succeeded to create, let alone maintain, such a universal empire, "there hardly appears to have been any long course of Time, in which some People or other did not either actually obtain, or at least attempt to procure to themselves sovereign Sway over the whole."[145]

But even if it was the clear and present danger of French hegemony that occasioned Davenant to write his essay, he tried to refute the arguments in favor of universal monarchy in more principled philosophical terms than did many of his contemporaries.[146] Contrary to what Mexia had argued in his *Historia Imperial*, universal monarchy was unlikely to bring security, prosperity and peace to the peoples subjected to its rule. Rather the opposite: "[w]hich way soever we consider great Empires (whether in their Infancy, in their blooming youth, in their Manhood and full Strength, or in their declining Age) we shall find Mankind ... afflicted with Wars, Famine, Bloodshed, Thraldom, and Devastations."[147] Nor would universal empire bring prosperity other than to its center, while its constituent kingdoms and provinces

[142] Daniel Defoe, *The Interests of the Several Princes and States of Europe consider'd, with Respect to the Succession of the Crown of Spain, and the Titles of the Several Pretenders Thereto Examin'd* (London, 1698), 22.

[143] Defoe, *Interests of the Several Princes and States of Europe*, 29.

[144] Charles Davenant, *An Essay upon Universal Monarchy. Written in the year 1701 soon after Lewis the Fourteenth had settled his grandson Philip de Bourbon upon the throne of Spain* (London: James, John and Paul Knapton, 1734), 30–31.

[145] Ibid., 32. [146] Ibid., 60. [147] Ibid., 63.

will end up overburdened by taxes and impoverished. Davenant then disputed the main argument for universal monarchy, namely that it would put an end to wars among states and thus bring lasting peace to the world. Yet quite regardless of the moral qualities of its ruler, the cost and trouble of maintaining such a universal monarchy "were a greater Weight upon the World, than now and then a War could."[148] Instead the proper antidote to constant war is the balance of power, "[a]s the Earth is now divided into several Kingdoms, principalities and States, between them wars will happen, but the weaker fortify themselves by Alliances with the stronger so that (unless some great Oppressor rises up to disturb the World with his ambition) we have many more years of Peace than of War."[149] Unsurprisingly, therefore, the doctrine of balance of power was not only a recipe for resisting Spanish attempts at hegemony, but also a centerpiece of a British imperial ideology favoring free commercial exchange on the seas.[150]

In this section we have seen how aspirations to world domination and universal monarchy in Europe were challenged on a variety of grounds during the seventeenth century. The Spanish bid for empire in the Americas was contested on the grounds of its incompatibility with the precepts of natural law and the natural liberty of men, and the successive quests for universal monarchy in Europe were resisted with reference to the natural liberty of states and their right to wage preventive war in defense of that liberty. As I will argue in the next section, from this debunking of imperial ambition followed not the wholesale demise of empires and the rise of states but attempts to argue that there existed an international system of states in Europe and a world of colonial empires on its outside. Thus, the emergence of a recognizably international realm in Europe corresponded with the re-conceptualization of the non-European world into one of overseas empires characterized by commercial competition between European imperial powers.

The End of Empire?

By the mid eighteenth century, the prospect of a universal monarchy was no longer perceived as a threat by European powers, although

148 Ibid., 69. 149 Ibid., 69.

150 David Armitage, *The Ideological Origins of the British Empire* (Cambridge: Cambridge University Press, 2000), 142–144.

it still inspired fear among those few city republics that struggled to maintain their independence amid ongoing great power rivalry.[151] The final rhetorical blow to the idea of universal monarchy had come from no one less than Montesquieu. Asking whether any European people was designated to rule over the others, he found this idea to be morally impossible. Advances in technology had made nations increasingly equal in military power while the development of international law had made war increasingly disadvantageous to victors as well as vanquished. Since overseas commerce had superseded war as the main source of wealth and power, European states had to adapt to the demands of commercial competition or perish. Hence territorial conquest was no longer an issue.[152]

In Europe, the balance of power was now widely espoused in theory and practice as the way to maintain peace and international order while preserving the liberty of individual states. As Emer de Vattel argued in his *Droit de Gens* (1758), "[t]he continual attention of sovereigns to every occurrence, the constant residence of ministers, and the perpetual negotiations, make of modern Europe a kind of republic, of which the members – each independent, but all linked together by the ties of common interest – unite for the maintenance of order and liberty." The ultimate warrant of this international order was the balance of power "which is understood such a disposition of things, as that no one potentate be able absolutely to predominate, and prescribe laws to the others."[153] Should any power try to dominate the others, "other states have a right to anticipate him: and if the state of war declares in their favour, they are justifiable in taking advantage of this happy opportunity to weaken and reduce a power too contrary to the

151 Richard Whatmore, *Against War and Empire: Geneva, Britain, and France in the Eighteenth Century* (New Haven: Yale University Press, 2012).

152 Charles-Louis Secondat de Montesquieu, "Réflexions sur la Monarchie Universelle." [1734] in *Œuvres Completes*, Tome II, Édition de Roger Caillois (Paris: Pléiade, 1951), 19–38, esp. 20–23.

153 Emer de Vattel, *The Law of Nations, Or, Principles of the Law of Nature, Applied to the Conduct and Affairs of Nations and Sovereigns, with Three Early Essays on the Origin and Nature of Natural Law and on Luxury.* [1758] Edited and with an introduction by Béla Kapossy and Richard Whatmore (Indianapolis: Liberty Fund, 2008), III.III. § 47, 496. See also Isaac Nakhimovsky, "Vattel's Theory of the International Order: Commerce and the Balance of Power in the Law of Nations." *History of European Ideas* 33, no. 2 (2007): 157–173.

equilibrium, and dangerous to the common liberty."[154] Enlightenment historians saw this emergent system of states as the outcome of successful resistance against bids for universal monarchy. As Robertson argued in his *History of the Reign of the Emperor Charles V* (1769), a modern system of states in Europe had first emerged as a result of the opposition by other European powers against the imperial designs by Charles V. Thus, it was an unintended consequence of his great ambition that "[n]o prince was so much superior to the rest in power, as to render his efforts irresistible, and his conquests easy…the advantages possessed by one state were counterbalanced by circumstances favourable to others and this prevented any from attaining such superiority as might have been fatal to all."[155] But this contestation of power had also galvanized Europe into a unity, since "[t]he nations of Europe in that age, as in the present, were like one great family: there were some features common to all, which fixed a resemblance; there were certain peculiarities conspicuous in each, which marked a distinction."[156] And as Edward Gibbon remarked some years later in his *Decline and Fall of the Roman Empire* (1776–1778), in sharp contrast to the Roman Empire, "the division of Europe into a number of independent states, connected, however, with each other, by the general resemblance of religion, language, and manners, is productive of the most beneficial consequences to the liberty of mankind."[157]

But beyond the confines of a Europe held together by common laws and customs, the enterprise of empire was well and alive. As Pocock has argued, to Enlightenment historians, "the advent of a commerce-generating civil society in all parts of what they chose to terms 'Europe' was the guarantee that neither ancient empire, medieval empire and

[154] Vattel, *Law of Nations*, III.III. § 49, 498.

[155] William Robertson, *The History of the Reign of the Emperor Charles V, with a View of the Progress of Society in Europe, from the Subversion of the Roman Empire to the Beginning of the Sixteenth Century*, Vols. I & II. [1769] (London: Routledge, 1857), Vol. II, 470. For an analysis, see Frederick G. Whelan, "Robertson, Hume, and the Balance of Power." *Hume Studies*, 21, no. 2 (1995): 315–332.

[156] Robertson, *The History of the Reign of the Emperor Charles V*, Vol. II, 470.

[157] Edward Gibbon, *The Decline and Fall of the Roman Empire*. Vol. 1 (New York: Modern Library, s.a.), 72–3. For an analysis, see John Robertson, "Gibbon's Roman Empire as a Universal Monarchy: The Decline and Fall and the Imperial Idea in Early Modern Europe." in Rosamond McKitterick and Roland Quinault, (eds.) *Edward Gibbon and Empire* (Cambridge: Cambridge University Press, 1997), 247–70.

papacy, or early modern universal monarchy and religious warfare, would return and plague them, and they knew that oceanic commerce and European empire in other continents were part of their modern world."[158] But even as the great commercial empires had superseded the old dreams of territorial conquest and aggrandizement in Europe, some Enlightenment historians and philosophers maintained that commercial empire abroad served to sustain despotism at home, and that these institutions should either be reformed, or altogether abolished and replaced with political institutions that would better cater to the interests of humankind as a whole.[159] As we shall see in the next chapter, such arguments would soon became commonplaces of revolutionary rhetoric in America and France.

Perhaps the most widely read account of the rise commercial empires during this period was the *Histoire philosophique et politique des établissements et du commerce des Européens dans les deux Indes* (1770) by the Abbé Guillaume-Thomas Raynal.[160] While Enlightenment historians such as Robertson had focused primarily on the transition from competing claims to empire to a system of states in Europe, Raynal provided a detailed account of the political and economic consequences of the intensified intercourse between European states and the rest of the world brought about by circumnavigation and the discoveries. As Pocock has noted, the *Histoire des Deux Indes* was the first genuinely global history.[161] At the center of this global history was the assumption that commercial exchange was a great

158 Pocock, *Barbarism and Religion* IV: *Barbarians, Savages, and Empires*, 231.

159 See Sankar Muthu, *Enlightenment against Empire*. (Princeton: Princeton University Press, 2003), chs. 2 & 3; Sankar Muthu, "Conquest, Commerce, and Cosmopolitanism in Enlightenment Political Thought." in Sankar Muthu (ed.) *Empire and Modern Political Thought* (Cambridge: Cambridge University Press, 2012), 199–231.

160 A collaborative work by Raynal, Diderot and others, *L'Histoire des Deux Indes* appeared in several editions, with significant changes and additions being made to the editions of 1774 and 1780. Despite being poorly translated, I have used the translation of the 1774 edition by Justamond. For notable differences between editions, see Girolamo Imbruglia, "Civilisation and Colonisation: Enlightenment Theories in the Debate between Diderot and Raynal." *History of European Ideas* 41 no. 7 (2015): 858–882.

161 J. G. A. Pocock, "Commerce, Credit, and Sovereignty: The Nation-State as Historical Critique." in Béla Kapossy (ed.), *Markets, Morals, Politics: Jealousy of Trade and the History of Political Thought* (Cambridge, MA.: Harvard University Press, 2018), 265–284, at 272.

civilizer of nations, but also a source of economic and political disparities among them and their inhabitants.[162] Thus, while it is true that "those states, that have been commercial, have civilized all the rest", intensified commerce has also meant that "some nations, that were of no consequence, are become powerful; others, that were the terror of Europe, have lost their authority."[163] Raynal then proceeded to explore the historical connections between commerce and civilization by tracing the history of empire from Rome to his own contemporaneity. Thus, we learn that the Romans had "promoted an intercourse between different nations, not by uniting them by the ties of commerce, but by imposing upon them the same yoke of subordination," and that during the Middle Ages, "[t]he single maxim, that the pope had a right to the sovereignty of all empires, sapped the foundation of all society and public virtue."[164] Thus neither the Roman Empire nor the Christian empire of the Middle Ages were worthy of emulation. Instead it was the Portuguese discoveries during the fifteenth century that had paved the way for the rise of the transcontinental commercial empires of the modern age, so that "[i]f Vasco de Gama had not made his discoveries, the spirit of liberty would have been again extinguished, and probably without hopes of a revival."[165] Much of the success of the Portuguese had depended on the generous liberties granted to the people by its kings, who "raised the spirit of the nation still higher, by treating the nobility in some measure upon a footing of equality, and by setting bounds to their own authority."[166]

Whereas Spain had extended its empire in the Americas by brute force and governed it according to the old model of territorial sovereignty, the Portuguese had discovered in the course of their eastward expansion that it "was necessary to establish a system of power and commerce, which, at the same time that it was extensive enough to take in all objects, should be so well connected, that all the parts of the grand edifice intended to be raised, should mutually strengthen each

[162] For an analysis, see Kenta Ohji, "Civilisation et Naissance de l'Histoire Mondiale Dans l'Historie des Deux Indes de Raynal." *Revue de Synthèse* 129 no. 1 (2008): 57–83.

[163] Abbé Guillaume-Thomas-François Raynal, *A Philosophical and Political History of the Settlements and Trade of the Europeans in the East and West Indies*. trans. by J. O. Justamond (London: W. Strahan and T. Cadell, 1783), I.I, 2 & 4.

[164] Raynal, *Philosophical and Political History*, I.I, 9 & 31.

[165] Ibid., I.I, 124. [166] Ibid., I.I, 146.

other."[167] Where the traditional model of territorial aggrandizement had failed to produce the desired economic benefits, commercial exchange was capable of connecting different parts of the world into a coherent and governable whole. But to Raynal, commercial exchange was but another way of conquest, albeit perhaps of a less brutal kind. The right of conquest now applied to commercial enterprises and private companies as much as to sovereigns, sometimes with unexpected outcomes. Hence the Portuguese empire was soon beset by decay as a consequence of "the vices and folly of some of their chiefs, the abuse of riches and of power."[168] "Thus the Portuguese lost the foundation of all real power, which consist in agriculture, natural industry, and population, and there was consequently no proportion between their commerce and the means of keeping it up."[169] After having been conquered by Spain and having their colonial possessions taken over by the Spanish Crown, Portugal lapsed into obscurity and lost its commercial edge. Instead, we witness the rise of the Dutch and the English, who gradually perfected the idea of commercial empire much to the chagrin of the French. Again, much of this success hinged on republican liberties of the Dutch, who in "[t]he ambition of giving greater stability and extent to her enterprises, excited in the republic a spirit of conquest… her connections embraced the universe, of which, by toil and industry, she became the soul. In a word, she had attained the universal monarchy of commerce."[170]

In this chapter, we have seen how construction of a global political space during the sixteenth century created the preconditions for rival claims to universal sovereignty in Europe as well as overseas. The ensuing attempts to bridle aspirations to universal sovereignty by appeals to natural rights and liberties, the balance of power, and public international law issued in the conceptualization of a system of states in Europe and the construction of an external arena of colonial empires. All major European powers had now established vast overseas empires that recognized few limits to their authority, and which were governed according to the same legal norms and practices derived from the rights of conquest and occupation that had been used to justify European expansion ever since the first wave of conquests in the sixteenth century.[171]

[167] Ibid., I.I, 105. [168] Ibid., I.I, 206. [169] Ibid. I.I, 223.
[170] Ibid. V.XII, 424–25
[171] See Andrew Fitzmaurice, *Property, Sovereignty, and Empire, 1500–2000* (Cambridge: Cambridge University Press, 2014).

To the extent that empires and states were perceived as distinct forms of polity at this time, it was because they now existed in different spaces, were composed of different populations, and were ruled according to different principles and standards of legitimacy. While European states were based on principles of indivisible sovereignty and territorial demarcation, colonial empires presupposed that sovereignty was divisible and boundless in principle and possible to extend over vast spaces and discontinuous polities and populations. Since these empires had grown out of European states, critics were quick to point out that the non-European world had become a factory outlet for the relentless quest for power and wealth that had made lasting peace and order difficult if not impossible to attain in Europe for centuries. The stateless parts of the world which had long been within the scope of the law of nations were now gradually removed from its purview with the rising conviction that this law applied to sovereign and civilized states only.[172]

But the world of empires and the world of states were nevertheless interconnected through commerce and other modes of exchange. Although such exchange had supposedly brought the benefits of civilization to the non-European world, it had also given rise to enormous disparities between those worlds. If indeed empire abroad went hand in hand with despotism at home, possible remedies were now becoming increasingly available in legal theory. As I will describe in the next chapter, those who wanted to break free from their imperial masters could now do so by declaring independence and seek international recognition of their claims. Given the Enlightenment critique of empire and despotism, those who wanted to raise such claims to independence could now do so armed with fresh notions of liberty and doctrines of sovereignty, and eventually boost these further with reference to notions of nationhood and self-determination.[173]

[172] See Jennifer Pitts, "Empire and Legal Universalisms in the Eighteenth Century." *American Historical Review* 117, no. 1 (2012): 92–121; Jennifer Pitts, *Boundaries of the International. Law and Empire* (Cambridge, MA.: Harvard University Press, 2018), 118–147.

[173] For an overview of some of these possibilities and their emergence, see Anthony Pagden, "Fellow Citizens and Imperial Subjects: Conquest and Sovereignty in Europe's Overseas Empires", *History & Theory* 44, no. 4 (2005): 28–46.

3 *Empire and Independence c.1776–c.1825*

Introduction

To some authors, a recognizably modern international system in Europe emerged only with the Vienna settlement of 1815. The end of the Napoleonic wars marked the end of empire in Europe and a transition to a system of sovereign and territorially bounded states. In the words of Harry Hinsley, the significance of the struggle against Napoleon was that "it was the newer ideas of the eighteenth century that were ultimately strengthened, the older programme of universal European monarchy ... that was destroyed."[1] Other scholars have pointed to the fact that the signatories to the Vienna settlement maintained overseas empires whose legitimacy had been challenged by the American and French Revolutions, issuing in the dismantling of their empires and the creation of new states in the Americas and a corresponding expansion of international society to include them.[2] The American Declaration of Independence of 1776 constituted what was to become the United States of America out of the thirteen seceding colonies and paved the way for their inclusion into what was still a European international society, all while plugging this newborn

[1] Francis Harry Hinsley, *Power and the Pursuit of Peace: Theory and Practice in the History of Relations between States* (Cambridge: Cambridge University Press, 1967), 190.

[2] See, for example, Adam Watson, "New States in the Americas." in Hedley Bull and Adam Watson (eds) *The Expansion of International Society* (Oxford: Clarendon Press, 1984), 127–141; David Armitage and Sunjay Subrahmanyam (eds.) *The Age of Revolutions in a Global Context, c. 1760–1840* (Houndsmills: Palgrave Macmillan, 2010); Christopher A. Bayly, *The Birth of the Modern World 1780–1914. Global Connections and Comparisons* (Oxford: Blackwell, 2004, 86–120; Jürgen Osterhammel, *The Transformation of the World. A Global History of the Nineteenth Century* (Princeton: Princeton University Press, 2014), ch. 8. For a historiographical overview, see Trevor Burnard, "Empire Matters? The Historiography of Imperialism in Early America, 1492–1830." *History of European Ideas* 33 no. 1 (2007): 87–107.

federal republic into an expansive orbit of transatlantic commerce and civilization.[3] As David Armitage has shown, the American Declaration of Independence was disseminated widely and inspired many subsequent declarations of independence across the world during the century to come. As he has argued, "the declarations of independence issued around the globe since the late eighteenth century mark a major transition in world history: in this era a world of states emerged from a world of empires."[4] Thus the Age of Revolutions provided other examples of wars of secession and struggles for independence, some of them successful and others not. In Saint Domingue, what started as a slave revolt in 1791 soon evolved into a wholesale social upheaval through a selective appropriation of the egalitarian promises of the French Revolution, and eventually issued in a declaration of independence in 1804.[5] Following the French invasion of the Iberian peninsula in 1808, the civil wars and wars of independence that swept across Latin America led to the demise of the Spanish empire and the emergence of more than a dozen new states in the 1820s which styled themselves republics.[6] Being the only remaining monarchy on the continent, Brazil declared independence in 1822 to preserve Braganza rule when João VI returned to Portugal from his exile in Rio de Janeiro during the Peninsular war. In Europe struggles for independence were

3 See David M. Golove, and Daniel J. Hulsebosch, "Civilized Nation: The Early American Constitution, the Law of Nations, and the Pursuit of International Recognition." *New York University Law Review* 85 (2010): 932–1066; Mikulas Fabry, *Recognizing States: International Society and the Establishment of New States since 1776* (Oxford: Oxford University Press, 2010); Peter S. Onuf and Nicholas Greenwood Onuf, *Federal Union, Modern World: The Law of Nations in an Age of Revolutions, 1776–1814* (Madison: Madison House, 1993).

4 David Armitage, *The Declaration of Independence. A Global History* (Cambridge, MA.: Harvard University Press, 2007), 104.

5 See, for example, David Geggus, "The Caribbean in the Age of Revolution." in Armitage and Subrahmanyam, *Age of Revolutions*, 59–82; Laurent Dubois, *Avengers of the New World. The Story of the Haitian Revolution* (Cambridge MA.: Harvard University Press, 2004); Robin Blackburn, "Haiti, slavery, and the age of the democratic revolution." *The William and Mary Quarterly* 63, no. 4 (2006): 643–674; Julia Gaffield (ed.) *The Haitian Declaration of Independence: Creation, Context, and Legacy* (Charlottesville: University of Virginia Press, 2016).

6 See Jeremy Adelman, *Sovereignty and Revolution in the Iberian Atlantic* (Princeton: Princeton University Press, 2006); Gabriel Paquette, "The Dissolution of the Spanish Atlantic Monarchy." *The Historical Journal* 52, no. 1 (2009): 175–212; Hilda Sabato, *Republics of the New World. The Revolutionary Political Experiment in 19th-Century Latin America* (Princeton: Princeton University Press, 2018).

less successful with Greece and Belgium being the only new states to emerge in the aftermath of the Vienna settlement.

In this chapter, I will argue that what has been made to look like a phase in the transition from a world of empires to a world of states by authors such as Hinsley and Armitage looked different to many of those involved, who were more inclined to view this as a contest between different forms of empire and different imperial powers. Pursuing this argument, I will focus on claims to independence and their recognition during the Age of Revolutions. Since declarations of independence were but claims to sovereignty understood in terms of independence from external interference, their success hinged on the extent to which that equation of sovereignty with external independence was accepted as a valid ground for international recognition and admission into what was in the process of becoming an international society. Declarations of independence are thus best understood as speech acts which, to achieve their intended outcome – recognition by the relevant parties – presuppose a shared understanding of what such independence means and what it entails in diplomatic and legal practice. Since such shared understanding is contingent on the meaning of independence and its connections to other legal and political concepts, the success of any given declaration of independence in turn hinges on its ability to align this meaning with prevailing requirements of legal recognition. But since these latter requirements were in constant flux during this period, claims to independence involved interpreting these with reference to the more fundamental legal and political principles these claims were believed to embody or express. This implied that since these principles also were intensely contested during the same period, claims to independence are meaningful only against the backdrop of the more general disputes about the nature of political authority, the sources of its legitimacy, and the limitations of its scope that together have made it possible to demarcate the Age of Revolutions in time and space.[7]

Thus, as I shall argue in this chapter, to understand how declarations of independence became viable roads to statehood, we need to situate them in the broader context of contemporary legal theory and political rhetoric from which those declarations emerged and gained traction. As I will show, the possibility of independence was as much conditioned by the changing norms of recognition as it was shaped by

[7] See Sabato, *Republics of the New World*, 30–33.

largely simultaneous attempts to de-legitimize various forms of empire and imperialism by revolutionaries as well as their critics. Consonant with more general changes in political language during this period, the notion of independence takes on a new meaning that makes it possible to raise claims to independence in terms that make it possible to reconcile their recognition with the expansion and consolidation imperial rule. The trajectory of the concept of independence tracks that of liberty more generally and can perhaps with some simplification be described in terms of a transition from a republican to a liberal understanding.[8] In the former understanding, independence entails not only a right to not be dominated by any other state but also a right to participate in the affairs of the larger whole of which each state form part. In the latter, independence equals little but a right to non-interference by other states within an international society based on contractual agreements between formally equal parties. If independence as non-interference presupposed a contractual form of association that did not rule out hierarchical and unequal relations between formally equal parties, then the expansion of international society meant little but a continuation of imperial relations with other means. But before I can proceed to analyze how the changing understanding of independence affected the prospects of attaining international recognition and what such inclusion into international society entailed, I will say a few words about what these claims to independence were *not* about.

First, claims to independence did not issue from anything like modern states, nor did they bring such entities into immediate existence. As Jeppe Mulich has pointed out, while the revolutions in the Atlantic world brought an end to earlier forms of colonialism and paved the way for claims to independence, this still took place within a framework of hierarchical and imperial relations, so that "autonomy did not mean nationhood and revolution did not spell the end of empire."[9] So although struggles for independence brought wholesale reconfigurations of sovereignty in the Atlantic world and ushered in the emergence of a dozen or so new polities in Latin America, these new polities did

8 See, for example, Quentin Skinner, *Liberty Before Liberalism* (Cambridge: Cambridge University Press, 1998); Philip Pettit, *Republicanism: A Theory of Freedom and Government* (Oxford: Oxford University Press, 1997).

9 Jeppe Mulich, "Empire and Violence: Continuity in the Age of Revolution." in Tarak Barkawi, and George Lawson (eds.), *The International Origins of Social and Political Theory* (Bingley: Emerald Publishing, 2017), 181–204, at 186.

not conform to contemporary legal standards of what sovereign statehood ought to entail and had therefore to embark on long and arduous struggles to refashion themselves in such a direction in the hope of being accepted as rough equals by their European counterparts.[10] At the time of independence, the authority structures of these new-born states still reflected the forms of divisible sovereignty and legal pluralism that had characterized the imperial order into which these polities until recently had been firmly embedded. Behind proud declarations of independence were often profound uncertainties about the precise locus of sovereign authority, who were subjected to it, as well as about its territorial extension and boundaries.[11]

Second, another reason why claims to independence ought not to be taken as indicative of a transition from empires to states is that these polities did not contain homogenous peoples or nations. Although sometimes cast in the name of this or that people or nation, the rhetoric of independence did rarely if ever correspond to sociocultural facts on the ground. Colonial communities were far from homogeneous and had long been based on practices of unequal inclusion that precluded the formation of nations or peoples in any modern sense, which made claims to nationhood hollow at best. As David Armitage has remarked, "[t]he American Declaration, like its successor declarations, was a document of state-making, not of nation-formation."[12] Although the American declaration of independence made mention of a people, there was nothing to indicate that this "people" was

[10] See Arnulf Becker Lorca, *Mestizo International Law. A Global Intellectual History 1842–1933* (Cambridge: Cambridge University Press, 2014); Liliana Obregón, "Between Civilisation and Barbarism: Creole Interventions in International Law." *Third World Quarterly* 27 no. 5 (2006): 815–832; Liliana Obregón, "Completing Civilization: Creole Consciousness and International Law in Nineteenth Century Latin America." in Anne Orford (ed.), *International Law and Its Others* (Cambridge: Cambridge University Press, 2006), 247–264; Carsten-Andreas Schulz, "Civilisation, Barbarism and the Making of Latin America's Place In 19th-Century International Society." *Millennium* 42 no. 3 (2014): 837–859.

[11] See, for example, Jaime E. Rodriguez, *The Independence of Spanish America* (Cambridge: Cambridge University Press, 1998); Lauren Benton, *Law and Colonial Cultures. Legal Regimes in World History 1400–1900* (Cambridge: Cambridge University Press, 2002), 31–79; Lauren Benton and Richard J. Ross, (eds.) *Legal Pluralism and Empires, 1500–1850* (New York: New York University Press, 2013).

[12] Armitage, *Declaration of Independence*, 17.

conceived of as an acting subject, or as a source of democratic legitimacy. By the same token, subsequent declarations of independence in Latin America "mostly drew on Spanish understandings of sovereignty as residing in the autonomy of specific *pueblos* rather than in particular nations or states."[13] These *pueblos* were rarely united in their quest for independence, but such declarations were often motivated fear and self-interest among local elites. As Jeremy Adelman has noted, "independence *did not* signify that large numbers of people grew clearer about what they did want as a precondition for rejecting what they did not."[14] It is therefore misleading to interpret appeals to nationhood by those who fought for independence as an indication that something akin to modern nations were in the process of being formed during this period.[15] Hence, since there were no peoples or nations present at this point in time that could be involved in a struggle to determine their own fate, it would be misleading to equate declarations of independence with pleas for national self-determination, especially given that the legal doctrine of self-determination gained traction only later in the nineteenth century.[16] Thus, even in those instances in which claims to independence were couched in the language of nationhood, it was hardly the case that among recognizing parties "[t]heir settled existence was taken as conclusive evidence of the will of their respective people to constitute them."[17]

Third, something similar goes for the question of citizenship during the quest for independence. American colonial societies were stratified along racial lines with European and creole elites at the top, and Indians, those of mixed race, and slaves at the bottom. European settlers and creole elites occupied a precarious top position within the imperial hierarchy. As Joshua Simon has argued, "[a]t once dominant as Europeans within American colonies, and dominated as Americans

13 Ibid., 121.

14 Jeremy Adelman, "Iberian Passages: Continuity and Change in the South Atlantic." in *The Age of Revolution in Global Context*, 59–64, at 81.

15 See Benedict Anderson, *Imagined Communities. Reflections on the Origin and Spread of Nationalism* (London: Verso, 1983), 47–66.

16 Eric D. Weitz, "Self-Determination: How a German Enlightenment Idea Became the Slogan of National Liberation and a Human Right." *The American Historical Review* 120 no. 2 (2015): 462–496; compare Jörg Fisch, *The Right of Self-determination of Peoples: The Domestication of an Illusion* (Cambridge: Cambridge University Press, 2015), 69–90.

17 Fabry, *Recognizing States*, 50.

within European empires, Creoles were neither colonizers nor colonized, but both."[18] Although the latter saw independence as a way of escaping imperial domination, they also saw it as a threat to the internal hierarchy and gave rise to fears that it would lead to a slave revolt as had been the case in Haiti. In terms of citizenship rights, the Constitution of Cádiz of 1812 had stipulated that sovereignty resided in a Spanish nation "composed of Spaniards from both hemispheres" but was ambiguous concerning *what* the rights of citizenship consisted of as well as *who* was entitled to citizenship.[19] Whereas that constitution granted representation of the Spanish American possessions to the Cortes, their influence was perceived as too limited to make any difference to colonial affairs by creole elites. Consequently their "leaders demanded *equality* rather than *independence*; they sought *home rule*, not *separation* from the Spanish Crown."[20] Given this colonial legacy and the variegated racial makeup of imperial populations, once independence had been attained and Latin American republics had been formed, attempts to define citizenship were ridden with contestation and arbitrariness, thus compromising one of the main promises of the American revolutions, that of popular sovereignty.[21] In Latin America, the leaders of new republics thus faced the dual challenge of legitimizing political authority by inventing peoples and nations all while delimiting its territorial scope through the drawing of boundaries.[22]

But if the road from empires to states was not as straight as some authors have led us to believe, what was really at stake in the making of

[18] Joshua Simon, *The Ideology of Creole Revolution. Imperialism and Independence in American and Latin American Political Thought* (Cambridge: Cambridge University Press, 2017), 24; Jorge Cañizares-Esguerra, "Racial, Religious, and Civic Creole Identity in Colonial Spanish America." *American Literary History* 17, no. 3 (2005): 420–37.

[19] "The Cádiz Constitution of 1812." in Sarah C. Chambers and John Charles Chasteen (eds.), *Latin American Independence. An Anthology of Sources.* (Indianapolis: Hackett Publishing, 2010), 96–107, at 97.

[20] Rodriguez, *Independence of Spanish America*, 2.

[21] Tamar Herzog, *Defining Nations: Immigrants and Citizens in Early Modern Spain and Spanish America* (New Haven: Yale University Press, 2008); Tamar Herzog, "Communities Becoming a Nation: Spain and Spanish America in the Wake of Modernity (and thereafter)." *Citizenship Studies* 11, no. 2 (2007): 151–172; Hilda Sabato, "On Political Citizenship in Nineteenth-Century Latin America." *American Historical Review* 106, no. 4 (2001): 1290–1315.

[22] Sabato, *Republics of the New World*, 22–49.

new states during the Age of Revolutions? Even if claims to independence were but ways of redefining the parameters of imperial rule, the fact remains that these claims brought a host of new states into existence and expanded the orbit of international society outside its European point of origin. As I will argue in this chapter, the relative success of claims to independence was made possible by changes in meaning of the concept of independence itself. These changes were brought about by a creative appropriation of legal principles that allowed leaders of wannabe states to jump through the windows of opportunity that their interpretations of the geopolitical situation created. From this point of view, declarations of independence are best understood as claims to sovereignty whose success would depend on being recognized as such, not as expressions of national identities or popular wills, since nations and peoples were still waiting to emerge in those places where declarations of independence were promulgated. Declarations of independence could only succeed by aligning these with emerging norms of international recognition and the attempts to delegitimize imperial rule that were in vogue during this period. From this it follows that if we want to understand the making of new states during this period, we should focus less on the domestic makeup of wannabe states and focus more on the underlying changes in international legal norms that made declarations of independence look like a viable strategy to those who wanted to shake off the imperial yoke. And to understand why such a shaking off began to look both possible and desirable at the end of the eighteenth century, we need to understand how the attempts to delegitimize empire and imperial rule that accompanied the American and French Revolutions impacted the interpretation of the very same legal norms. It will then become plain why claims to independence were understood by contemporaries not as pointing towards a transition to a world of states and towards the creation of an international society, but rather toward a transition from an older form of territorial empire based on direct rule to a new maritime and commercial form based on more indirect influence over nominally independent or semi-sovereign states.

The rest of this chapter is organized as follows. In the next section, I will briefly describe the principal features of the European legal order at the advent of the revolutions and the meaning that the concept of independence had acquired within this legal context. I will then go on to describe the contours of revolutionary and counter-revolutionary rhetoric and the attempts to delegitimize imperial rule in which both revolutionaries and their critics were engaged, and how this polemic spilled over into a tension between two distinct conceptions of independence and international order. I will end by describing how a selective uptake of these conceptions came to constitute the immediate intellectual context in which the claims to independence by Latin American states were raised and recognized by Britain in the aftermath of the Napoleonic wars.

From Independence to Recognition

As I argued in the previous chapter, a common way to resist aspirations to universal monarchy was to claim that European states formed part a wider community held together by shared legal norms and designated to safeguard the liberty of individual states by means of the balance of power. These themes were further articulated in legal and political thought during the latter part of the eighteenth century and came to exercise a considerable influence on revolutionaries on both sides of the Atlantic. For example, in an early and influential attempt to mythologize the Peace of Westphalia, Gabriel Bonnot de Mably maintained that the Treaty of Westphalia in 1648 represented a constitutional moment at which European states had entered into a federation and was the foundation upon which all subsequent treaties between them had been built. What happened in Westphalia was "the finest, most learned, and profound negotiation which was yet made among men. The treaties of Münster and Osnabruck are the fundamental law of the empire, and the basis on which liberty was established. It is the foundation the public law Europe."[23] Within that legal framework, "the independence of all sovereigns is equal, and ought everywhere to be equally respected. A great prince, who takes pleasure exacting such submission from little states...does by his conduct imprudently teach all Europe that he esteems more the rights of force than of justice?"[24] Mably here conjures up a republican international order in which the independence of states is understood as the absence of domination, warranted by the public law of Europe

23 Gabriel Bonnot, Abbé de Mably, *The Principles of Negotiations: or, An Introduction to the Public Law of Europe Founded on Treaties* (London: London: James Rivington and James Fletcher, 1758), 188. For a background, see Martti Koskenniemi, *To the Uttermost Parts of the Earth. Legal Imagination and International Power 1300–1870* (Cambridge: Cambridge University Press, 2021), 417–421.

24 Mably, *The Principles of Negotiations*, 88–89.

and modelled on the virtuous example of the Roman republic, which had "waged war only to secure and strengthen the empire of laws among men, and make them happy."[25] To Mably, unbridled international commerce would inevitably lead to an unequal distribution of wealth and power within as well as among states, thereby subverting the precious balance of power and the liberty of individual states in Europe.[26] For this reason "[t]he project of having alone the empire of the sea, and monopolizing all sorts of commerce, is no less chimerical, or less destructive, that the project of universal monarchy on the continent."[27] As we shall see in the next section, this contention was to become a cornerstone of Napoleonic foreign policy against the perceived global dominance of Great Britain.

But the most influential legal theorist in this context was Emer de Vattel. Although he maintained that the legal personality of states derived from their internal constitution, he took external independence to be a necessary condition of their sovereign equality within the larger republic he believed that European states now together constituted.[28] This is already evident in the very first pages of *Le Droit de Gens* (1758), where he stated that:

> every nation that governs itself, under what form soever, without dependence on any foreign power, is a sovereign state. Its rights are naturally the same as those of any other state. Such are the persons who live together in a natural society, subject to the law of nations. To give a nation a right to make an immediate figure in this grand society, it is sufficient that it be

25 Mably, *The Principles of Negotiations*, 42.

26 See, for example, Julie Ferrand and Arnaud Orain, "Abbé de Mably on Commerce, Luxury, and Classical Republicanism." *Journal of the History of Economic Thought* 39, no. 2 (2017): 199–221; István Hont, "The Rich Country – Poor Country Debate in the Scottish Classical Political Economy." in István Hont and Michael Ignatieff (eds.) *Wealth & Virtue. The Shaping of Political Economy in the Scottish Enlightenment* (Cambridge: Cambridge University Press, 1983), 271–315; Christopher Brooke, "Eighteenth-century Carthage." in Béla Kapossy, Isaac Nakhimovsky and Richard Whatmore (eds.) *Commerce and Peace in the Enlightenment* (Cambridge: Cambridge: Cambridge University Press, 2017), 110–124.

27 Mably, *The Principles of Negotiations*, 71.

28 See Ben Holland, "The Moral Person of the State: Emer de Vattel and the Foundations of International Legal Order." *History of European Ideas* 37 no. 4 (2011): 438–445; Ben Holland, *The Moral Person of the State. Pufendorf, Sovereignty, and Composite Polities* (Cambridge: Cambridge University Press, 2017), 120ff.

really sovereign and independent, that is, that it govern itself by its own authority and laws.[29]

As he went on to explain, European states no longer form "a confused heap of detached pieces, each of which thought herself very little concerned in the fate of the others, and seldom regarded things which did not immediately concern her."[30] The transition to a modern legal order had been facilitated by the practices of diplomatic intercourse and balance of power that warranted the independence of states within what through centuries of intercourse had evolved into one great republic. But the insistence on the regulating force of the balance of power made it hard to reconcile the notion that states were independent actors whose primary duty was self-preservation with the idea that they were also subject to the law of nations, all while every state was supposed to strive for moral perfection and international harmony in accordance with the laws of nature.[31] Perhaps precisely because of those tensions, *Le Droit de Gens* was read and appropriated for a wide range of ideological purposes during the Age of Revolutions when there apparently was a Vattel for every weather.[32] But since the world of Vattel was primarily a world of sovereign states of a yet undetermined spatiotemporal scope, he had little to say about empires or about European imperial expansion on other continents.[33] From this silence some authors have inferred the disappearance of the concept of empire from international law. For example, according to Emmanuelle Jouannet, with the rise of the modern state, the concept of empire loses its original Roman connotations and ceases to

[29] Emer de Vattel, *The Law of Nations, or, Principles of the Law of Nature, Applied to the Conduct and Affairs of Nations and Sovereigns, with Three Early Essays on the Origin and Nature of Natural Law and on Luxury.* [1758]. Edited and with an introduction by Béla Kapossy and Richard Whatmore (Indianapolis: Liberty Fund, 2008), I.I.§4, 83. For a background, see Koskenniemi, *To the Uttermost Parts of the Earth*, 860–872.

[30] Vattel, *Law of Nations*, III.III. § 47, 496.

[31] For his attempt to resolve these tensions, for example Ian Hunter, "Vattel's Law of Nations: Diplomatic Casuistry for the Protestant Nation." *Grotiana* 31, no. 1 (2010): 108–140; Richard Devetak, "Law of Nations as Reason of State: Diplomacy and the Balance of Power in Vattel's "Law of Nations." *Parergon* 28, no. 2 (2011): 105–128.

[32] I owe this expression to Lauren Benton.

[33] See Jennifer Pitts, *Boundaries of the International. Law and Empire* (Cambridge, MA.: Harvard University Press, 2018), 68–91.

organize political experience until it finally disappears from the political and legal register. By the end of the Napoleonic wars, the concept of empire becomes but a fiction, albeit a potent one. In its place enters the new legal and political reality of the sovereign state as a moral person, and an international system of such states as its natural correlate.[34] But whereas Vattel's universalism was limited by his conception of a European states system, he nevertheless provided some of the most important conceptual resources for those who wanted to raise claims to independence from imperial powers on other continents. The first and perhaps most important of these was his rendition of sovereignty in terms of external independence, a conception which was to be weaponized by revolutionaries and conservatives of all stripes in Europe and the Americas during this period. A second innovation that would be used to legitimize struggles for independence was his highly malleable conceptualization of civil war. When a civil war "produces in the nation two independent parties, who consider each other as enemies, and acknowledge no common judge", this entails that "they stand therefore in precisely the same predicament as two nations, who engage in a contest, and, being unable to come to an agreement, have recourse to arms."[35] This implies that whenever hostilities during a war of secession had reached a certain tipping point, those in favor of independence could confidently claim that theirs was no mere rebellion or civil war, but an *international* contest between legal equals that should be judged according to the norms of international rather than public law.[36] Hence, as would become obvious during the American revolution, claiming independence and going international in the process of doing so were but two sides of the same coin. A third valuable

[34] Emmanuelle Jouannet, "The Disappearance of the Concept of Empire. Or, the Beginning of the End of Empires in Europe from the 18th century." Presentation at the Conference A Just Empire? Rome's Legal Legacy and the Justification of War and Empire in International Law, Commemorative Conference on Alberico Gentili (1552–1608). New York University School of Law, 13–15 March 2008.

[35] Vattel, *The Law of Nations, or, Principles of the Law of Nature, Applied to the Conduct and Affairs of Nations and Sovereigns, with Three Early Essays on the Origin and Nature of Natural Law and on Luxury*. [1758]. Edited with an introduction by Béla Kapossy and Richard Whatmore. (Indianapolis: Liberty Fund, 2008), III.XVIII, 293.

[36] On this point, Se David Armitage, *Civil Wars. A History in Ideas* (New York: Knopf, 2016), 128–34.

resource was his innovative conceptualization of the right of intervention. Contrary to widespread belief, Vattel did not maintain that sovereignty entailed an unconditional right to non-intervention but instead provided a series of reasons *for* intervention, for example in states whose governments threatened their own populations, were savage by their very nature, or generally disruptive of the legal order and balance of power in Europe.[37] In such cases intervention would be called for in order to safeguard the security of other states as well as to maintain international order:

> If then there is anywhere a nation of a restless and mischievous disposition, ever ready to injure others, to traverse their designs, and to excite domestic disturbances in their dominions, it is not to be doubted that all the others have a right to form a coalition in order to repress and chastise that nation, and to put it forever after out of her power to injure them.[38]

During the Age of Revolutions, what constituted such a restless and mischievous disposition was entirely in the eyes of the beholder. Such justifications of intervention came in handy for those who wanted to end the spread of revolutionary fervor but could equally easily be harnessed to support struggles for independence by arguing that restlessness and mischief were characteristic of imperial powers. Hence, by defining sovereignty in terms of external independence from other states Vattel not only presupposed the existence of an international realm, but also furnished the conceptual resources necessary for anyone wanting to enter that realm by raising claims to sovereignty by declaring themselves independent of other powers. Should this result in civil war all the better, since this made it possible to *internationalize* the conflict in question.

This was a marked difference from the early modern order. Until this point, jurists had not had to bother much about what counted as a state and what did not. As James Crawford has argued in his seminal account of how states have been created in international law, recognition had "no separate place in the law of nations before the middle of the eighteenth century. The reason for this is clear: sovereignty, in

[37] See Lorenzo Cello, "The Legitimacy of International Interventions in Vattel's the Law of Nations." *Global Intellectual History* 2 no. 2 (2018): 105–123; Luke Glanville, "Responsibility to Perfect: Vattel's Conception of Duties beyond Borders." *International Studies Quarterly* 61 no. 2 (2017): 385–395.

[38] Vattel, *Law of Nations*, 289.

its origin merely the location of supreme power within a particular territorial unit ... necessarily came from within and did not require the recognition of other States or princes"[39] While I have disputed the accuracy this claim elsewhere, Crawford is right to argue that that a recognizably modern theory of international recognition did not emerge until the Age of Revolutions, and then precisely in response to the legal challenges prompted by the equation of sovereignty with external independence.[40] This being so since if sovereignty is supposed to derive from external rather than domestic sources, it becomes contingent on relations between states and thereby also an *international* rather than a domestic phenomenon.[41]

But there was yet no such connection between sovereignty understood as independence and the need for international legal recognition. This took a few more steps in the evolution of legal theory. The first partition of Poland in 1772 – an event which was to loom large in revolutionary rhetoric as an example of the abuse of sovereignty – put a problem that had long haunted elective monarchies into relief. While dynastic succession in hereditary monarchies did not normally give rise to any need for legal action by other states, such a need could arise if a ruler was elected and derived his rank or title from his people rather than from his predecessor, or, if that rank or title had been conferred on him by a foreign power. These possibilities became even more pertinent in those cases when foreign rulers opposed the election of a prince in another state on grounds that he would be unlikely to honor treaties. Poland was a case in point, where foreign powers had been involved in endless disputes about the election of kings since the beginning of the eighteenth century, disputes that had culminated in its first partition. As Johann Heinrich Gottlob von Justi then argued, in such cases foreign powers had a duty to recognize such states as legal persons on the same grounds as they had a duty to recognize

39 James Crawford, *The Creation of States in International Law* (Oxford: Oxford University Press, 2007), 12.

40 Jens Bartelson, "Recognition: A Short History." *Ethics & International Affairs* 30, no. 3 (2016): 303–321.

41 See Stéphane Beaulac, "Emer de Vattel and the Externalization of Sovereignty." *Journal of the History of International Law* 5 vol. 2 (2003): 237–292; Stéphane Beaulac, *The Power of Language in the Making of International Law: The Word Sovereignty in Bodin and Vattel and the Myth of Westphalia* (Leiden: Martinus Nijhoff Publishers, 2004).

hereditary monarchies and were also under a strict obligation not to intervene in their domestic affairs.[42]

During this period, the principles of dynastic legitimacy were being challenged by claims to popular sovereignty and ideas of democratic legitimacy, thereby altering the ideological context in which claims to independence could be raised and staked. Political authority could no longer be persuasively justified with reference to royal lineage or transcendent principles, but was increasingly believed to reside in the people, often quite regardless of how this people was to be defined and demarcated in practice.[43] In this revolutionary ideological context, claiming independence on behalf of a people was a potent way of garnering support for such claims, domestically as well as internationally. Thus, another difficult issue faced by international lawyers of this era concerned the legal consequences of claims to independence founded on notions of popular sovereignty. Here the appropriation of Vattel's definition of sovereignty as external independence made it easier to legitimize such claims to an international audience and made it difficult for European states to contest these on purely legal grounds.[44] Although not entirely without precedent, the most challenging case in this regard was posed by the American Declaration of Independence in 1776. While its purpose was to perform the independence it declared, it took considerable legal deliberation before the intended outcome was achieved.[45] But whereas discussions of recognition until this point had been focused on dynastic rights of succession, the German law

[42] Johann Heinrich Gottlob von Justi, *Historische und Juristische Schriften*, Vol. 1 (Frankfurt & Leipzig: Garbe, 1760), 185ff. For an analysis, see C. H. Alexandrowicz, "The Theory of Recognition *In Fieri*." *British Yearbook of International Law* 34 (1958): 176–198.

[43] See, for example, Mlada Bukovansky, *Legitimacy and Power Politics: The American and French Revolutions in International Political Culture* (Princeton: Princeton University Press, 2010); J. Samuel Barkin and Bruce Cronin, "The State and the Nation: Changing Norms and the Rules of Sovereignty in International Relations." *International Organization* 48, no. 1 (1994): 107–130.

[44] See Peter S. Onuf and Nicholas Greenwood Onuf, *Federal Union, Modern World: The Law of Nations in an Age of Revolutions, 1776–1814* (Madison: Madison House, 1993); Arnulf Becker Lorca, "Universal International Law: Nineteenth-Century Histories of Imposition and Appropriation." *Harvard International Law Journal* 51 no. 2 (2010): 475–552.

[45] See David Armitage, *Foundations of Modern International Thought* (Cambridge: Cambridge University Press, 2013), 191–214.

professor Johann Christian Wilhelm von Steck now focused on the rights of new-born states. Although a mere declaration of independence was not itself a sufficient ground for granting the United States independence, Steck maintained that once Britain had renounced sovereignty over its colonies and thereby implicitly recognized their *de facto* independence, other states were obliged to treat the United States as a free and equal sovereign state, and had no rights to intervene in its domestic affairs even should they not recognize its right to independence.[46] Furthermore, and now capitalizing on Vattel's notion of civil war, once it had been recognized by other powers, the declaration of independence implied that what had started as a war of secession was turned into a war between formal equals and therefore fell within the purview of international law, an implication that would inspire many who would later fight wars of secession against imperial powers.[47]

This point was made even more forcefully by the German jurist and diplomat Georg Friedrich von Martens in his *Precis du Droit des Gens Modernes de l'Europe* (1789). In those cases "that a province, or territory, subjected to another state, refuses obedience to it, and endeavours to render itself independent ... a foreign nation does not appear to violate its perfect obligations nor to deviate from the principles of neutrality" if it "treats as sovereign him who is actually on the throne, and as an independent nation, people who have declared, and still maintain themselves independent."[48] From this Martens concluded that "when a nation acknowledges, expressly or tacitly, the independence of the revolted state ... foreign powers have no more right to oppose the revolution, nor is even their acknowledgement of its validity necessary."[49] As Charles Alexandrowicz summarized the legal implications of these combined claims to independence and popular sovereignty, "the problem of recognition was formulated in a manner to show that the disturbance of the static legal order, which

[46] Johann Christian Wilhelm von Steck, "Versuch von Erkennung der Unabhängikeit einer Nation, und eienes Staates." in Johann Christian Wilhelm von Steck, *Versuche über Verschiedene Materien politischen und rechtlicher Kenntnisse* (Berlin, 1783), 49–56.

[47] Armitage, *Civil Wars*, 145–147.

[48] Georg Friedrich von Martens, *A Compendium of the Law of Nations Founded on the Treatises and Customs of the Modern Nations of Europe*. trans. by William Cobbett (London: Cobbett and Morgan, 1802), 81.

[49] Martens, *Compendium*, 82.

had prevailed in the past during the period of dynastic legitimism, was not allowed to prevent the reconciliation of new political changes with the tentative principles of a flexible and potentially progressive law."[50]

The next step was to argue that international recognition of claims to independence was indeed *constitutive* of statehood rather than but a polite way of reluctantly acknowledging facts already established on the ground. The philosophical underpinnings of this view were furnished by Hegel's *Grundlinien der Philosophie des Rechts* (1820), in which he held that the "state is the absolute power on earth; each state is consequently a sovereign and independent entity in relation to others. The state has a primary and absolute entitlement to be a sovereign and independent power *in the eyes of others*, i.e. *to be recognised* by them."[51] This being so, since "without relations to other states, the state can be no more an actual individual, than an individual can be an actual person without a relationship with other persons."[52] While the legitimacy of the state and its authority is wholly an internal matter, "it is equally essential that this legitimacy should be supplemented by recognition on the part of other states. But this recognition requires a guarantee that the state will likewise recognise those other states which are supposed to recognise it."[53] The Hegelian view of recognition was echoed and spread by Henry Wheaton in his influential *Elements of International Law* (1836), a work that made the connections between notions of independence, international recognition, and international society appear watertight and the worldwide spread of which contributed greatly to the contagion of sovereignty. Sovereignty, he argued, "is acquired by a State either at the origin of the civil Society of which it consists or when it separates itself lawfully from the community of which it previously formed a part and on which it was dependent."[54] And conversely, "[t]he internal sovereignty of a State does not, in any degree, depend upon its recognition by other States. A new State, springing into existence, does not require the recognition of other States to confirm its internal sovereignty."[55] But although internal

[50] Alexandrowicz, "Theory of Recognition *In Fieri*", 191.
[51] Georg Wilhelm Friedrich Hegel, *Elements of the Philosophy of Right* (Cambridge: Cambridge University Press, 1991), 366–367.
[52] Hegel, *Elements of the Philosophy of Right*, 366–367. [53] Ibid.
[54] Henry Wheaton, *Elements of International Law* (Boston: Little, Brown & Co., 1866), I.II, §21, 31.
[55] Ibid., I.II, §21, 32.

sovereignty does not stand in need of recognition by other actors, its external sovereignty "may require recognition by other States in order to render it perfect and complete."[56] In the case of new states, this implied that "where a revolted province or colony has declared and shown its ability to maintain its independence, the recognition of its sovereignty by other foreign States is a question of policy and prudence only."[57] But whenever recognition had been forthcoming from the relevant parties, what states looked like on the inside now became wholly irrelevant to the question of their sovereignty:

> whatever be its internal constitution, or form of government, or whoever may be its rulers, or even if it be distracted with anarchy, through a violent contest for the government between different parties among the people, the State still subsists in contemplation of law, until its sovereignty is completely extinguished by the final dissolution of the social tie, or by some other cause which puts an end to the being of the State.[58]

But as Wheaton added, should a state desire "to enter into that great society of nations ... such recognition becomes essentially necessary to the complete participation of the new State in all the advantages of this society."[59] Thus, to Wheaton, international legal recognition was not only essential to complete and perfect the fact of external independence, but also for wannabe states to attain membership in an international society much less dense than the kind of republic envisaged by his pre-revolutionary predecessors. Whereas Mably and Vattel had assumed that sovereignty originated from within states and that such internal sovereignty was necessary to attain recognition and membership of international society, Wheaton argued that the reverse held true. States were entitled to inclusion in international society by virtue of having their claims to sovereignty recognized by other states regardless of the makeup of their domestic political institutions. Wheaton had thus subtly yet effectively turned the world of Vattel inside out, legitimizing struggles for independence from direct imperial rule while simultaneously sanctioning new forms of indirect imperial rule. But notably, those passages were written before standards of civilization had been created to raise the bar of recognition and membership of international society. Because within his international society of formally equal states, some states were clearly less sovereign than others

[56] Ibid., I.II, §22, 33. [57] Ibid., I.II, §26, 40–41. [58] Ibid., I.II, § 20, 32.
[59] Ibid., I.II, §21.

by virtue of their dependence on their more powerful peers: "States which are thus dependent on other States, in respect to the exercise of certain rights, essential to the perfect external sovereignty, have been termed semi-sovereign States."[60] This, and other similar gradations of sovereignty were to provide legal sanction of indirect forms of imperial governance during much of the remaining nineteenth century.[61]

Delegitimizing Empire

Both the American and French Revolutions contributed to the spread of the Enlightenment critique of imperial rule on the grounds that it was despotic and its methods of rule arbitrary. In this way revolutionary rhetoric added fresh complications to the relationship between empire and independence on both sides of the Atlantic. Whereas the American Revolution was seen by both its advocates and its critics as a revolution *against* empire and in favor of independent government, the French Revolution was seen as a revolution against empire by some of its advocates but as one in *favor* of empire by many of its critics. But through its unintended consequences, its effect was rather the reverse. Whatever efforts new-born states in the Americas undertook to fulfill the membership requirements of an emergent international society – by entering into commercial treaties and by honing their diplomatic skills – their sovereignty and their ability to honor treaties were often held in doubt by their European counterparts.[62] But among the liberal internationalists of the day, there was an expectation that the dismantling of European empires and the emergence of new states in the Americas would help increase the scope of free commerce to replace the zero-sum rivalry between mercantilist powers, in the hope of thereby eliminating what had long been seen as a major cause of war among states.[63]

60 Ibid., I.II, § 34, 54.
61 See, for example, Lauren Benton, "From International Law to Imperial Constitutions: The Problem of Quasi-sovereignty, 1870–1900." *Law and History Review* 26 no. 3 (2008): 595–619; Arthur Learoyd, "Configurations of Semi-Sovereignty during the Long Nineteenth Century." in Jens Bartelson, Martin Hall and Jan Teorell (eds.) *De-Centering State Making. Comparative and International Perspectives* (Cheltenham: Edward Elgar, 2018), 155–174.
62 Onuf and Onuf, *Federal Union, Modern World*, 122.
63 Ibid., 100; Istvan Hont, *Jealousy of Trade: International Competition and the Nation-state in Historical Perspective* (Cambridge, MA.: Harvard University Press, 2005), 447–528.

Both revolutions had profound consequences for how the international realm was conceived, and the meaning of independence was intensely contested by revolutionaries and their critics alike. Authors on both sides mobilized available resources within the legal framework described in the previous section to further their own causes. While they all agreed that the revolutionary wars had disrupted the old legal order, they were in profound disagreement as to the nature of that order, the causes of its disturbance, and the means of its preservation or restoration. Those issues were to be settled at the Congress of Vienna in 1815, with far-reaching consequences for the possibility of attaining international recognition of claims to independence by new states. As I will argue in the next section, the Vienna settlement marked the transition from what remained of an older republican understanding of independence to what was in the process of becoming a modern liberal understanding of the meaning of the same concept. To the extent that the French Revolution had fueled quests for independence in Europe, counter-revolutionary rhetoric helped to re-entrench principles and practices according to which statehood depended less on legal recognition and more on principles of dynastic succession. Yet simultaneously, the same rhetoric had a reverse impact on how claims to independence raised by polities *outside* Europe were received, as indicated by the increased willingness to recognize Latin American states in the 1820s.

The connection between independence and international order was made explicit not only in the American Declaration of Independence itself, but in many of the pamphlets written to justify its cause to a broader audience. As Paine argued in *Common Sense* (1776), the desire to escape hereditary monarchy and imperial rule means that "the cause of America is in great measure the cause of all mankind."[64] Since its colonization, America "hath been the asylum for the persecuted lovers' of civil and religious liberty from every part of Europe. "Hither have they fled, not from the tender embraces of the mother, but from the cruelty of the monster; and it is so far true of England, that the same tyranny which drove the first emigrants from home, pursues their descendants still."[65] America should strive to become independent of Britain not only to escape tyranny, but also to disentangle itself

[64] Thomas Paine, *Common Sense* (Girard, KA.: Haldeman-Julius, s.a.), 13.
[65] Ibid., 40.

from the destructiveness of European power politics. Any submission to Britain "tends directly to involve this Continent in European wars and quarrels and set us at variance with nations who would otherwise seek our friendship, and against whom we have neither anger nor complaint." Since "our plan is commerce," Paine continues, that "will secure us the peace and friendship of all Europe; because it is the interest of all Europe to have America a free port."[66]

From these general arguments in favor of independence Paine moved on to list the reasons why this ought to issue in a *declaration* of independence rather than in any other means of assertion. The first of these reveals a reliance on the legal grounds for international recognition discussed in the previous section. Since "[i]t is the custom of Nations, when any two are at war, for some other powers, not engaged in the quarrel, to step in as mediators, and bring about the preliminaries of a peace; But while America calls herself the subject of Great Britain, no power, however well disposed she may be, can offer her mediation. Wherefore, in our present state we may quarrel on forever."[67] The second reason had to do with how to harness the imbalances of power in favor of independence: "It is unreasonable to suppose that France or Spain will give us any kind of assistance, if we mean only to make use of that assistance for the purpose of repairing the breach, and strengthening the connection between Britain and America; because, those powers would be sufferers by the consequences."[68] A third and most important reason was the obvious interest to have the struggle for independence acknowledged as a struggle between legal equals rather than as a mere act of rebellion: "While we profess ourselves the subjects of Britain, we must, in the eyes of foreign nations, be considered as Rebels. The precedent is somewhat dangerous to their peace, for men to be in arms under the name of subjects; we, on the spot, can solve the paradox; but to unite resistance and subjection requires an idea much too refined for common understanding."[69] Paine could here draw on Vattel's reconceptualization of civil war, by arguing that the American Revolution was hardly a revolution properly speaking, but a conflict between two formal equals that should be settled with reference to the law of nations rather than by means of public law. The fourth and final reason concerned the economic benefits expected to ensue from such a declaration that would entice other states to

[66] Ibid., 42. [67] Ibid., 73. [68] Ibid. [69] Ibid., 74.

recognize it, by "assuring all such Courts of our peaceable disposition towards them, and of our desire of entering into trade with them; such a memorial would produce more good effects to this Continent than if a ship were freighted with petitions to Britain."[70]

And as Paine noted a couple of years later in his *Letter to the Abbé Raynal* (1782), the rise of commerce had brought the end of the age of conquest, "[t]he world has undergone its divisions of empire, the several boundaries of which are known and settled. The idea of conquering countries, like the Greeks and Romans, does not now exist; and experience has exploded the notion of going to war for the sake of profit."[71] To Paine, even the current state of war with Britain was preferable to continuing dependence. In economic terms, the American Revolution had made it plain that "[i]n a state of dependence, and with a fettered commerce, though with all the advantages of peace, her trade could not balance itself, and she annually run into debt. But now, in a state of independence, though involved in war, she requires no credit; her stores are full of merchandize, and gold and silver are become the currency of the country."[72]

The French Revolution gave rise to similar hopes for independence among those Enlightenment writers who had been criticizing European imperialism in the name of progress and humanity.[73] The spread of revolutionary ideas should not only bring an end to despotism, but also to the worldwide system of conquest and domination. As Condorcet expressed his hopes for progress in the name of a united mankind, a "glance at the present state of the globe reveals, in the first place, that the principles of the French Constitution are accepted already by every enlightened person."[74] To him, the American and French Revolutions were but harbingers of a coming worldwide abolition of imperial rule and despotism, since "the liberty that the French and North American

70 Ibid., 75.

71 Thomas Paine, *Letter addressed to the Abbé Raynal on the Affairs of North America, in which the mistakes in the Abbé's account of the revolution of America are corrected and cleared up* (Boston, MA.: Benjamin Edes & Sons, 1782), 43–44.

72 Ibid., 26.

73 See Sankar Muthu, *Enlightenment Against Empire* (Princeton: Princeton University Press, 2003).

74 Marie Jean Antoine Nicolas de Caritat, Marquis de Condorcet, *Sketch for a Historical Picture of the Progress of the Human Mind: Tenth Epoch*. trans. by Keith Michael Baker *Daedalus* 133 no. 3 2004: 65–82, at 66.

republics have both the real interest and the power to bring to African and Asian commerce, and how they must necessarily spring either from the newly acquired good sense of the European nations or from their obstinate attachment to their commercial prejudices."[75]

But what was the point of juxtaposing empire and independence in the way some Enlightenment authors did? To some scholars, the French Revolution was above all a revolution in favor of the modern nation-state insofar as it called forth the nation as the ultimate source of sovereignty and brought it to coincide with the boundaries of the territorial state.[76] As we shall see in the following chapters, such an imagined congruence between nation and state became a regulative idea behind claims to national self-determination during the second half of the nineteenth century and lasted well into the twentieth. Yet there are reasons to question whether there was such an easy transition from empires to states. In what remains of this chapter, I will focus on how the revolutionaries and their critics differed in their interpretations of the French Revolution and its consequences for international order and the conditions under which independence could be attained. As has been pointed out by David Armitage and Emma Rothschild, this debate can be understood as a clash between two distinct conceptions of empire rather than as one between empire and state as distinct forms of political association: between older conceptions of territorial empire based on conquest on the one hand, and new conceptions of maritime empire based on overseas commerce on the other.[77] These conceptions implied different ideas about independence might mean,

[75] Condorcet, *Sketch for a Historical Picture of the Progress of the Human Mind*, 68.

[76] Robert Wokler, "Contextualizing Hegel's Phenomenology of the French Revolution and the Terror." *Political Theory* 26 no. 1 (1998): 33–55; Robert Wokler, "The Enlightenment and the French Revolutionary Birth Pangs of Modernity." in Björn Wittrock, Johan Heilbron and Lars Magnusson (eds.) *The Rise of the Social Sciences and the Formation of Modernity* (Dordrecht: Springer, 1998), 35–76. István Hont, "The Permanent Crisis of a Divided Mankind: 'Contemporary Crisis of the Nation State' in Historical Perspective." *Political Studies* 42, no. 1 (1994): 166–231. See also William H. Sewell, *A Rhetoric of Bourgeois Revolution: The Abbé Sieyès and "What Is the Third Estate?"* (Durham, NC: Duke University Press, 1994).

[77] See David Armitage, "The Elephant and the Whale: Empires of Land and Sea." *Journal for Maritime Research* 9 no. 1 (2007): 23–36; Emma Rothschild, "Language and Empire, c. 1800." *Historical Research* 78 no. 200 (2005): 208–229.

under what conditions it could be legitimately attained, and when it could be said to be threatened by other actors.

Once it became clear that the ambitions of the French revolutionaries recognized no boundaries, it was tempting to view the French Revolution as another shot at universal monarchy threatening the independence of other states. As the revolution progressed and its spirit spread, it was met with opposition on the grounds that it violated the law of nations and subverted the balance of power that was supposed to underpin European legal order. Famously, to Burke, what made the French Revolutionary wars different from earlier attempts at territorial aggrandizement was the fact that they originated in the usurpation of a legitimate monarchical government: "It is not France extending a foreign empire over other nations: it is a sect aiming at universal empire, and beginning with the conquest of France."[78] Rather than being confined to France, "the spirit of aggrandizement, and consequently the spirit of mutual jealousy seized upon all the coalesced Powers" until the precarious balance of power that had kept Europe together had been all but ruined.[79] Peace with this revolutionary beast is therefore impossible, since "[b]y this means the proposed fraternity is hustled in the crowd of those treaties, which imply no change in the public law of Europe, and which do not upon system affect the interior condition of nations."[80] Above all, the Revolution had been disruptive of all those laws and conventions that had long been conducive to peace and amity among European states, since the "[r]evolution was made, not to make France free, but to make her formidable; not to make her a neighbour, but a mistress; not to make her more observant of laws, but to put her in a condition to impose them."[81] And as Burke concluded in his fourth *Letter on a Regicide Peace* (1796), revolutionary France "is not an enemy of accident, that we have to deal with. Enmity to us and to all civilized nations is wrought into the very stamina of its constitution."[82] Burke, who up to this point had subscribed

[78] Edmund Burke, "Letter II. On the Genius and Character of the French Revolution as it Regards Other Nations." in Edmund Burke, *Letters on a Regicide Peace, Select Works of Edmund Burke*. Vol. 3 (Oxford: Clarendon Press, 1874–1878), 153–190, at 157.

[79] Ibid., 159. [80] Ibid., 168. [81] Ibid., 169.

[82] Edmund Burke, "Letter IV. Against Eden's *Some Remarks on the Apparent Circumstances of the War in the Fourth Week of October 1795*." in Edmund Burke, *Letters on a Regicide Peace, Select Works of Edmund Burke*. Vol. 3, (Oxford: Clarendon Press, 1874–1878), 307–393, at 376–377.

to a Vattelian notion of sovereignty as external independence and had advocated a policy of non-intervention in British imperial affairs, now invoked a right to intervene in the affairs of France on the grounds that it had stepped outside the European legal order and subverted the balance of power in Europe.[83]

To counteract these and other criticisms, the French diplomat Alexandre d'Hauterive soon provided an official justification of the French foreign policy under Napoleon. In *De l'état de la France, à la fin de l'an VIII* (1800), he forcibly argued that the European legal order had been thoroughly destabilized already well before the French Revolution, and that the revolutionary wars were but justifiable responses to its already manifest decay. The principles enshrined in the Peace of Westphalia had been corroded and the balance of power underpinning it subverted, first by the rise of the Russian empire and then by the elevation of Prussia to great power status. But the most decisive moment in this process of subversion had been "the prodigious extension of the colonial and maritime system in the four quarters of the globe", a process that had started with "discoveries and remote conquests" and now was ushering in "the domination of one maritime power and the dependence or subjugation of every other."[84] This rise of maritime power had in fact been made possible by the Peace of Westphalia itself, to which England had not been party so as to "prove that at that time continental policy was everything, and the maritime system nothing."[85] Cromwell had laid the foundation of that maritime system through the promulgation of the Navigation Act of 1651, which had restricted colonial trade to England. Met with little opposition from other powers, this had created "an indissoluble union between the powers of the state and the commercial interest of

[83] See Jennifer Pitts, *Boundaries of the International. Law and Empire* (Cambridge, MA.: Harvard University Press, 2018), 93–107; Jennifer Pitts, *A Turn to Empire* (Princeton: Princeton University Press, 2005), 63–85.

[84] Alexandre Maurice Blanc de Lanautte, Comte d'Hauterive, *State of the French Republic at the End of the Year VIII*. trans. by Lewis Goldsmith (London: J. S. Jordon, 1801), 4 & 16. For a background to this debate, see Murray Forsyth, "The Old European States-System: Gentz versus Hauterive." *The Historical Journal* 23 no. 3 (1980): 521–538; Rothschild, "Language and Empire".

[85] d'Hauterive, *State of the French Republic*, 18.

the nation."[86] Thus, and not unlike Paine before him, d'Hauterive maintained that this had given rise to a corrupt system of commercial expansion and rivalry that served the monopolistic interests of England to the detriment of the prosperity and well-being of the rest of humanity. Not only had the maritime commercial system gained preponderance over the continental territorial system when it came to power and wealth, but so had England in relation to the rest of the world:

> The ships of England cover every sea; she sends soldiers, arms, gold, and emissaries, over the four quarters of the world; there exists not a colony so remote as not to be threatened by her distant expeditions; there is no empire, however estranged to European connections, to which she does not labour to procure access, and secure to herself exclusive establishments.[87]

Thus England is "justly suspected of aiming at the universal empire of maritime commerce, and acquiring by means of that empire an all-powerful influence over the social and political interests that belong both to the system of commerce by land, and the political and administrative system of every state."[88] These systemic convulsions had undermined the public law of Europe and the continental balance of power upon which it rested, so "that, at the time immediately preceding the revolution, a public system of general safety in Europe no longer existed but in appearance; that the revolution did no more than loudly proclaim its extinction."[89] Thus the causes of revolution were not to be found in the imperfections of the French state and its government, but rather in disturbances of the continental balance of power that had occurred as a consequence of the expansion of the English overseas empire. The alliance then formed against revolutionary France was but a coalition which history "will distinguish by the name of a conspiracy against the independence of a single nation, or that of a solemn and premeditated abjuration of all the rules of public law."[90] Thus France was in her right to wage war "to dissolve a confederacy, the enemy of the repose of Europe; it made war to obtain peace."[91] Since the system of commercial rivalry rested upon an act of usurpation and was perpetuated by a compact of idleness among the bystanders, it should be overthrown and replaced by a system of commercial exchange more congenial to the interests of other European states and eventually all

[86] Ibid., 21. [87] Ibid., 119. [88] Ibid., 130. [89] Ibid., 33–34.
[90] Ibid., 71. [91] Ibid., 89.

of humankind. Hence this compact of idleness may be broken only by "one great power, which, at the same time that it breaks its own fetters, may rouse those that are most disposed and best able to follow the example: this power is France."[92] To this contention he added a proposal to reform the system of maritime commerce in order to undo English dominance by putting an end to the practice of privateering and enforcing the rights of neutral commerce during war.[93]

The Prussian diplomat Friedrich von Gentz – who had translated Burke's *Reflections on the Revolution in France* to German – was quick to attempt a wholesale refutation of the above claims. In *Von dem politischen Zustande von Europa vor und nach der Revolution* (1801), von Gentz disputed the extent to which the Treaty of Westphalia had established a system of public law in Europe, to what extent any subsequent events actually had contributed to its dissolution, and finally, whether any public law could be said to be in effect at the onset of the French Revolution. As he went on to argue, the Treaty of Westphalia could not, neither in intent nor in effect, have provided the legal foundations of a republican or federative system in Europe, since "it did not include all the nations even then important; and still less did it embrace all the relations of the states which it did include" and whatever federal principles it had embodied had already been violated by the ambitions of Louis XIV.[94] While there was no doubt that the entrance of Russia and the rise of Prussia had added their fair share of complications to European great power politics, this had little or nothing to do with what had been agreed upon in Westphalia. But most importantly, the rise of the commercial and colonial system had not

[92] Ibid., 145–146.

[93] See Isaac Nakhimovsky, The "Ignominious Fall of the European Commonwealth: Gentz, Hauterive, and the Armed Neutrality of 1800." in Koen Stapelbroek (ed.), *Trade and War: The Neutrality of Commerce in the Inter-State System, Collegium. Studies across Disciplines in the Humanities and Social Sciences* Vol. 10, (2011): 212–28; Isaac Nakhimovsky, *The Closed Commercial State: Perpetual Peace and Commercial Society from Rousseau to Fichte* (Princeton: Princeton University Press, 2011), ch. 2; Richard Whatmore, "Liberty, War and Empire: Overcoming the rich state-poor state problem 1789–1815." in Béla Kapossy, Isaac Nakhimovsky and Richard Whatmore (eds.) *Commerce and Peace in the Enlightenment* (Cambridge: Cambridge: Cambridge University Press, 2017), 216–243.

[94] Friedrich von Gentz, *On the State of Europe Before and After the French Revolution* (London, 1802), 10 & 13.

compromised the articles of that treaty, since "[t]he new relations which it created, were all of them such as had never been thought of at the treaty of Westphalia; such as were then neither foreseen nor conjectured; and such as in every respect were beyond the sphere of the system of public law."[95] Since most European powers had been involved in overseas expansion, the influence of the commercial system was not the result of British imperial ambition alone. Rather than a threat, the rise of the commercial system was a source of independence and prosperity: "Hence the independence of remote climes, not created nor cultivated for us only, and the new sources of opulence to which Europe is invited by their freedom and independence."[96] While the commercial system had certainly produced rivalries among European states, this was not the prime cause of the French Revolution. Although the latter had been facilitated by social discord within France, the main cause was to be found in the appetite for progressive political reform gone astray. Before the revolution, "Europe possessed, in every reasonable sense of the word, a federative constitution, a political balance, and a law of nations."[97] And France, despite its claims of being threatened by other great powers, was at that time enjoying great security and the amount of political influence most appropriate to its standing. From this followed a maxim according to which whenever the "conduct of France endangers the security and independence of other nations, the opposition of England is consistent with the interests of Europe."[98]

This analysis of the French revolutionary wars and their consequences was further elaborated in his *Fragmente aus der neuesten Geschichte des politischen Gleichgewichts* (1806). Now the task was less to refute revolutionary rhetoric as it was a matter of finding a viable way to restore the lost balance of power in Europe. Whereas before the outbreak of revolutionary wars "no person succeeded in prescribing laws to Europe, and...all apprehension even of the return of universal dominion, was gradually banished from every mind."[99] But as a consequence of the French quest for empire that

[95] Ibid., 41. [96] Ibid., 43–44. [97] Ibid., 93. [98] Ibid., 157.
[99] Friedrich von Gentz, *Fragments upon the Balance of Power in Europe* (London: M. Peltier, 1806), 65.

had disrupted the European balance, it had become "a duty, in the whole state confederacy, to exercise an immediate influence on the internal relations of a kingdom" in order to restore the European balance.[100] To achieve this, the concept of a balance of power was given a distinct Vattelian touch by referring to "that constitution subsisting among neighbouring states more or less connected with one another; by virtue of which no one among them can injure the independence or essential rights of another, without meeting with effectual resistance on some side."[101] Yet this definition made it easy to concede to the revolutionaries that the first partition of Poland in 1772 indeed had sacrificed the norm of non-intervention on the altar of great power politics.[102]

With the proclamation of the Empire in 1804, it became increasingly clear to the political elites in Europe that Napoleon was bent on erecting some kind of universal empire not limited to the European continent.[103] As Biancamaria Fontana has argued, while this was an attempt to reconcile French supremacy with "the vision of peaceful sisterhood of European nations" it "remained inextricably bound with the revolutionary heritage and the universalistic tradition of the Enlightenment; it represented a novel, distinctly modern project of European hegemony."[104] Yet for all its apparent novelty, to Benjamin Constant this was but an unfortunate and anachronistic return of wars of conquest to the modern world.[105] Constant – who had drawn the famous distinction between the liberty of the ancients and that of the moderns – saw the revolution as little but a perverse attempt to revive the former in a world already conclusively tilted in favor of the latter. Whereas the freedom of the ancients was essentially republican liberty premised on the right to participation in the political affairs of the

[100] Ibid., 112–113. [101] Ibid., 55. [102] Ibid., 74.

[103] See Philip Dwyer, "Napoleon and the Universal Monarchy." *History* 95 no. 319 (2010): 293–307; Martyn P. Thompson, "Ideas of Europe during the French Revolution and Napoleonic Wars." *Journal of the History of Ideas* 55 no. 1 (1994): 37–58.

[104] Biancamaria Fontana, "The Napoleonic Empire and the Europe of Nations." in Anthony Pagden (ed.), *The Idea of Europe. From Antiquity to the European Union* (Cambridge: Cambridge University Press, 2002), 116–128, at 122–124.

[105] For a background, see Anthony Pagden, "Fellow Citizens and Imperial Subjects: Conquest and Sovereignty in Europe's Overseas Empires." *History & Theory* 44 no. 4 (2005): 28–46.

city republic, modern liberty was based on civil rights that protected citizens from undue interference by political authority under the rule of law.[106] The same distinction was implicit in his analysis of international order. In *De l'Esprit de Conquête et de l'Usurpation dans leur Rapports avec la Civilisation Européenne* (1814), Constant started by arguing that although wars of conquest once were natural to the peoples of antiquity given the condition of scarcity they found themselves in, the age of commerce "must necessarily replace that of war, as the age of war was bound to precede it." In order to lead nations to war in the age of commerce, "it is necessary to overturn the situation in which they find themselves, which can scarcely be done without inflicting many evils upon them."[107] It was obvious that usurpation was the crowning of those evils which had brought the spirit of conquest back into life, as it was that "a government given up to the spirit of invasion and conquest must corrupt a part of the population to secure its active services in its own enterprises."[108] The Napoleonic revival of empire had shifted the tradeoff between diversity and homogeneity in favor of the latter, the effect of conquest being to instill uniformity on the conquered, since the "interests and memories that arise from local customs contain the germ of resistance that authority is reluctant to tolerate and that it is anxious to eradicate."[109] In modern wars of conquest, this admiration of uniformity has turned into a dogma, so that when "[a]pplied to all parts of an empire, this principle must necessarily apply also to all those countries this empire may conquer."[110] In contrast to the diversity that had characterized the great empires of antiquity, which were "demanded by nature and consecrated by experience", the modern desire for homogeneity makes empires virtually indistinguishable from nations, since "[t]he great empire is nothing independently of its provinces, in the same way as "[t]he whole nation is nothing separated from the parts that compose it."[111] Thus modern empires posed a threat to the independence of particular communities

[106] Benjamin Constant, "The Liberty of the Ancients Compared with That of the Moderns." in Benjamin Constant, *Political Writings*. edited by Biancamaria Fontana (Cambridge: Cambridge University Press, 1988), 308–328.

[107] Benjamin Constant, "The Spirit of Conquest and Usurpation and Their Relation to European Civilization." in Benjamin Constant, *Political Writings*. edited by Biancamaria Fontana (Cambridge: Cambridge University Press, 1988), 51–148, at 52–53.

[108] Ibid., 63–64. [109] Ibid., 74. [110] Ibid. [111] Ibid., 77 & 78.

in a way that the empires of antiquity never had been able to do. To Constant, the interruption of peaceful relations between the commercial nations of modern Europe caused by the revival of the spirit of conquest was thus nothing but an unmitigated disaster, to be averted only by treaty between those nations "that wished simply to be free, and that nation against which the universe would fight only to compel her to be just."[112]

Several things were at stake in the debate between those who defended the French revolutionary policy and their many opponents. First, although authors on both sides were debunking imperial aggrandizement on the grounds that it inevitably threatens the independence of individual polities, the conceptions of empire singled out for criticism reflected the differences between empires of land and sea as they were conceptualized by contemporaries. Whereas the French were claiming that the chief threat to independence came from the relentless expansion of maritime and commercial empire by the British, the critics of the French revolution saw the sudden revival of wars of conquest and territorial aggrandizement as the main threat to the independence of polities. To them, the French Revolution was a *conservative* revolution insofar as it aimed to preserve the prerogatives of territorial empire in a world in which global commercial exchange already had superseded the former as the main source of wealth and power. Second, although these authors were in some agreement that the European states system ought to be based on the principles of public law and the balance of power which together would safeguard the independence of individual states, that independence meant very different things to them. To Paine and d'Hauterive, the boundless expansion of commercial empires did not only threaten the independence of France and other European polities, but also that of peoples in those parts of the world that had been involuntarily pulled into the orbit of transnational commerce and subjugated by the agents of empire, whether private or public. To von Gentz and Constant, the rise of maritime empires and the global spread of commercial exchange were rather the very preconditions of independence, in so far as they granted new polities the right to enter mutually beneficial relationships of commercial exchange with metropolitan powers, and perhaps also into an expansive international society based on the formal equality of states and the rule of international law. To

112 Ibid., 83.

them, the French fought in vain to preserve principles and practices that already had been consigned to the dustbin of history by the world-wide spread of commercial exchange. But however different their understandings of empire and independence, the above authors were in broad agreement that whatever settlement that could be reached should try to *restore* some of the features of the international order that they believed had existed *before* the French Revolution, however much they differed about the characteristics of that order and the legal principles upon which it had been based.

Becoming Independent

The Congress of Vienna in 1815 and the ensuing congress system were conceived to restore the balance of power in Europe without inviting back the continuous struggle for preponderance that had long animated great power politics in Europe. Yet this settlement produced different outcomes in different parts of the world. In Europe, the Vienna settlement brought back the principles dynastic legitimacy center stage and gave its signatories the right if not the duty to intervene in other states to suppress internal disturbances or tendencies to revolutionary upheaval.[113] From then on, anyone aspiring to independence in Europe faced an uphill struggle, with little likelihood of success lest they could navigate the treacherous waters of contemporary geopolitics with great skill and jump through those few windows of opportunity that presented themselves. This was no more evident than in the Greek struggle for independence from the Ottomans, which right from its start became caught in the rivalry between Britain and Russia until it eventually was crowned with success thanks to the support of the former. Other struggles for independence in the Balkans were less successful, instead producing a host of semi-sovereign entities formally within the auspices of the Ottoman empire while being under *de facto* control of other powers.[114]

113 See Hinsley, *Power and the Pursuit of Peace*, 186–212; Brian E. Vick, *The Congress of Vienna: Power and Politics after Napoleon* (Cambridge, MA.: Harvard University Press, 2014); Stella Ghervas, *Conquering Peace: From the Enlightenment to the European Union* (Cambridge, M.A.: Harvard University Press, 2021), 82–147.

114 See Peter Haldén, "A Non-Sovereign Modernity: Attempts to Engineer Stability in the Balkans 1820–90." *Review of International Studies* 39 no. 2 (2013): 337–359.

In Latin America, however, the aftermath of the Napoleonic wars produced different outcomes. Although what came to be known as the Western Question was not addressed directly within the congress system, it nevertheless reflected a profound tension between continental and Atlantic powers that kept their diplomats busy during the coming decade. Whereas the Holy Alliance supported continuing Spanish sovereignty over its Latin American possessions with reference to principles of dynastic legitimacy, the United States and Great Britain initially remained neutral and advocated non-intervention in the civil wars now in the process of tearing those possessions apart. In the United States, this neutrality eventually translated into arguments for independence and recognition modelled on their own historical experience. As John Quincy Adams argued, "[t]here is a stage in such contests when the parties struggling for independence, have … a right to demand its acknowledgement by neutral parties, and when the acknowledgement may be granted without departure from the obligations of neutrality."[115] In Britain, Lord Castlereagh had argued against interventions to suppress revolts already during the early days of the congress system, and was therefore more inclined to maintain that while Spain and Portugal still enjoyed *de iure* sovereignty over their possessions, they could not expect Britain to intervene on their behalf to counteract the cascade of independence claims now emanating from Latin America. Yet this neutrality was far from extending international legal recognition to those entities. Such recognition was proposed by James Monroe only once the province of Florida had been wrestled from the hands of Spain and Latin American revolutionaries had attained *de facto* independence.[116] And in what was to become a decisive break with the principles of dynastic legitimacy enshrined in the congress system, the British foreign secretary George Canning finally recognized the independence of the Spanish provinces of Colombia and Rio de la Plata in 1824, and in 1825 that of Brazil.

But the road leading there was all but smooth. The collapse of Spanish empire in Latin America had produced a volatile situation in

[115] Letter from John Quincy Adams to James Monroe, August 24, 1818. in Worthington Ford (ed.), *Writings of Quincy Adams*, Vol. 6 (New York: MacMillan, 1916), 442–443. Quoted in Fabry, *Recognizing States*, 55.

[116] For a background, see Brian Loveman, "U.S. Foreign Policy toward Latin America in the 19th Century." *Oxford Research Encyclopedia of Latin American History* (Oxford: Oxford University Press, 2016).

which local struggles for independence intersected with geopolitical rivalries between European great powers. As Rafe Blaufarb has noted, "The Western Question was thus less about the question of independence per se than about how the conflict would affect the geopolitical order. The question was given urgency by the fear that Britain would achieve global hegemony by turning South America into a 'second Hindoustan'."[117] For their part, British decisions to recognize the independence of Latin American states were constrained by the conflicting imperatives of maintaining the status quo after the end of the Napoleonic wars and the simultaneous fear of losing control over the profitable trade with Latin American states. Both France and Russia feared that such independence would usher in British dominance in the Atlantic, while the United States was concerned with counteracting European influence in the Western hemisphere. Hence nothing in the geopolitical context made British recognition come easy. Canning even had strong reasons to postpone the recognition of Latin American states in the hope of preventing a French invasion of Spain, but once such an invasion was underway anyway recognition became easier, and even more so when Ferdinand VII had been reinstated on the throne in 1823.[118]

The intellectual context in which these claims to independence were raised and recognized deserves some attention, especially since this indicates the extent to which the attainment of independence depended on the happy confluence of legal norms and revolutionary rhetoric. As Simon has argued, the ideology of the creole revolutions was both anti-imperial and imperial in character, reflecting the ambiguous position of the creole elites within the imperial order. While they opposed imperial rule on the grounds of the inequalities and domination it imposed upon colonial populations, creole authors simultaneously wanted to preserve the privileges they enjoyed in relation to the non-European parts of these populations. Creole revolutionaries "argued that rebellion against European rule was a legitimate means of preserving a set of privileges more expansive than the particular

117 Rafe Blaufarb, "The Western Question: The Geopolitics of Latin American Independence." *American Historical Review* 112 no. 3 (2007): 742–763, at 747.

118 See Norihito Yamada, "George Canning and the Spanish Question, September 1822 to March 1823." *The Historical Journal* 52 no. 2 (2009): 343–362.

rights of Englishmen and Spaniards, but less inclusive than the universal rights of man."[119]

The first claims to independence were raised against the backdrop of the failed attempts at imperial reform in Spanish America, and the invasion of the Iberian Peninsula by Napoleon in 1808. In response to Napoleon's decision to grant the Spanish crown to his brother Joseph, a *Junta Central* was formed in Seville which claimed authority over the overseas possessions. Yet when the American provinces were not granted equal representation, this issued in protests and the creation of local *juntas* to protect Spanish interests in the Americas. In the *Memorial de Agravios* (1809) Camilo Torres articulated the creole grievances in detail, reminding the *Junta* that "our parents ... by means of indescribable labors, discovered, conquered, and populated this New World for Spain."[120] In the province of Caracas and elsewhere, this dissatisfaction led to an overthrow of Spanish authorities and the establishment of a *de facto* independent local *junta*. Simón Bolívar, who had been sent to London in 1810 on behalf of that *junta* to seek British protection against a feared French invasion, instead opted to request full British recognition of Venezuelan independence. Having had his request turned down by Wellington's elder brother, foreign secretary Richard Wellesley, Bolívar returned to his native Caracas to fight for independence only to face defeat and disbandment of his revolutionary forces two years later.[121] Meditating on the causes of defeat from his brief exile in Cartagena, these were not to be found in the strength of the enemy forces but in the inherent weakness of the federal constitution which Venezuela had adopted more or less unabridged from North America: "although it is the most perfect and the most suitable for guaranteeing human happiness in society, is notwithstanding the form most inimical to the interest of or emerging states." This being so, since "our fellow citizens are not yet ready to take on the full and independent exercise of their rights, because they lack the political

[119] Simon, *Ideology of Creole Revolution*, 33.

[120] José Camilo de Torres, *Representacion del Cabildo de Bogota Capital del Nuevo Reino de Granada a la Suprema Junta Central de Espana*, 1809 (Bogota: N. Lora, 1832). Quoted in Simon, *Ideology of Creole Revolution*, 36.

[121] For the context of Bolívar's writings, see Humberto R. Núñez Faraco, "The Entanglements of Freedom: Simón Bolívar's Jamaica Letter and Its Socio-political Context, (1810–1819)." *Global Intellectual History* 3, no. 1 (2018): 71–91; Simon, *Ideology of Creole Revolution*, 17–47.

virtues marking the true citizen of a republic."[122] Rather than mobilizing the people into a cohesive and virtuous unity, the federal constitution had contained the seeds of factionalism and insurrection that made Venezuela an easy prey for its inner and outer enemies. Hence the only remedy against discord and disintegration was a centralized and authoritarian government.[123] As Simon has noted on this solution, "the union served a double purpose, fortifying American independence against external threats, while preserving the internal hierarchies the American states inherited from their imperial forebears."[124]

After having failed to liberate Cartagena from royalist forces in 1815, Bolívar fled to Jamaica from where he wrote to Lord Wellesley in another attempt to garner British support for his cause and composed his most famous statement in favor of South American independence, the *Carta de Jamaica* (1815). Even at the imminent threat of Spanish reconquest, he maintained that "[t]he destiny of America is irrevocably fixed; the tie that bound her to Spain is severed, for it was nothing but an illusion biding together the two sides of that vast monarchy."[125] The current state of America was thus "similar to the circumstances surrounding the fall of the Roman empire, when each breakaway province formed a political system suitable to its interests and situation."[126] Already when it was evident that the Spanish empire was crumbling, Europe, "with an eye to rational foreign relations, should have prepared and carried out the project of American independence, not only because world equilibrium demands it but because this is the legitimate and sure way to acquire overseas markets."[127] Consequently, Bolívar continued, "we were justified in expecting all civilized nations to rush to our aid, helping us achieve a goal whose advantages are mutual to both hemispheres."[128] Long deprived of their natural liberty, South American peoples could not be expected to maintain "in proper balance the difficult undertaking of a republic",

[122] Simón Bolívar, "The Cartagena Manifesto: Memorial Addressed to the Citizens of New Granada by a Citizen from Caracas." in David Bushnell (ed.), *El Libertador. Writings of Simon Bolívar* (Oxford: Oxford University Press, 2003), 33–11, at 6.

[123] Bolívar, "The Cartagena Manifesto", 7.

[124] Simon, *Ideology of Creole Revolution*, 39.

[125] Simón Bolívar, "The Jamaica Letter: Response from a South American to a Gentleman from This Island." in David Bushnell (ed.) *El Libertador. Writings of Simon Bolívar* (Oxford: Oxford University Press, 2003), 12–30, at 13.

[126] Ibid., 18. [127] Ibid., 16. [128] Ibid., 16.

and therefore stood in need of the "stewardship of paternalistic governments to cure the wounds and ravages of despotism and war."[129] But to avoid the trappings of a tyrannical government, Americans should nevertheless prefer a republican to a monarchical government. Ideally the entire continent ought to be divided into a number of smaller republics, whose unique quality is "their permanence, while large ones suffer a variety of changes, always tending toward empire."[130] Although more than ready to shake off the Spanish yoke but still too internally divided and isolated from the rest of the world, the independence of such republics would only be possible "[w]hen we are at last strong, under the auspices of a liberal nation that lends us its protection, then we will cultivate in harmony the virtues and talents that lead to glory; then we will follow the majestic path toward abundant prosperity marked out by destiny for South America."[131] That liberal nation was of course Great Britain. As he had written to Wellesley, "England, almost exclusively, will see prosperity flowing back to her shores from this hemisphere must depend, almost exclusively, on her as benefactress."[132]

Similar arguments were repeated in his *Discurso de Angostura* (1819), but now addressed to an audience of domestic legislators. Comparing the constitution of Venezuela with that of North America, "no matter how enticing this magnificent federalist system may seem to be … [o]ur moral constitution did not yet possess the necessary consistency to receive the benefit of a completely representative government."[133] As Bolívar went on to explain, "the existence of a government depends not on its political theory, or its form, or its administrative mechanism, but on its appropriateness to the nature and character of the nation for which it is instituted."[134] Yet nevertheless any future government must be republican: "[i]ts bases must be the sovereignty of the people, the division of powers, civil liberty, the proscription against slavery, the abolition of monarchy and privileged classes."[135] But the promises of

[129] Ibid., 23–24. [130] Ibid., 25. [131] Ibid., 30.

[132] Simón Bolívar, "Letter to Sir Richard Wellesley: An Appeal for Support." in David Bushnell (ed.) *El Libertador. Writings of Simon Bolívar* (Oxford: Oxford University Press, 2003), 153–155, at 154.

[133] Simón Bolívar, "The Angostura Address." in David Bushnell (ed.) *El Libertador. Writings of Simon Bolívar* (Oxford: Oxford University Press, 2003), 31–53, at 38.

[134] Ibid., 42. [135] Ibid., 40.

popular sovereignty could not be realized immediately since the contours of that people were still in abeyance: "[i]t is impossible to say with certainty to which human family we belong. Most of the indigenous peoples have been annihilated. The European has mixed with the American and the African, and the African has mixed with the Indian and the European."[136] As Simon has noted, Bolívar had not only to come to terms with an imperial legacy of misrule, but also to cope with "the challenges involved in governing a racially stratified society renegotiating its terms of existence after the shock of independence."[137] But even if that independence was still waiting to be recognized by the British government, its warriors and defenders are "armed not only with justice but also with full military strength" thanks to the "unlimited generosity of certain foreign citizens who have seen humanity suffer and the cause of reason languish."[138]

By appealing to the prosperity that free trade with independent Latin American states could be expected to bring to the British, Bolívar plugged right into a tradition of economic thought that depicted direct colonial rule as economically inefficient and detrimental to the interests of the metropolis. As I described in the previous chapter, that tradition had taken its beginning with the criticism of empire by early political economists such as Davenant and Defoe, who argued that the Spanish colonial system not only was illegitimate, but that its monopolistic trade policies that made its decline inevitable. As William Petty had put this point with reference to Britain in his *Political Arithmetick* (1690), the main impediment to the greatness of England "is that the territories thereunto belonging, are too far asunder, and divided by the sea into many several Islands and Countries."[139] This made direct rule over those territories impractical and costly, since "small divided remote Governments,

136 Ibid., 38–39. On his conception of nationality, see Simon Collier, "Nationality, Nationalism, and Supranationalism in the Writings of Simón Bolívar." *Hispanic American Historical Review* 63 no. 1 (1983): 37–64; Sara Castro-Klarén, "Framing Pan-Americanism: Simon Bolivar's Findings." *New Centennial Review* 3 no. 1 (2003): 25–53.

137 Simon, *Ideology of Creole Revolution*, 103.

138 Ibid., 52.

139 William Petty, *Political Arithmetick: or A Discourse Concerning the Value of Lands, People, Buildings ... As the Same Relates to Every Country in General, but More Particularly to the Territories of His Majesty of Great Britain, and His Neighbours of Holland, Zealand, and France* (London: R. Clavel, 1690), 87.

being seldom able to defend themselves, the Burthen of protecting them all, must lye upon the chief Kingdom England."[140] To him and his successors in the Scottish Enlightenment, for colonialism to be viable, the profit ensuing from trade with the colonies must outweigh the cost of their protection. Since monopolistic trade of the kind practiced by Spain at the time was unsustainable on such terms, it ought to be replaced by a system of free trade. Adam Smith made this point most clearly when he stated that "[t]he exclusive trade of the mother countries tends to diminish, or, at least, to keep down below what they otherwise rise to, both the enjoyments and industry of all those nations in general, and of the American colonies in particular."[141] The possession of colonies is thus justifiable only on condition that they contribute their own defense as well as that of their mother country. On that score, European policies had been a failure, since "the defense of their colonies has generally occasioned a very considerable distraction of the military force of those countries ... such colonies, therefore, have been a source of expense and not of revenue to their respective home countries."[142] Direct rule under conditions of monopolistic trade was simply bad business, whereas free trade with independent states was a source of mutual prosperity and security: As Jeremy Bentham had argued in a series of open letters addressed to the Spanish government in 1822, profit from colonial trade would only accrue when it was free and did not involve the subjection of either party.[143]

During the regency heydays when Bolívar was seeking British protection and recognition of states in Latin America, contentions like the above were often used to challenge mainstream monopolistic imperial ideology from inside the pages of *The Edinburgh Review*. Coupled with a widespread conviction in London that Spanish colonial rule long had bordered on the despotic and barbaric, the resources needed to advocate the independence of the new-born republics were now available, even if this amounted to a simultaneous repudiation of Spanish sovereignty

[140] Ibid., 88.
[141] Adam Smith, *An Inquiry into the Nature and Causes of the Wealth of Nations*, ed. by Edwin Cannan, Vol. 2 (London: Methuen, 1904), § 268, 94.
[142] Ibid., § 271, 94–95.
[143] Jeremy Bentham, "Rid Yourselves of Ultramaria." in Philip Schofield (ed.), *Colonies, Commerce, and Constitutional Law: Rid Yourselves of Ultramaria and Other Writings on Spain and Spanish America* (Oxford: Clarendon Press, 1995), Letter III.

but which at the time was judged to be all but lost anyway.[144] This was all evident in a speech held in the House of Commons by the prominent lawyer and Whig politician James Mackintosh in June 1824 against the backdrop of a petition from the merchants of London to "recognise the Independence of the States in those countries for have in fact established Independent Governments."[145] As Mackintosh pointed out, such recognition had the backing of the "first rank of the mercantile community" – signatories included the Barings, the Goldsmiths, and, notably, David Ricardo – so that the "the mass of private interest engaged in our trade with South America is so great as to render it a large part of the national interest."[146] Hence the recognition of American states should not be confined to a formal acknowledgement of their independence from the Spanish crown, since "it is not by formal stipulations or solemn declarations that we are to recognize the American States; but by measures of practical policy which imply that we acknowledge their independence...to deal with them in every respect as commonwealths entitled to admission into the great society of civilized States."[147] Recognizing the new-born states in Latin America was not only legally warranted given that those states now possessed stable governments and a modicum of internal tranquillity, but it was also in the obvious interest of Britain "to protect the trade and navigation of her subjects; to acquire the best means of cultivating friendly relations with important countries, and of composing by immediate negotiation those differences which might otherwise terminate in war."[148] This would also benefit the states being recognized, since commerce being "the real civilizer and emancipator of mankind ... to open South America to the commerce of the world, is in reality not

[144] For an analysis, see Gabriel Paquette, "The Intellectual Context of British Diplomatic Recognition of the South American Republics, c. 1800–1830." *Journal of Transatlantic Studies* 2 no. 1 (2004): 75–95.

[145] Substance of the speech of Sir James Mackintosh in the House of Commons, June 15, 1824. *On presenting a petition from the merchants of London for the recognition of the independent states established in the countries of America formerly subject to Spain* (London: Longman, Hurst, Rees, Orme, Brown and Green, 1824), 1. For the legal context of his argument and its reception, see Martin Clark, "A Conceptual History of Recognition in British International Legal Thought." *British Yearbook of International Law* 87 no. 1 (2017): 18–97, esp. 30–35.

[146] Ibid., 2 & 57.

[147] Ibid., 6. [148] Ibid., 8.

merely to multiply the enjoyments and comforts of her people, but to render them partakers of the arts, and knowledge, and morality, and liberty of civilized men."[149] And conversely, Bolívar envisaged that the unification of New Granada and Venezuela would become a "unifier, center, emporium for the human family, sending out to the entire earth the treasures of silver and gold hidden in her mountains, extracting health and vitality from her lush vegetation for the suffering men of the old world."[150] Consequently, when Latin American states eventually were recognized by Britain, it was by means of treaties of commerce and amity rather than by any other available diplomatic means.[151]

The new states in Latin America were thus admitted into international society, yet on unequal terms. Although their status as Western colonial societies qualified them as civilized, the racial composition of their populations and the fragility of their domestic institutions disqualified them from full membership in the community of civilized states.[152] Soon after independence, however, creole elites took upon themselves to bring their states up to European standards by completing the process of civilization and making them conform to the norms of territorial sovereignty.[153] But by aspiring to recognition and protection on the terms described above, Bolívar was also unwittingly contributing to new forms of imperial rule that would eventually cancel his own visions of a creole empire or Panamerican community. As some historians of Latin American independence have pointed out, the willing acceptance of free trade brought new-born states in Latin America right into the orbit of British informal empire.[154] But so did also his homegrown creole imperialism. To the dangers of individual liberty within new-born states corresponded with a conception of sovereignty according to which states could well be formally independent

149 Ibid., 68. 150 Bolívar, "Angostura Address", 53.

151 Fabry, *Recognizing States*, 60.

152 Schulz, "Civilization, Barbarism and the Making of Latin America's Place in 19th- Century International Society."

153 Obregón, "Completing Civilization", 250–255; Carsten-Andreas Schulz, "Territorial sovereignty and the End of Inter-cultural Diplomacy along the 'Southern frontier'." *European Journal of International Relations* 25 no. 3 (2019): 878–903.

154 See, for example, John Gallagher and Ronald Robinson, "The Imperialism of Free Trade." *Economic History Review* 6 no. 1 (1953): 1–15; Matthew Brown (ed.), *Informal Empire in Latin America: Culture, commerce and capital* (Oxford: Blackwell, 2008).

yet nonetheless being subjected to other states precisely by virtue of owing their independence and recognition and protection by them. And by arguing that the non-white parts of the population were not mature enough to enjoy the fruits of liberty and popular sovereignty, Bolívar was issuing a license for paternalistic rule in states whose populations were divided along the lines of race and class, or which otherwise failed to conform to the republican ideals of virtuous conduct.

As Lauren Benton and Lisa Ford have argued, new practices of granting independence changed the terms of imperial rule and the nature of empire. Rather than merely being but a state blown big through successive territorial conquests, empire could now be better understood as a system of nominally independent states constituted by legal recognition from the imperial center and upheld through protection by its overseas agents. All the way from Uruguay to Tahiti, the many middlemen of the British empire were busy extending British influence by promoting claims to sovereignty of new states and creating regional formations of semi-sovereign entities whose legal status Wheaton was about formalize. Hence granting independence to new polities was not only perceived as a way of dismantling what remained of Spanish imperial authority, but also as a clever and cost-effective method of reinforcing British imperial rule by outsourcing the responsibility for its exercise to nominally sovereign entities in Asia and the Americas.[155]

Independence now meant something different than it had meant to Mably and Vattel. Yet it was the equation of sovereignty with external independence that had made it possible to reconcile independence and empire in the first place. Although the Vienna settlement brought a momentary end to imperial aggrandizement in Europe and a revival of the idea that European states were united in a community aimed at the preservation of order and natural liberty, the emergence of new states in the Americas gave impetus to new notions of international society constituted by international recognition and held together by contractual arrangements between parties. This tendency was evident in subsequent attempts by Latin American lawyers to adjust the rules of international law to accommodate the new states and safeguard their independence, something which required a reconceptualization

[155] Lauren Benton and Lisa Ford, *Rage for Order. The British Empire and the Origins of International Law 1800–1850* (Cambridge, MA.: Harvard University Press, 2016), 148–179.

of the relationship between independence and recognition.[156] As the formidable lawyer and educator Andrés Bello argued in his *Principios de derecho de gentes* (1832), "[t]he *independence* of a nation consists in not receiving laws from another nation, and its *sovereignty* in the existence of a supreme authority that directs and represents it."[157] Yet from the viewpoint of international law, what matters to statehood is that "every nation which governs itself under any form whatsoever, and which has the ability to communicate directly with other nations, is in their eyes an independent and sovereign state."[158] Hence, if statehood is partly constituted through international recognition, it followed that "if a new state appears as the result of the colonization of a recently discovered country, or of the dismemberment of an old state, the other states need only discover whether the new association is in fact independent ... if this is the case, they cannot in justice refuse to recognize it as a member of the society of nations."[159] To the same extent that independence is an offer no other state can refuse, no state "is permitted to dictate to another the form of government, religion, or administration it must adopt, nor call it to account for anything that happens among its citizens or between the government and its subjects."[160] But whereas Bello was acutely sensitive to the dangers posed to new-born states by foreign intervention, he nevertheless maintained that independence was possible to reconcile with unequal contractual arrangements between parties, so that in the rank of sovereign states "[w]e must include in this number even states that are linked to another more powerful state by an unequal alliance, in which the more powerful state is given more honor in exchange for the aid it gives to the weaker state."[161] Likewise, since a state retains its identity as a moral person regardless of whom happens to rule it, its obligations to other states and their subjects remain the same, and especially so in case of extraterritorial protection. Citing Palmerston approvingly, Bello concurred that "protection of its subjects is an

[156] See Louise Fawcett, "Between West and Non-West: Latin American Contributions to International Thought." *International History Review* 34 no. 4 (2012): 679–704.

[157] Andrés Bello, "Principles of International Law." in *Selected Writings of Andrés Bello*, edited by Ivan Jakšić (Oxford: Oxford University Press, 1997), 229–254, at 241. On the influence of Bello, see Ivan Jakšić, *Andrés Bello: Scholarship and Nation-building in Nineteenth-century Latin America* (Cambridge: Cambridge University Press, 2006).

[158] Ibid., 243. [159] Ibid., 244. [160] Ibid., 246. [161] Ibid., 243.

unquestionable right of every sovereign state, when they have been damaged in their persons or their interests by the government of another, and especially in the case when their pecuniary credits have not been satisfied."[162] Hence what has been made to look like a formative period in the transition from a world of empires to a world of states can equally well be interpreted as the rise of a new form of empire, based on unequal modes of exchange and extraterritoriality characteristic of maritime and commercial empire. But by becoming international under those conditions, Latin American leaders had to relinquish the possibilities of political association that had presented themselves briefly during the revolutionary struggle against Spain. The ideas of continental unity that had animated the thought and action of Bolívar and his fellow travelers were now becoming distant dreams, and ideas of a creole empire or cosmopolitan community relegated to realm of the ideal.

[162] Ibid., 253.

4 *Empire and Self-Determination, c.1820–c.1919*

Introduction

In the previous chapter, I argued that whereas recognition of new states in the Americas brought an expansion of international society, this could equally well be interpreted as a continuation of imperial relations with other means. Latin American polities did not become international by virtue of becoming independent from the empire of Spain, but rather by being integrated into a commercial empire being built by the British. In this chapter, I will pursue a similar line of argument with regard to the claims to national self-determination that first emerged in the aftermath of the First World War and then spread across the world until the right to self-determination finally was enshrined in international law in the latter half of the twentieth century.[1] These claims were distinct from earlier claims to independence insofar as they made reference to a nation or people in whose name these claims were raised, and by doing so implied that nation and state ought to coincide within the same territory. As we saw in the previous chapter, the recognition of independence in the Americas required only that sovereignty had been transferred from the metropolis to the colonial polity in question but left questions about the precise locus and scope of that sovereignty unanswered. By contrast, to make sense of claims to *national* self-determination it is necessary to examine the entire range of underlying

[1] See, for example, Jörg Fisch, *The Right of Self-determination of Peoples: The Domestication of an Illusion* (Cambridge: Cambridge University Press, 2015), 190ff; Eric D. Weitz, "Self-determination: How a German Enlightenment Idea Became the Slogan of National Liberation and a Human Right", *The American Historical Review* 120 no. 2 (2015): 462–496; Volker Prott, *The Politics of Self-Determination. Remaking Territories and National Identities in Europe, 1917–1923* (Oxford: Oxford University Press, 2016); Maja Spanu, "The Hierarchical Society: The Politics of Self-Determination and the Constitution of New States after 1919." *European Journal of International Relations* 26 no. 2 (2020): 372–396.

assumptions about the nature of the prospective bearers of sovereignty – nations, peoples, and states – that made such claims to possible to raise and recognize as legitimate in the first place. In this chapter, I will do this with reference to the most widespread conceptions of nationality and self-determination during the second half of the nineteenth century until the Paris Peace Conference in 1919, arguing that doing this is crucial to understanding how a modern international realm was conceptualized into existence.

Extant accounts have almost invariably constructed the rise of self-determination as key phase in the transition from a world of empires to a world of states and the expansion of international society. As I mentioned in the previous chapter, the starting point of this process has been located to the French Revolution and its notions of nationhood and nationality. For example, to Harry Hinsley, while the Napoleonic wars had overthrown the early modern states system, the peace settlement of 1815 inaugurated a modern international system in Europe.[2] Although the Conference System was designed with the explicit aim to prevent future attempts at imperial expansion by saddling great powers with the obligation to preserve the balance of power, it was accompanied by the emergence of modern nations and the spread of nationalist ideologies. Whereas some of these ideologies were based on notions of nationality that made allegiance to common political institutions the sole criterion of membership, others were based on imagined socio-cultural and linguistic commonalities among peoples. Yet within this view, nothing like modern nations or nationalism could have evolved without the prior presence of the territorial state. As Hinsley argued, "it follows from the nature and function of the state that in the only definition of empire that is universally valid – the rule of one government over more than one social group that state has begun as an empire ... from its need to adjust the increasing mixture of its cultural composition or because of the widening of its class differences or in its search for defence against the imperialism of neighbouring states."[3] Nations could emerge only when states had successfully assimilated all differences and created sufficiently homogeneous populations: "The political community and the political loyalty have become national

[2] Francis Harry Hinsley, *Nationalism and the International System* (London: Hodder and Stoughton, 1973), 82ff.

[3] Ibid., 29.

only when … the state has developed beyond being an empire – than which the nation is usually less extensive and more cohesive."[4] On this account, a modern international realm emerged with the transition from empires to nation-states, a process propelled by the spread of nationalist ideologies.

Similarly, to James Mayall, the decisive factor behind the making of the modern international system was the rise of popular sovereignty and the demise of dynastic principles of legitimacy in international society. Although the territorial state and the international system remained essentially the same, "nationalists moved into the building which had previously been occupied by dynastic rulers and religious authorities… they were more often forced to accommodate their own plans to the existing structure, than they were able to rebuild the international system in their own image."[5] By the same token, according to Rodney Bruce Hall, the *ancien regimes* of Europe faced a crisis of legitimacy during the late eighteenth century that led to the gradual replacement of the principle of territorial and dynastic sovereignty with that of national and popular sovereignty, and the slow and painstaking consolidation of an international system based on national identities and democracy in the aftermath of the Revolution of 1848.[6] A similar emphasis on changing principles of legitimacy can be found in a more recent book by Barry Buzan and George Lawson, who argue that "nationalism was usually corrosive of dynastic rule … [n]ot only did sovereignty shift from ruler to people, but the territory of the state became identified with the history and location of the people rather than being determined by hereditary rights or dynastic nuptials."[7] Since most empires were based on dynastic principles of rule, undermining the legitimacy of the latter had a destabilizing impact on the former. Thus, according to Buzan and Lawson, "[n]ationalism also transformed international order by establishing the nation-state as the principal unit of international politics."[8]

[4] Ibid., 30.

[5] James Mayall, *Nationalism and International Society* (Cambridge: Cambridge University Press, 1990), 26.

[6] Rodney Bruce Hall, *National Collective Identity: Social Constructs and International Systems* (New York: Columbia University Press, 1999), 133–172.

[7] Barry Buzan and George Lawson, *The Global Transformation. History, Modernity, and the Making of International Relations* (Cambridge: Cambridge University Press, 2015), 116.

[8] Ibid., 118.

This argument finds additional support in historical accounts of the long nineteenth century. As Christopher Bayly has pointed out in his seminal synthesis, by the end of the nineteenth century, "the state was now regarded as an embodiment of the nation, and the nation or race was assumed to be the key actor on the world stage."[9] A similar point has been made by Jürgen Osterhammel, to whom "[t]he nineteenth century saw the birth of international relations as we know it today", largely because of the nation-state, "a special kind of state organization, which first emerged in the nineteenth century and began to spread hesitantly and unevenly around the world...[i]nternational politics in the nineteenth century was acted out between 'powers' organized party as nation-states, partly as empires."[10] After these empires had been all but abolished in Europe, "colonial empires were a transitional form on the way to a mature international community of states...and hence the midwife of a postimperial international order."[11] Thus, even if the nineteenth century was not yet the age of nation-states, it was during this period that modern nation-states were formed and rose to prominence in the international order.[12]

Likewise, intellectual historians have seen the French Revolution and especially its aftermath as decisive in this regard. Thus, according to Robert Wokler, "[h]erein lay the establishment of the first genuinely modern state, in the sense in which it has become a nation-state, plucked from the womb of the *ancien regime* by its own offspring who, in transfiguring their delegated powers and hence their own identity, brought a new world into being."[13] Similarly, to István Hont, the French Revolution marked an inaugural moment in the final transition from empires to states. To him, "[t]he primary sense of the 'nation-state' is that it is the opposite of empire, defined as a kind of territorial state-system within which entire populations or

[9] Christopher A. Bayly, *The Birth of the Modern World 1780–1914. Global Connections and Comparisons* (Oxford: Blackwell, 2004), 265.

[10] Jürgen Osterhammel, *The Transformation of the World. A Global History of the Nineteenth Century* (Princeton: Princeton University Press, 2014), 394.

[11] Ibid., 396. [12] Ibid., 406–12.

[13] Robert Wokler, "Contextualizing Hegel's Phenomenology of the French Revolution and the Terror." *Political Theory* 26, no. 1 (1998): 33–55, at 39; see also Robert Wokler, "The Enlightenment and the French Revolutionary Birth Pangs of Modernity", in Björn Wittrock, Johan Heilbron and Lars Magnusson (eds.), *The Rise of the Social Sciences and the Formation of Modernity* (Dordrecht: Springer, 1998), 35–76.

nations ... are also considered as either superiors or inferiors."[14] Thus, from this point of view, the emergence of the modern international system was intertwined with the rise of modern nationalism, as long as we assume that the latter "is primarily a political principle, which holds that the political and national unit should be congruent."[15] Finally, and according to Charles Tilly, in practice such congruence was the result of revolutionary situations in which established authority structures were challenged, and in which "the challenger was either resisting a demand for cultural assimilation into the state or demanding political autonomy on behalf of an explicitly stated cultural distinctness."[16]

Since much explanatory power hinges on the meanings attributed to the concepts of empire, state, and nation, the above accounts raise another set of questions which often has been glossed over by historians and students of international relations alike. They usually start out from the basic assumption that the transition from a world of empires to a world of nation states was a process through which political authority was *nationalized* as a consequence of changing norms of legitimacy and the fresh claims to national self-determination emanating from these. But since it remains enigmatic how and why these underlying norms changed in the first place, there is something paradoxical about self-determination, for, as Nathaniel Berman has asked, "how can international law recognize a right accruing to an entity which, by its own admission, lacks international legal existence?"[17] Since justifications of self-determination presuppose some prior definition of that very self which is supposed to determine its own fate, studying the emergence of the principle of self-determination makes it necessary to study how that particular kind of self was created by

[14] István Hont, "The Permanent Crisis of a Divided Mankind: 'Contemporary Crisis of the Nation State' in Historical Perspective." *Political Studies* 42, no. 1 (1994): 166–231, at 172. See also William H. Sewell, *A Rhetoric of Bourgeois Revolution: The Abbé Sieyès and "What Is the Third Estate?"* (Durham, NC: Duke University Press, 1994).

[15] Ernest Gellner, *Nations and Nationalism* (Ithaca: Cornell University Press, 1983), 1.

[16] Charles Tilly, "States and Nationalism in Europe 1492–1992", *Theory and Society* 23, no. 1 (1994): 131–146, at 134.

[17] Nathaniel Berman, "Sovereignty in Abeyance: Self-determination and International law." *Wisconsin International Law Journal* 7, no. 1 (1988): 51–105, at 52.

fusing nation and state together into a *prima facie* coherent unity. Such is the task of the present chapter.

Let us begin by noting that the very term "nation-state" had to wait for its first appearance in the English language until 1895 and then was used to denote "a numerous body of human beings permanently united by common inhabitation of a definite territory and by the establishment of an all-comprehending relation of sovereign and subject."[18] When crafting this definition, the author was able to capitalize on a concept which had been formulated some twenty years earlier by the Swiss lawyer Bluntschli, who then argued that the principle of nationality "is not content with the State protecting national language, custom, and culture, but demands that the State itself should become national. Absolutely stated, it comes to this: Every People has a call and a right to form a State. As mankind is divided into a number of Peoples, the world must be divided into the same number of States."[19] But long after this concept had come into wide enough currency, its use was still beset by ambiguities and profound tensions. Granted that the concept of nation-state refers to a congruence of political authority and community within the same portion of territory, this raises the question of how such congruence was conceptualized into existence and how it became perceived as a constitutive feature of the modern international system.[20] Given that this ideal of congruence was met with opposition from statesmen such as Lord Acton and Klemens von Metternich its final triumph becomes even more enigmatic.

In this chapter I will try to answer these questions by analyzing how connections between the concepts of state and nation were forged in legal and political theory and practice until this ushered in a modern doctrine of national self-determination in the beginning of the twentieth century. Since notions of nationality and nationhood began to exercise a measurable influence on international law and political

[18] Charles M. Platt, "A Triad of Political Conceptions: State, Sovereign, Government." *Political Science Quarterly* 10 no. 2 (1895): 292–323, at 298.

[19] Johann Kaspar Bluntschli, *The Theory of the State* (Oxford: Clarendon Press, 1885), 95.

[20] This congruence has remained an important topic even to contemporary theorists of nationalism. See, for example, Andrew Vincent, *Nationalism and Particularity* (Cambridge: Cambridge University Press, 2002), 36–61; Bernard Yack, *Nationalism and the Moral Psychology of Community* (Chicago: University of Chicago Press, 2012), 96–112.

practice first during the processes of Italian and German unification, my focus will be on how such connections were created and used to understand and motivate political and legal action, roughly from the start of the *risorgimento* to the end of the First World War.[21] As I will try to show, however, none of the authors conventionally saddled with the responsibility for having brought the transition from empires to nation states about would have recognized any sharp distinction or contradiction between these concepts. Not only were some European empires struggling to turn themselves into nation-states at this point, but nascent nation-states such as Italy and Germany were embarking on imperial adventures outside Europe.[22] But although self-government had long been denied non-European peoples on the grounds of their immaturity and lack of civilization, the ideal of congruence of nation and state quickly spread across the world and issued in claims to national self-determination by colonial and peripheral polities at the end of the First World War. Since most of these claims were unsuccessful, the ways in which self-determination was put into practice merely perpetuated imperial relations between European and non-European peoples. But remaining within the increasingly shaky confines of European empires, these peoples were in the process becoming international precisely by virtue of being denied access to international society on *equal* terms, a logic which would culminate in the decolonization of Asia and Africa in the twentieth century.

In making this argument, I will first explore how international lawyers tried to accommodate the many tensions between territorial and national interpretations of sovereignty, arguing that although these tensions were provisionally resolved in favor of the notion of nationality this did little to change the grounds on which international recognition was granted in principle. I will then describe how the congruence

[21] For a similar take on nationalism, see Isaiah Berlin, "Nationalism: Past Neglect and Present Power", in H. Hardy (ed.), *Against the Current. Essays in the History of Ideas* New York: Viking Press, 1980), 333–355.

[22] See, for example, Neil Evans, "'A World Empire, Sea Girt': The British Empire, State, and Nations, 1780–1914." in Stefan Berger and Alexei Miller (eds.) *Nationalizing Empires* (Budapest: Central European University Press, 2015), 31–97; Stefan Berger, "Building the Nation among Visions of German Empire", in Berger and Miller, *Nationalizing Empires*, 247–308; Andrea Komlosy, "Imperial Cohesion, Nation-Building, and Regional Integration in the Habsburg Monarchy." in Berger and Miller, *Nationalizing Empires*, 369–428.

of nation and state underwriting these efforts was conceptualized by the many philosophers, historians, and nationalist agitators who often had their own political stakes in bringing it about. Finally, I will explore how the worldwide dissemination of this ideal conditioned attempts to reconceptualize empire after the Great War, and how this produced some of the first conceptions of a modern international system.

Recognizing Nationality

Modern theories of sovereignty have an ambiguous scope. Although claims to sovereignty often encompass peoples as well as territories, these entities are not always assumed to coincide. Whereas early modern theories of sovereignty were primarily concerned with the subjects of sovereign authority regardless of where these happened to find themselves, a modern concept of sovereignty is taken to refer primarily to the existence of supreme authority within a bounded territory regardless of whom happens to be there.[23] According to Jordan Branch, such practices of territorial demarcation were not consolidated until after the Congress of Vienna in 1815.[24] This ambivalence was reflected in doctrines of international recognition, which initially made few references to the territorial scope of sovereignty and contained few commitments as to the proper locus of sovereignty when stipulating requirements for international legal recognition. To authors like Wheaton and his predecessors, it was quite sufficient for an entity aspiring to sovereign statehood to display a semblance of *de facto* independence from other states to merit formal legal recognition and observance of non-intervention from these. There was no requirement to the effect that state and nation ought to coincide within the same territory, since according to Wheaton, "[a] State is also distinguishable

[23] See, for example, Annabel S. Brett, *Changes of State: Nature and the Limits of the City in Early Modern Natural Law* (Princeton: Princeton University Press, 2011);11–36; Stuart Elden, *The Birth of Territory* (Chicago: University of Chicago Press, 2013); Lauren Benton, *A Search for Sovereignty: Law and geography in European empires, 1400–1900* (Cambridge: Cambridge University Press, 2010), 1–39; Jens Bartelson, *Sovereignty as Symbolic Form* (London & New York: Routledge, 2014).

[24] Jordan Branch, *The Cartographic State: Maps, Territory, and the Origins of Sovereignty* (Cambridge: Cambridge University Press, 2013), 135–138.

from a Nation, since the former may be composed of different races of men, all subject to the same supreme authority."[25]

As a consequence, and as Quincy Wright would later remark from a safe temporal distance, "[t]he political right of revolution, the legal right of recognition, and the policy of recognizing *de facto* governments, suggested by the American Declaration of Independence and Monroe Doctrine, were increasingly recognized by all states during the nineteenth century, and marked a considerable change in the practice of international law from that of the age of imperialism."[26] But as I argued in the previous chapter, the quests for independence that took place during the first half of the nineteenth century in Latin America and elsewhere were struggles to achieve statehood rather than pleas for *national* self-determination strictly speaking. For example, as Hugh Seton-Watson laconically remarked on Greek independence in 1830, "[a] Greek state now existed, but a Greek nation still had to be made."[27] But although the *de facto* principle constituted a valid ground for international recognition, the way in which it was applied in political practice was about to change. Since the meaning of sovereignty and non-intervention now could be interpreted in other than strictly territorial terms, those in favor of national self-determination could argue that nations or peoples rather than states ought to be the locus of sovereign authority, and that other states therefore were obliged to grant recognition to such entities once they had attained *de facto* control over the government of a given state.

Hence there was an unresolved tension in international law, captured not without sarcasm by Mountague Bernard when he described what

25 Henry Wheaton, *Elements of International Law* (Boston: Little, Brown & Co., 1866), 30.

26 Quincy Wright, "Recognition and Self-Determination", *Proceedings of the American Society of International Law at Its Annual Meeting*. Vol. 48 (Cambridge: Cambridge University Press, 1954), 23–37, at 27; see also Quincy Wright, "Some Thoughts about Recognition," *American Journal of International Law* 44, no. 3 (1950): 548–559.

27 Hugh Seton-Watson, *Nations and States: An Enquiry into the Origins of Nations and the Politics of Nationalism* (London: Taylor & Francis, 1977), 114. As some colleagues kindly have pointed out, this most likely alludes to a remark allegedly made by Massimo d'Azeglio: "Fatta l'Italia, bisogna fare gli Italiani", the authenticity of which has been disputed by Stephanie Malia Hom, "On the Origins of Making Italy: Massimo D'Azeglio and 'fatta l'Italia, bisogna fare gli italiani'." *Italian Culture* 31 no. 1 (2013): 1–16.

was at stake in the *Risorgimento* thus: "in the controversy between Count Cavour and Baron Schleinitz, each insists on non-intervention, but each uses it as a weapon against the other; the former applies it to nations, the latter to States; the one maintains that there ought *to be* no interference in Italy, the other that there ought *to have been* none in Naples."[28] At the end of the day it was Cavour who went back home with the precious prize to Vittorio Emanuele II, but not before an important requirement of recognition had been added by the British foreign secretary Lord Russell: "When the formation of this state shall be announced to Her Majesty, it is hoped that the government of the king will be ready to show that the new monarchy has been erected in pursuance of the deliberate wishes of the people of Italy."[29] In the rest of this section, I will describe attempts to turn nationality into a legal ground of international recognition, arguing that however unsuccessful these were, they nevertheless contributed to the naturalization of the nation-state as the predominant locus of political authority in the modern world.

A first step towards translating a nationalist interpretation of sovereignty into political practice had been taken by Charles-Louis Napoléon Bonaparte in 1848, four years before he became Napoleon III, when he decided that French foreign policy would be based on a *principe des nationalités*, which meant that some peoples were entitled to self-rule on grounds of their nationality and national belonging. Although this principle was arbitrarily invoked in order to debunk Austrian sovereignty claims during the *Risorgimento* as well as in support of German unification, it was met with domestic opposition on the grounds that a unified Italy and Germany would constitute major threats to French security and imperial interests.[30] But since this doctrine contained no

28 Mountague Bernard, *On the Principle of Non-Intervention. A Lecture Delivered in the Hall of All Souls College* (Oxford & London: J. H. Parker, 1860), p. 3.

29 Letter from Russell to D'Azeglio, March 31, 1861. Quoted in Mikulas Fabry, *Recognizing States. International Society and the Establishment of New States since 1776* (Oxford: Oxford University Press, 2010), 91.

30 See, for example, Roger Price, *The French Second Empire: An Anatomy of Political Power* (Cambridge: Cambridge University Press, 2001), 405–464; James Summers, *Peoples and International Law* (Leiden: Brill, 2013), 107–124; Ian Brownlie, "An Essay in the History of the Principle of Self-determination", in C. H. Alexandrowicz (ed.) *Studies in the History of the Law of Nations* (Dordrecht: Springer, 1970), 90–99; Otto Pflanze, "Nationalism in Europe, 1848–1871." *The Review of Politics* 28, no. 2 (1966): 129–143.

clear conception of what constituted the basis of nationality, it was open to creative interpretation and application. As Napoleon III could confidently retort to his critics, in order not to challenge French predominance, issues of nationality should be settled pragmatically in each individual case, since "nationalities do not define themselves solely in terms of language and race: they depend especially on the configuration and conformity of ideas born of common interests and a shared history."[31] Thus the point of nationality was to reinforce French imperial designs at the expense of its rivals, and in effect sacrificing the independence of its allies in the process, something which became all too apparent after the Franco-Prussian war.

But the notion of nationality was soon twisted into a justification of national independence by Italian lawyers supportive of unification. To Pasquale Mancini, who was deeply involved in the process of unification and in the drafting of Italy's first Civil Code, the primary subject of international law was not sovereign states, but rather distinct peoples sharing the same unified territory, traditions, and language. As he argued in an inaugural lecture in Turin: "The complex of these elements, in fact, consists in the very nature of each population, and causes among the members of the national consortium, a particular intimacy both material and moral, and it creates a more intimate community of law, which is impossible to exist between individuals of different nations."[32] But a given people "do not form a nation without the moral unity of a common thought, a prevailing idea that forms a society."[33] Thus to exist as a nation presupposes a consciousness of its existence among its members, a common consciousness that the existence of a people does not require. This entailed that governments should represent nations rather than states. Since nations were constituted from within they could warrant freedom a way that states could not.[34]

[31] Letter to Ollivier, November 7, 1867, quoted in Price, *French Second Empire*, 406.

[32] Pasquale Stanislao Mancini, *Della nazionalità come fondamento del diritto delle genti. Prelezione al corso di diritto internazionale e marittimo pronunziata nella Regia Università di Torino* [1851] (Torino: Giappachelli, 1994), 37–38. Translated by Elisabetta Fiocchi Malaspina, "Teaching International Law during the Italian Unification: a New Discipline for a New State," *Miscellena Historico-Iuridica* 13, no. 1 (2014): 143–158, at 149.

[33] Mancini, *Della nazionalità come fondamento del diritto delle genti*, 43–44.

[34] For the context of Mancini's theory, see Liliana Obregón Tarazona, "Writing International Legal History: An Overview." *Monde(s)* 7, no. 1 (2015): 95–112.

Similar views of the paramount importance of nationality to international law were entertained by Count Mamiani, whom Cavour had appointed minister of education to Sardinia-Piedmonte in 1860. He began his restatement of the principle of nationality in *II Nuovo Diritto Europeo* (1859), by arguing that "with the maturity of civilization, it appears that nations alone are to constitute the true and mighty individual members of the great human family."[35] Like Mancini, his conception of the nation was based on a delicate blend of objective and intersubjective elements. Originally sprung from families, "a certain identity of their nature and their fortunes came to display itself, and gave birth to one same language, one same genius in arts and letters, with many common usages and traditions, and some substantial homogeneity."[36] But in contrast to Mancini, the causes conducive to the rise of nations were not purely internal and cultural in character, but also external and geopolitical, given that "[a]nother cause of this movement has been the need which they have felt of strengthening themselves against other peoples which are excessively aggrandized by fortune or by conquests."[37] According to Mamiani, this meant that only states with "a certain permanent moral unity" and a "spontaneous and assiduous concurrence of minds and wills" that comes with nationality are likely to endure. Because "if we go by experience, we shall see that it is by nations that States are ordinarily founded, and that close political conjunctions of races different in breed, in tongue and in temperament, seldom get so far."[38] The implications of this mode of reasoning for Italian independence were straightforward, since there is "a maxim of international law that where there is not any competent moral unification or any spontaneous social communion…there is violence but not justice, there is conquest but not self-renunciation."[39]

Similar views of the legal purchase of nationality evolved in the context of German unification. In his *Allgemeine Statslehre* (1875–6) Bluntschli provided a philosophical elaboration of this principle, and thereby a belated legal justification of the integration of Schleswig-Holstein into the German Confederation.[40] Tracing the origin of the

35 Terenzio Count Mamiani della Rovere, *Rights of Nations, or The New Law of European States Applied to the Affairs of Italy*. trans. by Roger Acton (London: W. Jeffs, 1860), IV, 39.

36 Ibid., 39. 37 Ibid., 41. 38 Ibid., 45. 39 Ibid., 47.

40 Martti Koskenniemi, *The Gentle Civilizer of Nations: The Rise and Fall of International Law 1870–1960* (Cambridge: Cambridge University Press, 2001), 64.

notion of nationality back to the French Revolution, Bluntschli argued that "it was trodden under foot at the Restoration. The Congress of Vienna, with utter disregard of national rights, distributed fragments of great peoples among the restored dynasties."[41] But during the processes of Italian and German unification, "[t]he impulses to nationality were roused more strongly than ever before, even among the masses, and demanded satisfaction in politics. Peoples desired to give their union a political form and to become Nations."[42] Hence according to Bluntschli, the fact that Italians and Germans had "begun to demand recognition for the rights of nationalities (*Nationale Rechte*) implies an advance in civilisation."[43]

In the philosophical parts of his treatise – inspired by his teacher Savigny – Bluntschli set out to explain how a people could attain nationhood and statehood. The essence of a people, he maintained, "lies in its civilisation (*Kultur*): its inner cohesion and its separation from foreign peoples spring mainly from development in civilisation, and express spirit and themselves chiefly in influencing its conditions."[44] But in order to become a nation proper, a given people must first attain statehood, since "[b]y a Nation (*Volk*) we generally understand a society of all the members of a State as united and organised in the State. The Nation comes into being with the creation of the State. It is the consciousness, more or less developed, of political connection and unity which lifts the Nation above the People."[45] Yet at the end of the day, "how far a people is able and worthy to form a State, cannot in the imperfect condition of international law be decided by any human judgment, but only by the judgment of God as revealed in the history of the world. As a rule it is only by great struggles, by its own sufferings and its own acts, that a nation can justify its claim."[46] But still the conditions of success were laid bare by means of a distinction largely coeval with that between civilized and uncivilized peoples, since "only those peoples in which the manly qualities, understanding and courage, predominate are fully capable of creating and maintaining a national State. Peoples of more feminine characteristics are, in the end, always governed by other and superior forces."[47] The legal import of the principles of nationality and self-determination was thus confined to Europeans only; the others had to suffer what they must.

[41] Bluntschli, *Theory of the State*, 99. [42] Ibid. [43] Ibid., 93. [44] Ibid., 89.
[45] Ibid., 90. [46] Ibid., 106. [47] Ibid., 103.

To elevate the ambiguous principle of nationality into a ground for international recognition was for obvious reasons an urgent concern of Italian and German lawyers but had also some resonance outside their spheres of immediate intellectual influence. Among them was Francis Lieber, who conveyed similar notions of nationhood to what proved to be a receptive American audience.[48] As he informed his readers, the word nation "means, in modern times, a numerous and homogeneous population ... permanently inhabiting and cultivating a coherent territory, with a well-defined geographic outline, and a name of its own – the inhabitants speaking their own language, having their own literature and common institutions."[49] Without such a distinctive national character "[s]tates cannot obtain that longevity and continuity of political society which is necessary for our progress."[50] A mankind divided into nations was a potent bulwark against future empire and a precondition of international cooperation, since "[t]he multiplicity of civilized nations, their distinct independence (without which there would be enslaving Universal Monarchy), and their increasing resemblance and agreement, are some of the great safeguards of our civilization."[51] This multiplicity of nations was now in the process of evolving into an international community. According to Lieber, "[t]he civilized nations have come to constitute a community, and are daily forming more and more a commonwealth of nations, under the restraint and protection of the law of nations, which has begun to make its way even to countries not belonging to the Christian community, to which the Law of Nations had been confined."[52]

In one of the most ambitious attempts to insert the notion of nationality into the heart of international law, Pasquale Fiori maintained that whereas a congruence of nation and state was morally desirable, it was not necessary to the legal personality of the former. In the second edition of his *Nuovo Diritto Internazionale Pubblico* (1865/1885), Fiore distinguished rather sharply between nations and states. Whereas the former is "a moral being which results from a conjoining of natural elements which mostly are those of race, language,

[48] See, for example, James Farr, "Francis Lieber and the Interpretation of American Political Science." *Journal of Politics* 52, no. 4 (1990): 1027–1049.

[49] Francis Lieber, *Fragments of Political Science on Nationalism and Inter-Nationalism* (New York, Scribner, 1868), 8.

[50] Ibid. [51] Ibid., 20–21. [52] Ibid., 22.

and the character of customary traditions," the latter is "a political organism formed by a certain amount of men reunited on the same territory, with the proper means to defend the right of the members of the association, and the power necessary to take responsibility for its own actions in relation to other states."[53] And although "nationality is the most perfect organic principle and the most efficacious of moral unity", the application of this principle was far from straightforward since "to admit the principle of nationalities as a legal principle for the organization of humanity would require that the idea of nationality was a legal conception whose nature was to indicate, in every contested instance, a line of demarcation to determine the limits of this or that nationality."[54] Yet since this rarely if ever was possible, the principle of nationality was open to abuse as indicated by its usage by those German authors who "have come to regard race as the decisive factor, perhaps with the intention of subsequently applying the theory to justify certain territorial aggrandizements."[55] Yet regardless of the inevitable arbitrariness of national lines of demarcation, any peace treaty including cessation of territory which has not taken the will of its inhabitants into consideration will "confound people absolutely heterogenous in terms of race, origin, culture, language and nationality [and] will therefore create a permanent ferment of unrest and anarchy."[56] Thus, in order to bring about the congruence of state and nation necessary to legal order, the principle of nationality ought to be codified in international law. As Fiore argued in his final treatise first published in 1890, "[n]o sovereign, on the basis of treaties, dynastic interests or prescription, can properly maintain the right to set bounds to the liberty of people of the same nationality who wish to unite politically in conformity with their national aspirations."[57] And from this it followed that "[i]nternational law should protect the

[53] Pasquale Fiore, *Nouveau Droit International Public Suivant des Besoins de la Civilization Moderne*, Vol. I. trans. by Charles Antoine (Paris: A. Durand et Pedone-Lauriel, 1885), § 287–289, 255–256.

[54] Ibid., §276, 245, § 298, 259. [55] Ibid., § 284, 252.

[56] Pasquale Fiore, *Nouveau Droit International Public Suivant des Besoins de la Civilization Moderne*, Vol. II. trans. by Charles Antoine, (Paris: A. Durand et Pedone-Lauriel, 1885), §1065, 461.

[57] Pasquale Fiore, *International Law Codified and Its Legal Sanction; or, The Legal Organization of the Society of States* (New York: Baker, Voorhis, & Co, 1918), I, § 93, 119.

formation of national states, safeguard the rights of people of the same nationality and should see that the national aspirations spontaneously and constantly asserted are not repressed by deception or force."[58] Yet this right did not extend beyond the confines of civilized states. Although Fiore did insist that uncivilized peoples were within the purview of international law, he maintained that "colonization and colonial expansion cannot be questioned" and "that civilized countries, in order to find new outlets for their ever increasing activity, need to extend their present possessions and to occupy those parts of the earth which are not of any use to uncivilized peoples."[59]

But as Brownlie and Koskenniemi have pointed out, although the widespread application of the principle of nationality had given rise to profound changes that could no longer easily be accommodated within international law, attempts to codify this principle into law were largely unsuccessful.[60] For example, as John Westlake maintained, "the indefiniteness and instability of all the characters on which nationalities are based are a conclusive objection to founding international rights on nationality, as was proposed by many eminent Italian jurists at the time when the unity of their country was being achieved. Nationalities, though often important in politics, must be kept outside international law."[61] Yet Westlake tacitly assumed that states and nations ought to be congruent, since a nation, "means a state considered with reference to the persons composing it. Such also is the usual meaning of the word in the English language when civilised people are spoken of."[62] Perhaps Lassa Oppenheim was more realistic in his assessment of the impact of nationality when he held that "the principle of nationality is of such force that it is fruitless to try to stop its victory. Wherever a community of many millions of individuals, who are bound together by the same blood, language, and interests, become so powerful that they think it necessary to have a State of their own, in which they can live according to their own ideals and can build up a national civilisation, they will certainly get that

[58] Ibid., I, § 94, 119. [59] Ibid., I, §15, 46.

[60] Brownlie, "History of the Principle of Self-Determination", 94; Martti Koskenniemi, *The Gentle Civilizer of Nations: The Rise and Fall of International Law 1870–1960* (Cambridge: Cambridge University Press, 2001), 63, 67.

[61] John Westlake, *International Law, Vol. 1: Peace* (Cambridge: Cambridge University Press, 1910), 5.

[62] Ibid., 3.

State sooner or later."[63] As Matthew Craven has rightly pointed out, during this period "[t]he competence to confer and withhold nationality was still regarded as a matter falling within the domain of domestic jurisdiction in the sense that international law neither required such conferral in any particular case nor prohibited its withdrawal."[64] But however unsuccessful the above attempts to accommodate the principle of nationality within international law ultimately were, it remains to describe what made these attempts possible in the first place. This makes a brief detour back to the French Revolution and its immediate aftermath necessary.

The Contagion of Nationality

There is a wide agreement that the French Revolution changed the grounds on which claims to sovereignty could be legitimized. It has been pointed out that by identifying the people or nation as the bearer of sovereignty, the ideologues of the Revolution also created the preconditions for what was to become a lasting fusion of nation and state.[65] Hence, in this section, I shall describe how this congruence of nation and state was conceptualized in different national contexts and how the desired result – the nation-state – then was related to contemporary conceptions of empire and imperial rule. As I shall argue, the way in which this relationship was conceived was hardly a matter of distinction or contradiction, but more often a question of entanglement and mutual reinforcement. Sometimes this implied that empires were conceived of in national terms, but more often it meant that the imagined congruence of nation and state was used to legitimize imperial rule over non-European peoples believed unable to attain such a congruence for themselves.

63 Lassa Oppenheim, *International Law. A Treatise* (London & New York: Longmans, Green & Co, 1905), 74.

64 Matthew Craven, "Statehood, Self-determination, and Recognition." in Malcolm D. Evans, (ed.), *International Law* (Oxford: Oxford: Oxford University Press, 2010), 203–251, at 222.

65 See, for example, Chimène I. Keitner, "National Self-Determination in Historical Perspective: The Legacy of the French Revolution for Today's Debates." *International Studies Review* 2, no. 3 (2000): 3–26; Robert Wokler, "The Enlightenment and the French Revolutionary Birth Pangs of Modernity", in Johan Heilbron, Lars Magnusson, and Björn Wittrock, (eds.) *The Rise of the Social Sciences and the Formation of Modernity: Conceptual Change in Context, 1750–1850* (Dordrecht: Springer 1998), 35–76.

In this context it is important to remember how this congruence was conceptualized into existence. As Martin Thom has described in vivid detail, this was largely a consequence of a historiographical transition during the late eighteenth and early nineteenth century that brought a transvaluation of the ancient city-state. From having served as a template for Enlightenment political thought, the ancient city-state was sidelined in the historical writing of revolutionaries and romantics. In its place gradually emerged the nation modelled on the tribe, the liberty of the republic replaced by that of the people, the virtues of cosmopolitan urbanity with those of the rustic countryside.[66] Yet those authors who wanted to bring state and nation to coincide had to explain how these entities were supposed to hang together. Whereas some assumed that the state was prior to and constitutive of nations and national identities, others assumed that the state derived its existence or at least its legitimacy from nations and national identities. Whereas the former solution came naturally to those subscribing to contractual views of sovereign authority, the latter solution presupposed that nations existed prior to and independent of any political authority. Those taking the latter route were thus challenged to provide evidence of the existence of such pre-political nations by accounting for their historical continuity and their cultural distinctness.[67] This implied that whenever there was a perceived mismatch between the scope of sovereign authority and the composition of the corresponding community, some version of nationalism would most likely be invoked in order to bestow sovereign authority with a semblance of political legitimacy.[68] Hence the above options gave rise to two distinct conceptions of nationhood, one republican and the other nationalist in character. Whereas those who assumed that states were constitutive of nations conceptualized the latter as a voluntary association predisposed to contest sovereign authority whenever it was found lacking in popular consent, those who took nations to be constitutive of states conceptualized the former as a primordial community of belonging predisposed to contest

66 See Martin Thom, *Republics, Nations and Tribes* (London: Verso: 1995).

67 See Keitner, "National Self-Determination in Historical Perspective", 17–18, 21–22; Bernard Yack, "Popular Sovereignty and Nationalism." *Political Theory* 29, no. 4 (2001): 517–536.

68 For the origins of these ideas, see Erica Benner, "Nationalism: Intellectual Origins", in John Breuilly (ed.), *The Oxford Handbook of the History of Nationalism* (Oxford: Oxford University Press, 2013), 37–55.

sovereign authority whenever it was found insufficiently expressive of its transcendent will. During the second half of the nineteenth century, these conceptions came to represent profound and lasting challenges to the legitimacy of the international order as well as that of individual governments in Europe and elsewhere.[69]

An early republican rendering of the congruence of nation and state was made by Abbé Sieyès in a pamphlet entitled *Qu'est-ce que le Tiers Etat* (1789).[70] Written in response to the vexed constitutional problem of *where* in the social body popular sovereignty was located once the monarch was gone, Sieyès maintained that the nation ought to be understood not as the locus of this sovereignty but as its very source, its constituent power (*pouvoir constituant*).[71] To him, the nation comprised all productive strata of society but excluded the nobility and the clergy from the purview of political power, since to be part of the nation "one must be either by untainted by privileges of any sort, or else relinquish them immediately and completely."[72] This nation was to be an association of free individuals united into a single body and articulating a common will. Although such "[i]ndividual wills still constitute its origin and form its essential components...[t]he community needs a common will; without *singleness* of will it could not succeed in being a willing and acting body."[73] Hence, being a constituent rather than a constituted power, "[t]he nation is prior to everything. It is the source of everything. Its will is always legal; indeed it is the law itself."[74] Although this nation was originally intended to be a purely voluntary association, its realization in time required the homogenization of its members and the cultivation of a cult of nationality as a precondition of its singularity and sovereignty.[75] And because a "nation

69 Matthew Craven, "Statehood, Self-determination, and Recognition", in Malcolm D. Evans, (ed.), *International Law* (Oxford: Oxford University Press, 2010), 203–251, esp. 230–231.

70 See Moran M. Mandelbaum, "The Fantasy of Congruency: The Abbé Sieyès and the 'nation-state' problématique revisited." *Philosophy & Social Criticism* 42, no. 3 (2016): 246–266; Jens Bartelson, *The Critique of the State* (Cambridge. Cambridge University Press, 2001), 40–43.

71 See, for example, Lucia Rubinelli, *Constituent Power. A History* (Cambridge: Cambridge University Press, 2020), ch. 1.

72 Comte Emmanuel Joseph Sieyès, *What Is the Third Estate?* Trans. by M. Blondel and edited by S. E. Finer (London: Pall Mall Press, 1964), 71.

73 Ibid., 121. 74 Ibid., 124.

75 Hont, "Permanent Crisis of a Divided Mankind", 194; Lucien Jaume, "Citizen and State under the French Revolution", in Quentin Skinner and Bo Stråth

is always in a state of nature and, amidst so many dangers, it can never have to many possible methods of expressing its will", Sieyès had furnished a potent way of conceptualizing the connection between state and nation that seemed to avoid the obvious difficulties that came with positing the nation as the ultimate locus of sovereign authority and which would continue to resonate in political and legal thought for much of the coming century.[76]

Another major attempt to conceptualize nation and state as congruent was made by Hegel. To him, the French Revolution was but a moment of liberation through which the French nation came to determine its own fate by appropriating the state for its own ends. The spirit of a nation, he argued in *Grundlinien der Philosophie des Rechts* (1820) "is both the law which permeates all relations within it and also the customs and consciousness of the individuals who belong to it."[77] But the nation cannot exist without a state any more than the state can exist without the nation, "[s]ince the being-for-itself of the actual spirit has its existence in this independence, the latter is the primary freedom and supreme dignity of a nation."[78] What followed from this was the final amalgamation of nation and state, so that "[t]he nation state [*das Volk als Staat*] is the spirit in its substantial rationality and immediate actuality, and is therefore the absolute power on earth; each state is consequently a sovereign and independent entity in relation to others."[79] To Hegel, the congruence of nation and state was not only an abstract ideal but also the final objective of world history insofar as the nation-state was the triumphant form of political life.

Neither Sieyès nor Hegel had much to say about the European empires of their own time, most likely because they did not consider

(eds.) *States and Citizens: History, Theory, Prospects* (Cambridge: Cambridge University Press, 2003): 131–144; David A. Bell, *The Cult of the Nation in France: Inventing Nationalism, 1680–1800* (Cambridge, MA: Harvard University Press, 2001); Sudhir Hazareesingh, *Saint-Napoleon. Celebrations of Sovereignty in Nineteenth Century France* (Cambridge, MA: Harvard University Press, 2004).

76 Sieyès, *What Is the Third Estate?*, 128. For the historical import, see Duncan Kelly, "Popular Sovereignty as State Theory in the Nineteenth Century." in Richard Bourke and Quentin Skinner (eds.), *Popular Sovereignty in Historical Perspective* (Cambridge: Cambridge University Press, 2016), 270–296.

77 Georg Wilhelm Friedrich Hegel, *Elements of the Philosophy of Right*. trans. by H. B. Nisbet (Cambridge: Cambridge University Press, 1991), § 274, 312.

78 Ibid., § 322, 359. 79 Ibid., § 331, 366–367.

these to be empires at all given their understanding of Rome and its legacy. In *Qu'est-ce que le Tiers Etat*, Sieyès used the term "empire" in a rather loose and metaphorical sense but made no mention of its concrete instantiations in the political world. But because of the revolutionary context of their lives and work, both authors were unwittingly involved in their making, albeit in different ways. Sieyès most famously so, since he was responsible for the dissolution of the Directorate, an event that made the Coup of 18 Brumaire possible and brought Napoleon Bonaparte to power. Hegel perhaps more indirectly so, since even though he had situated the French and Haitian revolutions in a world historical context, other parts of his work did indeed justify imperial and colonial rule outside Europe.[80] These parts of the world were forever beyond the scope of a history the *telos* of which was the nation-state. As Hegel argued when he compared different oriental empires in his *Vorlesungen über die Philosophie der Weltgeschichte* (1822–1830), since in India and China, "[t]he proper basis of the State, the principle of freedom is altogether absent: there cannot therefore be any State in the true sense of the term." As a consequence, neither the Chinese nor the Indian empire were close to attain the congruence required, because "if China may be regarded as nothing else but a State, Hindoo political existence presents us with a people, but no State."[81] Since non-European peoples were stuck in a state of despotism and lacked the historical consciousness necessary to escape this predicament on their own, they could attain freedom only if the Europeans first imposed their civilization on them.[82]

After the tumultuous events of 1848, it was no one less than Mill who brought this ideal down to earth and turned the congruence of nation and state into an almost axiomatic requirement of representative government. As he stated in *Considerations of Representative Government* (1861), "[a] portion of mankind may be said to constitute

[80] See, for example, Susan Buck-Morss, *Hegel, Haiti, and Universal History* (Pittsburgh: University of Pittsburgh Press, 2005); Jeanne Morefield, *Covenants without Swords: Idealist Liberalism and the Spirit of Empire* (Princeton: Princeton University Press, 2005), ch. 1.

[81] Georg Wilhelm Friedrich Hegel, *The Philosophy of History*. trans. by J. Sibree (Kitchener: Batoche Books, 2001), 179.

[82] Hegel, *The Philosophy of History*, 180. For an interpretation along these lines, see Alison Stone, "Hegel and Colonialism." *Hegel Bulletin* 41 no. 2 (2017): 247–270.

a nationality if they are united among themselves by common sympathies which do not exist between them and any others...[and]...desire to be under the same government, and desire that it should be government by themselves, or a portion of themselves, exclusively."[83] Such common sympathies may have many different causes, but the strongest of them was the "identity of political antecedents; the possession of a national history, and consequent community of recollections."[84] Although a sense of common identity could spring from many sources, the existence of nationhood was a necessary condition of legitimate and effective self-government, since "[w]here the sentiment of nationality exists in any force, there is a prima facie case for uniting all the members of the nationality under the same government, and a government to themselves apart."[85] And conversely, whenever a population is not sufficiently homogenous, self-government becomes virtually impossible, since "[a]mong a people without fellow-feeling, especially if they read and speak different languages, the united public opinion necessary to the working of representative government cannot exist."[86] Hence, and as a general principle of government, it is "a necessary condition of free institutions that the boundaries of governments should coincide in the main with those of nationalities."[87] Thus, to Mill, the congruence of nation and state was neither merely an abstract ideal nor a desirable historical end state, but was instead a precondition of representative government and thus also a requirement of self-determination.

But to Mill and other proponents of popular sovereignty such as de Tocqueville, notions of nationality and national self-government were in no way categorically opposed to ideas of empire and imperial rule. To de Tocqueville, it was rather the other way around. The power and prestige of the French nation required its expansion on other continents and the suspension of indigenous rule there.[88] Although Mill did not justify empire on overtly nationalist grounds, his conception of self-government was such that most non-European peoples were exempted on the grounds that they had not attained the degree of

[83] John Stuart Mill, *Considerations on Representative Government* (New York: Henry Holt & Co, 1873), 308.

[84] Ibid., 308. [85] Ibid., 310. [86] Ibid. [87] Ibid., 313.

[88] See Alexis de Tocqueville, *Writings on Empire and Slavery*. edited by Jennifer Pitts (Baltimore: Johns Hopkins University Press, 2001). For his differences with Mill on this issue, see H. O. Pappé, "Mill and Tocqueville." *Journal of the History of Ideas* 25, no. 2 (1964): 217–234, esp. 223.

civilization necessary.[89] As he made this point in *A Few Words on Non-Intervention* (1859): "Nations which are still barbarous have not got beyond the period during which it is likely to be for their benefit that they should be conquered and held in subjection by foreigners. Independence and nationality, so essential to the due growth and development of a people further advanced in improvement, are generally impediments to theirs."[90] As for the government of colonial dependencies, Mill divided the latter into two main categories, those mature enough for self-determination and those not: "Some are composed of people of similar civilization to the ruling county, capable of, and ripe for representative government, such as the British possessions in America and Australia, Others, like India, are still at a great distance from that state."[91] Whereas "colonies of European race" ought to "possess the fullest measure of internal self-government", beyond those civilized nations capable of nationality and self-determination, we find "conditions of society in which a vigorous despotism is in itself the best mode of government for training the people in what is specifically wanting to render them capable of a higher civilization."[92] Thus, since nationality was an achievement of progress and civilization rather than a trait latent in all societies, self-determination could not be granted to barbarous or uncivilized peoples. This being so since "barbarians have no right as a *nation*, except a right to such treatment as may, at the earliest possible period fit them for *becoming one*."[93] Barbarous or uncivilized peoples had thus to remain under paternalistic tutelage by European powers until they had acquired the traits believed by their masters to be necessary to good government and self-determination. Since it had become an almost "universal condition of the more backward populations to be either held in direct subjection

[89] See Uday Singh Mehta, *Liberalism and Empire: A Study in Nineteenth-century British Liberal Thought* (Chicago: University of Chicago Press, 1999); Jennifer Pitts, *A Turn to Empire: The rise of Imperial Liberalism in Britain and France* (Princeton: Princeton University Press, 2005), ch. 5; Duncan Bell, "John Stuart Mill on Colonies." *Political Theory* 38, no. 1 (2010): 34–64; Beate Jahn, "Kant, Mill, and Illiberal Legacies in International Affairs." *International Organization* 59, no. 1 (2005): 177–207.

[90] John Stuart Mill, "A Few Words on Non-Intervention", in *The Collected Works of John Stuart Mill.* Volume XXI. ed. by John M. Robson (Toronto: University of Toronto Press, London: Routledge and Kegan Paul, 1984), 118–119.

[91] Ibid., 336–337. [92] Ibid., 338 & 346. [93] Ibid., 119.

by the more advanced, or to be under their complete political ascendency", it was now imperative to provide them with "the best attainable present government, and with the conditions most favorable to future permanent improvement."[94] As Uday Metha has described the implications of Mill's position, "the possession of nationhood became a mark of civilization. That and only that could entitle a people to any sort of recognition. By making nationality in the political sense a mark of civilization, Mill helped shaped one of the enduring features of post-nineteenth century politics."[95]

Less well known is the fact that Mill also maintained that even those settler colonies deemed sufficiently civilized for self-government should nevertheless be kept within the bounds of empire, because such an arrangement would be a first step "toward universal peace and general friendly co-operation among nations" and would render "war impossible among a large number of otherwise independent communities, and...hinders any of them from being absorbed into a foreign state, and becoming a source of additional aggressive strength to some rival power."[96] This conception of empire as a union of internally independent settler communities would soon be superseded by even more grandiose visions in which a transcontinental community of Anglo-Saxons would be subjected to a common political authority within a global state.[97] Yet the former and more internationalist visions of empire would later became hard to distinguish from conceptions of an international system based the principle of national self-determination. It then became, as Metha has noted, a supreme irony that "nationality, while it legitimized colonial power, also became the principal language in which colonialism was resisted."[98] But as we shall see in the

94 Mill, *Considerations on Representative Government*, 347; Mehta, *Liberalism and Empire*, 46–76; Pitts, *Turn to Empire*, 138–146.

95 Pratap Bhanu Mehta, "Liberalism, Nation, and Empire: The Case of J. S. Mill", in Sankar Muthu (ed.), *Empire and Modern Political Thought* (Cambridge: Cambridge University Press, 2012), 232–269, at 246.

96 Mill, *Considerations on Representative Government*, 342.

97 See Duncan Bell, *The Idea of Greater Britain: Empire and the future of world order, 1860–1900* (Princeton: Princeton University Press, 2007), esp. 178–227; Duncan Bell, "The Victorian Idea of a Global State", in Duncan Bell, (ed.) *Victorian Visions of Global Order: Empire and International Relations in Nineteenth-century Political Thought* (Cambridge: Cambridge University Press, 2007), 159–185.

98 Mehta, "Liberalism, Nation, and Empire", 260.

next section, what these critics have neglected is the extent to which successful claims to self-determination merely implied that new-born nation-states remained trapped within the confines of imperial rule by being integrated within a global system of free trade.

The international ramifications of the desired congruence of nation and state were most clearly pronounced in the works of Mazzini, whose revolutionary pleas for national self-determination against empire and despotism enjoyed a wide appeal not only in Europe but elsewhere as well.[99] Deeply involved in and arguably also the chief ideologist of Italian unification, Mazzini saw the Italian struggle as part of a wider process of national awakening and emancipation all over Europe. As he proclaimed in 1849, "We need to establish a Holy Alliance of the Peoples and oppose it to the existing league of princes. We need to set the *foundations* for democracy."[100] The prime vehicle for such emancipation and the *sine qua non* of democratic government was the nation-state. As Mazzini had argued already in 1832, "[t]he nation is the only sovereign ... the nation alone has the inviolable right to *choose* its own institutions, to *correct* them and *change* them, when they no longer correspond to its needs and no longer contribute to social and intellectual *progress*."[101] In order to create a republic in which the nation was truly sovereign in this sense, it was necessary first to create a people by abolishing privilege and "raise to the level of religion the dogma of equality."[102] To Mazzini, although the people in whose name the revolution was to be undertaken was prepolitical insofar as it antedated the republican institutions that were to be born through revolution, "the multitude of individuals does not

[99] See, for example, contributions to Christopher A. Bayly and Eugenio F. Biagini, *Giuseppe Mazzini and the Globalization of Democratic Nationalism 1830–1920* (Oxford: Oxford University Press, 2008); H. S. Jones, "The Idea of the National in Victorian Political Thought." *European Journal of Political Theory* 5, no. 1 (2006): 12–21.

[100] Giuseppe Mazzini, "Toward a Holy Alliance of the Peoples", in Stefano Recchia and Nadia Urbinati (eds.) *A Cosmopolitanism of Nations. Giuseppe Mazzini's Writings on Democracy, Nation Building, and International Relations* (Princeton: Princeton University Press, 2009), 117–131, at 121.

[101] Giuseppe Mazzini, "On the Superiority of Representative Government." in Stefano Recchia and Nadia Urbinati (eds.), *A Cosmopolitanism of Nations. Giuseppe Mazzini's Writings on Democracy, Nation Building, and International Relations* (Princeton: Princeton University Press, 2009), 39–52, at 50.

[102] Mazzini, "On the Superiority of Representative Government", 43.

yet constitute a Nation, unless it is directed by common principles, governed by the same laws, and united in a fraternal bond."[103] That unity under common principles and laws is what "associate a multitude of men and transform them into a homogenous whole. Without it there is no *nation*, but only a *crowd*."[104] In order to enact the will of the nation it is necessary to elect deputies to a national assembly, and "any restrictions brought to the exercise of its power ... would contradict the principle of national sovereignty."[105] Like many others who were trying to weld nation and state together at this time, Mazzini did not and perhaps could not distinguish between ethnic and civic conceptions of nationality. Rather his notion of nationhood was based on a historical congruence of pre-political commonalities of language and culture with common political allegiances, a notion of nationality not unlike those formulated by Vico and Herder before him.[106] As he forcefully made this point, "[l]anguage, territory, and race are just indications of *nationality*. They remain unstable when they are not all combined...they need to be supported by a specific historical tradition and by the development of a collective life that results in a common character."[107]And given the immediate political context of Italian unification, Mazzini had no reason to conceptualize the state in terms independent of the nation thus defined since its concrete existence safely could be taken for granted. Rather the upshot of his project was to provide an ideologically persuasive account of how such nations could *turn themselves into states* through democratic revolutions in favor of national self-determination.[108]

Still more important to our present concerns are the internationalist dimensions of Mazzini's political thought.[109] While Mazzini thought

[103] Ibid., 48. [104] Ibid. [105] Ibid., 51.

[106] See Bruce Haddock, "State and Nation in Mazzini's Political Thought." *History of Political Thought* 20, no. 2 (1999): 313–336.

[107] Giuseppe Mazzini, "Nationalism and Nationality." in Stefano Recchia and Nadia Urbinati (eds.), *A Cosmopolitanism of Nations. Giuseppe Mazzini"s Writings on Democracy, Nation Building, and International Relations.* (Princeton: Princeton University Press, 2009), 62–65, at 65.

[108] See David G. Rowley, "Giuseppe Mazzini and the Democratic Logic of Nationalism." *Nations and Nationalism* 18, no. 1 (2012): 39–56.

[109] Stefano Recchia and Nadia Urbinati, "Giuseppe Mazzini's International Political Thought." in Stefano Recchia and Nadia Urbinati (eds.), *A Cosmopolitanism of Nations. Giuseppe Mazzini's Writings on Democracy, Nation Building, and International Relations* (Princeton: Princeton University

that "to revive the nationality of different peoples is an indispensable condition for the progressive advancement of our epoch", any such revival had to be undertaken with respect to the reciprocal rights of other nations to revive themselves on equal terms.[110] The ultimate task of a democratic revolution was that of promoting the association of different countries so that "[f]ree and equal Peoples will help one another, each will be able to benefit from the resources that others possess in the pursuit of their common civilization and progress."[111] Thus an important objective of Italian foreign policy consisted in "promoting the principle of Nationality as the supreme foundation of international order and as a guarantee of future peace."[112] Hence international peace and order were only possible among democratic nations, yet such peace and order were but stepping stones towards a wider moral and political community that eventually would comprise all mankind regardless of cultural and other differences between nations. Since these differences were historically contingent and therefore mutable, progressive development would eventually "lead to the fusion of all members of Humanity in the awareness of a common origin, a common law, and a common goal."[113] Finally, and in contrast to his Enlightenment predecessors, Mazzini saw no contradiction

Press, 2009), 1–30; Nadia Urbinati, "The Legacy of Kant: Giuseppe Mazzini's Cosmopolitanism of Nations." in Chistopher A. Bayly and Eugenio F. Biagini, *Giuseppe Mazzini and the Globalization of Democratic Nationalism 1830–1920* (Oxford: Oxford University Press, 2008), 11–36; Maurizio Isabella, "Mazzini's Internationalism in Context: From the Cosmopolitan Patriotism of the Italian Carbonari to Mazzini's Europe of the Nations." in Christopher A. Bayly and Eugenio F. Biagini, *Giuseppe Mazzini and the Globalization of Democratic Nationalism 1830–1920* (Oxford: Oxford University Press, 2008), 37–58.

110 Giuseppe Mazzini, "Humanity and Country." in Stefano Recchia and Nadia Urbinati (eds.), *A Cosmopolitanism of Nations. Giuseppe Mazzini's Writings on Democracy, Nation Building, and International Relations* (Princeton: Princeton University Press, 2009), 53–57, at 53.

111 Giuseppe Mazzini, "Nationality and Cosmopolitanism." in Stefano Recchia and Nadia Urbinati (eds.), *A Cosmopolitanism of Nations. Giuseppe Mazzini's Writings on Democracy, Nation Building, and International Relations* (Princeton: Princeton University Press, 2009), 57–62, at 61.

112 Giuseppe Mazzini, "Principles of International Politics." in Stefano Recchia and Nadia Urbinati (eds.), *A Cosmopolitanism of Nations. Giuseppe Mazzini's Writings on Democracy, Nation Building, and International Relations* (Princeton: Princeton University Press, 2009), 224–240, at 232.

113 Mazzini, "Humanity and Country", 55.

between the aspirations of nationality and those of humanity, since as he repeatedly maintained, "[h]umanity constitutes the *end* and the nation the *means*."[114]

But the development of nationalities was far from even across the European continent. Whereas some peoples had already acquired a firm sense of nationality and nationhood, other obviously lagged behind: "There are some races, such as the Slavs ... whose lives thus far have been a vague anticipation of things to come."[115] Thus a unified Italy had a civilizing mission of its own waiting. Its foreign policy should aim to "establish an alliance with the Southern Slavs and with the entire Hellenic element." The need for civilization was even larger outside Europe, something which made it necessary to "systematically increase the Italian influence at Suez and Alexandria ... [and to] ... invade and colonize the Tunisian lands when the opportunity presents itself."[116] So beyond the proud proclamations of the virtues of democracy and internationalism, dreams of empire were still not far away in Mazzini's mind, since "[a]lready in the past, the flag of Rome was unfurled on top of the Atlas Mountains, after Carthage had been vanquished, and the Mediterranean became known as *Mare nostrum*. We were masters of that entire region until the fifth century. Today the French covet it and they will soon have it if we don't get there first."[117]

Similar republican and internationalist sensibilities were reflected in contemporary attempts to reconcile nation and state in French political thought. For example, although Michelet held that the national characteristics of a people derived from climate and natural circumstances,

[114] Giuseppe Mazzini, "Nationalism and Nationality." in Stefano Recchia and Nadia Urbinati (eds.), *A Cosmopolitanism of Nations. Giuseppe Mazzini's Writings on Democracy, Nation Building, and International Relations* (Princeton: Princeton University Press, 2009), 62–65, at 63. For the tension between conceptions of nationality and humanity in nineteenth century political thought, see Sankar Muthu, *Enlightenment Against Empire* (Princeton: Princeton University Press, 2003); Jens Bartelson, *Visions of World Community* (Cambridge. Cambridge University Press, 2009), esp. 115–140; Georgios Varouxakis, "'Patriotism,' 'Cosmopolitanism' and 'Humanity' in Victorian Political Thought." *European Journal of Political Theory* 5 vo. 1 (2006): 100–118.

[115] Mazzini, "Humanity and Country," 57.

[116] Giuseppe Mazzini, "Principles of International Politics," 238–239.

[117] Ibid., 239.

such pre-political nations nevertheless required a state as a medium of their realization. As he argued in *Le Peuple* (1845), "[t]he Patria, the City, far from being opposed to nature, are for that soul of the people which dwells therein, the single and all-powerful means of realizing its nature, giving it, at once, the vital starting-point and the liberty of development."[118] To Michelet, such national belonging did not preclude the formation of international and cosmopolitan sentiments among peoples belonging to distinct nations. Rather it was a way of fostering them: "The more man advances, the more he enters into the spirit of his country, and the better he contributes to the harmony of the globe ... one's native country forms the necessary initiation to the country of all mankind."[119] Pursuing a similar republican agenda in his *Qu'est-ce qu'une Nation* (1882), Renan made one of the few attempts during this period to define (and defend) the idea of the nation-state in voluntaristic terms. Having noted that the modern ideas of nation and nationality were of recent vintage, Renan went on to debunk definitions of nationhood that were based on commonalities of language, race, religion, and territorial belonging. Although the boundaries of states and the composition of populations had varied greatly across time and were contingent on the "profound complications of history" generated by endless conquests, a modern nation was in essence nothing but "a spiritual principle, a soul", constituted by a "rich legacy of memories" on the one hand, and "a present-day consent, the desire to live together" on the other.[120] In his famous definition, "[a] nation is therefore a large-scale solidarity, constituted by the feeling of the sacrifices that one has made in the past and of those that one is prepared to make in the future."[121] What made nation and state fit so neatly together was the fact that they had been joined in collective memory since time immemorial by virtue of the tacit consent of successive generations.

118 Jules Michelet, *The People*. trans. by C. Cocks (London: Longman, Brown, Green, and Longmans, 1846), 140. For analyses, see Alain Pons, "De la 'nature commune des nations' au Peuple romantique. Note sur Vico et Michelet." *Romantisme* 5, no. 9 (1975): 39–49; Pierre Nora, "Michelet, ou l'Hysterie Identitaire." *L'Esprit Créateur* 46, no. 3 (2006): 6–14.

119 Ibid., 140.

120 Ernest Renan, "What Is a Nation?" in Geoff Eley and Ronald Grigor Suny, (eds.) *Becoming National: A Reader* (Oxford: Oxford University Press, 1996), 42–55, at 52.

121 Ibid., 53.

It is worth noting that however much in vogue notions of nationality were in Europe, they were also met with fierce opposition, especially in the aftermath of the revolutions of 1848. Although many historians have focused on the rise of nationalism during this period, the triumph of the nation-state form was far from certain at this point.[122] For example, during the process of Italian unification, the legitimacy of nationality was contested on the grounds that it threatened local autonomy and civic identities in a way Habsburg dominance supposedly did not.[123] In Britain, Victorian liberals regarded the congruence of nation and states with some suspicion as attempts to bring such congruence about were perceived as threats both to integrity of the empire and to minority rights on the European continent.[124] Perhaps its most famous critic was Lord Acton, who traced the lineage of the national idea back to the French Revolution and the restoration. To Acton, the quest for national unity ran counter to both dynastic tradition and natural liberty. The creation of national states "overrules the rights and wishes of the inhabitants, absorbing their divergent interests in a fictitious unity; sacrifices their several inclinations and duties to the higher claim of nationality, and crushes all natural rights and all established liberties for the purpose of vindicating itself."[125] Hence "its course will be marked with material as well as moral ruin."[126] As we will note in the next chapter, this kind of criticism would reappear with a conservative twist in mid-twentieth century debates about decolonization and nationhood in Africa and Asia.

The republican and cosmopolitan tenets salient in the works of Mazzini and Michelet were virtually absent from contemporary

122 For an overview of recent research, see Axel Körner, "Beyond Nation States: New Perspectives on the Habsburg Empire." *European History Quarterly* 48 no. 3 (2018): 516–533.

123 See Maurizio Isabella, "The Political Thought of a New Constitutional Monarchy: Piedmont after 1848." in Douglas Moggach and Gareth Stedman Jones (eds.) *The 1848 Revolutions and European Political Thought* (Cambridge: Cambridge University Press, 2018), 383–404.

124 See Georgios Varouxakis, "1848 and British Political Thought on The Principle of Nationality." in Douglas Moggach and Gareth Stedman Jones (eds.) *The 1848 Revolutions and European Political Thought* (Cambridge: Cambridge University Press, 2018), 140–161.

125 Lord Acton, "Nationality." [1862] in *The History of Freedom and Other Essays*, edited with an introduction by John Neville Figgis. (London: MacMillan, 1907), 270–300, at 288.

126 Ibid., 299.

attempts to align nation and state in German political thought. In the German context, the desired congruence of nation and state found support in new modes of historical writing that depicted this congruence as an inevitable consequence of revolutionary and violent geopolitical competition among European powers.[127] For example, to Leopold von Ranke, the greatest achievement of the French Revolution had been "the fact that nationalities were rejuvenated, revived, and developed anew. They became part of the state, for it was realized that without them the state could not exist."[128] To him, there could be no history apart from the history of nation-states and their violent intercourse. Another more ominous example of this view can be found in the works of Heinrich von Treitschke, whose combustible cocktail of essentialist nationalism and state fetishism made him notorious in Britain as one of the founders of *Realpolitik* and the architect behind aggressive German foreign policy.[129] As he argued in a series of lectures delivered in Berlin from 1874 onwards, the rise of nationality was rooted in a revulsion against the imperial ambitions of Napoleon, which had been an "unhappy attempt to transform the multiplicity of European life into the arid uniformity of universal sovereignty has produced the exclusive sway of nationality as the dominant political idea."[130] But now Italy and Germany offered edifying examples of peoples attaining national unity and statehood out of the ashes of that failed empire. Treitschke identified two forces working in history to bring about the congruence of nation and state. First there was "the tendency of every State to

[127] See Reinhart Koselleck, "Historical Criteria of the Modern Concept of Revolution." in Reinhart Koselleck, *Futures Past: On the Semantics of Historical Time.* (Cambridge, MA.: MIT Press, 1985), 39–54; Georg G. Iggers, *The German Conception of History: The National Tradition of Historical Thought from Herder to the Present* (Middletown: Wesleyan University Press, 1968).

[128] Leopold von Ranke, "*The Great Powers.*" in Theodore H. von Laue (ed.) *Leopold Ranke: The Formative Years* (Princeton: Princeton University Press, 1950), 181–218, at 181 & 215.

[129] See, for example, John Bew, *Realpolitik: A History* (Oxford: Oxford University Press, 2016), 69–76; Hans Kohn, "Treitschke: National Prophet." *The Review of Politics* 7, no. 4 (1945): 418–440; Karl H. Metz, "The Politics of Conflict: Heinrich von Treitschke and the Idea of 'Realpolitik'." *History of Political Thought* 3 no. 2 (1982): 269–284.

[130] Heinrich von Treitschke, *Politics*, Vol. 1. trans. by Blanche Dugdale and Torben de Bille (New York: Macmillan, 1916), 21.

amalgamate its population in speech and manners into one single mould, and secondly, the impulse of every vigorous nationality to construct a State of its own."[131] This tendency in favor of congruence was not accidental but almost providential, since "that Nation and State should merge into one is the tendency of all great nations." But whereas this tendency towards congruence was characteristic of the history of European nations, it was virtually absent from other continents. This being so since the "superiority of Western culture arises from the fact that Western Europe has larger compact ethnological masses, while the East is the classic soil for the fragments of nations."[132] To Treitschke and Hegel, because of the impossibility of any real and spontaneous congruence of nation and state, all empires of the East were condemned to lasting despotism unless subjected to the liberating force of European civilization.

Hence, in those cases in which different nations were united within the same state, "the one which wields the authority should also be the superior in civilization ... [and the] ... form of Government by which the coexistence of several nations within one State can be made bearable is a wise Despotism, which keeps them all in a lethargy."[133] European expansion on foreign shores and imperial domination had therefore been conducive to the formation of a system of states in Europe, since "the feeling of fellowship was quickened among the European States when the Caucasian race began to form a great aristocracy for the subjugation of the savage peoples."[134] Since the successful establishment of settler colonies on other continents had been decisive in the struggle for power among European states, "every colonizing effort which retains its single nationality has become a factor of immense importance for the future of the world. Upon it depends the share which each people will take in the domination of the earth by the white races."[135] To Treitschke, it was unthinkable that non-European peoples should be ever able to govern themselves or achieve national self-determination: "The civilizing of a barbarian people is the best achievement. The alternatives before it are extirpation or absorption

131 Treitschke, *Politics*, Vol. 1, 272. 132 Ibid., 273.
133 Ibid., 282–283 & 292.
134 Heinrich von Treitschke, *Politics*, Vol. 2. trans. by Blanche Dugdale and Torben de Bille (New York: Macmillan, 1916), 569.
135 Treitschke, *Politics*, Vol. 1, 119.

into the conquering race."[136] To Treitschke, it is not only the case that non-European peoples lack nation-states simply because they are racially inferior and uncivilized. Rather their racial inferiority allows them to be absorbed or extirpated for European powers to fulfill *their* historical destiny by consolidating themselves into nation-states and dominate the rest of the world. To Germany this was a matter of great importance, since until recently it "had too small a share of the spoils in the partition of non-European territories among the Powers of Europe, and yet our existence as a State of the first rank is vitally affected by the question whether we can become a power beyond the seas."[137]

When his disciple and successor Friedrich Meinecke later recounted the ideological sources of German unification in his *Welburgertum und Nationalstaat* (1907), this process was portrayed as a transition from the cosmopolitan delusions of the Enlightenment through an awakening of the German national spirit to the unification of the *Reich* under Bismarck. Doing this, Meinecke describes how nations and states come to converge through the interplay of historical forces and human action. Although there is a difference between cultural nations which are "primarily based on some jointly experienced cultural heritage" and political nations that "are primarily based on the unifying force of a common political history and constitution," it was the historical destine of the former to find its institutional expression in the latter.[138] As Meinecke further argued, "[f]or as far as political nations are concerned, they arise not only through a demand for self-determination but also through the quit workings of the state and through a shared political life within the same political system."[139]

[136] Ibid., 121. On Treitschke's role in the institutionalization of racism, see Andrew Zimmerman, "Race and World Politics: Germany in the Age of Imperialism, 1878–1914." *The Oxford Handbook of Modern German History* (Oxford: Oxford University Press, 2011), 359–376.

[137] Ibid., 33.

[138] Friedrich Meinecke, *Cosmopolitanism and the National State*. trans. by Robert B. Kimber (Princeton: Princeton University Press, 1970), 10. For an analysis and a background, see Troy RE. Paddock, "Rethinking Friedrich Meinecke's Historicism." *Rethinking History* 10, no. 1 (2006): 95–108; Duncan Kelly, "'The Goal of that Pure and Noble Yearning.' Friedrich Meinecke's Visions of 1848", in Douglas Moggach and Gareth Stedman Jones (eds.), *The 1848 Revolutions and European Political Thought* (Cambridge: Cambridge University Press, 2018), 293–321.

[139] Ibid., 13.

Whenever a strong sense of political community exists in such a state, "the population of a state has become a political nation and the state a national state."[140]

Meinecke then traced the trajectory of the German cultural nation from the Seven Years War to its final unification, emphasizing the extent to which the spread of the idea of the national state provided this process with historical momentum. In ideational terms this implied that there was an unbroken continuity from Hegel's first conceptualization of the nation-state to its final realization by Bismarck. According to Meinecke, Hegel had considered "state and nation so closely related to each other that the essential purpose in the existence of a nation is to be a state, and a nation that has not achieved the form of a state has no real history."[141] But it fell upon Ranke to substantiate this abstract ideal and turn into a principle of historical writing, thereby essentializing the notion of nationhood and nationality, since "a nation is not based on self-determination but on pre-determination."[142] Such pre-determination implied that Ranke conceived nations as individual subjects endowed with a capacity to act at their own behest, but only until we reach a penultimate point when "[w]e no longer feel the strength of the nation forming the state but rather the strength of the state forming the nation."[143] What had prompted the rise of the national state and the spread of claims to self-determination all over Europe was "the conquering French national state, which, nourished on universal, cosmopolitan ideas, tried to bring states and nations under its universal domination."[144] Although Romanticism had "summoned up the spirits of the past against the despised rational and cosmopolitan spirit", the real opposition to the Napoleonic empire sprung from nativistic foundations, arising from the "fanaticism of half-civilized nations…a fanaticism that rejected the modern cultural elements of this world empire."[145] Hence, in the final analysis, "the goal to which everything is directed is an all-inclusive community of the German national state, a community so strong that it is able to tolerate, utilize, and overcome all the separate nationalities of its individual members."[146] But even if the realization of that congruence of nation and state represented the highest form of political association, this did not preclude that

[140] Ibid., 13. [141] Ibid., 198. [142] Ibid., 205. [143] Ibid., 211.
[144] Ibid., 214. [145] Ibid., 229. [146] Ibid., 374.

nation-states like Germany entered the arena of world politics with the intent of forming empires of their own.[147]

Despite their obvious ideological differences and the different national contexts in which they were active, the ways in which the authors discussed in this section conceptualized the nation-state into existence were remarkably similar. In some contexts, the promise of a congruence between nation and state was seen as an antidote to imperial domination and a necessary step towards popular sovereignty and national unification. In other contexts, the ideal of congruence was seen as a source of national power and glory and a justification for the domination of other peoples. In still other contexts, the imagined congruence of state and nation furnished a fresh idiom in which the dusty republican and cosmopolitan ideals of the previous century could be revitalized and legitimized. Hence notion of the nation-state was extremely versatile insofar as it could contain and to some extent reconcile a wide array of ideological positions, thereby amplifying positions that would perhaps otherwise not have gained traction as easily among European elites of the day. Consequently, the nation-state came abundant with recipes for its own radicalization.

The many ways in which nation and state were glued together also display some interesting similarities. To the authors discussed above, the congruence of nation and state was literally a matter of time. Consonant with the historicist sentiments of the age, there was a wide agreement that such congruence had a temporal dimension and was the outcome of historical processes. What was disputed was the extent to which these processes were self-propelled or whether they needed to be pushed forward by means of reforms or revolutions, yet everyone seemed to agree that the nation-state was the both the vehicle of historical progress as well as its ultimate outcome. To some authors – notably Hegel, Mill, and Mazzini – this progress was closely connected to notions of civilizational advancement, whereas to others – notably Ranke and Treitschke – the nation-state represented a historical culmination of great power politics as well as the prime instrument for its continuation into the future. This made it possible for these

[147] See, for example, Winfried Baumgart, "German Imperialism in Historical Perspective." in Arthur J. Knoll and Lewis H. Gann, *Germans in the Tropics: Essays in German Colonial History* (New York: Greenwood, 1987), 151–164.

authors to reconceptualize the divide between the West and the rest in historicist terms. Rather than being an immutable spatial divide, the separation between a world composed of homogenous, territorially demarcated, and civilized nation-states from a world consisting of heterogenous, territorially unbounded, and uncivilized polities was now thought to be malleable according to the logic of historical progress and the spread of civilization enabled by that logic. To authors of a more republican and internationalist inclination, this implied that non-European peoples could possibly come to fulfill the requirements of self-determination at some point in the future provided the right kind of paternalistic guidance by their European masters. But to more die-hard nationalist authors the emphasis on the congruence of nation and state provided but another justification of imperial expansion during the late nineteenth century scramble for colonies in Africa and elsewhere. Since non-European polities could not hope to attain the political maturity required for self-government on their own, they had to remain under imperial rule if not permanently so at least for a foreseeable future. But although imperial rule frequently was justified with reference to the backwardness of non-European peoples as indicated by their lack of nation-states, such justifications reinforced the idea that the nation-state represented the most advanced form of political association and hence something worthy of aspiration among those who had yet to attain the coveted congruence of nation and state. As Matthew Craven has noted, the delimitation of a sphere of European nation-states, and the application of prescriptive criteria of statehood to polities outside that sphere have been a core problem of international law since then.[148]

Globalizing Nationality

One of the first references to *national* self-determination was made by Lenin in 1914 with the objective of uniting workers of different nationalities in Russia against the Tsarist suppression of minorities. He then maintained that "by examining the historical and economic conditions of the national movement, we shall inevitably reach the conclusion that self-determination of nations means the political separation of the nations from alien national bodies, the formation of an

[148] Craven, "Statehood, Self-Determination, and Recognition," 247.

independent national state."[149] As we shall see in the next chapter, this notion was to become an important weapon in the socialist struggle against the imperialist world order. Self-determination – along with the ideal of non-domination it entailed – was to become the linchpin of decolonization in Asia and Africa during the second half of the twentieth century. In this section, I shall describe how the notion of self-determination was appropriated by Woodrow Wilson and disseminated to the colonial world where it was used to galvanize anti-colonial nationalist rhetoric. Doing this, I will emphasize the modular aspect of modern nationalism and the ensuing ability of the nation-state form to travel to forever new contexts.[150]

The First World War was not only a contest between empires but also produced a worldwide crisis of empire. The war had mobilized millions of imperial subjects on all sides, some of them in the hope that their participation in the war would issue in greater autonomy. Failure to deliver on these hopes severely undermined the legitimacy of empires even on the winning side.[151] In Europe, the principle of self-determination seemed to triumph after the war, when Poland was resurrected as an independent state while Czechoslovakia and the embryo of what was to become Yugoslavia were carved out of the remains of the Austro-Hungarian empire, while Alsace-Lorraine was returned to the French. As Sarah Wambaugh enthusiastically noted, "[t]he war has rescued the principle of self-determination from its academic retirement…One hears no longer that it is a doctrine which does not concern international law; for it grows obvious to the world that everything which concerns sovereignty concerns international law."[152]

149 Vladimir Ilyich Lenin, *The Right of Nations to Self-Determination* (Moscow: Foreign Languages Publishing House, 1947), 10. For analyses, see Fisch, *Right of Self-Determination of Peoples*, 116–122; Weitz, "Self-Determination," 485–489.

150 See Manu Goswami, "Rethinking the Modular Nation Form: Toward a Sociohistorical Conception of Nationalism." *Comparative Studies in Society and History* 44 no. 4 (2002): 770–799.

151 See Robert Gerwarth and Erez Manela, "The Great War as a Global War: Imperial Conflict and the Reconfiguration of World Order, 1911–1923." *Diplomatic History* 38 no. 4 (2014): 786–800.

152 Sarah Wambaugh, *The Doctrine of National Self-determination: A Study of the Theory and Practice of Plebiscites with a Collection of Official Documents*, Vol. 1 (New York: Oxford University Press, 1919), lii.

Yet the implementation of the principle of self-determination gave rise to numerous disputes over territory and identity on the fringes of Europe, some of them resulting in protracted ethnic wars.[153] Not all national groups were allowed self-determination but were instead subject to minority protections to avoid legitimizing secession and further fragmentation. This had far-ranging implications in those cases in which state and nation were not congruent and served to reinforce the norm that they ideally ought to be congruent, thereby naturalizing the nation-state as the basic building block of the international realm. As Eric Weitz has argued, "[t]he result was the creation of an international system that prized the homogeneity of populations under the state...rather than the acceptance of multi-ethnicity as the preeminent form of society under dynastic rule."[154] But what had originally been a principle tailored to fit a uniquely European experience was soon appropriated by leaders of colonial polities who now argued that since their populations constituted nations in this sense they were entitled to self-determination under the new principles of international law that were being proposed at the Paris Conference.[155] In this section, I shall describe these claims and their reception by Western leaders in the aftermath of the First World War, arguing that whereas this episode did little to change the relations between imperial powers and colonial peoples in the short term, it was nevertheless crucial as the dissemination of the idea of self-determination made becoming international hard to refuse for any group of people wanting to resist imperial domination in the decades to come.

The swift global spread of the idea of self-determination testified to the success of Woodrow Wilson's wartime rhetoric. In a series of speeches delivered to Congress towards the end of the Great War, he had famously proclaimed the contours of a new international order based on the equality of nations and the consent of the governed. By equating the consent of the governed with the Leninist notion of

153 See Volker Prott, *Politics of Self-Determination*, 113–211.

154 Eric D. Weitz, "From the Vienna to the Paris System: International Politics and the Entangled Histories of Human Rights, Forced Deportations, and Civilizing Missions." *The American Historical Review* 113 no. 5 (2008): 1313–1343, at 1315.

155 See Arnulf Becker Lorca, *Mestizo International Law. A Global Intellectual History 1842–1933* (Cambridge: Cambridge University Press, 2014), 225–262.

self-determination, Wilson skilfully appropriated the latter for his own liberal internationalist purposes and assumed that it already was a force to be reckoned with in international affairs.[156] His Fourteen Points thus included a call for an "impartial adjustment of all colonial claims, based upon a strict observance of the principle that in determining all such questions of sovereignty the interests of the populations concerned must have equal weight with the equitable claims of the government whose title is to be determined."[157] But although Wilson did not exclude non-European peoples from the right of self-government and was generally averse to European imperialism, he was not prepared to abolish the imperial system altogether but insisted that non-European peoples would attain self-government through gradual reform under the auspices of the League of Nations rather than through a worldwide revolution as proposed by Lenin.[158] Some of this was much in line with how the principle of nationality had been interpreted earlier, yet there were some differences between these explicitly racialized interpretations and those inherent in the newly fashioned idea of self-determination. As Trygve Throntveit has pointed out, "Wilson was less troubled by the postponement of freedom for many oppressed populations than our postcolonial sensibilities can easily stomach, but not because he considered oppression their racial destiny."[159] However, the fact that Wilson was opposed to European imperialism did not imply that he was against empire *per se*. As Robert Gerwarth and Erez Manela have argued, he and his successors "imagined a global imperium of nation-states, interlocked within a system of international organization and governed by the principles of free

[156] See Erez Manela, "Imagining Woodrow Wilson in Asia: Dreams of East-West Harmony and the Revolt against Empire in 1919." *American Historical Review* 111 no. 5 (2006): 1327–1351.

[157] Speech delivered to Congress January 8, 1918, reprinted in *The Bases of Durable Peace as voiced by President Wilson* (Chicago: The Union League Club of Chicago, 1918), V, 15.

[158] See, for example, Erez Manela, *The Wilsonian Moment. Self-Determination and the International Origins of Anticolonial Nationalism* (Oxford: Oxford University Press, 2007), 19–55; Derek Heater, *National Self-Determination: Woodrow Wilson and His legacy* (London: Macmillan, 1994); Allen Lynch, "Woodrow Wilson and the Principle of 'National Self-Determination': A reconsideration." *Review of International Studies* 28 no. 2 (2002): 419–436.

[159] Trygve Throntveit, "The Fable of the Fourteen Points: Woodrow Wilson and National Self-determination." *Diplomatic History* 35 no. 3 (2011): 445–481, at 470.

trade."[160] Not very different from what the British had tried to create in Latin America a century earlier, this new empire of states had some resemblance to prior efforts to globalize the Monroe Doctrine.[161]

It was against this backdrop that Wilson fought to establish the mandates system at the Paris conference. Yet the claims to self-determination raised by colonial polities were different from those raised during the Latin American and Greek struggles for independence a century earlier. While the latter had been based on often vague claims to territorial possession and had been recognized by other states to the extent that these claims were deemed successful, the recognition of self-determination presupposed that such claims could be legitimized with reference to the will of a given people to govern itself within territorial boundaries that had to be determined simultaneously.[162] In this way, the principle of self-determination became the foundation of both domestic as well as international legitimacy, so that sovereignty could only be justified with reference to the will of a distinct people or nation, and pleas for international recognition had to be made at the behalf of a distinct people or nation in order to be met with success. This meant that any colonial polity aspiring to self-determination had to make credible claims that it constituted a nation in at least some of the senses of this term discussed in the previous section, something which compelled their leaders to craft and promote their own local brands of nationalism and to make their often-diverse polities look like nations in the eyes of Western lawyers and politicians. As anti-imperialist sentiments took on a truly transnational character after the Great War, anticolonial nationalism spread rapidly and soon culminated in pleas for self-determination in Asia and elsewhere.[163]

But since those colonial polities which raised claims to self-determination still had to confront the obstacles posed by the standard

[160] Gewarth and Manela, "The Great War as a Global War," 798.

[161] Juan Pablo Scarfi, "In the Name of the Americas: The Pan-American Redefinition of the Monroe Doctrine and the Emerging Language of American International Law in the Western Hemisphere, 1898–1933." *Diplomatic History* 40 no. 2 (2016): 189–218.

[162] Fisch, *Right of Self-Determination of Peoples*, 126–159.

[163] See, for example, Manela, "Imagining Woodrow Wilson in Asia"; Manela, *The Wilsonian Moment*, 55–75; Erez Manela, "Asia in the Global 1919: Reimagining Territory, Identity, and Solidarity." *The Journal of Asian Studies* 78 no. 2 (2019): 409–416.

of civilization, their quest for self-determination was much of an away-game.[164] Especially so since the requirements of international legal recognition had been articulated on basis of ethnology, or the "science of races" as its foremost proponent James Lorimer had named it. Having defined the law of nations as the "realization of the freedom of separate nations by the reciprocal assertion and recognition of their real powers," Lorimer had elaborated the grounds for recognition and membership in international society.[165] Drawing on findings from the "science of races," he raised the question whether "in the presence of ethnical differences which for jural purposes we must regard as indelible, we are entitled to confine recognition to those branches of alien races which consent to separate themselves from the rest, and ... to accept our political conceptions."[166] To answer this question, Lorimer had divided humanity into three distinct spheres – the civilized, the barbarous, and the savage – to which corresponded three distinct levels of recognition. Full recognition extended to all European states and their colonies insofar they were populated with people of European birth or descent; partial recognition extended to Turkey and those Asian states that retained their independence; while the "sphere of natural, or mere human recognition extends to the residue of mankind; though we ought, perhaps, to distinguish between the progressive and the non-progressive races." Thus, the international lawyer is "not bound to apply the positive law of nations to savages, or even to barbarians ... but he is bound to ascertain the points at which ... barbarians and savages come within the scope of partial recognition."[167] With the principle of nationality never being formally integrated into international law, such gradations of civilization were still common

[164] Brett Bowden, "The Colonial Origins of International Law. European expansion and the Classical Standard of Civilization." *Journal of the History of International Law* 7, no.1, (2005): 1–23; Gerrit W. Gong, *The Standard of Civilization in International Society* (Oxford: Oxford University Press, 1984); Koskenniemi, *Gentle Civilizer of Nations*, 98–178.

[165] James Lorimer, *The Institutes of the Law of Nations. A Treatise of the Jural Relations of Separate Political Communities* (Edinburgh: William Blackwell and Sons, 1883), 3. For analyses, see Martti Koskenniemi, "Race, Hierarchy and International Law: Lorimer"s legal science." *European Journal of International Law* 27 no. 2 (2016): 415–429; Martin Clark, "A Conceptual History of Recognition in British International Legal Thought." *British Yearbook of International* Law 87 no. 1 (2017): 18–97, esp. 49–55.

[166] Lorimer, *Institutes*, 98. [167] Ibid., 102.

stock among many international lawyers. But after the end of the First World War, these gradations became increasingly contested as leaders of colonial polities started to develop and defend their own notions of civilization, and semi-peripheral countries like Persia, China, and Turkey began to protest and re-negotiate their unequal treaties with European powers.[168]

As Arnulf Becker Lorca has shown, already before the Paris Conference started, African and Asian leaders had petitioned Woodrow Wilson, and president of the conference French premier George Clemenceau for self-determination on the grounds that their polities indeed did meet the requirements of nationhood and the standards of civilization, however homegrown the latter sometimes turned out to be. For example, W. E. B. Du Bois – a former student of Treitschke's and now leader of the Pan-African movement – argued that peoples of African descent should be granted self-determination whenever their level of civilization so permitted. In letters sent to both Wilson and Clemenceau, Du Bois urged that European powers should cede their African possessions and allow for "the establishing of a great Independent State in Africa, to be settled and governed by Negroes."[169] In India anticolonial nationalism had a longer pedigree, stretching back to the nineteenth century.[170] As Karuna Mantena has argued "[w]hat began as an internal critique of British rule on grounds of exclusion and inequality developed into more critical considerations about pathologies resulting from the very fact of empire."[171] Thus, in a popular pamphlet first published in 1909, Mohandas Gandhi advocated full Indian independence but rejected Western civilization

[168] See Liliana Obregón, "The Civilized and the Uncivilized." in *The Oxford Handbook of the History of Public International Law*, ed. by Anne Peters and Bardo Fassbender (Oxford: Oxford University Press, 2012), 917–939; Becker Lorca, *Mestizo International Law*, 244–251; Ian Clark, *International Legitimacy and World Society* (Oxford: Oxford University Press, 2007), 83–130.

[169] W. E. B. Du Bois, "Letter from W. E. B. Du Bois to Premier of France (1918)." quoted in Becker Lorca, *Mestizo International Law*, 243.

[170] See, for example, Christopher A. Bayly, *Recovering Liberties: Indian Thought in the Age of Liberalism and Empire* (Cambridge: Cambridge University Press, 2011); Nazmul S. Sultan, "Self-Rule and the Problem of Peoplehood in Colonial India." *American Political Science Review* 114 no. 1 (2020): 81–94.

[171] Karuna Mantena, "Popular Sovereignty and Anticolonialism." in Richard Bourke and Quentin Skinner (eds.), *Popular Sovereignty in Historical Perspective* (Cambridge: Cambridge University Press, 2016), 297–319, at 309.

and its concept of statehood on the grounds that they would but perpetuate patterns of imperial domination.[172] To avert these dangers, Gandhi envisaged a decentralized peasant democracy firmly anchored in those village communities that had long been a paramount Hindu political institution.[173] As Shruti Kapila has shown in detail, much Indian political thought during the early struggles for independence was characterized by this rejection of the state. As she has argued, "[a] violent fraternity was thus born at the limits and ends of colonial covenants, that circumvented, if it did not destroy, liberal ideas of contract, positing instead the ambivalence of intimacy and hostility centered on the anti-statist political subject."[174] Yet others were less suspicious of Western notions of nation and state. Influenced by the republican nationalism of Mazzini, Lajpat Rai – another founding father of the Indian independence movement – welcomed the formation of the League of Nations "for maintaining the peace of the world, and fostering the development of different nationalities on the principle of Self-Determination."[175] Rai demanded "an absolutely unmolested opportunity of autonomous development for India similar to that accorded to the various nationalities within the Austro-Hungarian and Ottoman Empires."[176] He then went on to argue that the different peoples of India constituted a single nation in its own right, because "[e]thnologically they are descended from the same race", and sharing "the same blood, the same language, the same

[172] Mohandas K. Gandhi, *Hind Swaraj or Indian Home Rule* (Ahmedabad: Navajivan Press, 1938), 20–41.

[173] See Mantena, "Popular Sovereignty and Anticolonialism"; Karuna Mantena, "On Gandhi's Critique of the State: Sources, Contexts, Conjunctures." *Modern Intellectual History* 9 no. 3 (2012): 535–563.

[174] Shruti Kapila, *Violent Fraternity. Indian Political Thought in the Global Age* (Princeton: Princeton University Press, 2021), 9.

[175] Lala Lajpat Rai, *Self-Determination for India* (New York: India Home Rule League of America, 1919), 5. For analyses of Mazzini's influence on Rai and the independence movement in general, see Fabrizio de Donno, "The Gandhian Mazzini: Democratic Nationalism, Self-Rule, and Non-Violence." in Christopher A. Bayly and Eugenio F. Biagini, *Giuseppe Mazzini and the Globalization of Democratic Nationalism 1830–1920*. (Oxford: Oxford University Press, 2008), 374–398; Claude Markovitz, "Cosmopolitanism and Imperialism in Nineteenth-Century British India." *Humanity: An International Journal of Human Rights, Humanitarianism, and Development* 12, no. 1 (2021): 47–58.

[176] Rai, *Self-Determination for India*, 6.

civilization, literature, customs, and traditions."[177] Rai backed this view with ample quotes from British scholars who had recently argued that India constituted a distinct and continuous civilization thanks to its common Sanskrit and Hindu heritage. Echoing Mill, Rai could thus maintain with some confidence that "a nationality is constituted when the people are animated by sympathies which make them co-operate with one another more willingly than with other people and desire to be under the same government."[178] And in what seemed to be a proactive blow to less erudite detractors, he added that "according to Sir Henry Maine, the idea of Nationality was first derived from India, and it travelled westwards."[179] But the kind self-determination desired by Rai and his fellow travelers was still limited in scope, since "[u]pon the principles we have discussed we claim that the British Parliament should enact a complete Constitution for India conceding autonomy within the British Commonwealth."[180] And in a concluding tribute to Spencer, Rai maintained that "[s]uch a system embodies a higher and a nobler ideal ... the ideal of a world-wide Empire of amity not an Empire of enmity."[181]

These early shots at self-determination indicated the extent to which the concepts of nationhood and civilization could be stretched beyond their established connotations and turned against colonial masters. As one Korean nationalist argued, "[t]he Korean people forms today a homogeneous nation, having their own civilization and culture, and having constituted one of the historical states in the Far East for more than four thousand and two hundred years."[182] To this was added a memorandum in which it was further asserted that "it is as much to Korea as to China – the other historic state now under deadly assault by Japan – that the Japanese owe not a little of their cultural development and the thoughts and ideals which have nourished their mind and enabled them to capture greatness."[183] Although the Egyptian delegation was not allowed to travel to Paris to participate in negotiations, its leader Saad Zaghloul first bombarded Wilson and Clemenceau with pleas for self-determination and then co-authored a memorandum on Egyptian national claims to be presented at the

[177] Ibid., 8. [178] Ibid., 10. [179] Ibid., 10. [180] Ibid., 12. [181] Ibid., 13.
[182] Quoted in Lorca, *Mestizo International Law*, 239.
[183] *The Claim of the Korean People and Nation for Liberation from Japan and for the Reconstitution of Korea as an Independent State*. Memorandum, Paris, April 1919.

conference in his absence. In an appeal to the foreigners residing in Egypt, Zaghloul declared that "[w]e desire complete independence, exclusive of all foreign domination, in order that, under a constitutional regime, we may correct the wrongs that the government of a foreign Power has caused to our society, whether deliberately, whether by the nature even of the interference."[184] In a dispatch to the British prime minister Lloyd George, Zaghloul emphasized that "[w]hatever may be its present weakness, a nation with a civilisation so ancient will always preserve, before the world, its prestige and its title to the gratitude of the world."[185] And as he begged Clemenceau, "[m]ust the Conference not listen to the Egyptian people whose civilization is very ancient and who would have been independent for almost a century had not the European Concert forced them to remain under Ottoman suzerainty?"[186] In the bold memorandum submitted to the participants at the Paris conference, Zaghloul went on to question the very coherence of the standard of civilization by arguing that the international legal order now taking shape "cannot continue to distinguish between nations, some to be made free and others to be doomed to slavery, only because the Western mind has been pleased for long centuries to trace limits, both ethnic and geographic."[187] But in a more modestly phrased appeal to the diplomatic corps in Cairo, his claim to self-determination was circumscribed by the recognition that "Egypt would consider herself highly honored to place her independence under the guarantee of the Society of Nations, and to contribute thus, in the measure of her means, to the realization of the new ideas of Justice and of Right."[188] Thus, Indian and Egyptian leaders did not only claim to speak on behalf of their respective peoples, but claimed that their respective peoples constituted nations in the by now accepted sense of this term. To this they added that their nations not only constituted civilizations in a generic sense of this term, but also possessed characteristics of civilization in a sense fully on a par with or even superior to that of their colonial masters.

[184] Egyptian Delegation, *Collection of Official Correspondence from November 11, 1918 to July 14, 1919*, (Paris, 1919), 14.
[185] Ibid., 26. [186] Ibid., 71–72.
[187] Egyptian Delegation, *The Egyptian National Claims. A Memorandum Presented to the Peace Conference by the Egyptian Delegation Charged with the Defence of Egyptian Independence* (Paris, 1919), 4.
[188] Egyptian Delegation, *Collection of Official Correspondence*, 11.

A blunter way to debunk the standard of civilization was by claiming that the Europeans were themselves uncivilized. What had transpired during the war gave ample evidence of uncivilized behavior on their part, evidence which was easily turned into arguments as to why their rule not only was illegitimate, but also essentially morally corrosive to emergent nations outside Europe. In another letter to Clemenceau, Zaghloul expressed his desire to submit evidence of atrocities committed by British troops in Egypt, so that "The Conference will ... be in a position to judge whether, after such treatment, the Egyptians should be expected to live under the British Protectorate."[189] He then expected the British to "rise in indignation and condemn atrocities committed in its name against a people with a glorious past, a people whose country is not a *res nullius*, open to exploration and of which the first occupant has the free disposition."[190] Exposing such uncivilized behavior was not only a way of discrediting European claims to superiority in general, but also a way of justifying claims to self-determination by undermining the legitimacy not only of direct colonial rule but also that of mandates and protectorates.[191]

These contestations of civilization soon spilled over into a wholesale assault on another popular imperial ideology of this time, which was based on the idea that Europeans had a mission to civilize non-European peoples by virtue of their superior scientific knowledge, technology, and moral dispositions. The Great War provided strong reasons to doubt such claims. As Michael Adas has argued, "years of carnage in the very heartlands of European civilization demonstrated that the Europeans were at least as susceptible to instinctual, irrational responses and primeval drives as the people they colonized."[192] Among those leading this assault on the civilizing mission of the West was no one less than the 1913 Nobel Laureate Rabindranath Tagore, who warned against the materialist excesses and mechanistic modes of government by means of which Westerners had constituted themselves into one single nation, in "that aspect which a whole

[189] Egyptian Delegation, *Collection of Official Correspondence*, 82. Also Manela, *Wilsonian Moment*, 63–76.

[190] Ibid., 85–86. [191] Becker Lorca, *Mestizo International Law*, 251–258.

[192] Michael Adas, "Contested Hegemony: The Great War and the Afro-Asian Assault on the Civilizing Mission Ideology." *Journal of World History* 15 no. 1 (2004): 31–63, at 41.

population assumes when organized for a mechanical purpose."[193] This had allowed the West to expand into those parts of the world that knew nothing of such nations at the expense of their primeval and more spiritual ways of life, so that "[w]hen this organization of politics and commerce, whose other name is the Nation, becomes all powerful at the cost of the harmony of the higher social life, then it is an evil day for humanity."[194] To Tagore, nations and national belonging was not a universal characteristic of humankind but a peculiar feature of Western civilization closely associated with its spirit of conflict and conquest, "[b]ecause this civilization is the civilization of power, therefore it is exclusive, it is naturally unwilling to open its sources of power to those whom it has selected for its purposes of exploitation."[195] Having entered places altogether innocent of such corrupt conceptions such as India, "the Nation of the West forges its iron chains of organization which are the most relentless and unbreakable that have ever been manufactured in the whole history of man."[196] The remedy was not therefore to emulate Western civilization but to blend its few fruits with the spiritual traditions of the East.[197]

But these petitions and protestations were in vain, at least in the short run. None of the leaders discussed above was received at the Paris Conference and most of their claims were left unrecognized by European powers, which instead agreed on establishing the mandates system into which former German possessions in Africa and leftovers from the Ottoman empire would be integrated. As has been pointed out by Jeanne Morefield and Jacob Kripp, the mandates system was based on a profoundly racialized conception of international order. To its architect Jan Smuts, placing the lesser races under European tutelage was necessary to avert the dangers that race war and miscegenation posed to white supremacy and global order.[198] Still the Wilsonian emphasis on the consent of the governed as the basis of domestic and

[193] Rabindranath Tagore, *Nationalism* (London: Macmillan, 1917), 19. For an analysis of his work and its impact, see Michael Collins, *Empire, Nationalism, and the Postcolonial World: Rabindranath Tagore's writings on history, politics and society* (Abingdon: Routledge, 2013).

[194] Ibid., 23. [195] Ibid. [196] Ibid., 37. [197] Ibid., 52–53.

[198] Jeanne Morefield, *Empires without Imperialism: Anglo-American Decline and the Politics of Deflection* (Oxford: Oxford University Press, 2014), 171–200; Jacob Kripp, "The Creative Advance Must Be Defended: Miscegenation, Metaphysics, and Race War in Jan Smuts's Vision of the League of Nations." *American Political Science Review* 116 no. 3 (2022): 940–953.

international legitimacy called for new ways of legitimizing imperial rule that at least purported to take the interests of colonial peoples into consideration if only to deprive anticolonial nationalism of some of its fertile soil. This prompted European powers to reconceptualize their justifications of empire and imperial rule and to recalibrate the methods of colonial governance accordingly.

For example, in Britain, where the League of Nations was mainly seen as a means to preserve and extend British influence in the world, some of the federalist schemes for a Greater Britain that had been articulated in the late nineteenth century now provided the conceptual resources for reconceptualizing the empire in terms of a commonwealth. The venerable imperial historian Reginald Coupland was most explicit in this regard. Lamenting the spread of nationalism and pleas for self-determination across the world, he went on to claim that "the ideal of national freedom must be harmonized with the ideal of international unity."[199] To Coupland, the best way of achieving such harmony was by using the British commonwealth as a template for the wider international system now taking shape. The commonwealth was uniquely suited in this regard because it is "nothing else than an attempt, on a wider scale than anything that has preceded it, to solve that insistent problem of nationality; an endeavour to keep a motley company of nations living contentedly together both in freedom and in unity; a unique experiment in international relations."[200] Similarly, it is perhaps no coincidence that the need to provide visions of empire with fresh ideological foundations coincided with the first attempts to institutionalize international relations as an academic discipline in Britain and the United States. These attempts had begun already before the war and were born out of the often explicitly racist study of the relations between the European powers and the rest of the world that had dominated academic departments during the late nineteenth century.[201]

199 Reginald Coupland, *The Study of the British Commonwealth. An Inaugural Lecture Delivered before the University of Oxford* (Oxford: Clarendon Press, 1921), 9.

200 Ibid., 10.

201 See the contributions to David Long and Brian C. Schmidt (eds.), *Imperialism and Internationalism in the Discipline of International Relations* (Albany, NY.: SUNY Press, 2005); Robert Vitalis, "The Noble American Science of Imperial Relations and its Laws of Race Development." *Comparative Studies*

One of its founding fathers was particularly invested in the process of imperial rejuvenation. Alfred Zimmern – who had contributed to the foundation of the League of Nations before becoming the first professor of international politics at Aberystwyth in 1919 – spent a collection of lectures titled *The Third British Empire* (1926) to reconceptualize the Empire as a commonwealth whose "foundations are securely laid on the rock of human nature ... which correspond to what men and nations really are, rather than to any artificial schemes in our own minds."[202] But to do so, Zimmern had to defuse the principle of nationality by disconnecting it both from contemporary conceptions of race as well as from the doctrine of self-determination. To Zimmern, race and nationality were different things which should not be conflated in theory and never coincided in practice outside the inflammatory rhetoric of nationalist leaders.[203] By the same token, nationality was not a license for self-determination, since there was no necessary connection between belonging to a nation and being subject to a government.[204] Thus the "theory of the nation-state is unsound ... because it is based on a confusion ... between government and nationality, between free institutions and national institutions."[205] By contrast, the viability and legitimacy of the British Commonwealth derived from the fact that it had been able to overcome this vicious confusion, so that "far from associating and confusing government

in Society and History 52 no. 4 (2010): 909–938; Robert Vitalis, *White World Order, Black Power Politics* (Ithaca: Cornell University Press, 2016); Peter Marcus Kristensen. "Subject Matters: Imperialism and the Constitution of International Relations." *Review of International Studies* (2022): 1–23.

202 Alfred Zimmern, *The Third British Empire*. (London: Humphrey Milford, 1926), 144. For analyses, see Mark Mazower, *No Enchanted Palace: The End of Empire and the Ideological Origins of the United Nations* (Princeton: Princeton University Press, 2009), 66–100; Jeanne Morefield, *Covenants Without Swords: Idealist liberalism and the Spirit of Empire* (Princeton: Princeton University Press, 2004), 175–204; John Donald Bruce Miller, "The Commonwealth and World Order: The Zimmern Vision and after." *Journal of Imperial and Commonwealth History* 8, no. 1 (1979): 159–174.

203 Alfred Zimmern, "Nationalism and Internationalism" [1918], in *Prospects of Democracy and other Essays* (London: Chatto & Windus, 1929), 76–94. See also Tomohito Baji, "Zionist Internationalism? Alfred Zimmern's Post-racial Commonwealth." *Modern Intellectual History* 13, no. 3 (2016): 623–651.

204 Alfred Zimmern, "Nationality and Government." [1918] in *Nationality and Government, and other Wartime Essays* (London Chatto & Windus, 1918), 32–60.

205 Zimmern, *The Third British Empire*, 130.

with nationality it has recognized that the whole art of government consists in bringing different kinds of people, different nations, different groups, different religions, different cultures, under a single law... under an international system ... of justice."[206] In short, to Zimmern, there was little to distinguish his vision of the Commonwealth both from earlier ways of understanding the British Empire *and* from the new international system that was emerging under the auspices of the League of Nations. Indeed, these entities seemed to appear on a continuum with little clear water between them.

The mandates system was an important part of that order insofar as it contributed to the continuation not only of racial hierarchies but to the perpetuation of empire. As Susan Pedersen has remarked, "whatever purposes the mandates system had been devised to serve, extending the right of self-determination was not one of them."[207] Although the mandates system was supposed to make imperial rule more benevolent, it never prepared subject populations for self-rule or endorsed any serious plans to create independent states out of mandated territories.[208] Cobbled together to defuse virulent claims for self-determination, the mandates system was a waiting room in which colonial peoples were condemned to languish while imperial powers reconciled their claims to sovereignty over the non-European world. But as Pedersen has emphasized, the main import of the mandates system was that it contributed to the internationalization of a range of political issues which previously had been exclusively within the purview of domestic or imperial politics by relocating them to what was an international realm in becoming. Thus "the League helped make the end of empire imaginable, and normative statehood possible, not because the empires willed it so...but because that dynamic of internationalization changed everything – including how 'dependent peoples' would bid for statehood [and] what 'statehood' would henceforth mean."[209]

In this chapter, I have contested the claim that a recognizably modern international realm only emerged in the aftermath of the First World War, and then as a consequence of the rapid rise and spread of

[206] Zimmern, *The Third British Empire*, 131.

[207] Susan Pedersen, *The Guardians. The League of Nations and the Crisis of Empire* (Oxford: Oxford University Press, 2015), 3.

[208] Ibid., 402. [209] Ibid., 406.

nationalism during the second half of the nineteenth century. A closer look at authors in different national contexts thought responsible for having articulated the principle of nationality and thereby effecting a transition from empire and nation-state by tilting standards of legitimacy in favor of the latter seems instead to indicate that most of them envisaged the nation-state as but a continuation of empire by other means. Hence what from a transitionist point of view has been made to look like a formative moment in the consolidation of a modern international system in Europe and the starting point of its spread to Asia and Africa looks more like a process through which imperial relations were reproduced on a global scale by turning the nation-state into *the* template of political order, compelling peripheral polities to reinvent themselves into such entities in the hope of obtaining legal recognition from their masters.

5 *The Empire of the International*

Introduction

In the previous chapter, we saw how the notion of nationality – the imagined congruence of state and nation – was invoked by European powers to justify the exclusion of non-European polities from the international system on the grounds that they failed to meet the requirements of self-government. Although Wilsonian promises of self-determination had opened the door to the inclusion of colonial peoples, claims to independence raised by non-European polities in the immediate aftermath of the First World War were largely unsuccessful. Many non-European polities were put in the waiting room of history or included on unequal terms which only further fueled anti-colonial sentiments and produced waves of political unrest that lasted through the interwar years. Still the spread of ideas of self-determination and nationalism and the creation of the mandates system reflected a broader trend towards the internationalization of the world.

In this chapter, I will discuss the process of decolonization after the end of the Second World War. According to what has become the established view of this process, successful claims to self-determination by Asian and African peoples replaced imperial hierarchies of unequal inclusion with a global and more inclusive international system based on the sovereign equality of its member states.[1] This narrative often locates the critical point of transition to the Bandung Conference in 1955, which has been described as a counterpoint to the Westphalian myth insofar as it provides the modern international system with an alternative point of origin. As some international lawyers recently have argued, the Bandung Conference "was when international law became truly 'universal.' It was the moment during which the majority of the people in the world either lived within a state ... or were fighting to

[1] For an excellent overview, see Jan C. Jansen & Jürgen Osterhammel, *Decolonization: A Short History* (Princeton: Princeton University Press, 2017).

form an independent state that was supported by international law. In this sense, it might make more sense to describe our contemporary international order as *Bandungian* rather than *Westphalian*."[2] To other scholars, the Bandung Conference was important insofar as it helped to push the postwar international order in a less Eurocentric direction. For example, as Amitav Acharya has argued, "[t]he Bandung conference's extension of universal sovereignty and its realisation of a substantial Afro-Asian consensus ... on issues such as decolonisation and human rights ... constitute a powerful act of agency by the non-Western countries."[3] Even those who believe that the Bandung Conference has been unduly mythologized have been willing to concede its importance "as a nexus where commitments to decolonization meet the challenges and practices of postcolonial politics" so that "the diverse and often contentious meanings of Bandung help us better understand the cardinal points of international relations in the twentieth century."[4] Indeed, "from Bandung to the structure of the United Nations, the fault lines of the postcolonial moment had a long afterlife that remained vibrant and contentious through the course of the Cold War period."[5] Yet underlying the anti-imperialist rhetoric and its emphasis on non-interference and development was an affirmation of the Western notion of the nation-state as the ultimate goal of self-determination, thereby turning domestic minorities into aliens and outsiders.[6]

[2] Luis Eslava, Michael Fakhri, and Vasuki Nesiah, "The Spirit of Bandung." in Luis Eslava, Michael Fakhri, and Vasuki Nesiah (eds.) *Bandung, Global History, and International Law. Critical Pasts and Pending Futures* (Cambridge: Cambridge University Press, 2017), 3–32, at 16.

[3] Amitav Acharya, "Studying the Bandung Conference from a Global IR perspective." *Australian Journal of International Affairs* 70 no. 4 (2016): 342–357, at 354. See also See Seng Tan and Amitav Acharya, (eds.) *Bandung Revisited: The Legacy of the 1955 Asian-African Conference for International Order* (Singapore: National University Press, 2008).

[4] Quỳnh N. Phạm and Robbie Shilliam, "Reviving Bandung." in Quỳnh N. Phạm and Robbie Shilliam (eds.) *Meanings of Bandung: Postcolonial orders and decolonial visions.* (London: Rowman & Littlefield, 2016), 3–20, at 17.

[5] Eslava et al., "The Spirit of Bandung," 19. For a similar argument, see Ahmad Rizky Mardhatillah Umar, "Rethinking the Legacies of Bandung Conference: Global Decolonization and the Making of Modern International Order." *Asian Politics & Policy* 11 no. 3 (2019): 461–478.

[6] See, for example, Antony Anghie, "Bandung and the Origins of Third World Sovereignty," in in Luis Eslava, Michael Fakhri, and Vasuki Nesiah (eds.) *Bandung, Global History, and International Law. Critical Pasts and Pending Futures* (Cambridge: Cambridge University Press, 2017), 535–551;

The main themes of the Bandung Conference were echoed in the 1960 UN Declaration of the Granting of Independence to Colonial Peoples and Countries, a resolution that proclaimed that "[t]he subjection of peoples to alien subjugation, domination and exploitation constitutes a denial of fundamental human rights, is contrary to the Charter of the United Nations and is an impediment to the promotion of world peace and co-operation." It called for immediate steps to be taken "in Trust and Non-Self-Governing Territories or all other territories which have not yet attained independence, to transfer all powers to the peoples of those territories, without any conditions or reservations, in accordance with their freely expressed will and desire, without any distinction as to race, creed or colour, in order to enable them to enjoy complete independence and freedom."[7] This language further resonated in the UN Covenant on Political and Civil Rights and the Covenant on Economic, Social and Cultural Rights, which in their final form stated that "[a]ll peoples have the right of self-determination. By virtue of that right they freely determine their political status and freely pursue their economic, social and cultural development."[8] In this way, the once contested principle of national self-determination was elevated into a universal right, and the responsibility for its implementation fell heavily on colonial powers. As these covenants stated, "[t]he States Parties to the present Covenant, including those having responsibility for the administration of Non-Self-Governing and Trust Territories, shall promote the realization of the right of self-determination, and shall respect that right, in conformity with the provisions of the Charter of the United Nations."[9]

As Edward Keene has remarked, in contrast to the League of Nations, the United Nations was "envisioned as, or quite rapidly became, an organization of *all* the world's peoples, with universal participation in the projects of preserving peace and developing global

Itty Abraham, "Bandung and State Formation in Post-Colonial Asia", in See Seng Tan and Amitav Acharya, (eds.) *Bandung Revisited: The Legacy of the 1955 Asian-African Conference for International Order.* (Singapore: National University Press, 2008), 48–68.

7 United Nations, *Declaration on the Granting of Independence to Colonial Countries and Peoples*, 1960, Articles 1 & 5.

8 United Nations, *International Covenant on Civil and Political Rights*, 1966, Article 1, § 1.

9 Ibid., § 3.

civilization."[10] But since this globalization of the international system had to be achieved while respecting the sovereign equality of every state along with its right to develop whatever kind of political and economic system it deemed fit, the postwar international system came to embody two normative principles that sometimes were hard to reconcile: "that the sovereign independence of state should be respected, so as the encourage the toleration of political and cultural differences; and that their sovereignty should be divided, so as to facilitate the promotion of civilization."[11] Differences in terms of race and civilization no longer constituted valid grounds for exclusion, and these categories were replaced with those of culture and ethnicity when making sense of differences within and between states. As Cary Fraser has aptly summarized the upshot of this process, "decolonization marked a shift in global consciousness from notions of racial hierarchy as a fundament of human society to the search for human community by transcending race."[12]

Decolonization in this sense was made possible by making self-determination a universal right, a process met with some initial resistance by colonial powers at the San Francisco Conference.[13] The legal codification of self-determination brought a series of corresponding changes to the practices of international recognition. Whereas earlier practices of recognition had excluded many non-European polities on the grounds that they lacked the characteristics of civilization or sovereignty, such exclusions were no longer considered admissible given the right of self-determination and the emphasis on sovereign equality in the UN Charter. As Mikulas Fabry has argued, the right to self-determination implied that former colonies "were being acknowledged more or less automatically because the new global political climate could not tolerate the institution of formal empire, and not as a result of appraisal in terms of some

[10] Edward Keene, *Beyond the Anarchical Society. Grotius, Colonialism and Order in World Politics* (Cambridge: Cambridge University Press, 2002), 136.

[11] Ibid., 143–144.

[12] Cary Fraser, "Decolonization and the Cold War," in Richard H. Immerman and Petra Goedde (eds.) *The Oxford Handbook of the Cold War* (Oxford: Oxford University Press, 2013), 469–485, at 482.

[13] See Jörg Fisch, *The Right of Self-determination of Peoples: The Domestication of an Illusion* (Cambridge: Cambridge University Press, 2015), 190ff; Eric D. Weitz, "Self-determination: How a German Enlightenment Idea Became the Slogan of National Liberation and a Human Right." *The American Historical Review* 120 no. 2 (2015): 462–496.

substantive standards."[14] But the right of self-determination was still prone to paradox in the same way as it had been before, since the self that was supposed to determine itself was itself undetermined. Who was to enjoy the right to self-determination was in practice restricted to polities whose territories already had been demarcated by their masters and which often were culturally heterogeneous communities with weak governments. In this context "[r]ecognition by third parties turned into a formality regardless of how viable or unviable new states might have appeared."[15] But even if many criteria of *de facto* statehood were downplayed or ignored during the process of decolonization, the notion of nationality remained important insofar as many claims to self-determination were based on an imagined congruence of state and nation within the territory inherited from colonial powers. As Hendrik Spruyt has pointed out, "[n]ational self-determination meant independence for the territorial unit constructed by the former imperial master, not self-determination for ethnic groups within that territorial unit…[t]he existing constitutive rule of sovereign territoriality defined the range of international behaviors that nationalists could adopt, and entailed particular domestic strategies to simultaneously deny local ethnic and subnational claims."[16] This legal indeterminacy gave rise to a tension between the principles of territorial integrity and those of national self-determination which in turn fueled conflicts within as well as between new states as they tried to make nation and state converge to qualify as a nation-states proper.[17] Yet as I will try

[14] Mikulas Fabry, *Recognizing States. International Society and the Establishment of New States Since 1776* (Oxford: Oxford University Press, 2010), 148. Also, Martin Clark, "A Conceptual History of Recognition in British International Legal Thought." *British Yearbook of International* Law 87 no. 1 (2017): 18–97, esp. 94–97.

[15] Ibid., 157.

[16] Hendrik Spruyt, "The End of Empire and the Extension of the Westphalian System: The normative basis of the modern state order." *International Studies Review* 2 no. 2 (2000): 65–92, at 79 & 80. See also Lydia Walker, "Decolonization in the 1960s: On legitimate and illegitimate nationalist claims-making." *Past & Present* 242 no. 1 (2019): 227–264; Eric Lewis Beverley, "Introduction: Rethinking Sovereignty, Colonial Empires, and Nation-States in South Asia and Beyond." *Comparative Studies of South Asia, Africa and the Middle East* 40 no. 3 (2020): 407–420.

[17] For an analysis of the legal complications involved, see Samuel Kwaw Nyameke Blay, "Self-determination versus Territorial Integrity in Decolonization." *New York University Journal of International Law and Politics* 18 (1985): 441–472.

to show, the imperative of congruence was less a question of legality but more a matter of political legitimacy, as many commentators took for granted that national unity was a condition of possible democracy.

But what was the final outcome of decolonization, and how should it be understood in the wider context of global intellectual history? In contrast to those established interpretations that claim that decolonization either brought a more inclusive and equal international system, or, that decolonization merely meant that unequal relations between the West and the rest were reproduced in economic terms, I will argue that the globalization of the international system brought about by decolonization equally well can be interpreted as fulfilment of older visions of empire insofar as the global international system is the first political system of a truly universal and planetary scope. Whereas the distinction between a world of states and a world of empires earlier had been coeval with the bifurcation of global space into a civilized European inside and an uncivilized non-European outside, the universalization of the nation-state form brought about by decolonization made this bifurcation impossible to sustain since it was difficult to explain how the international system could retain its defining characteristic as the locus of civilization once its constitutive and supposedly uncivilized outside was gone.

Similar arguments have already been pursued by others. For example, according to Adom Getachew, anticolonial nationalists were not content to build their own independent states but were also involved in a struggle to overcome international hierarchy and create an international order free from domination. As she has summarized this ambition, "[c]entral to this combination of nation-building and worldmaking was the view that the global project of European empire had radically transformed the economic and political conditions of the modern world in ways that required a similarly global anticolonial project."[18] Although these attempts at worldmaking were largely unsuccessful, they highlighted the many ways in which imperial and hierarchical relations were perpetuated and continued to be constitutive of an international system of formally equal states. In a similar way, as Jaakko Heiskanen has recently argued, the transition from a world of empires to a world of states did not imply that the

[18] Adom Getachew, *Worldmaking after Empire: The Rise and Fall of Self-determination* (Princeton: Princeton University Press, 2019), 24.

former vanished, rather that it was sublated, since "the imperial order that preceded the international order was not simply effaced without remainder. Instead, the imperial structures are retained within the new order and continue to animate international relations from within ... The formation of the modern international order is a dialectical moment that both negates and preserves the imperial order that came before."[19]

In this chapter I would like to pursue this line of argument to its logical conclusion by arguing that decolonization in effect if not in intention turned *the international system into an empire in its own right*. Many of those functions conventionally thought to distinguish empires from other kinds of polity were taken over by the international system once it was conceptualized as global and boundless in scope. The characteristic mechanism of imperial rule – the *divide et impere* – was now institutionalized in the guise of the invisible hand of international anarchy that kept states in a condition of constant competition for security and power and socialized them into relative similarity under the banner of a global civilization. The multicultural makeup characteristic of the empires of the past was now enshrined in the principles of tolerance and non-interference, and the traditional trade-off between sociocultural diversity and governability was resolved with reference to the idea of sovereign equality. Hence formal empire vanished not because it had become illegitimate but because it had become redundant at a moment when the international system itself fulfilled old visions of universal rule.

When making this argument, I will join forces with those who maintain that decolonization ought to be situated in a global context of interaction between a variety of interlocutors.[20] From this point of view, the globalization of the international system *cum* empire was not the result of an imposition of Western ideas and institutions on the colonial peoples of the non-Western world, but consequences of

[19] Jaakko Heiskanen, *The Ethnos of the Earth: Nationalism, Ethnicity, and International Order* (Dissertation, POLIS, University of Cambridge, 2020), 11.

[20] See, for example, Martin Thomas and Andrew S. Thompson, "Rethinking Decolonization: A New Research Agenda for The Twenty-first Century." in Martin Thomas and Andrew S. Thompson (eds.) *The Oxford Handbook of the Ends of Empire* (Oxford: Oxford University Press, 2019), 1–26; Arnulf Becker Lorca, *Mestizo International Law. A Global Intellectual History 1842–1933* (Cambridge: Cambridge University Press, 2014).

the creative appropriation of these ideas and institutions coupled with a selective understanding of postcolonial state making by Western commentators on the other. The rest of this chapter is organized as follows. In the next section, I will analyze some major statements by anticolonial leaders, emphasizing how their appropriation of nationalist and anti-imperialist ideas helped them to justify their nationalist and internationalist projects of self-determination. In the third section, I describe how the process of decolonization and its outcomes were understood by Western commentators and social scientists, emphasizing the extent to which these were interpreted in narrow nationalist terms and quickly assimilated to contemporary concerns with the modernization and development of new states against the backdrop of superpower rivalry and looming threats from the Soviet Union. In the final section, I will describe how the outcome of decolonization came to be conceptualized in terms of a universal international system by students of international relations, and how the concomitant confinement of non-European peoples into nation-states produced a profound sense of loss and entrapment among postcolonial scholars.

Remaking the World

What was at stake in claims to self-determination among those who raised them? As some scholars have pointed out, achieving independence and international recognition were rarely conceived as ends in themselves, but as stepping-stones to achieve greater things, ranging from economic development to a brave new world order free from Western or capitalist domination. As Getachew has noted, "the emergence of the nation-state as the normative unit of international order also provided occasion to rethink the conditions in which a system of states might overcome imperial domination and hierarchy."[21] Many anticolonial nationalists were aware that formal independence offered little protection against the continuing encroachment of their former colonial masters, and took this opportunity to argue in favor of a wholesale reform of the international system in a more egalitarian direction. According to Getachew, rather than amounting to an expansion of the Westphalian system, the "anticolonial account of self-determination marked a radical break from the Eurocentric model

[21] Getachew, *Worldmaking after Empire*, 4.

of international society and established nondomination as a central ideal of a postimperial world order."[22] Pleas for self-determination were intended to bring about a radical transformation of the world order and the eventual abolition of its remaining yet informal elements of hierarchy and domination. Thus "[d]ecolonization understood as a revolutionary project ... required remaking the international order that sustained relations of dependence and domination. Nation-building was to be situated and realized through worldmaking."[23]

But decolonization was also a matter of *appropriating* international norms for the purpose of state making and international reform in a historical context that best can be described as highly averse to this kind of endeavor. First, the fact that the international system was bifurcated along the ideological and political fault lines of the Cold War meant that each superpower was more than happy to offer their own neo-imperial recipes for state making to anticolonial leaders. As a leading historian of this period has pointed out, this implied that "there were two hegemonic models of development on offer when the new states were being created...[that] ... offered a road to high modernity through education, science, and technological progress."[24] Second, anticolonial leaders faced domestic constraints as a consequence of centuries of colonial rule. As Odd Arne Westad has pointed out, "[t]he whole entity that the new leaders were trying to fill with their own content was a colonial construct: its borders, its capital city, its official language."[25] Yet colonial rule had often defined the contours and composition of colonized spaces well in advance of independence. As Mahmood Mamdani has argued, imperial powers had in many cases created political communities "in which colonized groups were subdivided into territorial homelands and made subject to separate legal regimes. These divisions were drawn along lines of cultural and ethnic distinction, thereby transforming ethnic groups into administrative-political units known as tribes."[26] Anticolonial leaders thus faced

[22] Ibid., 11. [23] Ibid., 17.

[24] Odd Arne Westad, *The Global Cold War: Third World Interventions and the making of our times* (Cambridge: Cambridge University Press, 2005), 92. Also Jeremi Suri, "The Cold War, Decolonization, and Global Social Awakenings: Historical intersections." *Cold War History* 6 no. 3 (2006): 353–363.

[25] Ibid., 90.

[26] Mahmood Mamdani, *Neither Settler nor Native. The Making and Unmaking of Permanent Majorities* (Cambridge, MA.: Harvard University Press, 2020), 11.

the double challenge of turning the heterogenous spaces handed over to them by their masters into states in any recognizable sense of this term while simultaneously avoiding being sucked into the dysfunctional dynamics of ongoing superpower rivalry while doing so.

As I will argue in this section, many of those who struggled to attain independence responded to these challenges by going international. Much like their interwar predecessors, anticolonial leaders projected their expectations for the future onto the international realm, whose existence they took to be necessary to their realization.[27] Although new states in Asia and Africa soon entered into various co-operative arrangements – the foundation of the Non-Aligned Movement in 1961 and of the Organization of African Unity in 1963 being exemplary institutional embodiments of anticolonial internationalism – in order to reform the international system and provide alternatives to superpower rivalry, they were also quick to capitalize on their newly acquired international recognition by using norms of non-intervention as a protective shell for their attempts at state making at home.[28] Hence the universalization of the nation-state form was less a result of its imposition from the outside, but more a matter of the appropriation of the idea of self-determination in the hope of overcoming troubled colonial legacies at home while keeping imperial powers – old as well as new – at bay. In this process, international organizations in general and the United Nations in particular were instrumental insofar as they functioned as clearinghouses for colonial polities aspiring to international legal recognition. As such these organizations were actively involved in the production of new sovereign states.[29] But as state making in Asia and Africa progressed, the internationalist aspirations of anticolonial leaders waned. As Jeffrey Byrne has argued, anticolonial internationalism "transformed from a transnational mode of cooperation that evaded and subverted the authority of the colonial

[27] See Manu Goswami, "Imaginary Futures and Colonial Internationalisms." *American Historical Review* 117 no. 5 (2012): 1461–1485.

[28] Luke Glanville, "The Myth of 'traditional' Sovereignty." *International Studies Quarterly* 57 no. 1 (2013): 79–90; Luke Glanville, *Sovereignty and the Responsibility to Protect: A New History* (Chicago: University of Chicago Press, 2013), 132–170.

[29] See Eva-Maria Muschik, "Managing the World: The United Nations, Decolonization, and the Strange Triumph of State Sovereignty in the 1950s and 1960s." *Journal of Global History* 13 no. 1 (2018): 121–144.

state into an international cooperation that legitimized and zealously defended the authority of the postcolonial state."[30] Given the strong internationalist commitments of this first generation of anticolonial leaders, this outcome appears enigmatic, but, as we will note below, perhaps less so if we consider the pressures of nationalist ideologies and superpower rivalry.

Those who embarked on the road to Bandung were in for a bumpy ride as they had to navigate the treacherous waters of this rivalry while struggling to create states out of the polities handed down to them by centuries of imperial rule. Despite the vastly different circumstances faced by anticolonial leaders in their quest for independence and international recognition, their responses demonstrated some remarkable similarities. Disappointed with the many promises of liberal internationalism in general and those of Wilsonian self-determination in particular, this generation of anti-imperialist statesmen and intellectuals combined beliefs in the virtues of their pre-colonial traditions and institutions with theories of imperialism – notably those of Lenin and Hobson – to which they added selected tenets of European nationalism described in the previous chapter. Although these ingredients were blended in different proportions, the resulting understandings of self-determination converged on a set of basic assumptions about the world and the place of postcolonial states within it. First, following Lenin and Hobson, many postcolonial leaders believed that imperialism and colonialism were products of the capitalist *modus operandi* of the modern international system rather than attributable to the evil designs of individual imperial powers, even if this in no way implied that the latter were innocent. Second, anticolonial leaders shared a conviction that achieving national unity was necessary in the remaking of colonial territories into states even if not directly compelled in this direction by international legal norms. Third, anticolonial leaders were in broad agreement that the sociocultural divisions that posed obstacles to national unification were but consequences of imperial rule rather than being pre-colonial in origin. Taken together, this set of beliefs predisposed many anticolonial leaders to channel their political ambitions into the nation-state form while trying to reform the international system. Hence anticolonial nationalism and internationalism were but

[30] Jeffrey James Byrne, *Mecca of Revolution: Algeria, Decolonization, and Third World Order* (Oxford: Oxford University Press, 2016), 10.

two sides of the same coin, but tensions between these aspirations opened up a conceptual space which at least momentarily could be filled with alternatives that did not conform to the nation-state form. In many cases, these alternatives initially seemed more desirable than the nation-state and were also prominent in early anti-imperialist rhetoric.

Among the first on the road to Bandung was the would-be Indonesian president Sukarno, whose relentless struggle for independence would put many of the conflicting pressures described above into sharp relief. Well before proclaiming independence from the stairs of his house in 1945, Sukarno had been busy reconciling the many conflicting social, political, and religious forces that long had made Indonesian unity look utopian. To Sukarno, the driving forces of imperialism were economic rather than political in character. As he argued in an early essay that defined the parameters of an independence to come, "the primary cause of colonization is not the desire for fame nor the wish to see the world; nor is it the longing for freedom, nor population pressures faced by the colonizers in their own countries…The prime cause of colonization is the search for gain."[31] Not only had Sukarno to face deep religious and regional divisions in the vast archipelago he wanted to turn into a nation-state, but his would-be fellow travelers were torn between *prima facie* incompatible ideological positions. Thus, questions arose whether "[i]n colonial territories can the Nationalist movement be joined with the Islamic movement, which essentially denies the nation? Can it be allied with Marxism, which proclaims an international struggle?"[32] Sukarno's answer to these questions was clearly in the affirmative, yet it took considerable stretching of the concept of the nation and some equally creative reinterpretation of its purported rivals to provide a persuasive script for national unification. Taking Renan's notion of the nation as his template, Sukarno argued that in order to constitute a nation, "a people must have shared a common history; secondly, a people must possess the will and desire to live as one."[33] The kind of nationalism envisaged by Sukarno was to him different in spirit from its Western form. Whereas Eastern nationalism

[31] Sukarno, "Nationalism, Islam, and Marxism." [1926] trans. by Karel H. Warouw and Peter D. Weldon. With an introduction by Ruth T. McVey (Ithaca, Modern Indonesia Project, Cornell University, 1970), 35. For the road to Indonesian independence, see Bernhard Dahm, *Sukarno and the struggle for Indonesian independence* (Ithaca: Cornell University Press, 1969).

[32] Ibid., 38. [33] Ibid.

was based on a true love of humanity, Western nationalism "is an aggressive nationalism, a nationalism that only pursues its own selfish interests ... [that] ... will certainly end in its own destruction."[34] By contrast, since both Marxist and Islam in their essence aspire to transcend all national boundaries, their reconciliation with nationalism will temper the parochial tendencies of the latter and add a necessary international dimension to the struggle for independence and non-domination. Indeed, the transnational forces of Pan-Islamism and Marxism must be harnessed to promote the cause of independence, in order "to lift Islam from its present state of humiliation and decay" and, by the same token, for "workers in Asian countries to be able to have the freedom to build true socialist movements, these countries must be free."[35] From this point of view, formal independence was but a first yet indispensable step towards freedom from imperial domination, and that freedom could only be secured within a broader international context of transnational revolution and reform.

More erudite than his comrade in arms, the coming vice-president Mohammed Hatta also emphasized the economic causes of imperialism but added some sophistication to that analysis. To him, the Indonesian struggle for independence had to be understood in the context of an ongoing liberation of Asia from Western dominance. The spirit of revolution, first unleashed by Japanese expansionism and then exacerbated by Wilsonian promises of self-determination, had engulfed the Asian continent from India to Turkey and was now descending upon Indonesia.[36] To Hatta, the international realm was defined by a struggle for power, a struggle which was the cause of "the formation of states, of the crumbling of worldwide empires into a number of smaller independent sovereign states, and last but not least the cause of subjection of the one state by the other."[37] In current world affairs this conflict was manifest in the colonial situation and the antithesis between the white and the colored races underlying it, an antithesis that could be resolved only through a violent struggle for

[34] Ibid., 42. [35] Ibid., 48 & 59.

[36] Mohammed Hatta, "Indonesia in the Middle of the Asian Revolution." [1923] in *Portrait of a Patriot. Selected Writings of Mohammed Hatta* (The Hague: Mouton, 1972), 17–26.

[37] Mohammed Hatta, "The Economic World Structure and the Conflict of Power." [1926] in *Portrait of a Patriot. Selected Writings of Mohammed Hatta* (The Hague: Mouton, 1972), 36–57, at 36.

independence on behalf of the colonized peoples of color.[38] Although Hatta shared the belief that "the main cause of colonial expansion lies in the great need for supplies of the colonizing people", this "policy of robbery" had its roots in the structure of the international system whose primitive lawlessness made the weak prey to the strong, since in "international societies every action of the strongest could be called a right."[39] From this it followed that the struggle for independence would never succeed as long as it paid naïve tribute to the principles of humanity, but that it had to be based on "existing *racialism* and conflicts of interest".[40] Hence, to Hatta, "there is no other means for the colony to escape this humiliating situation of slavery than by means of violence."[41] In the wider international context this implied that "western imperialism must be destroyed for the sake of humanity and...it is the duty of every colonized nation to shake off the foreign yoke."[42]

To Sukarno and Hatta, none of the above could be accomplished in isolation but required cooperation among colonized peoples. It was therefore necessary to situate the Indonesian struggle for independence in the long chain of events that together formed the rise of the Eastern nations, and to translate this struggle into a common ethos for the postcolonial world. Having had Indonesian independence recognized in 1949, Sukarno further emphasized the necessity of an international ethics of independence in his opening speech at the Bandung conference. At the moment of independence, he argued, "we were suddenly confronted with the necessity of giving content and meaning to our independence. Not material content and meaning only, but also ethical and moral content, for independence without ethics and without morality would be indeed a poor imitation of what we sought."[43] The moral code that ought to govern independence would be "the subordination of everything to the well-being of mankind" which presupposed that new states would be united "by a common detestation of colonialism in whatever form it appears. We are united by a common detestation of racialism. And we are united by a common determination to preserve and stabilise peace in the world."[44] To Sukarno, this was all the more urgent given the increasing interdependence of the

[38] Ibid., 39. [39] Ibid., 42 & 44. [40] Ibid., 45. [41] Ibid., 50. [42] Ibid., 55.
[43] Sukarno, opening address to the Bandung Conference, April 18, 1955 (Jakarta: Ministry of Foreign Affairs, 1955), 3.
[44] Ibid., 4.

modern world, in which states "depend one upon the other and no nation can be an island unto itself. Splendid isolation may once have been possible; it is so no longer. The affairs of all the world are our affairs, and our future depends upon the solutions found to all international problems, however far or distant they may seem."[45]

Next to embark on the road to Bandung was Jawaharlal Nehru. But as we may recall from Chapter 4, well before him, Gandhi had envisioned independent India in terms of a decentralized peasant democracy rather than as a modern nation-state. During the interwar years, others had voiced skepticism of about sovereign statehood and argued that Indian independence rather ought to be conceived along pluralist and federalist lines. Perhaps foremost among these authors was Radhakamal Mukerjee, whose anticolonial federalism was based on a conceptualization of popular sovereignty in pluralist terms that rendered the state as little but an obstacle to the effective exercise of that sovereignty within a federation of village republics. Inspired by contemporary British pluralists such as Laski and Cole, Mukerjee argued that social groups existed independently of and stood in no need of authorization from the sovereign state. The Indian village community, he maintained, "representing as it does the integration of the needs and interests of diverse classes and functional groups, has created for itself permanent and constituted organs of the common life as well as bodies of customs which regulate the rights and duties of individuals to the group and of the groups to one another."[46] This federalist and pluralist vision of an Indian polity once independence had been attained was very different from the statist and nationalist one that would eventually prove victorious.

To Nehru, by contrast, achieving independence and development implied creating a nation-state of precisely the kind that the federalists abhorred and conceptualizing popular sovereignty accordingly in terms of national democracy. While doing this, Nehru demonstrated the extent to which going international was instrumental and perhaps

[45] Ibid., 6.

[46] Radhakamal Mukerjee, *Democracies of the East. A Study in Comparative Politics* (London: P. S. King & Son, 1923), 157. For analyses, see Karuna Mantena, "Popular Sovereignty and Anticolonialism." in Richard Bourke and Quentin Skinner (eds.) *Popular Sovereignty in Historical Perspective* (Cambridge: Cambridge University Press, 2016), 297–319; Nazmul S. Sultan, "Between the Many and the One: Anticolonial Federalism and Popular Sovereignty." *Political Theory* 50 no. 2 (2022): 247–274.

necessary to achieve independence on such terms. As Martin Bayly has shown, Nehru could draw upon a rich tradition of Indian international thought that was both anticolonial and internationalist in spirit and which had been institutionalized in the Indian Council for World Affairs prior to independence.[47] In this context, going international entailed a strong commitment to anti-imperialism. As Nehru noted ahead of the decision whether India should remain part of the Commonwealth after independence, "[s]o far the West or Europe has been the centre of political activity and dominated the politics of the world. Therefore, their disputes and their quarrels and their wars have dominated the world."[48] In Nehru's vision of the future to come, "Europe can no longer be the centre of the world, politically speaking...Europe belongs to the past and the centre of world history, of political and other activities, shifts elsewhere."[49] To Nehru, this was not only indicative of a coming shift in the global distribution of power in favor of Asia, but also in the *modus operandi* of the international system as a whole. Since the international system could not generate conflicts on its own – or so he believed – the recurrence of war was the result of a long cycle of bad karma initiated by European powers through their obsession with power, their rivalries, and constant conquests. As he argued in *The Discovery of India* (1946), postcolonial states should avoid getting sucked into this dynamic, and instead pursue peaceful cooperation, since "[i]f there is no co-operation there is bound to be friction with its inevitable results. Co-operation can only be on a basis of equality and mutual welfare, on a pulling-up of the backward nations and peoples to a common level of well-being and cultural advancement, on an elimination of racialism and domination."[50] In the case of India, this implied a strong commitment to the idea of non-alignment. As Nehru had stated already on the eve

47 Martin J. Bayly, "Lineages of Indian International Relations: The Indian Council on World Affairs, The League of Nations, and the pedagogy of internationalism." *International History Review* 44 no. 4 (2022): 819–835.

48 "We Have not Bound the Future Down", May 17, 1949, in Jawaharlal Nehru, *Selected Speeches* Vol. 1, September 1946–May 1949. (Publications Division. Ministry of Information and Broadcasting, Government of India, 1949), 291.

49 Ibid., 294–295

50 Jawaharlal Nehru, *The Discovery of India* [1946] (New Delhi: Oxford University Press, 1989), 540.

of independence, "[w]e propose...to keep away from the power politics of groups, aligned against one another, which have led in the past to world wars and which may again lead to disasters on an even vaster scale."[51] To counteract these possibilities, Nehru advocated close cooperation between Asian countries, and the Asian Relations Conference he hosted in 1947 was in many ways the first manifestation of postcolonial solidarity.[52] As Nehru claimed when planning it, "closer relations between Asian countries have become so absolutely essential that...we may as well take a lead in it, because whichever way you look at it, India happens to be the centre of all this."[53] Although Nehru faced a range of political constraints deriving from the legacy of colonial rule, his international engagements made it possible to circumvent some of these by performing independence internationally before it had become established domestically.[54] Thus it is obvious from his speeches that he envisaged international cooperation and non-alignment as *conditions* of independence rather than as its end results. As he went on to argue in another speech, "we believe that peace and freedom are indivisible and the denial of freedom anywhere must endanger freedom elsewhere and lead to conflict and war."[55] Hence the abolition of imperial domination abroad was the *sine qua non* of non-domination at home, so "that in our external, internal or domestic policy, in our political policy, or in our economic policy, we do not propose to accept anything that involves in the slightest degree dependence on any other authority."[56] As Bhikhu Parekh has pointed

[51] Broadcast from New Delhi, September 7, 1946, in Jawaharlal Nehru, *Selected Speeches* Vol. 1, September 1946-May 1949. (Publications Division. Ministry of Information and Broadcasting, Government of India, 1949), 2–3.

[52] See Vineet Thakur, "An Asian Drama: The Asian Relations Conference, 1947." *The International History Review* 41 no. 3 (2019): 673–695.

[53] Jawaharlal Nehru, "Inter-Asian Relations." *India Quarterly* 2 no. 4 (1946): 323–327, at 323.

[54] See, for example, Judith M. Brown, "Nehru-the Dilemmas of a Colonial Inheritance." in Jost Dülffer and Marc Frey (eds.) *Elites and Decolonization in the Twentieth Century* (Houndsmills, Basingstoke: Palgrave Macmillan, 2011), 177–194.

[55] Broadcast from New Delhi, September 7, 1946 in Jawaharlal Nehru, *Selected Speeches* Vol. 1, September 1946-May 1949. (Publications Division. Ministry of Information and Broadcasting, Government of India, 1949), 2–3.

[56] "Meeting Ground of East and West", March 8, 1949, in Jawaharlal Nehru, *Selected Speeches* Vol. 1, September 1946–May 1949. (Publications Division. Ministry of Information and Broadcasting, Government of India, 1949), 244.

out, Nehru's insistence that India should remain non-aligned and seek to develop its own foreign policy was both "a necessary expression and an indispensable means of preserving Indian independence... [and]... the common ground on which Indians of different ideological persuasions could be united." A policy of non-alignment was necessary in order serve the internationalist imperative to "open up and reconstitute the international system on a broader basis."[57]

Anticolonial leaders wanted to escape not only their imperial masters, but also the international system which they believed had made imperialism and colonialism possible. Their escape route went by emphasizing the transnational character of their struggle, then by appealing to a community of new-born states for support, and finally by plugging into the international system in the hope of being able to reform it from within. With Sukarno and Nehru among the organizers, the Bandung conference was but a first step towards achieving these objectives. Being to some extent a reaction to Western indifference to Asian concerns during the early phase of the Cold War, the Bandung Conference was characterized by ritualized diplomatic performances and later mythologized by posterity as a decisive moment in decolonization. Its most tangible outcome was the *Dasasila Bandung*. To some extent building on the UN Charter, this declaration put additional emphasis on the rights of non-intervention and non-interference, along with a renewed insistence on the "recognition of the equality of all races and of the equality of all nations large and small" as well as the "promotion of mutual interests and cooperation" among Third World states.[58]

Tropes of international equality and non-domination also figured pre-eminently in rhetoric of independence among African leaders and were often connected to pleas for African unity. To Julius Nyerere, anticolonial nationalism ran the risk of reproducing imperial divisions if not tempered by a fair dose of internationalism. As he maintained in

[57] Bhikhu Parekh, "Nehru and the National Philosophy of India." *Economic and Political Weekly* 26 no 1/2 (1991): 35–48, at 43.

[58] Final Communiqué of the Asian-African conference of Bandung (April 24, 1955), 7. See also Naoko Shimazu, "Diplomacy as Theatre: Staging the Bandung Conference of 1955." *Modern Asian Studies* 48 no. 1, 2014: 225–252; Robert Vitalis, "The midnight ride of Kwame Nkrumah and other fables of Bandung (Ban-doong)." *Humanity: An International Journal of Human Rights, Humanitarianism, and Development* 4 no. 2 (2013): 261–288.

a talk ahead of Tanzanian independence at Chatham House, "[w]e find that our country must learn to think as a nation, and we are faced with the question of organization and of getting the hundred and twenty tribes to think of themselves as one people."[59] But as he later described the quest for national unity, "we have constantly warned ourselves against the snares of the imperialist whose policy is 'divide and rule'. Whenever we have asked for our right to govern ourselves it has been the imperialist who has told us that we are not ready because we still have tribal, religious, communal and other differences. At the same time it has been the imperialist who has encouraged these divisions in order to continue and rule a weak and divided people."[60] Escaping this predicament and achieving true independence could only be done through international cooperation. Hence Nyerere maintained that Tanganyika should join the United Nations and become a member of the Commonwealth but relinquish membership in the latter should his plans for African unity be realized.[61] By contrast, African unity and international cooperation under the auspices of the United Nations were fully compatible, since, as he argued, "[w]e have our responsibilities towards all those other African states with which our links are bound to be so close; and further, even the newest of nations has, in these days, duties towards all the nations upon earth and opportunities to influence by example the policies even of the most powerful."[62] Thus Nyerere believed that the creation of a United States of Africa would be but a political expression of a sense of unity already manifest among African peoples and would allow these peoples to outgrow the legacies of imperialism together. To him, "[i]ndissoluble African unity is the stone bridge which would enable us all to walk in safety over this whirlpool of power politics, and enable us to carry more easily the

[59] Julius Nyerere, Address at Chatham House, 29 July 1959, in C. C. Harris and Julius Nyerere, "Tanganyika Today." *International Affairs* 36 no. 1, 35–47, at 43

[60] Julius Nyerere, "Freedom and Unity," *Transition* 14, 1964, 40–45, at 42.

[61] Julius Nyerere, "Tanganyika and the Commonwealth." December 1961, in Julius Nyerere, *Freedom and Unity: Uhuru na Umoja; a selection from writings and speeches, 1952–65* (Dar es Salaam: Oxford University Press, 1967), 137–137.

[62] Julius Nyerere, "Receiving the Instruments of Independence." December 8, 1961, in Julius Nyerere, *Freedom and Unity: Uhuru na Umoja; a selection from writings and speeches, 1952–65* (Dar es Salaam: Oxford University Press, 1967), 142–143, at 142.

economic and social loads which now threaten to overwhelm us."[63] The policies intended to achieve these objectives were outlined before the General Assembly in December 1961, when Nyerere started by noting that "the fact that we have been a Trust Territory under British administration has greatly helped us to achieve our independence in the way we have achieved it."[64] The foreign policy of a new-born Tanzania would recognize the fundamental importance of the United Nations, because "[w]ithin this assembly every nation is an equal, and we believe that in this lies the unique character of the United Nations" and hence be based on "our basic and continued opposition to colonialism anywhere on our continent or in any other part of the world."[65] To this was added the imperative of staying out of the Cold War at all costs, since Tanzanians were "anxious to see that the nations of our continent are not used as pawns in conflicts which very often do not concern them at all."[66] Yet turning the above principles into viable policies required considerable latitude in the conduct of domestic politics, since "[w]e believe further that there is no question but that the maintenance of law and order in society depends upon there being one supreme authority which is accepted by the majority and which, if need be, can assert its authority on a dissenting minority."[67] This desire for supreme authority soon manifested itself in the creation of a socialist one-party state and an emphasis on self-reliance. As one of the appendices to *The Arusha Declaration* (1967) stated in no uncertain terms, "[i]ndependence means self-reliance. Independence cannot be real if a nation depends upon gifts and loans from another for Its development."[68] To Nyerere, the international system and the United Nations were the conveyor belt of those ambitions, and also

63 Julius Nyerere, "A United States of Africa." *Journal of Modern Africa Studies* 1, no. 1, 1963, 1–6, at 1.

64 Julius Nyerere, "Independence Address to the United Nations." December 14, 1961, in Julius Nyerere, *Freedom and Unity: Uhuru na Umoja; a selection from writings and speeches, 1952–65*. (Dar es Salaam: Oxford University Press, 1967), 144–156, at 144–145.

65 Ibid., 148 & 150. 66 Ibid., 154. 67 Ibid., 154.

68 *The Arusha Declaration and TANU's Policy on Socialism and Self Reliance* (Dar es Salaam: Publicity Section, Tanganyika African National Union, 1967). For this development, see Andreas Eckert, "Julius Nyerere, Tanzanian Elites, and the Project of African Socialism." in Jost Dülffer and Marc Frey (eds.) *Elites and Decolonization in the Twentieth Century* (Houndsmills, Basingstoke: Palgrave Macmillan, 2011), 216–240.

permissive causes of the supreme authority deemed necessary for their realization.

The internationalist dimension of self-determination and independence was perhaps even more pronounced in West Africa. Already in 1953, West African politicians launched the *Mouvement des Independants de Outre-Mer*, that warned against basing the struggle for independence on narrow forms of nationalism and instead tried to identify forms of political association that could transcend the nation state.[69] The coming premier of Senegal, Mamadou Dia, was most explicit on this score when he argued that although the anticolonial revolution and the making of new nations in Africa were "attributable to nationalism over which Western Europe has lost its monopoly" this also had made it necessary to "discard racist theories that claim to base the national vocation on the race or the people."[70] In their place Dia advocated the formation of multinational states, since "[i]t is perfectly obvious that the nation as a collective vocation within African dimensions necessarily groups diverse countries and peoples."[71] To his companion and eventual nemesis Léopold Senghor, the concentric circles of human community extended far beyond the confines of the territorial nation-state and called for the creation of multilayered forms of sovereignty to match the communal realities of African political life. In 1945, while taking part in the drafting of the new French constitution, Senghor argued that West Africans were part of a more inclusive French imperial community, which, although once built by coercion and domination, now stood a chance to realize the French revolutionary promises of equal citizenship for all inhabitants of French overseas territories under conditions of cultural diversity.[72]

69 Frederick Cooper, "Alternatives to Nationalism in French Africa, 1945–1960." in Jost Dülffer and Marc Frey (eds.) *Elites and Decolonization in the Twentieth Century* (Houndsmills, Basingstoke: Palgrave Macmillan, 2011), 110–137.

70 Mamadou Dia, *The African Nations and World Solidarity*. trans. by Mercer Cook (New York: Praeger, 1961), 3 & 5.

71 Dia, *The African Nations and World Solidarity*, 6.

72 Robert Lemaignen, Léopold Sédar Senghor, and Prince Sisowath Youtévong, *La Communauté Impériale Française* (Paris: Éditions Alsatia, 1945). For a detailed account of attempts to redefine the French empire, see Frederick Cooper "Alternatives to Empire: France and Africa after World War II." in Douglas Howland and Luise White (eds.) *The State of Sovereignty: Territories, Laws, Populations* (Bloomington: Indiana University Press), 94–123.

When the extension of political and social rights to African subjects caused fear in Paris that it would undermine the sovereignty of the French Republic, Senghor and Dia opted for a federal solution that would allow overseas territories considerable autonomy in relation to the metropole.[73] To Dia, it was obvious that the African struggle for independence marked the beginning of a worldwide revolution, since "the chief feature of the revolution of the *Tiers-Monde* nations is its anticolonialist character" and because the rejection of colonialism necessitated the simultaneous rejection of capitalism.[74] Thus "independence is a means, a potent means, to enable proletarian nations to assure their rapid development by integrating modern economies into a world economy on the basis of equitable co-operation."[75] Whereas to Dia independence was a means to resist and eventually undo the capitalist world system that he believed had produced imperial rule, to Senghor Western socialism had to be recalibrated to fit uniquely African circumstances by means of his doctrine of *Négritude*. From having initially been tailored to resist attempts to assimilate Africans to French civilization, *Négritude* gradually evolved into a comprehensive worldview intended to render the African experience of sociopolitical life unique and distinctive.[76] As such, it offered a way of transcending divisions along the lines of tribe and religion, and held out the promise of cultural unity among African peoples. As Senghor expressed this hope on the eve of Senegalese independence: "From the states of Africa, today disunited, the Federation will make a single people with a single culture, renewed by French culture, a single people animated by the same faith and reaching toward the same goal, which is the realization of its collective personality."[77]

Although they disagreed about its precise terms, Dia and Senghor, along with Sekou Touré of Guinea and Félix Houphouët-Boigny of Côte d'Ivoire, were all convinced that some kind of federation

[73] Ibid., 119. [74] Dia, *The African Nations and World Solidarity*, 34.

[75] Ibid., 83.

[76] See Gary Wilder, *Freedom Time: Négritude, decolonization, and the future of the world* (Durham, NC.: Duke University Press, 2015); Léopold Sédar Senghor and Kenneth Kirkwood, "Negritude and African Socialism." in Pieter Hendrik Coetzee and Abraham Pieter Jacob Roux, (eds.), *The African Philosophy Reader* (London: Routledge, 1998): 438–448.

[77] *L'Afrique Nouvelle*, January 23, 1959. Quoted in Cooper, "Alternatives to Nationalism in West Africa, 1945–1960", 126. (translation modified).

represented a viable middle road between French domination and full independence, even at a time when the latter seemed inevitable. But in September 1958, and against the backdrop of escalating hostilities in Algeria, General Charles de Gaulle made African colonies an offer intended to be hard to refuse. Given pending revisions of the French constitution that threatened to terminate existing federal arrangements, French colonial subjects were asked in a series of referenda whether they wanted to stay connected to France on new terms or wanted to attain full independence. While most colonies accepted to become part of the newly constituted French Community, in Guinea the response to De Gaulle's offer was a resounding no which resulted in its immediate independence. As Sékou Touré had told de Gaulle in April the same year in what was to become a *pièce de résistance* of anticolonial rhetoric: "[t]here can be no dignity without liberty, for every subjugation, every imposed constraint degrades the man on whom it weighs, steals away a part of his humanity, and makes him into an inferior being. We prefer poverty in liberty to riches in slavery. What is true for man is also true for societies and peoples."[78] Since the new terms of association with France granted citizenship rights but no right of self-determination to African peoples, the French Community was soon abandoned in favor of full sovereignty by the other West African colonies as well.[79]

However, it soon became obvious to anticolonial leaders that formal independence would not automatically yield freedom from domination let alone economic development. Whereas the right of self-determination granted sovereignty and international recognition to colonial peoples, it was far from clear that this amounted to a clean break with their imperial masters other than in superficial legal terms. As Sekou Touré would argue in a talk at Chatham House, "[i]ndependence is a means to an end, and that end is security. If we fail to work for that we betray the cause of liberty. We are responsible to those for whom we work. Our aim must be the welfare of our population."[80] To many of the leaders of the newly independent states in Asia and Africa, formal

[78] Ahmed Sékou Touré, *Expérience Guinéenne et Unité Africaine* (Paris: Présence Africaine, 1961), 81–82.

[79] Cooper, "Alternatives to Nationalism in West Africa, 1945–1960", 127–131.

[80] Ahmed Sekou Touré, "The Republic of Guinea." Address at Chatham House, 13 November 1959, *International Affairs* 36 no. 2 (1960): 168–173, at 171.

independence but inaugurated a new phase of neo-colonialism. Such themes were systematically articulated by Kwame Nkrumah in his *Neocolonialism. The Last Stage of Imperialism* (1965), in which he argued that "[t]he essence of neo-colonialism is that the State which is subject to it is, in theory, independent and has all the trappings of outward sovereignty. In reality its economic system and thus its political policy is directed from the outside."[81] Hence neo-colonialism hollowed out independence, since "[a] state in the grip of neo-colonialism is not the master of its own destiny."[82] To the loss of *de facto* independence corresponded the lack of responsibility among former imperial powers, since for the latter, "it means power without responsibility, and for those who suffer from it, it means exploitation without redress."[83] Neo-colonialism, although made possible by the invisible hand of world capitalism, had a distinctive political dimension insofar as it allowed for a reiteration the old imperial practice of *divide et impere* by "breaking up former large united colonial territories into a number of small non-viable States which are incapable of independent development and must rely upon the former imperial power for defence and even internal security."[84] This in turn could but fuel geopolitical competition, since "neo-colonialism increases the rivalry between the great powers which was provoked by the old-style colonialism."[85] And although neo-colonialism was first put into practice by former imperial masters, it now radiated outwards from the new imperial center: the United States, whose seeming support for decolonization was but a foil for its own imperial ambitions. Since the rise of neo-colonialism coincided with the creation of welfare states in the developed world, this meant that "developed countries succeeded in exporting their internal problem and transferring the conflict between rich and poor from the national to the international stage."[86] Being the "last hideous gasp" of imperialism, the only way to resist neo-colonialism was through *unity*: "Primary and basic is the need for an all-union government on the much divided continent of Africa."[87]

Thus, by the end of the 1960s, it had become a commonplace among anticolonial statesmen and intellectuals that formal independence just

[81] Kwame Nkrumah, *Neo-Colonialism. The Last Stage of Imperialism* [1965] (London: Panaf, 1970), ix.
[82] Ibid., x. [83] Ibid., xi. [84] Ibid., xiii. [85] Ibid., xiv. [86] Ibid., 254.
[87] Ibid., 253.

marked the beginning of a long and arduous struggle against neocolonial forms of domination and exploitation. Even if some begged to disagree, many were convinced that this struggle required nothing less than wholesale social revolutions in postcolonial states to be successful. As a slightly radicalized Sékou Touré claimed in 1973, "real independence, requires first of all a decolonization of mentalities, the achievement of an autonomous policy, that is *political sovereignty* based on an ideology whose reference is the People."[88] Only with full popular sovereignty over the means of production could new states in Africa and elsewhere hope to achieve the final objective of decolonization, namely "the economic independence, the preservation against the imperialist rapacity of our resources which are numerous."[89]

The anticolonial leaders discussed above all shared a commitment to the idea of African unity, either as a precursor to independence or as its consequence. Whereas the contours and composition of this union were subject to much debate, its desirability was rarely questioned. A notable exception in this regard was Frantz Fanon, whose *Les Damnés de la Terre* (1961) poured cold water on what he took to be the naïve cosmopolitanism of the native bourgeoisies in postcolonial states. The attempts to achieve nationhood had not only failed to overcome but had in effect re-entrenched colonial divisions so that "the nation is passed over for the race, and the tribe is preferred to the state."[90] In this predicament "weakness, which is almost congenital to the national consciousness of underdeveloped countries, is not solely the result of the mutilation of the colonized people by the colonial regime. It is also the result of the intellectual laziness of the national middle class, of its spiritual penury, and of the profoundly cosmopolitan mold that its mind is set in."[91] To Fanon, African unity was but a fading illusion reflecting the inability

[88] Ahmed Sékou Touré, *Afrika and Imperialism* [Address delivered after the assassination of Amílcar Cabral] (Newark, NJ.: Jihad Publishing, 1973), 8.

[89] Ibid., 10.

[90] Frantz Fanon, *The Wretched of the Earth*. trans, by Constance Farrington (New York: Grove Weidenfeld, 1963), 148. For similar interpretations, see Inés Valdez, "Cosmopolitanism without National Consciousness is not Radical: Creolizing Gordon's Fanon through Du Bois." *Philosophy and Global Affairs* (2021); Julian Go, "Fanon's Postcolonial Cosmopolitanism." *European Journal of Social Theory* 16 no. 2 (2013): 208–225; Begüm Adalet, "Infrastructures of Decolonization: Scales of Worldmaking in the Writings of Frantz Fanon." *Political Theory* 50 no. 1 (2022): 5–31.

[91] Ibid., 148.

of postcolonial states to achieve a real national consciousness distinct from the corrupt nationalism promulgated by the elites, to the point that "African unity takes off the mask, and crumbles into regionalism inside the hollow shell of nationality itself."[92] The struggle for independence and emancipation from domination must therefore start at home before it can spill over into the realization of any transnational unity among African peoples. Ideas of such unity also rested on the premise that it depended racial distinctions. Yet precisely because of their vested interests, "[t]he national bourgeoisies, who are quite clear as to what their objectives are, have decided to bar the way to that unity…This is why we must understand that African unity can only be achieved through the upward thrust of the people, and under the leadership of the people, that is to say, in defiance of the interests of the bourgeoisie."[93] Thus African unity "is not the fact of a metaphysical principle but the awareness of a simple rule which wills that every independent nation in an Africa where colonialism is still entrenched is an encircled nation, a nation which is fragile and in permanent danger."[94] This implied that nationhood should be understood as a condition of possible internationalism rather than its negation, since "the building of a nation is of necessity accompanied by the discovery and encouragement of universalizing values…it is national liberation which leads the nation to play its part on the stage of history. It is at the heart of national consciousness that international consciousness lives and grows."[95]

Last but not least in this genealogy of freedom fighters stood Amílcar Cabral, who devoted his short life to the liberation of his native Guiné and its sister colony Cabo Verde from Portuguese domination. In a desperate attempt to cling to their overseas possessions in new and adverse geopolitical circumstances, the Salazar government had enacted a constitutional change in 1951 which recast the Portuguese empire as a single and indivisible transcontinental state, into which its colonies were legally incorporated as extensions of Portuguese mainland territory.[96] Through this devious

[92] Ibid., 158. [93] Ibid., 163. [94] Ibid., 246. [95] Ibid., 246–247.

[96] See Norrie MacQueen, "Belated Decolonization and UN Politics against the backdrop of the Cold War." *Journal of Cold War Studies* 8 no. 4 (2006): 29–56; Bruno Cardoso Reis, "Portugal and the UN: A Rogue State Resisting the Norm of Decolonization (1956–1974)." *Portuguese Studies*, 29 no. 2 (2013), 251–76; Norrie MacQueen, *The Decolonization of Portuguese Africa. Metropolitan Revolution and the Dissolution of Empire* (London: Longmans, 1997).

move, the Portuguese government could circumvent demands of self-determination enshrined in the UN charter by arguing that their overseas territories were *not* entitled to independence because their peoples *already* enjoyed self-determination by virtue of being citizens of the same Portuguese transcontinental state.[97] As Cabral described this arrangement, "[t]his disgraceful subterfuge totally contradicts all the geographic, historic, ethnic, social and cultural facts, and it even comes into conflict with the laws prevailing in the colonies concerning their practical relationship with Portugal."[98] Having detailed the innumerable injustices perpetrated by the Portuguese in Africa, Cabral demanded that Portugal should abide by the UN charter and recognize the right of self-determination and independence of its African colonies.[99] With little hope that the Lisbon government would yield without armed struggle, Cabral outlined a strategy for his *Partido Africano para a Independência da Guiné e Cabo Verde*. The foremost requirement for attaining independence was unity, whose basic principle "lies in the difference between the items", which implied that particular interests should be cast aside in "the sense of removing the enemy's potential for exploiting the contradictions there might be among our population in order to weaken the strength of ours that we must pit against that of the enemy."[100] Social unity was as much a condition of successful struggle as well as conversely, because "to have unity it is also necessary to struggle."[101] That struggle had to begin at home in order to stand a chance of success. As Cabral argued in a famous

[97] For the ideological justifications of this reconceptualization, see Jens Bartelson, "Acabando con el Imperio: Lusotropicalismo como ideología imperial." *Relaciones Internacionales* 30 (2015): 11–26; Cláudia Castelo, *O Modo Português de Estar no Mundo: O lusotropicalismo e a ideologia colonial portuguesa, 1933–1961* (Porto: Edições Afrontamento, 1998), 13–67.

[98] Amílcar Cabral, "The Facts about Portugal's African Colonies." [1960] in *Unity and Struggle: Speeches and Writings of Amílcar Cabral.* trans. by Michael Wolfers (London and New York: Monthly Review Press, 1979), 19. For an analysis of Cabral's thought, see Branwen Gruffydd Jones, "Race, Culture and Liberation: African Anticolonial Thought and Practice in the Time of Decolonisation." *The International History Review* 42 no. 6 (2020): 1238–1256.

[99] Ibid., 27.

[100] Amílcar Cabral, "Party Principles and Political Practice." in *Unity and Struggle: Speeches and Writings of Amílcar Cabral*, 29 & 31.

[101] Ibid., 33.

speech delivered in Havana in 1966, the struggle for independence was first and foremost a struggle against "the internal contradictions in the economic, social, cultural...reality of each of our countries."[102] Thus, national liberation required a simultaneous social revolution whose dynamic was "essentially determined and conditioned by the historical reality of each people. Victory is only achieved by the adequate resolution of the various internal contradictions characterizing this reality."[103] For those on the receiving end of imperial domination, this had resulted in the destruction or ostensible preservation of their primordial forms of life at the hands of European settlers, thereby feeding those internal social contradictions that would become the springboard of future liberation. The struggle for independence had also an indispensable cultural component, since colonial domination "arouses and develops the cultural alienation of a section of the populace either by the so-called assimilation of the indigenous people or by the creation of a social abyss between an indigenous elite and the popular masses."[104] From this followed a simple formula: "the national liberation of a people is the regaining of the historical personality of that people."[105] But as notions of transcontinental unity were further disseminated to legitimize Portuguese rule, attempts to divide and rule along sociocultural lines became difficult to pursue without giving rise to blatant contradictions which Cabral was quick to capitalize on rhetorically.[106] Yet what appeared as an isolated quest for independence in a small corner of the vast African continent had wide-ranging consequences insofar as it bestowed anticolonial struggles in the rest of lusophone Africa with their peculiar revolutionary fervor and eventually brought what remained of the last European empire to an abrupt end after *O Revolução dos Cravos* in 1974.

In this section we have seen how anticolonial rhetoric was based on a blend of primordialism, anti-imperialism, and nationalism. While some

[102] Amílcar Cabral, "The Weapon of Theory" ("Presuppositions and objectives of national liberation in relation to social structure"). Address delivered to the first Tricontinental Conference of the Peoples of Asia, Africa and Latin America held in Havana in January, 1966, in *Unity and Struggle: Speeches and Writings of Amílcar Cabral*, 119–137, at 120.

[103] Ibid., 122.

[104] Amílcar Cabral, "National Liberation and Culture." *Transitions* 45 (1974): 12–17, at 14.

[105] Cabral, "Weapon of Theory", 130.

[106] Cabral, "Party Principles and Political Practice", 35–44.

followed the familiar European template that prescribed a congruence of states and nations, others tried to find ways to transcend the limits of that template in favor of transnational forms of political association and multilayered forms of sovereignty. Some of those attempts found inspiration in existing imperial modes of indirect governance and found fleeting support in post-war efforts to redefine European empires – most notably the British and French – so as to accommodate pleas for equal social and political rights under the auspices of wider communities – federal or confederal – which with hindsight looked like little but halfway houses to independence.[107] But since the anti-colonialists discussed above were convinced that the causes of imperialism and colonialism were to be found in the *modus operandi* of international system as a whole rather than in the malign dispositions of their individual masters, their struggles for self-determination had a distinct international dimension as well. Not only did anticolonial thinkers and leaders project their expectations for the future onto the international realm, but that realm also provided the very vehicle for realizing claims to independence by means international recognition in a period when the latter came relatively cheap. Membership of the international system in turn raised the prospects of reforming that system in a more egalitarian direction by doing away with the remnants of empire and taming the global forces of capitalism. But membership also offered a protective shell for state making enterprises at home, since norms of non-intervention and non-interference could be used to keep would-be meddlers at bay: Sadly, many of the anticolonial leaders discussed in this section pushed states in an authoritarian direction in response to mounting domestic and international pressures to conform to either communist or capitalist models of legitimacy and development.

But by plugging into the modern international system, new states were quickly trapped by its *ius necessarium* insofar as they had been recognized precisely as *states* with continuous and bounded territories rather than as any other form of political association – real or imagined – and this irrespective of what they happened to look like on the inside, or what their leaders had in mind for the future of their peoples. Hence the window of opportunity for transforming the international system that had been opened in Bandung was being closed

[107] For an analysis, see Michael Collins, "Decolonisation and the 'Federal Moment'." *Diplomacy & Statecraft* 24 no. 1 (2013): 21–40.

once a critical number of colonial states had attained independence and international recognition. As Byrne has noted about this development, "the net result of decolonization was a dramatically more state-centric world order than had been true of even the very late colonial post-World War II years."[108]

Decolonization as Diffusion

In the decades following the end of the Second World War, the abolition of formal empire and colonialism was perceived as urgent and desirable across the ideological spectrum in the West. Some Western intellectuals embraced this cause with great enthusiasm and did their best to promote it. Perhaps foremost among them was Jean-Paul Sartre, whose anticolonial ethos inspired a generation of African leaders and galvanized opposition against the war in Algeria at home.[109] His peculiar blend of Marxism and existentialism emphasized the systemic sources of colonialism while insisting on the dialectical character of anticolonial struggle and its role in recovering authentic selves. As he argued it in his introduction to Albert Memmi's *Portrait du colonisé, précédé par Portrait du colonisateur* (1957), since colonialist society cannot integrate the natives without destroying itself, "the colonized must discover the unity in opposition to that society. The excluded human beings will affirm their exclusivity in national selfhood."[110]

But the emergence of new states also spurred host of analyses and commentaries from social scientists which often were linked to attempts to promote the modernization and development of new-born states. Being largely supportive of the anti-imperialist and anti-colonial causes, many of these commentaries assumed that the rise of new states marked the final stage in a longer transition from a world of empires to a world of states, and that such transition was a consequence of the diffusion of Western ideas and institutions to the non-Western world. From this it was concluded that successful self-determination – manifested in the creation of nation-states – depended

108 Byrne, *Mecca of Revolution*, 9.

109 See, for example, Azzedine Haddour, "Remembering Sartre." in Jean-Paul Sartre, *Colonialism and Neocolonialism* (London & New York: Routledge, 2006), 1–21.

110 Jean-Paul Sartre, "Introduction." in Albert Memmi, *The Colonizer and the Colonized* (Boston: Beacon Press, 1967), xxi–xxxi, at xxviii.

on how well these nation-states emulated Western ideas and institutions. In this section, I will analyze some of the main interventions in debates on modernization and development in the Third World that took place during decolonization.

In one of the first statements in this genre, *On Alien Rule and Self Government* (1960), political theorist John Plamenatz described self-determination in terms of the successful emulation of Western ideas among peoples subjected to colonial rule. "If it is right that governments should be responsible to the governed", Plamenatz argued, "then there is wrong for one people to impose their rule on another...[a]nd if democracy is, in the modern world, a condition of individual freedom, then alien rule is also incompatible with that freedom."[111] Yet since democracy and freedom undeniably are ideals of European origin, "to the extent that peoples of Asia and Africa subject to European rule demand independence for the sake of democracy and freedom, they can be said to be claiming against the West he right to imitate the West."[112] In that regard Asian and African peoples had no real choice, since they "cannot now return to what they used to be before the Europeans forced themselves upon them...[t]hough they resent European interference, they now no longer have, either for themselves or for their countries, the ambitions of their ancestors."[113] Hence the "aspiration and the desire for self-government are themselves effects of the process started by the Europeans."[114] Plamenatz was here thoughtlessly recycling the late nineteenth-century view according to which self-government required a certain degree of political maturity on behalf of the people in question, and believed that colonialism largely had been conducive to the attainment of such maturity.

Moving on to discuss the capacity for self-government among colonial peoples, Plamenatz outlined four criteria before discussing the extent to which colonial societies must possess them in order to qualify as states proper. Whereas the two first concerned governmental capacity in more general terms – such as the ability to protect trade and industry as well as the ability to provide "security of person and good government by the standards of western Europe"– the third concerned the extent to which their rulers are likely to respect the rules

[111] John Plamenatz, *On Alien Rule and Self Government* (London: Longmans, 1960), 1.
[112] Ibid., 2. [113] Ibid., 15. [114] Ibid., 16.

of international law however European in spirit and origin the latter might be.[115] Yet the most important criterion when considering whether a people aspiring to independence is fit for self-government is "the ability to work the institutions that make democracy and freedom effective."[116] The peculiarity of this criterion resided in the fact that it also served to justify continued alien rule on the grounds that many colonial societies lacked such institutions. Yet if "the subject people aspire to democracy and freedom, the alien rule ought, if possible, to see to it that they do not get independence under conditions likely to prevent their getting the freedom and democracy they want."[117] To the extent that the quest for self-government was facilitated by the rise of nationalism, that was because "the nation, as a self-conscious unit, is mostly the product...of common reactions to foreign rule."[118]

But the conditions most conducive to democratic government were more cultural than institutional in character as they depended on the nature of society rather than on the quality of government. Hence the freedom indispensable democracy presupposed that "all men are to be allowed to pursue their own good as they chose so it provided that their good require them to make other men subservient to themselves."[119] And however elitist his conception of democracy was, "[i]n a democracy which is genuine and enduring all classes and groups and professions are organized to make definite demands on one another and on government."[120] Finally, although his stated task was not to judge *which* societies were qualified for self-government, Plamenatz nevertheless issued some warnings to colonizers and colonized alike. The former were advised never "to hold on to a colony or dependency *at any cost*, even if it is still, by your standards very far from fit for self-government."[121] The latter were duly reminded that since the Europeans remained more powerful, "your strength lies chiefly in the fact that your subjection is against their principles" and cautioned them that if "the world were to be divided into the 'white' against the 'coloured' peoples, it is the coloured who would be the more in danger."[122]

Another example of commentaries in this genre is *From Empire to Nation* (1960) by political scientist Rupert Emerson, a pioneering work that paved the way for many later accounts of the process of decolonization. Emerson was even more adamant that the transition

[115] Ibid., 40 & 39–42. [116] Ibid., 47. [117] Ibid., 49. [118] Ibid., 88.
[119] Ibid., 61. [120] Ibid., 68. [121] Ibid., 206. [122] Ibid., 207 & 208.

from empires to states hinged on a diffusion of Western ideas and institutions, and that imperialism had been the prime vehicle for spreading European civilization to other continents. After the end of the Second World War which had "made self-determination a living principle for the non-European world", "non-white peoples of the earth had declared, in terms which no one could refute, that they were no longer prepared to accept the position of inferiority which lay at the heart of the imperialist system."[123] Whereas imperial expansion had been made possible by the superior power of the West, "the peoples who came under the sway of the white man should soon yearn to possess the secrets and the sources of his power for themselves."[124] They were thus left with a choice: "either to seek out and adopt these things from which the white man derived his power or to accept a subordination to which there was no foreseeable end and which might involve disintegration as well."[125] Hence the seeds of independence and self-determination had been sown by the imperial powers themselves, since "through global conquest the dominant Western powers worked to reshape the world in their own image and thus roused against themselves the forces of nationalisms which are both the bitterest enemies of imperialism and, perversely, its finest fruit."[126]

But where Plamenatz had given nationalism and nationhood only a cursory treatment and did not seem to regard them as indispensable to self-government, Emerson took them to be both cause and consequence of self-determination. Emerson understood nationalism and nationhood as distinct European creations the spread of which had been promoted by colonial rule. With few exceptions, leaders struggling for independence in Africa and Asia had done so by trying to achieve national unity where there had been no unity of this kind before. While colonial governments could offer rule of law at best, "[a] far deeper emotional appeal lay in the concept of the nation which the rising leadership brought back from its study of the West ... It offered not only a new community to unite societies in the process of atomization, but also a program of action in which the people themselves were the principal actors."[127] But whereas "the nationalist in

[123] Rupert Emerson, *From Empire to Nation. The Rise to Self-Assertion of Asian and African Peoples* (Cambridge, MA.: Harvard University Press, 1960), 2 & 1.
[124] Ibid., 10. [125] Ibid., 10. [126] Ibid., 16–17. [127] Ibid., 84–85.

Europe and some other parts of the world could appeal to reasonably clearly delimited people already in part aware of its identity ... the African nationalist still has before him the entire task of creating the nations in whose name he professes to speak."[128] Furthermore, since most colonial societies lacked the essential characteristics of modern statehood, national leaders faced a double challenge, since it is "inevitable that there should have been, and still should be, a great revolutionary struggle to secure a coincidence between state and nation."[129] The success of that struggle in turn required that colonial peoples were ready to relinquish all their other allegiances in the process, since "it is a characteristic feature of the national era that for most men the national allegiance takes precedence over all other claims made upon them when they are confronted by alternative choices of allegiance, as most strikingly in time of war."[130]

Yet the value of nationhood resided not only in the cohesion it could bestow on postcolonial states. Emerson, like many before him, was eager to point out that nationalism and nationhood had been mighty precursors to democratization in Europe and elsewhere. Yet the road from nationalism to democracy was far from straight. Emerson was quick to mention the many aberrant cases in which nationalism had instead engendered authoritarian forms of rule, yet he maintained that "[t]he experience of the modern world suggests that national unity has been a necessary condition of democracy, but that it is far from being a sufficient one." But European experiences "indicate that democracy has been at its best where history has shaped homogenous peoples who managed to dispose at a relatively early stage of some of the more urgent issues of national identity."[131] New Asian and African states were struggling not only to achieve national unity, but to make their still fragile states safe for democracy. Yet the mismatch between constitutional principles and political realities had "been rudely emphasized by the recent abandonment of democratic pretensions in several of the new states."[132] Again the hope for successful democratization laid in their ability to learn from their former masters, since "[w]ith the customary lag in overseas application, the doctrines and practices which evolve in the metropole will be applied in the colonies."[133] But quite irrespective of whether these states were yet democratic or not,

[128] Ibid., 94. [129] Ibid., 96. [130] Ibid., 97. [131] Ibid., 221.
[132] Ibid., 227–228. [133] Ibid., 229.

the "key factor common to all of them is that they have presented themselves to the world as nations – even though the observer may have occasional doubts as to how widely and deeply the sense of nationhood has penetrated."[134]

Both Plamenatz and Emerson described decolonization as a transition from empires to nation-states driven by the diffusion of Western ideas and institutions whose emulation was necessary to self-determination. Whereas Plamenatz placed his bets on the dissemination of Westminster-style democracy, Emerson took nationhood to be a necessary condition of both independence and democracy. Yet they were in broad agreement that the world emerging before their eyes was one composed of nation-states, and that these nation-states together formed a truly global international system. This elevation of the nation-state into the sole locus of legitimate authority was reinforced by the simultaneous naturalization of nationalism and nationhood in and out of academia. As we saw in the previous chapter, during the late nineteenth and early twentieth century, nationalism had been understood primarily as an *ideology* designated to promote the congruence of state and nation within the same territory. Yet curiously, although the Second World War had made the perils of nationalism plain to anyone, this spurred a renewed academic interest in nationalism that treated nationhood as a natural fact of the sociopolitical world rather than as a historical contingency of a distinctively European pedigree. As Hans Kohn had stated in his pioneering *The Idea of Nationalism* (1944), "[n]ationalism is a state of mind, permeating the large majority of a people, and claiming to permeate all its members; it recognizes the nation-state as the ideal form of political organization and the nationality as the source of all creative cultural energy and of economic well-being."[135] This naturalization of nationhood proceeded further with the publication of *Nationalism and Social Communication* (1953) by Karl Deutsch. Having criticized extant definitions of nationalism for being both subjective and vague, Deutsch suggested that nationality ought to be understood as nothing more than a consequence of social communication. If definitions of nationality in terms of language, character and history

134 Ibid., 418.

135 Hans Kohn, *The Idea of Nationalism. A Study in Its Origins and Background* (New Brunswick: Transaction Books, 2008), 16.

are open to exception, "merely the presence of sufficient communication facilities with enough complementarity to produce the overall result."[136] From this assumption he inferred that "[m]embership in a people essentially consists in wide complementarity of social communication."[137] For a people to turn into a nation-state requires a successful claim to sovereignty on its behalf, since "nationalities turn into nations when they acquire power to back up their aspirations… if their nationalistic members are successful, and a new or old state organization is put into their service, then at last the nation has become sovereign, and a, nation-state has come into being."[138]

To many social scientists at this time, it was obvious that the new states were beset by divisions of a magnitude that made the diffusion of democratic institutions and the creation of national identities to support them difficult. In contrast to anti-imperialist statesmen and intellectuals in Asia and Africa, Western social scientists were inclined to believe that these divisions were endogenous to colonial polities rather than products of imperial rule. In order to come to terms with decolonization, these authors tried to rinse the concept of nationhood from its ideological baggage in order to demonstrate its usefulness in a postcolonial context. But by doing so, they provided additional impetus to the already manifest tendency to regard the nation-state as the epitome of civilizational advancement and cultural sophistication. Although the fresh focus on the nation-state led to disputes about *what* a nation is or ought to be, it cancelled all doubt as to *that* it is or at least ought to be. In many new states, the ensuing quest for nationhood gave rise to permanent minorities and prompted their redescription as underdeveloped ethnic groups unfit for self-determination.

In the context of the Cold War, the feared fallout of independence gone astray prompted the Ford Foundation to grant support to the Committee for the Comparative Study of New Nations at the University of Chicago in 1963. Mobilizing brilliant minds in the social sciences under the chairmanship of Clifford Geertz, this committee was tasked with exploring the prospects of modernization and democratization within newly independent states. Its trademark publication

136 Karl W. Deutsch, *Nationalism and Social Communication: An inquiry into the foundations of nationality* (Cambridge, MA.: MIT Press, 1966), 97.
137 Ibid., 97. 138 Ibid., 105.

entitled *New States and Old Societies* appeared in 1963, edited by Geertz and featuring essays by Edward Shils and David Apter among others. As Shils argued in the introductory essay, in almost all of the new states "societies consist of relatively discrete collectivities – ethnic, communal, caste, religious, or linguistic – that have little sense of identity with one another or with the national whole."[139] They have not reached the "point where the people they rule have become nations, more or less coterminous with the state in territorial boundaries."[140] Geertz – who had extensive fieldwork experience from Indonesia – argued that new states were torn between the conflicting imperatives of achieving recognition of their unique identities on the one hand, and the practical imperatives of achieving order and development by building a dynamic state on the other. To Geertz, "[t]his tension takes a peculiarly severe and chronic form in the new states, both because of the great extent to which their peoples' sense of self remains bound up in the gross actualities of blood, race, language, locality, religion, or tradition, and because of the steadily accelerating importance in this century of the sovereign state as a positive instrument for the realization of collective aims."[141] To subordinate the desire for identity and recognition to the demands of sovereign statehood would be for the community in question "to risk a loss of definition as an autonomous person, either through absorption into a culturally undifferentiated mass or, what is even worse, through a domination by some other rival ethnic, racial, or linguistic community that is able to imbue that order with the temper of its own personality."[142] To Apter – who had done equally extensive fieldwork in Ghana and Uganda – many new states had responded to the challenges posed by independence and development not by adopting democratic and pluralist institutions, but by means of "new political forms...that have the effect of providing for the continuity, meaning, and purpose of an individual's

[139] Edward Shils, "On the Comparative Study of New States." in Clifford Geertz (ed.) *Old Societies and New States: The Quest for Modernity in Asia and Africa* (New York: The Free Press, 1963), 1–26, at 3.

[140] Ibid., 3.

[141] Clifford Geertz, "The Integrative Revolution: Primordial Sentiments and Civil Politics in the New States." in Clifford Geertz (ed.) *Old Societies and New States: The Quest for Modernity in Asia and Africa* (New York: The Free Press, 1963), 105–157, at 106.

[142] Ibid., 107.

actions."[143] This coalesced in the rise of "political religion", systems of belief which served to "strengthen authority in the state and weaken the flexibility of the society. Hence it becomes difficult to change from autocratic to more democratic and secular patterns of political organization and social belief."[144] Thus, what had initially been optimistic assessments of the prospects of the diffusion of Western institutions soon gave way to a fear that many new states were gravitating in an authoritarian and ultimately communist direction largely because of their lack of social cohesion and legitimate government. Hence it seemed all the more urgent to explore the conditions of modernization and development in more detail.

The academic interest in new states soon bifurcated along well-known disciplinary lines in the United States. Whereas anthropologists like Geertz advocated a more contextually sensitive and interpretative approach to modernization and development, others followed Shils in his positivist conviction that the proper study of modernization "must go beyond the meaning the events have to those who share in them" in favor of more attention to "patterns and structures, even when these are not perceived or appreciated by those who participate in them."[145] From this it followed that the comparative study of new states required "categories equally applicable to all states and societies...variations must be subsumable within these categories."[146] With the Committee on Comparative Politics of the Social Science Research Council having been formed in 1953, there was no shortage of young political scientists who responded to this call to arms. Among the volumes published under the auspices of this committee was *Political Culture and Political Development* (1965), edited by Lucian Pye and Sidney Verba, devoted to comparing states at different levels of development across the world.[147] Motivated by the fact that "the dramatic emergence of a host of new sovereign states has abruptly confronted statesmen with baffling questions about the nature of differences in the conduct of politics", the introduction promised to answer questions like to "what

[143] David E. Apter, "Political Religion in the New Nations." in Clifford Geertz (ed.) *Old Societies and New States: The Quest for Modernity in Asia and Africa* (New York: The Free Press, 1963), 57–104, at 59.

[144] Ibid., 59.

[145] Shils, "On the Comparative Study of New States", 6.

[146] Ibid., 13.

[147] Lucian W. Pye and Sidney Verba (eds.) *Political Culture and Political Development* (Princeton, NJ.: Princeton University Press, 1965).

extent is it possible to accelerate and direct political change, and how can traditional societies be best transformed into democratic polities?"[148] In a conscious effort to split the difference between the conflicting pressures of generalization and contextualization, contributors to this volume further developed the concept of *political culture* that had been introduced by Gabriel Almond almost a decade earlier.[149] The concept of political culture was now used to refer to "to the system of beliefs about patterns of political interaction and political institutions. It refers not to what is happening in the world of politics, but what people believe about those happenings."[150] When exploring the multiple connections between political culture and political development, the latter was taken to signify among other things "the creation of a viable nation-state capable of performing effectively in the modern world....[and]... the advance of liberty, popular sovereignty, and free institutions."[151] As Verba was able to conclude in a chapter widely regarded as path-breaking, the paramount challenge facing new states in this regard was the creation of national identities, since "[t]he creation of a national identity among members of a nation is the cultural equivalent of the drawing of the boundaries of the nation."[152]

Others took a more nomothetic approach to modernization and development, giving rise to what would later become known as modernization theory.[153] In contrast to the more interpretative approach characteristic of area studies, the focus was here on the general determinants of state making and democratization. As Seymour Martin Lipset argued in an article that came to define the parameters of much subsequent research, "economic development

[148] Ibid., 3–26, at 4.

[149] Gabriel A. Almond, "Comparative Political Systems." *Journal of Politics* 18 no. 3 (1956): 391–409. Also Gabriel A. Almond and Sidney Verba, *The Civic Culture: Political Attitudes and Democracy in Five Nations* (Princeton, NJ.: Princeton University Press, 1963).

[150] Sidney Verba, "Comparative Political Culture", in Lucian W. Pye and Sidney Verba (eds.) *Political Culture and Political Development* (Princeton, NJ.: Princeton University Press, 1965), 512–560, at 516.

[151] Pye, "Introduction", 12. [152] Verba, "Comparative Political Culture", 530.

[153] For an analysis, see Nils Gilman, *Mandarins of the Future: Modernization Theory in Cold War America* (Baltimore: Johns Hopkins University Press, 2003).

involving industrialization, urbanization, high educational standards, and a steady increase in the overall wealth of the society, is a basic condition sustaining democracy."[154] To this Lipset added the observation that "[t]he extent to which contemporary democratic political systems are legitimate depends in large measure upon the ways in which the key issues which have historically divided the society have been resolved."[155] David Apter – whose work now had gravitated in a nomothetic direction – found the clues to development and democratization in the gradual secularization of postcolonial societies and the abolition of political religion as a means of political mobilization in the developing world.[156] Finally, the notorious Walt Rostow, writing against the backdrop of "the grave difficulties encountered in Asia, the Middle East, Africa and Latin America by those who have tried to make government by consent of the governed operate", argued that political development in those regions had been hampered by "autocratic or totalitarian leaders who have chosen...to build their domestic politics on 'anti-imperialism'."[157] Instead of embarking on ideologically driven expansionist adventures, Rostow believed that the cure consisted in "the achievement of an effective sense of nationhood as the first challenge of following upon the legal establishment of statehood."[158] With a host of new states being studied either in isolation or in comparison with others, the focus was on the consequences of decolonization for new states in terms of state capacity and democratization, while the global consequences of the universalization of the nation-state form largely escaped attention outside of international law, which was struggling to accommodate new facts on the ground.[159]

Given the widespread conviction that formal empire was illegitimate, it is hard to find any strong objections to decolonization during this

[154] Seymour Martin Lipset, "Some Social Requisites of Democracy: Economic Development and Political Legitimacy." *American Political Science Review* 53 no. 1 (1959): 69–105, at 86.

[155] Ibid., 86.

[156] David E. Apter, *The Politics of Modernization* (Chicago: University of Chicago Press, 1965).

[157] Walt W. Rostow, *Politics and the Stages of Growth* (Cambridge: Cambridge University Press, 1971), 5 & 279.

[158] Ibid., 283.

[159] For recent analyses, see Jochen von Bernstorff and Philipp Dann (eds.) *The Battle for International Law: South-North Perspectives on the Decolonization Era* (Oxford: Oxford University Press, 2019).

period, despite the many dull scenarios painted by American social scientists. Yet a few voices deserve to be mentioned because of the thrust of their arguments and their later uptake. For example, although not opposed to decolonization as such, the lawyer Clyde Eagleton found the practices of international recognition problematic because of their inherent arbitrariness. Self-determination, he argued, "cannot be allowed to any group for the sole reason that the group chooses to claim it. The United Nations must inquire whether there is enough homogeneity or unity or common desire to hold the new state together; whether it has economic resources and political capacity; how far it can defend self against attack."[160] In a similar vein, now from the standpoint of constitutional rather than international law, Ivor Jennings maintained that colonial territories only should be granted independence on condition that they were economically self-reliant and had acquired sufficient administrative and other capacities.[161] To this one might add the fact that some American realists feared that self-determination might run counter to the national interest. Thus, as Philip Bell had argued already in 1952, that despite the American commitment to the principle of self-determination, "[s]upport, rather than general condemnation, of colonialism is clearly the path for the United States where such a relationship is the only feasible alternative because of meager resources, or where the relationship is not subject to dispute."[162]

Others were not convinced that a congruence of nation and state was desirable in a postcolonial context. To Elie Kedourie, nationalism was as much a recipe for discord and oppression in the non-European world as it had been in early twentieth century Europe. As he argued in *Nationalism* (1960), the modernization of non-Western societies has "worked to debilitate and destroy tribalism and its social and political traditions. The consequence is an atomized society which seeks in nationalism a substitute for the old order, now irrevocably lost."[163] The connection of mandates and trusts to promises of

[160] Clyde Eagleton, "Excesses of Self-determination." *Foreign Affairs* 31 no. 4 (1953): 592–604, at 602; Clyde Eagleton, "Self-determination in the United Nations." *American Journal of International Law* 47 no. 1 (1953): 88–93.

[161] W. Ivor Jennings, *The Approach to Self-government* (Cambridge: Cambridge University Press, 1956).

[162] Philip W. Bell, "Colonialism as a Problem in American Foreign Policy." *World Politics* 5 no. 1 (1952): 86–109, at 109.

[163] Elie Kedourie, *Nationalism* (Oxford: Blackwell, 1993), 107.

self-determination under the League of Nations had been especially unfortunate in this regard, since their very impermanence deprived governments of effective means to establish a viable political order in advance of independence. In sum, and echoing Lord Acton, "the attempts to refashion so much of the world on national lines has not led to greater peace and stability. On the contrary, it has created new conflicts, exacerbated tensions, and brought catastrophe to numberless people innocent of all politics."[164]

Still others worried about the norms of sovereign equality and non-interference underwriting decolonization. For example, concerned with the impact of decolonization on the Cold War, Raymond Aron argued that although the norm of sovereign equality "has justified the recognition of the formal equality of all peoples" once states are recognized as members of the United Nations, "their governments invoke the ideology of 'sovereign equality' in order to reject the interventions either of the other states or even of the international organization itself."[165] Thus Aron feared that postcolonial states would hide behind these principles in order to get away with things that would violate the spirit of the UN Charter as well as the will of the international community. Although objections like these were mostly ignored or even scorned by contemporaries, they would resurface some decades later in debates about the causes of state failure, as many postcolonial states seemed condemned to lasting weakness and dysfunction.[166]

In this section, I have outlined some of the more salient responses provoked by the quest for self-determination and the rise of new states in Asia and Africa during the decades following the end of the Second World War. Although not everyone shared the unbridled enthusiasm of Jean-Paul Sartre and his *rive gauche* friends, most of these responses reflected the extent to which imperial rule had been delegitimized and the right of self-determination accepted across the ideological spectrum in the West. Yet most scholars pondering the consequences of

164 Ibid., 133–134.

165 Raymond Aron, *Peace and War. A Theory of International Relations* [1966] (New Brunswick: Transaction Books, 2009), 743.

166 See, for example, Gerard Kreijen and Robert Y. Jennings, *State Failure, Sovereignty and Effectiveness: Legal lessons from the decolonization of sub-Saharan Africa* (Leiden: Brill Nijhoff, 2004); Arjun Chowdhury, *The Myth of International Order. Why weak states persist and alternatives to the State fade away* (Oxford: Oxford University Press, 2018).

decolonization did so convinced that to the extent that decolonization marked a transition from a world of empires to a world of states, this was due to the successful diffusion of Western political ideas and institutions. While those scholars sometimes disagreed about *which* of these ideas and institutions were the most important and how to best promote their diffusion, there was an underlying consensus to the effect that the nation-state was the only possible form into which these ideas and institutions could be diffused with the intended outcomes of stability and prosperity.

Hence the omnipresent emphasis on nationhood, and hence the many difficulties to dovetail that concept with those of state and territoriality in those new and alien contexts that made the careers of an entire generation of comparativists. By sharing the above beliefs, however, Western social scientists were not in a good position to grasp the upshot of the anticolonial ideologies that animated the quests for independence in Asia and Africa, and which continued to inform state making processes well into the 1970s. Whereas the former operated under the assumption that the social and political divisions that threatened the cohesion of new-born states were endogenous and primordial in character, the latter assumed that these were but the cumulated outcomes of the *divide et impere* tactics of colonial governments. And whereas some anticolonial leaders initially had argued that the nation-state ought to be supplemented with or perhaps even superseded by transnational forms of political association and multilayered forms of sovereignty, they had eventually to accept that the nation-state had become the predominant form of political association in the modern world, and that this had happened as a result of a contingent confluence of their own concerns with those of Western political scientists and lawyers rather than as a consequence of a diffusion and slavish emulation of Western forms.

The Postcolonial Moment

Initially the study of decolonization was almost exclusively focused on its consequences for postcolonial states and their former masters. This had been the province of area studies and comparative politics and few efforts were made to explore its consequences for the international system as a whole during the first decades after the Second World War. As Nicolas Guilhot has argued, academic international relations remained curiously silent about decolonization and its outcomes during this period.[167] A rare exception was Hans Morgenthau, who had dwelled extensively on imperialism in his *Politics Among Nations* (1948). But in response to decolonization, he added a new section to the 1960 edition in which decolonization was represented as a "reverse moment in which the objects of colonial expansion try to regain their independence and achieve a fundamental change in the relation of the white and the colored races."[168] The challenged posed by new states to Western dominance was of little concern to students of international relations until later. With colonialism being increasingly discredited, the preoccupation with imperialism and internationalism that had characterized the discipline in the interwar years gave way to a new focus on hegemony and dependence. Yet a few political realists were still busy producing arguments as to why enduring colonialism was in the national interest of the United States, or why some colonial territories were unfit for independence given the characteristics of their populations.[169]

When the dust had settled, students of international relations could safely start out from the assumption that the international system now was *global* in character, and that it was composed of *states* and nothing else. In Great Britain, the Commonwealth was believed to supersede the remains of the empire, constituting a "group of great nations which uses the strategic network and its communications but no longer depends upon a ubiquitous Royal Navy for its defence", as commonwealth historian Charles Carrington now defined it.[170] But as Robbie Shilliam has pointed out, there was a short step from such conceptions of the Commonwealth to the English School notion of an international society held together by common norms and values.[171] For example,

[167] Nicolas Guilhot, "Imperial Realism: Post-War IR theory and Decolonization." *The International History Review* 36 no. 4 (2014): 698–720.

[168] Hans Morgenthau, *Politics among Nations: The Struggle for Power and Peace* (New York: Knopf, 1960), 358.

[169] See David Long and Brian C. Schmidt, "Introduction." in David Long and Brian C. Schmidt, (eds.) *Imperialism and Internationalism in the Discipline of International Relations* (Albany: SUNY Press, 2005), 1–11; Guilhot, "Imperial Realism", 710–714.

[170] Charles E. Carrington, "Decolonization: The last stages." *International Affairs* 38 no. 1 (1962): 29–40, at 39.

[171] Robbie Shilliam, *Decolonizing Politics* (Cambridge: Polity Press, 2021), 121–126. See also Martin Wight, "International Legitimacy." *International Relations* 4 no. 1 (1972): 1–28.

taking the outcomes of decolonization for granted, Hedley Bull could state in *The Anarchical Society* (1977) that "the starting point of international relations is the existence of *states*, or independent political communities, each of which possesses a government and asserts sovereignty in relation to a particular portion of the earth's surface and a particular segment of the human population."[172] What was particular about this global international system, however, was the fact that it no longer reflected the values and norms of a single culture or civilization, but embodied a plurality of values that had to be reconciled in the interest of preserving world order, so that "the cosmopolitan culture on which it depends may need to absorb the non-Western to a much greater degree if it is to be genuinely universal and provide a foundation for a universal international society."[173] That humankind was naturally compartmentalized into an international system was equally evident to Kenneth Waltz, who believed that "[t]he enduring anarchic character of international politics accounts for the striking sameness in the quality of international life through the millennia."[174] Thus, the international system is global in the sense that it occupies all inhabitable planetary space, but also timeless in character not only because it lacked a history of its own but because it made history possible as constant quest for power and security. Since such an international system had no definitive point of origin, its abrupt transformation or demise was equally inconceivable. The enduring fact of international anarchy not only explained why states had to help themselves in order to survive, but also why they took on similar characteristics as a result of being socialized into the same system. Hence states are what anarchy makes of them, since "[a]narchy entails relations of coordination among a system's units, and that implies their sameness."[175] Since states are

[172] Hedley Bull, *The Anarchical Society. A Study of Order in World Politics* (London: Macmillan, 1977), 8. A few years later, however, Bull touched upon the systemic consequences of decolonization, see Hedley Bull, "The Emergence of a Universal International Society." in Hedley Bull and Adam Watson (eds.), *The Expansion of International Society*. Oxford: Oxford University Press, 1984), 117–126. For a commentary, see Stanley Hoffman, "Hedley Bull and His Contribution to International Relations." *International Affairs* 62 no. 2 (1986): 179–195.

[173] Ibid., 317.

[174] Kenneth N. Waltz, *Theory of International Politics* (Reading: Addison-Wesley, 1979), 66.

[175] Ibid., 93.

not very different in terms of the functions they perform, this implies that "distinctions among them arise principally from their varied capabilities."[176] From this point of view, the capabilities that mattered most were economic and military strength, implying that states could be ranked according to their relative capabilities in these domains, and that these capabilities, rather than their domestic makeup, defined the terms of their intercourse.

This international system was also supposed to be self-regulating and self-reproducing, so that attempts at imperial expansion were counter-balanced and every attempt to transcend the international system in favor of world government negated by its very structure. But there are other ways of looking at these assumptions than those encouraged by their authors and their many critics. Rather than marking the final step in the long and painstaking transition from a world of empires to one of states propelled by the diffusion of Western ideas and institutions, the globalization of the international system implied that its constitutive outside now was lost, pending the discovery of extraterrestrial life. Earlier in this chapter we saw how Getachew and Heiskanen interpreted this historical transformation not in terms of an abolition of hierarchical relations and the inauguration of a brave new world of global equality, but in terms of a *sublation* of those relations *within* the modern international system to the extent that empire became supervenient on the world of states rather than being its negation and antecedent. In what appears to be the last instance of the age-old logic of *translatio imperii*, empire in this new guise was floating free of its concrete instances of domination and exploitation, and its center could no longer be located to any determinate state or group of states – whether Western or capitalist, or both – but seemed instead to be fully decentered and little but a modality of power: it was an *imperium sine imperator*.[177]

My interpretation of the global consequences of decolonization is different. As I would like to suggest, the antithesis between a world of empires and a world of states was never resolved in favor of the latter with remnants of the former migrating into it. This being so because there is no such antithesis outside the theories of transition that have

176 Ibid., 97.

177 Compare Michael Hardt and Antonio Negri, *Empire* (Harvard University Press, 2000), xiv–xv.

been invented to legitimize the rise and spread of the modern international system in terms of historical progress. To my mind, the globalization of the international system could as well be interpreted as a process through which the international system becomes an empire in its own right by *replacing rather than containing* the imperial aspirations of the West. From this point of view, formal empires came to an end not because they represented an illegitimate form of rule but because they had become redundant in a world in which an international system fulfilled the functions formerly associated with imperial rule equally well. In this way the global international system could be seen as a fulfilment of the vision of universal political authority first set forth by Dante in *Monarchia*. The distinguishing mechanism of imperial rule – the practice of *divide et impere* – was now outsourced to the invisible hand of international anarchy that made sure that humankind lived divided by fear and suspicion: You do not need an emperor when you have a security dilemma. All that is took to turn international anarchy into an inescapable social fact was a belief in the indivisibility of both sovereignty and security, so that humankind could become what Jonathan Havercroft has aptly termed "captives of sovereignty."[178] The claims to universality and boundlessness characteristic of the great empires of the premodern past were now warranted by the planetary extension of the international system, and the multiculturalism thought to be the trademark of successful imperial rule was now reproduced in the norms of global tolerance and sovereign equality of states that accompanied the global spread of the international system.[179] In this way, the international system *cum* empire provided what looked like a final resolution to the trade-off between homogenization and diversity that had haunted the great empires of the past.

For colonial peoples who had been railroaded into this system by their leaders, that system *cum* empire now appeared as little but a giant outdoor prison into which large parts of humanity had been accidentally confined, first by means of colonialism proper and then through the emulation of Western institutions and practices that had followed upon independence. Hence a generation of postcolonial intellectuals

[178] Jonathan Havercroft, *Captives of Sovereignty* (Cambridge: Cambridge University Press, 2011).

[179] See Wendy Brown, *Regulating Aversion: Tolerance in the Age of Identity and Empire* (Princeton: Princeton University Press, 2009).

were characteristically ambivalent about the nation-state yet mostly silent about the international realm. For example, although Edward Said barely touches upon issues of nationhood and statehood in *Orientalism* (1978), he nevertheless produced a defense of Palestinian self-determination on nationalist grounds in other contexts.[180] Among the rather few sustained engagements with questions of nationhood and statehood we find *Nationalist Thought and the Colonial World* (1986) by Partha Chatterjee. As he asked in his opening salvo, "why is it that non-European colonial countries have no historical alternative but to try to approximate the given attributes of modernity when that very process of approximation means their continued subjection under a world order which only sets their tasks for them and over which they have no control?"[181] Nationalism and its many avatars were foremost among the trappings of modernity, because "even if it challenged the colonial claim to political domination, it also accepted the very intellectual premises of 'modernity' on which colonial domination was based."[182] To Chatterjee, postcolonial states had been constituted through a series of successive moments during which colonial peoples first were led to believe that the alleged backwardness of their societies could be overcome through the appropriation of Western attributes, and then were mobilized by their elites into national movements until all differences and contradictions eventually were glossed over in the name of national unity.[183] Yet his point was not to abandon the quest for community, but to disentangle its possibility from layers of orientalist imposition and selective appropriation of Western values. As Homi Bhabha remarked on this possibility, "it is only when the western nation comes to be seen…as one of the dark corners of the earth, that we can begin to explore places from which to write histories of peoples and construct theories of narration."[184] Hence it became imperative to recover the pre-colonial parts of the past that

[180] See Edward W. Said, *Orientalism* (New York: Pantheon Books, 1978), *passim*. For an analysis, see Jan Selby, "Edward W. Said: Truth, Justice and Nationalism." *Interventions: International Journal of Postcolonial Studies* 8 no. 1 (2006): 40–55.

[181] Partha Chatterjee, *Nationalist Thought and the Colonial World. A Derivative Discourse* (Minneapolis: University of Minnesota Press, 1986), 10.

[182] Ibid., 30. [183] Ibid., 49–52.

[184] Homi K. Bhabha, "Introduction: Narrating the Nation." in Homi K. Bhabha (ed.) *Nation and Narration* (London & New York. Routledge, 1990), 1–7, at 6.

could provide a source of identity and a ground for resistance against the Western world order. Yet such project required unmediated access to an authentic past uncontaminated by the universalizing histories of the West and their entanglement with imperialism and the nation-state. As Ashis Nandy then argued, the spread of historical consciousness had brought nothing but the "devaluation, marginalization, and liquidation of memories that cannot be historicized" and consequently narrowed down the range of conceivable alternatives within the more ahistorical cultures of the East.[185] Yet Chatterjee and Nandy were in broad agreement that in the case of India, Gandhi had carried the key to transcendence, albeit in different ways. To Nandy, it was Gandhi who had first broken out of the determinism of history, because "his concept of a free India, his solution to racial, caste and inter-religious conflicts and his concept of human dignity were remarkably free from the constraints of history."[186] To Chatterjee, that precious possibility had been sacrificed on the altar of independence during the moment of arrival, when "the relentless thrust of its nationalist thematic turned the Gandhian interventions into a mere interlude in the unfolding of the real history of the nation."[187] But as he later pointed out in *The Nation and Its Fragments* (1993), anticolonial nationalism had created "its own domain of sovereignty within colonial society well before it begins its battle with the imperial power."[188] By raising claims to sovereignty in the spiritual domain, anticolonial nationalists had been able counteract the material superiority of the West. After independence, those "autonomous forms of imagination of the community were...overwhelmed and swamped by the history of the postcolonial state."[189] At the end of the day, this posed a limit to what the attempts to recover authentic forms of community could hope to achieve. As Chatterjee added with noticeable lament, "[i]f the nation is an imagined community and if nations must also take the form of states, then our theoretical language must allow us to talk about community and

185 Ashis Nandy, "History's Forgotten Doubles." *History and Theory* 34 no. 2 (1995): 44–66, at 61.
186 Ashis Nandy, *The Intimate Enemy. Loss and Recovery of Self Under Colonialism* (Oxford: Oxford University Press, 1989), 62.
187 Chatterjee, *Nationalist Thought and the Colonial World*, 157.
188 Partha Chatterjee, *The Nation and Its Fragments. Colonial and Postcolonial Histories* (Princeton: Princeton University Press, 1993), 6.
189 Ibid., 11.

state at the same time. I do not think our present theoretical language allows us to do this."[190]

As the sense of historical entrapment grew among postcolonial scholars, so did their conviction that the nation-state was less a vehicle of emancipation but more an unwanted imposition that constricted the recovery of the self. As Dipesh Chakrabarty argued in *Provincializing Europe* (2000), "nationalist thought was premised on the assumed universality of the project of becoming individuals, on the assumption that individual rights and abstract equality were universals that could find home anywhere in the world."[191] But the successful appropriation of these universals presupposed a narrative of transition according to which societies devoid of those features could somehow catch up. Yet to even think about a historical transition in those terms "was to think in terms of these institutions at the apex of which sat the modern state, and to think about the modern or the nation-state was to think a history whose theoretical subject was Europe."[192] But the search for the holy grail of a political subjectivity untainted by colonial experience more often took place within predetermined if loosely defined national contexts, with modern India as the paragon of the postcolonial world. Much of this methodological nationalism derived from the same social and political imaginaries from which postcolonial scholars struggled hard to escape.[193] But the more of the present predicament that could be construed as undesirable remnants of colonial experiences, the less the prospects of recovery and possibilities of transcendence would seem. Merely shaking its invisible bars from the inside would not make this outdoor prison go away, only fuel further resentment against the West for having built it.

In this chapter, I have sketched a brief intellectual history of decolonization by situating it in a global context. Doing this, I have emphasized the extent to which claims to self-determination and independence were based on creative appropriations of the concepts of state and nation, and how the success of these claims hinged on coeval

190 Ibid.
191 Dipesh Chakrabarty, *Provincializing Europe. Postcolonial Thought and Historical Difference* (Princeton: Princeton University Press, 2000), 34.
192 Ibid., 34.
193 This in obvious contrast to works like Sheldon Pollock, *The Language of the Gods in the World of Men: Sanskrit, Culture, and Power in Premodern India* (Berkeley: University of California Press, 2006).

changes in the practices of international recognition, changes which to some extent occurred as a result of the petitioning of the United Nations by anticolonial leaders. What we in retrospect have come to call decolonization was the result of this feedback loop. Yet anticolonial nationalism was often accompanied by pleas to remake the international system. Many anti-imperialists were concerned with the systemic causes of imperialism and did not readily accept the nation-state form other than as a default option. Instead, they tried to imagine forms of political association that transcended the limits of the nation-state by developing schemes of transnational cooperation or regional unity, or by envisaging multilayered forms of sovereignty. Anticolonial leaders also gradually realized that formal independence would not automatically yield freedom from domination and economic development, which created additional incentives to reform what they saw as an international system biased to their disadvantage. But the success of the quest for independence not only presupposed the existence of an international realm that could be interpellated and a United Nations that could petitioned to extend membership in that realm at its behest. Since claims to self-determination issued in pleas for new and more egalitarian forms of international exchange, these claims were to some extent *constitutive* of the same international system they promised to subvert or at least reform. Hence the many attempts by antiimperialists to envisage and create alternative forms of political association that transcended the limits of the nation-state did not always fail on their own terms, but rather because of the systemic pressures to conform the very moment they achieved independence and thereby became part of a global international system *cum* empire. In this way, the imperatives of sovereignty and security triumphed over the spirit of internationalism that had prevailed during the first two decades of anticolonial struggles in Asia and Africa.

This outcome was further reinforced by the ways in which the making of new states was understood in Europe and the United States. Whatever their differences, commentators were united in the belief that the viability of new states depended on their ability to emulate Western ideas and institutions, and that the achievement of national unity was a necessary condition of both democratization and development. The standard way of achieving national unity during this period was through an alignment of state and nation within the same fixed territory. From this point of view, the nation-state was an offer you could not refuse lest you wanted to be stuck in the past and thereby become an easy target of foreign intervention. Although there was no lack of postcolonial intellectuals who tried to recover meaningful experiences of community untainted by the Western imaginaries of empire, nation and state, their own methodological nationalism, bequeathed to them by European social theory, rather perpetuated their sense of entrapment. Hence, in the last and concluding chapter, I will analyze some contemporary attempts to contest and move beyond the modern international system *cum* empire.

6 From the International to the Global and Beyond?

Introduction

In this book, I have shown how an international realm was conceptualized into existence by focusing on how actors from a wide variety of contexts have understood relations between different polities across time. While many existing accounts have described the emergence of an international realm as a result of a transition from a world of empires to a world of states, I have tried to show how the modern international realm was first conceptualized to make sense of rivalries between European empires in the global space opened by the discoveries and the cartographical and geographical revolutions of the fifteenth and sixteenth centuries. Hence the creation of a global space antedated and conditioned the emergence of the international realm. I then argued that the subsequent expansion of the international realm on other continents is best understood as a continuation of imperial relations by other means rather than in terms of the gradual inclusion of non-European polities into an international society based on sovereign equality. Although successful claims to independence and self-determination issued in the creation of new and nominally sovereign states in the non-European world during the nineteenth and twentieth centuries, the concepts of independence and self-determination were redefined in the process so as to accommodate empire and imperial relations to the point of the international system eventually becoming an empire in its own right, premised on the exclusion and marginalization of all forms of political association that did not conform to the nation-state form.

The Eurocentrism of academic international relations follows directly from the naturalization of the nation-state and the corresponding reification of the international realm. This implied that the study of international relations became based on the nation-state as the default form of political association. Those forms of political life that existed before its triumph or outside European continent could then only be understood either as deviations from or precursors to the nation-state, and hence received only scant attention from academic international relations. Once the international realm was globalized, what had been part of its constitutive outside was relegated to a premodern past and rendered inaccessible to inquiry other than by assimilation to the statist and implicitly nationalist categories of international relations. Those forms of political life that could not be fit into these categories were left to anthropologists and historians until international relations began to broaden its scope of inquiry only in the last decades. Still the non-European parts of the past seem to require a significant amount of conceptual stretching to become accessible to inquiry.[1]

As I have tried to demonstrate, the expansion of the international realm and the universalization of the nation-state form have been driven by constant contestations of political authority and its legitimacy. Such contestations have given rise new standards of legitimate authority which then have been creatively appropriated and translated into claims to independence and doctrines of international recognition. But the spread and appropriation of such new standards of legitimacy did not bring any straight transition from a world of empires to a world of states. Rather, forms of statehood and nationhood were in many cases perfectly able to coexist with and reinforce empire and imperial rule in theory and practice alike. But the final triumph of the nation-state occurred at the expense not only of precolonial forms of political association but also of a range of alternatives that had been proposed prior to and during the process of decolonization. Some of these alternatives have recently attracted interest by political theorists and historians, who have tried to recover these to demonstrate that such alternative forms once were and still remain viable alternatives to empires and nation-states.[2] But this leaves us with the task of explaining why the nation-state triumphed given the existence of a range of *prima facie* viable competitors – whether federal or confederal – some of which exercised a significant political appeal on colonizers

1 See, for example, Hendrik Spruyt, *The World Imagined: Collective Beliefs and Political Order in the Sinocentric, Islamic and Southeast Asian International Societies* (Cambridge: Cambridge University Press, 2020).

2 For an excellent overview, see Merve Fejzula, "The Cosmopolitan Historiography of Twentieth-Century Federalism." *Historical Journal* 64 no. 2 (2021): 477–500.

and colonized alike before and sometimes also during the process of decolonization.[3]

As I have tried to show in this book, the universalization of the nation-state as the main locus of sovereign authority was the result of the spread and creative appropriation of the belief that state and nation ought to be congruent within the same territory, however differently these component terms have been defined and understood by interlocutors across the world. Whether explicitly nationalist or not, anticolonial leaders were quick to embrace this ideal of congruence given that the territorial framework of sovereignty in most cases already had been handed down to them by their imperial masters, leaving anticolonial leaders with the challenge of reconciling their federalist or otherwise cosmopolitan visions of political order with the brute facts of territorial statehood. The idea according to which sovereignty ought to be territorially demarcated to be legitimate had found its way into doctrines of international recognition already during the Age of Revolutions, and the congruence of nation and state was later naturalized into a global gold standard of political legitimacy by modernization theory. Both superpowers could agree that the nation-state represented the proper end of decolonization as it left the principles of government and economic development unspecified and open to ideological and geopolitical competition. This made it increasingly difficult for anticolonial leaders to mobilize support – whether domestically or internationally – in favor of the creation of any form of political association that could not at least be packaged and sold as a nation-state, however weak its domestic authority structures and however divided its population initially might have been. While the nation-state offered a convenient shortcut to international recognition, the ideal of congruence offered a potent weapon for handling domestic opposition from ethnic and religious minorities which could be excluded or sidelined with reference to this ideal. Hence the final victory of the nation-state over its competitors appears to be an essential by-product of the world becoming international under very specific historical circumstances,

[3] See, for example, Gary Wilder, *Freedom Time: Négritude, Decolonization, and the Future of the World* (Durham: Duke University Press, 2015); Frederick Cooper, *Citizenship between Empire and Nation* (Princeton: Princeton University Press, 2015); Duncan Bell, *The Idea of Greater Britain: Empire and the Future of World Order, 1860–1900* (Princeton: Princeton University Press, 2007).

not a matter of historical necessity. It is thus possible to imagine a range of counterfactual circumstances under which decolonization might have produced more variegated outcomes. Had the spread of nationalism been less virulent in the early twentieth century and had the détente between the United States and the Soviet Union kicked in a decade or so earlier, decolonization might as well have given rise to a patchwork of regional federations and multicultural states with sovereignty shared within regional and international institutions. Many of those arrangements which with hindsight appear but halfway houses between imperial rule and full independence could have been frozen in time and then decolonized from within, as it were.

This analysis gives us reasons to reassess the role of nationalism in the making of the modern international system. As I argued in Chapter 4, although many accounts of nationalism have emphasized its importance in the making of European nation-states, these accounts have largely taken the congruence of nation and state to be an unproblematic point of departure. But as I have tried to show, nationalism also provides ample justifications for bringing such congruence about whenever it is deemed absent. This implies that nationalism should not be understood as an ideology to which individual states may appeal in search of nationhood or social cohesion, but rather as a constitutive feature of the international realm insofar as it naturalizes the nation-state as a condition of international relations proper. As Heiskanen has pointed out, "nationalism must also be continually summoned for international relations to be intelligible: without the figure of the nation, references to national interests, national security, national identity, or even the 'international' would be nonsensical."[4]

But where does this historical analysis leave us in theoretical terms? One upshot of my narrative has been to *provincialize* the international realm by making it look like an accidental outgrowth of European power politics into alien contexts rather than as a given framework for the study of world politics. The international system is originally a *regional* order which has taken on imperial features as a consequence of being globalized. But whereas previous accounts of the international system have portrayed the spread of the sovereign state as a result of

[4] Jaakko Heiskanen, "Spectra of Sovereignty: Nationalism and International Relations." *International Political Sociology* 13 no. 3 (2019): 315–332, at 317.

the violent imposition of territorial modes of rule on heterogeneous and often recalcitrant colonial spaces, this book has emphasized the extent to which the spread of the sovereign state was propelled by an active and creative appropriation of underlying notions of legitimate authority by elites in the non-European world, and how a selective uptake of these notions then conditioned the expansion of the international realm during the nineteenth and twentieth centuries. But does this entail that the international realm is best understood in anarchical or hierarchical terms? I would like to suggest that the answer to this question is relative to context and perspective, and to some extent lies in the eyes of the beholder, so that what looked like an international society based on sovereign equality at Chatham House in 1960 looked more like a neocolonial empire to the elites of Accra or Algiers at the same time. Much like the endlessly recycled drawing from Wittgenstein's *Philosophische Untersuchungen* (1953) that can be seen either as a duck or as a rabbit but never as both at the same time, the international realm can be understood in either hierarchical or anarchical terms but perhaps never both simultaneously. To Wittgenstein, such visual ambiguity was the result of us seeing different *aspects* of it depending on a blend of familiarity and imagination, so that "we interpret it, and *see* it as we *interpret* it."[5] To him, the necessary presence of interpretation indicates that "[t]he importance of this concept lies in the connexion between the concepts of 'seeing an aspect' and 'experiencing the meaning of a word'."[6] To Wittgenstein, what holds true of visual ambiguity also holds true of semantic ambiguity, so that how we name things will determine the range of possible interpretations available to us. In the present case, this implies that conceptualizing the international realm in either anarchical or hierarchical terms can help us make sense of what goes on within that realm at any given point in time but that it will also necessarily limit our understanding of that realm by taking the above principles to be exhaustive of the possibilities at hand. Describing the international realm in anarchical or hierarchical terms will therefore conceal the extent to which the international realm constitutes an empire in its own right precisely by

[5] Ludwig Wittgenstein, *Philosophical Investigations*. trans. by G. E. M. Anscombe (Oxford: Basil Blackwell, 1958), II:xi, 194. For a discussion, see Malcolm Budd, "Wittgenstein on Seeing Aspects." *Mind* 96 no. 381 (1987): 1–17.

[6] Ibid., II:xi, 214.

virtue of its naturalizing of these *prima facie* conflicting principles of political association. Taken together, these principles presuppose that humankind is naturally divided into nation-states and that these are stratified along the lines of power and wealth. These principles will also help conceal the fact that nations and states never have been fully congruent, but premised on exclusion and domination.

Becoming Global

In this section and the next, I will engage with some attempts to move beyond the international realm in favor of more encompassing and normative visions of world politics. If most accounts of the rise and spread of the international realm have presented us with a false choice between the authoritarianism of empire and the democracy of the nation-state, where does the present narrative leave us when it comes to the possibilities of transcending the international realm? A first implication is that the existence of an international realm should not be taken for granted as a framework for the academic study of world politics but must instead be understood as a contingent yet unintended outcome of prior quests for empire by European powers. A second and perhaps less obvious implication is that the nation-state cannot be regarded as the sole or privileged locus of democratic legitimacy. Not only because of its accidental lumping together of some people to the exclusion of others, but also because many nation-states depend on the ongoing marginalization of permanent minorities thereby effectively duplicating structures of empire and imperial rule under the banner of multiculturalism.[7] Hence the sources of legitimate political authority must be sought elsewhere, beyond the confines of the nation-state and the international realm.

Now many of those who have tried to venture beyond the international realm in search of alternatives have invoked the concept of the

[7] For arguments of this kind, see Arash Abizadeh, "On the Demos and its Kin: Nationalism, Democracy, and the Boundary Problem." *American Political Science Review* 106, no. 4 (2012): 867–882; Jens Bartelson, "Globalizing the Democratic Community." *Ethics & Global Politics* 1, no. 4 (2008): 159–174; Mahmood Mamdani, *Neither Settler nor Native. The Making and Unmaking of Permanent Majorities* (Cambridge, MA.: Harvard University Press, 2020); Adom Getachew, "The State's Imperial Shadows." *Ethics & International Affairs* 35 no. 4 (2021): 503–513.

global and its many cognates. Consequently, and thanks to its inherent ambiguity, references to a global realm now abound in the literature. Some authors use the term "global" to refer to a totality of all sociopolitical relations. Others take it to denote whatever phenomena believed to be of a planetary scope. Still others take the global to be coextensive with the concepts of the world or earth, whatever these in turn are taken to mean. But apart from the ambiguity that surrounds this concept, the ensuing efforts to redefine the study of international relations along global lines have raised questions about the relationship between the global realm – however defined – and our standard definitions of the international realm in either systemic or societal terms. Whether we take these concepts to be coeval or contradictory, attempts to come to terms with the relationship between the international and the global have had disturbing consequences for the study of international relations, which has become increasingly torn between statist and globalist definitions of its subject matter. Today this is no longer merely an academic issue but a major apple of discord in world politics, no mere disagreement about semantics or empirics, but a clash between two worldviews, each with different normative and ideological implications for how scholars should conceptualize world politics. But as I have argued in this book, the conceptualization of the international realm was made possible by the creation of a global space within which imperial rivalries could unfold and a constitutive outside from which the international realm could be gradually carved out and eventually globalized. In this section, I will discuss some attempts to recover the concept of globality as a framework for analyzing world politics, arguing that this becomes easier once the international realm has been provincialized. In the next section, I will pursue this line of argument further by discussing some recent attempts to shift the perspective from the global to the planetary.

Attempts to reach into the global realm in the search of alternatives to the modern international system have been subject to criticism on a variety of grounds. A first kind of criticism concerns the ontological and logical possibility of conceptualizing the global realm in *sui generis* terms. As Rob Walker has argued, the very idea of such a transition "betrays an elementary and even willful failure to understand what has been at stake in the specifically modern understanding of the unity within diversity and the diversity within unity expressed in the modern sovereign state and the system of sovereign states."[8] Thus, the idea of anything global does not represent "a progressive shift towards an enlightened reason", but rather "a specific account of the necessary relation between universality and particularity."[9] Hence attempts to conceptualize a global realm in independent terms cannot be but another way of imposing some particularistic vision of political order onto the world. In a similar vein, to Sergei Prozorov, the notion of anything global must founder on its logical impossibility. To him, if the world is posited as the sum total of all beings, "such a totality must by definition count itself among its members, otherwise it would not be the sum of *all* beings, since it would remain outside itself."[10] Yet this leads to inconsistency, since if we divide that world into those parts of the world that belong to themselves, such as the world itself, and those parts who do not belong to themselves, and then ask whether the latter group of beings belong to itself. But "if it does, it must count itself among its elements, which are defined by the property of *not* belonging to themselves. Yet, if it does not belong to itself, it must also count itself among its elements, which, after all, compose *all* the parts that do not belong to themselves."[11] Since the conceptualization of such a whole must include *itself* as a part of that whole, it is inconsistent on set-theoretical terms and cannot serve as a starting point for a coherent study of world politics.

A second kind of criticism concerns the normative implications of conceptualizing the global realm in such terms. Here the notion of anything global is subject to the objection that it is inherently parochial by virtue of being a Western invention. Global imaginaries have their own historical trajectories, intertwined with those universal histories that were written to legitimize empire and imperial rule and which also were instrumental in the making of the international realm.[12] Hence going global in search of redemption from the perils

[8] R. B. J. Walker, *After the Globe, before the World* (London & New York: Routledge, 2010), 30.

[9] Ibid., 30.

[10] Sergei Prozorov, *Ontology and World Politics: Void Universalism I* (London & New York: Routledge, 2013), 8.

[11] Ibid., 8.

[12] See, for example, David Christian, "The Return of Universal History." *History and Theory* 49 no. 4 (2010): 6–27; David Christian, "World History in Context." *Journal of World History* 14 no. 3 (2003): 437–458.

of the international realm is fraught with danger lest ghosts from the past should be invited back to animate the present. For example, as Bruno Latour has argued, because the notion of a globe is an imperial construct, it should provincialized and eventually abandoned in favor of a new conception of the *Earth*. The notion of a globe "is still the undisputed, authoritative, universal, external frame within which all geopolitical identities ... are situated in a recognisable place, a province side by side with all the other provinces."[13] Since the notion of a globe is a prerequisite for the process of localization and the breaking down of global space into distinct and supposedly impenetrable portions, "it defines an invisible power inside which everything else could be located even though the frame allowing the localisation remains totally invisible."[14] Thus, the global visions are imperial visions: "it is this exotic vision of nature that Europe, and then more generally the West, has sold to the rest of the world as the real, earthly, natural, material world."[15] As such, like any other badly designed product, it should be recalled so that it can be "debugged and refitted."[16] But Latour himself offers few clues as to what a de-bugged, non-imperial conception of the Earth would look like, or how it would be able to accommodate its many provinces in a non-biased way. Yet it would follow that any attempt to conceptualize the global would reflect a thinly veiled will to govern in the name of universal rights and values, and this regardless of traditional concerns for state sovereignty or norms of non-intervention. For example, as Jean Cohen has argued, the United Nations system has expanded the scope of its executive authority during the past decades. While this expansion was undertaken to alleviate human suffering and protect human rights, it has also infringed on the autonomy of states, suspended existing constitutional arrangements, and in some cases also violated individual rights. According to her, the tendency on behalf of global governance institutions to interfere in the domestic affairs of states has undermined the norm of sovereign equality among states and given rise to new forms of hierarchical rule on a global scale.[17] Finally, according

[13] Bruno Latour, "Onus Orbis Terrarum: About a possible shift in the Definition of Sovereignty." *Millennium* 44 no. 3 (2016): 305–320, at 307.

[14] Ibid., 314. [15] Ibid., 319. [16] Ibid.

[17] See Jean L. Cohen, *Globalization and Sovereignty: Rethinking Legality, Legitimacy, and Constitutionalism* (Cambridge: Cambridge University Press, 2012).

to Inés Valdez, however globalist in their aspirations, extant cosmopolitanisms have been prone to Eurocentrism insofar as they failed to engage "intellectual resources and political practices from outside the West" and have tended to focus exclusively on Western institutions – democratic states and international organizations – as the only vehicles for cosmopolitan reform.[18] Especially the neo-Kantians have remained blind to "regimes of imperial and postimperial domination" and to "transnational forms of solidarity and cooperation" that would require "exiting exclusionary domestic and international realms of politics."[19] Hence contemporary forms of cosmopolitanism are hard to distinguish from earlier ideologies of empire to the extent that they inadvertently legitimize domination and fail to take the perspectives of non-European peoples into consideration.

The above lines of criticism reflect profound concerns about the legitimacy of political authority in a globalized world. To its critics, whatever the global is supposed to contain makes it look very like a late-modern revival of old dreams of empire. Yet critics also tend to imply that the particularistic logic of identity which lies at the heart of the modern international realm is an inescapable feature of the political world, and hence that humankind is stuck in a condition in which violent conflict between actors is forever possible and perhaps even inevitable. That is, from the point when the existence of an international realm began to be taken for granted, every attempt to recover any sense of a sociopolitical whole over and above the multiplicity of states became vulnerable to the objection any such notion must necessarily be both parochial and utopian in character. Such a sociopolitical totality would be but an expression of a will to power emanating from deep inside the international system itself, invariably reflecting the Western conceptions of time and space upon which this system once was built in order to resolve the many tensions between waning imperialism and nascent nationalism during this transformative period.

This goes some way to explain why the international and the global realms ended up being thought of as either coextensive or contradictory, but also why the postcolonial critique of attempts to conceptualize global in *sui generis* terms has had so much apparent bite. But

[18] Inés Valdez, *Transnational Cosmopolitanism: Kant, Du Bois, and Justice as a Political Craft* (Cambridge: Cambridge University Press, 2019), 5.
[19] Ibid., 6.

it is easy to forget that the logic of identity responsible for this bite is a natural companion to the modern international system, its chief function being to restrict the scope of sovereignty claims to particular portions of space in order to resolve otherwise intractable conflicts between rivaling claims to universal empire that antedated the emergence of the international system. But if the rise and spread of that system is comprehensible only against the backdrop of a global frame, it follows that we should reverse their order of analytical priority accordingly and take a global frame of reference as the starting point of our analysis, however contingent and constructed that frame itself is. Thus, it makes sense to speak of a global realm or a global frame of reference in *sui generis* terms only because it was conceptualized into existence *before* an international realm was eventually carved out of it during the early modern period, not because its ontological status is different.

But criticisms of the possibility of anything recognizably global raises other questions about social ontology. If the global is nothing but a fig leaf invented to conceal and legitimize power claims by dominant actors in the international system, *where* more exactly does this contest between particularistic and universalistic visions of political order take place? Furthermore, granted that anything global is ontologically impossible or logically inconsistent, how do we make sense of the undeniable fact that people speak and act *as if* such a realm indeed does exist, thereby in effect if not intention co-creating the corresponding social fact? The fact that a global frame is always already implicit in those questions brings us back to the understanding of the global realm that constituted the starting point of this book. As Peter Sloterdijk has reminded us, "[n]o theoretical engagement with the present can undo that the earth has been circumnavigated and its peoples and cultures forced into mediation. In this sense, terrestrial globalization, like an axiom, is the first and only precondition of a theory of the present age."[20] Against this backdrop it is important to recall that people go about their business making new worlds in ways they deem fit for their own purposes, and in blissful disregard of the various constraints posed by set theory and critical theory. For better or worse, people are, to paraphrase José Saramago's *A Viagem do Elefante*, relentlessly "giving

[20] Peter Sloterdijk, *Globes: Spheres II*. trans. by Wieland Hoban (Cambridge, M.A.: MIT Press 2014), 936.

new worlds to the world."[21] As I have tried to show in this book, the process of becoming international can be understood as a paradigmatic instance of such collective worldmaking. But as I have also argued, that process generated a steady stream of non-statist and cosmopolitan visions in the conceptual space that was opened between the standard definitions of empire and state, ranging from the *grand design* of Sully via the creole cosmopolitanism of Bolívar to the *Négritude* of Senghor, each of these visions reflecting a characteristic willingness to engage with distant Others to expand the concentric circles of human community and senses of belonging accordingly. And as Adom Getachew and Inés Valdez have shown in their investigations of anticolonial thought, most modern anti-imperialisms have effectively exited both the domestic and international realms in their strong cosmopolitan commitments to a more equitable world order.[22] Hence what seems to be peculiar – but in no way unique – to the present is that many of the worlds that are being conceptualized today are based on the possibility of *dissolving* rather that transcending the divide between the domestic and the international spheres. In contrast to earlier forms of cosmopolitanism, the new worlds being imagined today are not based on attempts to recover lost forms of association from a distant precolonial past or on definitions of humankind in the singular. Rather, contemporary cosmopolitans emphasize how inclusive visions of political community must be formulated anew against the backdrop of a common human habitat. As Gerard Delanty and Aurea Mota have argued, "the human societies and the Earth have now forged a tenuous unity as well as a consciousness of that unity. The presuppositions of modernity are now once again called into question with the emergence of an entangled conception of nature and society, Earth and the world."[23]

Many contemporary proposals to remake the modern world can be understood as responses to this predicament. Whereas the international realm once was carved out in blatant disregard of both nature and most of humankind, contemporary cosmopolitans are concerned

[21] José Saramago, *The Elephant's Journey* (London: Vintage Books, 2010), 77.
[22] Adom Getachew, *Worldmaking after Empire: The rise and fall of self-determination* (Princeton: Princeton University Press, 2019); Valdez, *Transnational Cosmopolitanism.*
[23] Gerard Delanty and Aurea Mota, "Governing the Anthropocene: Agency, Governance, Knowledge." *European Journal of Social Theory* 20 no. 1 (2017): 9–38.

with both. As Achille Mbembe has argued, this predicament calls for a new form of critical thinking that "thinks its possibility outside of itself, aware of the limits of its singularity, within the circuit that always connects us to an Elsewhere."[24] Hence "if we must walk anew the paths of humanity in companionship with all the species, then it is perhaps necessary to begin by recognizing that at bottom there is no world or place where we are totally 'at home', masters of the premises."[25] As Mbembe concludes, "[h]umanity is not given. It is pulled up and created in the course of struggles."[26] In a similar vein, to overcome the Eurocentrism inherent in earlier universalisms, Valdez has proposed that cosmopolitanism must be transnational and therefore also "*grounded* in concrete experiences of oppression and the political practices of the struggle against it, including the conceptions of justice and practices freedom developed in the struggle."[27] Finally, rather than abolishing borders between states – and hence the international system wholesale – Paulina Ochoa Espejo has argued that borders should not be understood in terms of the identity and belonging of those they contain, but rather redefined in terms the territorial politics through which people relate to the places where they live, so that "those present in a certain area determine the precise location of local jurisdictional borders by following patterns of resource use."[28] To these postcolonial cosmopolitans, the bounded nation-state is no longer a source of democratic legitimacy or a privileged locus of political authority, yet there are no suggestions of alternative authority structures to replace it. The closest we come is when Espejo argues that the right of border control "depends primarily on the purely conventional recognition of current borders."[29] Yet even if conventions as such lack deeper moral grounding, "they do provide an important service in securing the conditions in which important individual interests can be realized. This very service grounds the authority of the international system and the legitimacy of specific borders."[30] Here a more critical cosmopolitan might object that justifying the right of border control

[24] Achille Mbembe, *Out of the Dark Night. Essays on Decolonization* (New York: Columbia University Press, 2021), 228.
[25] Ibid., 229. [26] Ibid.
[27] Valdez, *Transnational Cosmopolitanism*, 9.
[28] Paulina Ochoa Espejo, *On Borders: Territories, Legitimacy, and the Rights of place* (Oxford: Oxford University Press, 2020), 18.
[29] Ibid., 215. [30] Ibid., 216.

with reference to international conventions whose parties depend on other states for the recognition of their legal personality risk sending us into circles while providing a rather dubious service to those who are already adversely affected by this arrangement.

The absence of compelling cosmopolitan visions – visions that first decouple and then realign political authority and community at the global level – goes some way to explain why different brands of nationalism seem to be the gut response to the challenges faced by nation-states as a consequence of those same flows of capital, information, goods and people which just about two decades ago were celebrated as harbingers of a united humankind. One implication of the story I have told in this book is that if colonial peoples sleepwalked into nation-states as a result of the subscription to nationalist beliefs, first on behalf of European elites and then by their colonial counterparts, and that a host of alternative forms of political association were sidelined in the process, then it would follow that the possibility to escape this predicament will depend on the articulation of yet another sufficiently coherent worldview that is able to challenge the nation-state as the predominant locus of political authority and the sources of its legitimacy. Because if the practice of such contestation explains how we ended up where we happen to be right now, it might as well tell us where to go next: to the planetary.

Going Planetary?

A planetary perspective promises to escape the international by emphasizing the situatedness of human existence on earth prior to and independent of the global and international spheres. Not unlike Heidegger, many of those who are turning to the planetary are doing this to recover the earth as the *ground* of the human world. As Heidegger writes in *The Origin of the Work of Art* (1935), "[t]he earth is the spontaneous forthcoming of that which is continually self-secluding and to that extent sheltering and concealing. World and earth are essentially different from one another and yet are never separated. The world grounds itself on the earth, and earth juts through world."[31] But whereas the concepts of the world and the earth have

[31] Martin Heidegger, "The Origin of the Work of Art." in Martin Heidegger, *Basic Writings*, ed. by David Farrell Krell (New York: Harper Collins, 1993), 139–212, at 174.

been around for centuries, the category of the planetary seems of more recent vintage. Its emergence is closely related to if not conditioned by the explorations of space that begun with the launch of *Sputnik* into orbit in 1957. As Hannah Arendt then pointed out, "[t]he earth is the very quintessence of the human condition, and earthly nature... may be unique in the universe in providing human beings with a habitat in which they can move and breathe without effort and without artifice."[32] Hence the planetary can no longer be subsumed under the category of the world, a category which had long been used to capture the totality and the uttermost limits of human experience. Although the term "world" was long used to describe the planet earth and everything contained within it, the sudden emergence of a planetary perspective questions and to some extent reverses this conceptual hierarchy.[33] As Benjamin Lazier has described this fascinating shift, the possibility of viewing the earth from space inaugurated the Earthrise era, provoking a profound restructuring of the relationship between inherited conceptions of organic life and human artifice while making it imperative to think globally, since "the vision of the naked Earth is also the view of a globe in disguise, the greatest of organisms: a man-made planet."[34] Or, as Kelly Oliver has put it, with the Apollo missions and the photographs of Earth from space, "the *world* gave way to the *planetary* and the *global*."[35] As Oliver notes, this shift of perspective also marked the beginning of the modern environmental movement with its distinctive focus on the planet as a whole. Yet the ambition to save the planet from devastation presupposes "[t]he mastering gaze that imagines itself taking the whole Earth as its object... perpetuates and emboldens a notion of human subjectivity as standing apart from its objects – in this case the earth – and over against them as the subjects controlling the destiny of those objects."[36] But as Oliver concludes, the planetary perspective is characterized by a

[32] Hannah Arendt, *The Human Condition* (Chicago: University of Chicago Press, 1958), 2.

[33] See Sean Gaston, *The Concept of the World from Kant to Derrida* (London: Rowman & Littlefield, 2013), Chs. 1 & 6.

[34] Benjamin Lazier, "Earthrise; or, the Globalization of the World Picture." *American Historical Review* 116 no. 3 (2011): 602–630, at 609.

[35] Kelly Oliver, *Earth & World. Philosophy after the Apollo Missions* (New York: Columbia University Press, 2015), 3.

[36] Oliver, *Earth & World. Philosophy after the Apollo Missions*, 25.

fundamental ambivalence, since "[o]n the one hand, the technological achievement of launching ourselves into space and leaving earth's atmosphere leads to feelings of mastery and control. On the other hand, seeing the Earth as a 'tiny pea' from space leads to feelings of insignificance and alienation."[37] In the rest of this section, I will discuss how this ambivalence animates current attempts to conceptualize the planetary and how these in turn issue in a paradox when it comes to the possibility of moving beyond the international realm.

The planetary perspective has found further justification in the threat posed by anthropogenic climate change and the subsequent conceptualization of the *Anthropocene* as a new geological epoch characterized by a significant human impact on all Earth systems. As Paul Crutzen and Eugene Stoermer argued when coining this term, given the "still growing impacts of human activities on earth and atmosphere...it seems to us more than appropriate to emphasize the central role of mankind in geology and ecology by proposing to use the term 'anthropocene' for the current geological epoch."[38] Although there is no agreement when the Anthropocene first emerged, Paul Crutzen points to the Industrial Revolution as the breaking point when this unprecedented and decisive human impact on the biosphere began in earnest.[39] As has been pointed out by different scholars, the current international system is not well suited to handle the challenges posed by the Anthropocene. Not only did the international system emerge in tandem with the Anthropocene, but this system has also contributed to the geological crisis by generating economic competition while fostering problems of collective action. This has made it difficult for the discipline of international relations to confront the Anthropocene and its implications in a systematic and coherent way.[40] Here a recourse to the concept of the global

[37] Ibid., 243.

[38] Paul J. Crutzen and Eugene F. Stoermer, "The Anthropocene." *IGBP Newsletter* 41 (Royal Swedish Academy of Sciences, Stockholm, 2000), 17–18, at 17. Also Paul J. Crutzen, "Geology of Mankind." *Nature* 415, 23 (2002).

[39] Ibid.; Paul J. Crutzen, "Geology of Mankind".

[40] See, for example, Duncan Kelly, *Politics and the Anthropocene* (Cambridge: Polity Press, 2019); Olaf Corry and Hayley Stevenson, "IR and the Earth: Societal multiplicity and planetary singularity." in Olaf Corry and Hayley Stevenson (eds.) *Traditions and Trends in Global Environmental Politics* (Abingdon: Routledge, 2017), 1–25; Audra Mitchell, "Is IR Going Extinct?"

offers little hope in terms of escaping this predicament, since it is equally anthropocentric in character. Should we want to make sense of the Anthropocene and its implications, existing conceptualizations of the international and global realms are both insufficient insofar as they presuppose a differentiation between culture and nature as their condition of possibility, and privilege the former so as to rule out the possibility of humans being an active geological force as suggested by the idea of the Anthropocene.[41] This comes close to what William Connolly has described as being sociocentric: "to act as if cultural interpretation and social explanation can proceed without consulting deeply non-human, planetary forces with degrees of autonomy of their own."[42] Bruno Latour likewise warns against uncritically accepting inherited categories of thought when making sense of the planetary. As he has argued, "[i]f we swallow the usual epistemology whole, we shall find ourselves again prisoners of a conception of 'nature' that is impossible to politicize since it has been invented precisely to limit human action thanks to an appeal to the laws of objective nature that cannot be questioned."[43]

Hence the rise of the planetary as a theoretical category of thought and action to capture all that which has been rendered irrelevant by anthropocentric and sociocentric theories of the global. As Connolly describes this realm, it is a "series of temporal force fields, such as climate patterns, drought zones, the ocean conveyor system,

European Journal of International Relations 23 no. 1 (2017): 3–25; Cameron Harrington, "The Ends of the World: International relations and the Anthropocene." *Millennium* 44 no. 3 (2016): 478–498; Anthony Burke et al., "Planet Politics: A manifesto from the end of IR." *Millennium* 44 no. 3 (2016): 499–523; Dahlia Simangan, "Where is the Anthropocene? IR in a New Geological Epoch." *International Affairs* 96 no.1 (2020): 211–224.

41 See, for example, Dipesh Chakrabarty, "Planetary Crises and the Difficulty of Being Modern." *Millennium* 46 no. 3 (2018): 259–282; Madeleine Fagan, "Security in the Anthropocene: Environment, Ecology, Escape." *European Journal of International* Relations 23 no. 2 (2017): 292–314; Philipp Pattberg and Oscar Widerberg, "Theorising Global Environmental Governance: Key Findings and Future Questions." *Millennium* 43 no. 2 (2015): 684–705; David Chandler, "The Transvaluation of Critique in the Anthropocene." *Global Society* 33 no. 1 (2019): 26–44.

42 William E. Connolly, *Facing the Planetary: Entangled Humanism and the Politics of Swarming* (Durham: Duke University Press, 2017), 10.

43 Bruno Latour, *Down to Earth. Politics in the New Climactic Regime* (Cambridge: Polity Press, 2018), 75.

species evolution, glacier flows, and hurricanes that exhibit self-organizing capacities to varying degrees and that impinge on each other and human life in numerous ways."[44] To Latour, a planetary focus means that the project of globalization must be abandoned in favor of a geocentric conception of the human condition. As he has claimed, rather than transcending the divisions of the international, the forces of globalization and modernization have caused the current climate crisis and aggravated these divisions, generating unprecedented migration, inequalities, and geopolitical rivalries. For Latour, "[t]his is the new way in which we can experience the universal human condition – a wicked universality, to be sure, but the only one available to us, now that the previous universality, promised by globalization, seems to be receding from the horizon. The new universality consists in feeling that the ground is in the process of giving way."[45] To resolve this crisis poses the challenge of finding a way beyond customary attachments to the local and the waning ideal of the global, thereby escaping the current tension between nationalism and globalism. Latour here proposes a new concept of the Terrestrial and vests it with agency: "If the Terrestrial is no longer the framework for human action, it because it *participates* in that action."[46] To come terms with this capacity for action necessitates a wholesale change in perspective, ending the modern and distorted views of the global: "The Globe grasps all things from far away, as if they were external to the social world and completely indifferent to human concerns. The Terrestrial grasps the same structures from up close, as internal to the collectivities and sensitive to human actions, to which they react swiftly."[47]

In a similar vein, as Dipesh Chakrabarty has argued, "[i]n thinking of the last few centuries of human pasts and of human futures yet to come we need to orient ourselves to both what we have come to call the globe and to a new historical-philosophical entity called the planet."[48] The difference being that whereas the globe "is a humanocentric construction; the planet, or the Earth system, decenters the human."[49] Yet

[44] Connolly, *Facing the Planetary*, 7. [45] Latour, *Down to Earth*, 17.
[46] Ibid., 51. [47] Ibid., 76.
[48] Dipesh Chakrabarty, *The Climate of History in a Planetary Age* (Chicago: University of Chicago Press, 2021), 3.
[49] Ibid., 4.

the global and the planetary are interconnected through capitalism and technology, both of which are fueling increasing emissions "through the pursuit of industrial and postindustrial forms of modernization and prosperity."[50] As a consequence, "humans have acquired the capacity to interfere with planetary processes but not necessarily – at least not yet – the capacity to fix them."[51] Hence nature can no longer be understood as the inanimate backdrop against which human activity unfolds. As Chakrabarty goes on to explain, "the Anthropocene signifies the extent and duration of our species' modification of the earth's geology, chemistry, and biology."[52]

The social sciences have been unable to come to terms with this predicament because of their long-standing tendency to distinguish natural history from human history while retaining an exclusive focus on the latter. According to Chakrabarty, the concept Anthropocene makes such a distinction both pointless and misleading, and calls instead for a recognition of the fact that "humans are a force of nature in the geological sense."[53] Such a recognition must issue in a qualification of extant stories of globalization and an acknowledgement of the limits of human freedom as well as in a rethinking of the role of capitalism in bringing this new predicament about.[54] From this follows the need to understand the planetary realm in *sui generis* terms, independently of yet related to existing conceptions of the global. As Chakrabarty argues, "[t]he nature of this new category *planet* is best explored ... by distinguishing it from the idea of the globe with which it has often been identified in the past."[55] This being so, since "[t]he word *globe* as it has appeared in the literature on globalization is not the same as the world *globe* in the expression *global warming*."[56] Although the global and the planetary realms are interlocked as implied by the notion of the Anthropocene, they are distinct categories with very different ontologies. Whereas global thought has been preoccupied with issues of sustainability, planetary thinking is focused on habitability without reference to human beings. The question at its center "is *not* what life is or how it is managed in the interest of power but rather what makes a planet friendly to the continuous existence of complex life."[57] Ultimately the category of the planetary is about how "very long-term planetary

[50] Ibid. [51] Ibid., 5. [52] Ibid., 7. [53] Ibid., 31. [54] Ibid., 31–48.
[55] Ibid., 71. [56] Ibid. [57] Ibid., 83.

processes involving both the living and the nonliving have provided ... the enabling conditions for both human existence and flourishing."[58] This further entails that what goes on in the global and the planetary realms occurs in different yet overlapping temporal and historical frames. Whereas the global "refers to matters that happen within human horizons of time", planetary processes "operate on various timetables, some compatible with human times, others vastly larger than what is involved in human calculation."[59] As such, the category of the planetary requires us to abandon or at least revise notions of history and social theory to accommodate its meaning and temporality. As Chakrabarty points out, facing the planetary "would have to begin from the same old premise of securing human life but now ground itself in a new philosophical anthropology, that is, a new understanding of the changing place of humans in the web of life and in the connected but different histories of the globe and the planet."[60]

But does the planetary perspective really provide a viable starting point for thinking beyond the international? I think that the first thing to note about this perspective – at least in the guise in which it has recently gained traction in the humanities and the social sciences – is that it has been made possible by a reversal and reinforcement of the distinctions between organism and artifice and between nature and culture, rather than by a dissolution of these distinctions. In this regard the planetary perspective either presupposes or purports to bring about a subversion of the traditional hierarchy between the human and the nonhuman domains by conceptualizing of the latter domain as the unconstructed foundation of the former. But as Sean Gaston has pointed out, this subversion merely implies that the human domain reappears as the constitutive Other of the nonhuman.[61] In this sense, going planetary brings the argument of this book full circle, to the Copernican revolution and the simultaneous constitution of a global space within which struggles for universal sovereignty could unfold before the rise of a modern international realm. When viewed from a planetary perspective, the international realm is not only coextensive with the empire of the human over the nonhuman world but has also facilitated the exploitation and devastation of the latter by the

[58] Ibid., 85. [59] Ibid., 86. [60] Ibid., 91.
[61] Gaston, *Concept of World from Kant to Derrida*, 151–161.

former. Here the planetary perspective issues in paradox. This being so since the category of the planetary constitutes *both* the ontological foundation of the international realm *and* the horizon of its possible transcendence, chasing its own tail in what looks like an inescapable circularity. That circularity, however, might prove to be productive. Because the more inclined we are to believe that the international system as a human artifice is a permissive cause of most threats to human existence, the more it would seem that this system must contain the seeds of its own abolition.

Bibliography

Abizadeh, Arash. 'On the Demos and Its Kin: Nationalism, Democracy, and the Boundary Problem.' *American Political Science Review* 106 no. 4 (2012): 867–882.

Abraham, Itty. 'Bandung and State Formation in Post-Colonial Asia,' in See Seng Tan and Amitav Acharya (eds.) *Bandung Revisited: The Legacy of the 1955 Asian-African Conference for International Order*. Singapore: National University Press, 2008, 48–68.

Acharya, Amitav. 'Studying the Bandung Conference from a Global IR Perspective.' *Australian Journal of International Affairs* 70 no. 4 (2016): 342–357.

Acharya, Amitav and Barry Buzan. *The Making of Global International Relations*. Cambridge: Cambridge University Press, 2019.

Acton, Lord. 'Nationality,' in John Neville Figgis (ed.) *The History of Freedom and Other Essays*. London: MacMillan, 1907, 270–300.

Adalet, Begüm. 'Infrastructures of Decolonization: Scales of Worldmaking in the Writings of Frantz Fanon.' *Political Theory* 50 no. 1 (2022): 5–31.

Adas, Michael. 'Contested Hegemony: The Great War and the Afro-Asian Assault on the Civilizing Mission Ideology.' *Journal of World History* 15 no. 1 (2004): 31–63.

Adelman, Jeremy. 'An Age of Imperial Revolutions.' *The American Historical Review* 113 no. 2 (2008): 319–340.

Adelman, Jeremy. 'Iberian Passages: Continuity and Change in the South Atlantic,' in David Armitage and Sanjay Subrahmanyam (eds.) *The Age of Revolutions in Global Context, c. 1760–1840*. Basingstoke: Palgrave Macmillan, 2009, 59–64.

Adelman, Jeremy. *Sovereignty and Revolution in the Iberian Atlantic*. Princeton: Princeton University Press, 2009.

Adelman, Jeremy. 'Empires, Nations, and Revolutions.' *Journal of the History of Ideas* 79 no. 1 (2018): 73–88.

Alexandrowicz, Charles Henry. 'The Theory of Recognition *In Fieri*.' *British Yearbook of International Law* 34 (1958): 176–198.

Alighieri, Dante. *Monarchy*, edited by Prue Shaw. Cambridge: Cambridge University Press, 1996.

Almond, Gabriel A. 'Comparative Political Systems.' *Journal of Politics* 18 no. 3 (1956): 391–409.

Almond, Gabriel A. and Sidney Verba. *The Civic Culture: Political Attitudes and Democracy in Five Nations*. Princeton, NJ.: Princeton University Press, 1963.

Anderson, Benedict. *Imagined Communities. Reflections on the Origin and Spread of Nationalism*. London: Verso, 1983.

Anghie, Antony. 'Francisco De Vitoria and the Colonial Origins of International Law.' *Social & Legal Studies* 5, no. 3 (1996): 321–336.

Anghie, Antony. *Imperialism, Sovereignty and the Making of International Law*. Cambridge: Cambridge University Press, 2007.

Anghie, Antony. 'Bandung and the Origins of Third World Sovereignty,' in Luis Eslava, Michael Fakhri, and Vasuki Nesiah (eds.) *Bandung, Global History, and International Law. Critical Pasts and Pending Futures*. Cambridge: Cambridge University Press, 2017, 535–551.

Anon. *Discourses upon the Modern Affairs of Europe*. London, 1680.

Apter, David E. 'Political Religion in the New Nations,' in Clifford Geertz (ed.) *Old Societies and New States: The Quest for Modernity in Asia and Africa*. New York: The Free Press, 1963, 57–104.

Apter, David E. *The Politics of Modernization*. Chicago: University of Chicago Press, 1965.

Arendt, Hannah. *The Human Condition*. Chicago: University of Chicago Press, 1958.

Armitage, David. *The Ideological Origins of the British Empire*. Cambridge: Cambridge University Press, 2001.

Armitage, David. *The Declaration of Independence. A Global History*. Cambridge, MA.: Harvard University Press, 2007.

Armitage, David. 'The Elephant and the Whale: Empires of Land and Sea.' *Journal for Maritime Research* 9, no. 1 (2007): 23–36.

Armitage, David. 'Globalizing Jeremy Bentham.' *History of Political Thought* 32 no. 1 (2011): 63–82.

Armitage, David. *Foundations of Modern International Thought*. Cambridge: Cambridge University Press, 2013.

Armitage, David. *Civil Wars. A History in Ideas*. New York. Knopf, 2016.

Armitage, David et al. 'Interchange: Nationalism and Internationalism in the Era of the Civil War.' *Journal of American History* 98 no. 2 (2011): 455–489.

Armitage, David and Sanjay Subrahmanyam (eds.) *The Age of Revolutions in Global Context, c. 1760–1840*. Basingstoke: Palgrave Macmillan, 2009.

Aron, Raymond. *Peace and War: A Theory of International Relations*. New Brunswick: Transaction Books, 2009.

Arusha Declaration and TANU's Policy on Socialism and Self Reliance. Dar es Salaam: Publicity Section, Tanganyika African National Union, 1967.

Asian-African conference of Bandung, Final Communiqué. April 24, 1955.

d'Aubery, Antoine. *Justes Pretentions du Roi sur l'Empire*. Paris: Antione Bertier, 1667.

Bacon, Francis. 'Of Empire,' in Francis Bacon (ed.). *Essays, Civil and Moral*, Vol. II, Part I. New York: P. F. Collier & Son, 1909–1914.

Bacon, Francis. 'Of the True Greatness of Kingdoms and Estates,' in Francis Bacon (ed.), *Essays, Civil and Moral*, Vol. II, Part I. New York: P. F. Collier & Son, 1909–1914.

Baji, Tomohito. 'Zionist Internationalism? Alfred Zimmern's Post-racial Commonwealth.' *Modern Intellectual History* 13 no. 3 (2016): 623–651.

Barkawi, Tarak. *Soldiers of Empire*. Cambridge: Cambridge University Press, 2017.

Barkawi, Tarak and Mark Laffey. 'Retrieving the Imperial: Empire and International relations.' *Millennium* 31 no. 1 (2002): 109–127.

Barkin, J. Samuel and Bruce Cronin, 'The State and the Nation: Changing Norms and the Rules of Sovereignty in International Relations.' *International Organization* 48 no. 1 (1994): 107–130.

Barreto, José Manuel. 'Cerberus: Rethinking Grotius and the Westphalian System,' in Martti Koskenniemi, Walter Rech, and Manuel Jiménez Fonseca (eds.), *International Law and Empire: Historical Explorations*. Oxford: Oxford University Press, 2017, 149–175.

Bartelson, Jens. *The Critique of the State*. Cambridge. Cambridge University Press, 2001.

Bartelson, Jens. 'Globalizing the Democratic Community.' *Ethics & Global Politics* 1 no. 4 (2008): 159–174.

Bartelson, Jens. *Visions of World Community*. Cambridge: Cambridge University Press, 2009.

Bartelson, Jens. 'The Social Construction of Globality.' *International Political Sociology* 4 no. 3 (2010): 219–235.

Bartelson, Jens. *Sovereignty as Symbolic Form*. London & New York: Routledge, 2014.

Bartelson, Jens. 'Acabando con el Imperio: Lusotropicalismo como ideología imperial.' *Relaciones Internacionales* 30 (2015): 11–26.

Bartelson, Jens. 'Recognition: A Short History.' *Ethics & International Affairs* 30 no. 3 (2016): 303–321.

Baumgart, Winfried. 'German Imperialism in Historical Perspective,' in Arthur J. Knoll and Lewis H. Gann (eds.) *Germans in the Tropics: Essays in German Colonial History*. New York: Greenwood, 1987, 151–164.

Bayly, Christopher A. *The Birth of the Modern World 1780–1914. Global Connections and Comparisons*. Oxford: Blackwell, 2004.

Bayly, Christopher A. *Recovering Liberties: Indian thought in the Age of Liberalism and Empire*. Cambridge: Cambridge University Press, 2011.

Bayly, Christopher A. and Eugenio F. Biagini. *Giuseppe Mazzini and the Globalization of Democratic Nationalism 1830–1920*. Oxford: Oxford University Press, 2008.

Bayly, Martin J. 'Lineages of Indian International Relations: The Indian Council on World Affairs, The League of Nations, and the pedagogy of internationalism.' *International History Review* 44 no. 4 (2022): 819–835.

Beaulac, Stéphane. 'Emer de Vattel and the Externalization of Sovereignty.' *Journal of the History of International Law* 5 no. 2 (2003): 237–292.

Beaulac, Stéphane. *The Power of Language in the Making of International Law: The word sovereignty in Bodin and Vattel and the Myth of Westphalia*. Leiden: Martinus Nijhoff, 2004.

Becker Lorca, Arnulf, 'Universal International Law: Nineteenth-Century Histories of Imposition and Appropriation.' *Harvard International Law Journal* 51 no. 2 (2010): 475–552.

Becker Lorca, Arnulf. *Mestizo International Law. A Global Intellectual History 1842–1933*. Cambridge: Cambridge University Press, 2014.

Bell, David A. *The Cult of the Nation in France: Inventing Nationalism, 1680–1800*. Cambridge, MA: Harvard University Press, 2001.

Bell, Duncan. *The Idea of Greater Britain: Empire and the Future of World Order, 1860–1900*. Princeton: Princeton University Press, 2009.

Bell, Duncan. 'John Stuart Mill on Colonies.' *Political Theory* 38, no. 1 (2010): 34–64.

Bell, Duncan. 'Making and Taking Worlds,' in Samuel Moyn and Andrew Sartori (eds.) *Global Intellectual History*. New York: Columbia University Press, 2013, 254–279.

Bell, Duncan. (ed.) *Victorian Visions of Global Order: Empire and International Relations in Nineteenth-century Political Thought*. Cambridge: Cambridge University Press, 2007.

Bell, Philip W. 'Colonialism as a Problem in American Foreign Policy.' *World Politics* 5 no. 1 (1952): 86–109.

Belmessous, Saliha. (ed.) *Native Claims. Indigenous Law against Empire, 1500–1920*. Oxford: Oxford University Press, 2011.

Belmessous, Saliha. (ed.) *Empire by Treaty: Negotiating European Expansion, 1600–1900*. Oxford: Oxford University Press, 2014.

Benner, Erica. 'Nationalism: Intellectual Origins,' in John Breuilly (ed.) *The Oxford Handbook of the History of Nationalism*. Oxford: Oxford University Press, 2013, 37–55.

Bentham, Jeremy. *An Introduction to the Principles of Morals and Legislation*. Oxford: Clarendon Press, 1907.

Benton, Lauren. *Law and Colonial Cultures: Legal Regimes in World History, 1400–1900*. Cambridge: Cambridge University Press, 2002.
Benton, Lauren. 'From International Law to Imperial Constitutions: The Problem of Quasi-sovereignty, 1870–1900.' *Law and History Review* 26 no. 3 (2008): 595–619.
Benton, Lauren. *A Search for Sovereignty: Law and geography in European Empires, 1400–1900*. Cambridge: Cambridge University Press, 2009.
Benton, Lauren. 'Possessing Empire. Iberian claims and interpolity law,' in Saliha Belmessous (ed.) *Native Claims: Indigenous Law against Empire, 1500–1920*. Oxford: Oxford University Press, 2011, 19–40.
Benton, Lauren. 'Beyond Anachronism: Histories of International Law and Global Legal Politics.' *Journal of the History of International Law* 21 no. 1 (2019): 7–40.
Benton, Lauren and Adam Clulow. 'Empire and Protection: Making Interpolity Law in the Early Modern World.' *Journal of Global History* 12 no. 1 (2017): 74–92.
Benton, Lauren and Benjamin Straumann. 'Acquiring Empire by Law: From Roman Doctrine to Early Modern European Practice.' *Law & History Review* 28 no. 1 (2010): 1–38.
Benton, Lauren and Lisa Ford. *Rage for Order: The British Empire and the Origins of International Law 1800–1850*. Cambridge, MA.: Harvard University Press, 2016.
Benton, Lauren and Richard J. Ross. (eds.) *Legal Pluralism and Empires, 1500–1850*. New York: New York University Press, 2013.
Benton, Lauren, Adam Clulow, and Bain Attwood (eds.) *Protection and Empire*. Cambridge: Cambridge University Press, 2018.
Berger, Stefan. 'Building the Nation among Visions of German Empire,' in Stefan Berger and Alexei Miller (eds.) *Nationalizing Empires*. Budapest: Central European University Press, 2015, 247–308.
Berlin, Isaiah. 'Nationalism: Past Neglect and Present Power,' in H. Hardy (ed.) *Against the Current. Essays in the History of Ideas*. New York: Viking Press, 1980, 333–355.
Berman, Nathaniel. 'Sovereignty in Abeyance: Self-determination and International Law.' *Wisconsin International Law Journal* 7 (1988): 51–105.
Bernard, Mountague. *On the Principle of Non-Intervention. A Lecture Delivered in the Hall of All Souls College*. Oxford & London: J. H. Parker, 1860.
von Bernstorff, Jochen and Philipp Dann (eds.) *The Battle for International Law: South-North Perspectives on the Decolonization Era*. Oxford: Oxford University Press, 2019.
Béthune, Maximilien de. *Duc de Sully. Grand Design of Henry IV, from Memoirs of Maximilian de Béthune duc de Sully*. London: Sweet and Maxwell, 1921.

Beverley, Eric Lewis. 'Introduction: Rethinking Sovereignty, Colonial Empires, and Nation-States in South Asia and Beyond.' *Comparative Studies of South Asia, Africa and the Middle East* 40 no. 3 (2020): 407–420.

Bew, John. *Realpolitik: A History*. Oxford: Oxford University Press, 2016.

Bhabha, Homi K. 'Introduction: Narrating the Nation,' in Homi K. Bhabha (ed.) *Nation and Narration*. London & New York. Routledge, 1990, 1–7.

Blachford, Kevin. 'Revisiting the Expansion Thesis: International Society and the Role of the Dutch East India Company as a Merchant Empire.' *European Journal of International Relations* 26 no. 4 (2020): 1230–1248.

Blackburn, Robin. 'Haiti, Slavery, and the Age of the Democratic Revolution.' *The William and Mary Quarterly* 63 no. 4 (2006): 643–674.

Blaufarb, Rafe. 'The Western Question: The Geopolitics of Latin American Independence.' *American Historical Review* 112 no. 3 (2007): 742–763.

Blay, Kwaw Nyameke. 'Self-determination versus Territorial Integrity in Decolonization.' *New York University Journal of International Law and Politics* 18 (1985): 441–472.

Bluntschli, Johann Kaspar. *The Theory of the State*. Oxford: Clarendon Press, 1885.

Bodin, Jean. *Six Bookes of a Commonwealth*. trans. by Knolles. London: G. Bishop, 1606.

Bodin, Jean. *Method for the Easy Comprehension of History*. trans. by Beatrice Reynolds. New York: Columbia University Press, 1945.

Bonnot, Gabriel, Abbé de Mably. *The Principles of Negotiations: or, An Introduction to The Public Law of Europe Founded on Treaties*. London: James Rivington and James Fletcher, 1758.

Bosbach, Franz. 'The European Debate on Universal Monarchy,' in David Armitage (ed.) *Theories of Empire 1450–1800*. Farnham: Ashgate, 1998.

Botella-Ordinas, Eva. 'Exempt from Time and from Its Fatal Change': Spanish Imperial Ideology, 1450–1700.' *Renaissance Studies* 26 no. 4 (2012): 580–604.

Bowden, Brett. 'The Colonial Origins of International Law: European Expansion and the Classical Standard of Civilization.' *Journal of the History of International Law* 7 no. 1, (2005): 1–23.

Branch, Jordan. *The Cartographic State: Maps, Territory, and the Origins of Sovereignty*. Cambridge: Cambridge University Press, 2013.

Braun, Harald E. *Juan de Mariana and Early Modern Spanish Political Thought*. Aldershot: Ashgate, 2008.

Brett, Annabel S. *Liberty, Right and Nature: Individual Rights in Later Scholastic Thought*. Cambridge: Cambridge University Press, 1997, 165–204.

Brett, Annabel S. *Changes of State: Nature and the Limits of the City in Early Modern Natural Law*. Princeton: Princeton University Press, 2011.

Brett, Annabel S. 'The Space of Politics and the Space of War in Hugo Grotius's *De iure belli ac pacis*.' *Global Intellectual History* 1 no. 1 (2018): 33–60.

Brett, Annabel S. 'The Subject of Sovereignty: Law, Politics and Moral Reasoning in Hugo Grotius.' *Modern Intellectual History* 17 no. 3 (2020): 619–645.

Breuilly, John. 'Modern Empires and Nation-States.' *Thesis Eleven* 139 no. 1 (2017): 11–29.

Brooke, Christopher. 'Eighteenth-century Carthage,' in Béla Kapossy, Isaac Nakhimovsky and Richard Whatmore (eds.) *Commerce and Peace in the Enlightenment*. Cambridge: Cambridge University Press, 2017, 110–124.

Brown, Judith M. 'Nehru-the Dilemmas of a Colonial Inheritance,' in Jost Dülffer and Marc Frey (eds.) *Elites and Decolonization in the Twentieth Century*. Houndsmills, Basingstoke: Palgrave Macmillan, 2011, 177–194.

Brown, Matthew (ed.) *Informal Empire in Latin America: Culture, Commerce and Capital*. Oxford: Blackwell, 2008.

Brown, Wendy. *Regulating Aversion: Tolerance in the Age of Identity and Empire*. Princeton: Princeton University Press, 2009.

Brownlie, Ian. 'An Essay in the History of the Principle of Self-determination,' in C. H. Alexandrowicz (ed.) *Studies in the History of the Law of Nations*. Dordrecht: Springer, 1970, 90–99.

Buck-Morss, Susan. *Hegel, Haiti, and Universal History*. Pittsburgh: University of Pittsburgh Press, 2005.

Budd, Malcolm. 'Wittgenstein on Seeing Aspects.' *Mind* 96 no. 381 (1987): 1–17.

Bukovansky, Mlada. *Legitimacy and Power Politics: The American and French Revolutions in International Political Culture*. Princeton: Princeton University Press, 2010.

Bull, Hedley. *The Anarchical Society: A Study of Order in World Politics*. London: Macmillan, 1977.

Bull, Hedley. 'The Emergence of a Universal International Society,' in Hedley Bull and Adam Watson (eds.) *The Expansion of International Society*. Oxford: Oxford University Press, 1984, 117–126.

Bull, Hedley and Adam Watson, 'Introduction,' in Hedley Bull and Adam Watson (eds) *The Expansion of International Society*. Oxford: Clarendon Press, 1984.

Burbank, Jane and Frederick Cooper. *Empires in World History: Power and the Politics of Difference*. Princeton: Princeton University Press, 2010.

Burke, Anthony et al. 'Planet Politics: A manifesto from the End of IR.' *Millennium* 44 no. 3 (2016): 499–523.

Burke, Edmund. *Letters on a Regicide Peace, Select Works of Edmund Burke*, Vol. 3. Oxford: Clarendon Press, 1874–1878.

Burnard, Trevor. 'Empire Matters? The Historiography of Imperialism in Early America, 1492–1830.' *History of European Ideas* 33 no. 1 (2007): 87–107.

Bushnell, David (ed.) *El Libertador: Writings of Simon Bolívar*. Oxford: Oxford University Press, 2003.

Buzan, Barry and George Lawson. *The Global Transformation: History, Modernity, and the Making of International Relations*. Cambridge: Cambridge University Press, 2015.

Byrne, Jeffrey James. *Mecca of Revolution: Algeria, Decolonization, and Third World Order*. Oxford: Oxford University Press, 2016.

Cabral, Amílcar. 'National Liberation and Culture.' *Transitions* 45 (1974): 12–17.

Cabral, Amílcar. *Unity and Struggle: Speeches and Writings of Amílcar Cabral*. trans. by Michael Wolfers. London and New York: Monthly Review Press, 1979.

Campanella, Tommaso. *A Discourse Touching the Spanish Monarchy*. London: Philemon Stephens, 1654.

Cañizares-Esguerra, Jorge. 'Racial, Religious, and Civic Creole Identity in Colonial Spanish America.' *American Literary History* 17 no. 3 (2005): 420–437.

Cañizares-Esguerra, Jorge. *Nature, Empire, and Nation: Explorations of the History of Science in the Iberian World*. Stanford: Stanford University Press, 2006.

Cardoso Reis, Bruno. 'Portugal and the UN: A Rogue State Resisting the Norm of Decolonization (1956–1974).' *Portuguese Studies* 29 no. 2 (2013): 251–276.

Carrington, Charles E. 'Decolonization: The Last Stages.' *International Affairs* 38 no. 1 (1962): 29–40.

de Carvalho, Benjamin, Halvard Leira, and John M. Hobson. 'The Big Bangs of IR: The Myths that Your Teachers Still Tell You about 1648 and 1919.' *Millennium* 39 no. 3 (2011): 735–758.

Castelo, Cláudia. *O Modo Português de Estar no Mundo: O lusotropicalismo e a ideologia colonial portuguesa, 1933–1961*. Porto: Edições Afrontamento, 1998.

Castro-Klarén, Sara. 'Framing Pan-Americanism: Simon Bolivar's Findings.' *New Centennial Review* 3 no. 1 (2003): 25–53.

Cavallar, George. 'Vitoria, Grotius, Pufendorf, Wolff and Vattel: Accomplices of European Colonialism and Exploitation or True Cosmopolitans?' *Journal of the History of International Law* 10 no. 2 (2008): 181–209.

Cello, Lorenzo. 'The Legitimacy of International Interventions in Vattel's The Law of Nations.' *Global Intellectual History* 2 no. 2 (2018): 105–123.

Chakrabarty, Dipesh. *Provincializing Europe: Postcolonial thought and Historical Difference*. Princeton: Princeton University Press, 2000.

Chakrabarty, Dipesh. 'Planetary Crises and the Difficulty of Being Modern.' *Millennium* 46 no. 3 (2018): 259–282.

Chakrabarty, Dipesh. *The Climate of History in a Planetary Age*. Chicago: University of Chicago Press, 2021.

Chambers, Sarah C. and John Charles Chasteen (eds.) *Latin American Independence: An Anthology of Sources*. Indianapolis: Hackett Publishing, 2010.

Chandler, David. 'The Transvaluation of Critique in the Anthropocene.' *Global Society* 33 no. 1 (2019): 26–44.

Chatterjee, Partha. *Nationalist Thought and the Colonial World: A Derivative Discourse*. Minneapolis: University of Minnesota Press, 1986.

Chatterjee, Partha. *The Nation and Its Fragments: Colonial and Postcolonial Histories*. Princeton: Princeton University Press, 1993.

Chiong Rivero, Horacio. *The Rise of Pseudo-Historical Fiction: Fray Antonio de Guevara's Novelizations*. New York: Peter Lang, 2004.

Chowdhury, Arjun. *The Myth of International Order. Why Weak States Persist and Alternatives to the State Fade Away*. Oxford: Oxford University Press, 2018.

Christian, David. 'World History in Context.' *Journal of World History* 14 no. 3 (2003): 437–458.

Christian, David. 'The Return of Universal History.' *History and Theory* 49 no. 4 (2010): 6–27.

Clark, Ian. *International Legitimacy and World Society*. Oxford: Oxford University Press, 2007.

Clark, Martin. 'A Conceptual History of Recognition in British International Legal Thought.' *British Yearbook of International Law* 87 no. 1 (2017): 18–97.

Cohen, Jean L. *Globalization and Sovereignty: Rethinking Legality, Legitimacy, and Constitutionalism*. Cambridge: Cambridge University Press, 2012.

Collier, Simon. 'Nationality, Nationalism, and Supranationalism in the Writings of Simón Bolívar.' *Hispanic American Historical Review* 63 no. 1 (1983): 37–64.

Collins, Michael. 'Decolonisation and the "federal moment".' *Diplomacy & Statecraft* 24 no. 1 (2013): 21–40.

Collins, Michael. *Empire, Nationalism, and the Postcolonial World: Rabindranath Tagore's Writings on History, Politics and Society*. Abingdon: Routledge, 2013.

Condorcet, Marie Jean Antoine Nicolas de Caritat, Marquis de. Sketch for a Historical Picture of the Progress of the Human Mind: Tenth Epoch. trans. by Keith Michael Baker. *Daedalus* 133 no. 3, (2004): 65–82.

Connolly, William E. *Facing the Planetary: Entangled humanism and the Politics of Swarming*. Durham: Duke University Press, 2017.

Constant, Benjamin. *Political Writings*, edited by Biancamaria Fontana. Cambridge: Cambridge University Press, 1988.

Cooper, Frederick. 'Alternatives to Empire: France and Africa after World War II,' in Douglas Howland and Luise White (eds.) *The State of Sovereignty: Territories, Laws, Populations*. Bloomington: Indiana University Press, 2008, 94–123.

Cooper, Frederick. 'Alternatives to Nationalism in French Africa, 1945–1960,' in Jost Dülffer and Marc Frey (eds.) *Elites and Decolonization in the Twentieth Century*. Houndsmills: Palgrave Macmillan, 2011, 110–137.

Cooper, Frederick. *Citizenship between Empire and Nation*. Princeton: Princeton University Press, 2015.

Corry, Olaf and Hayley Stevenson. 'IR and the Earth: Societal Multiplicity and Planetary Singularity,' in Olaf Corry and Hayley Stevenson (eds.) *Traditions and Trends in Global Environmental Politics*. Abingdon: Routledge, 2017, 1–25.

Costa Lopez, Julia, Benjamin De Carvalho, Andrew Latham, Ayşe Zarakol, Jens Bartelson, and Minda Holm. 'In the Beginning There Was No Word (for it): Terms, Concepts, and Early Sovereignty.' *International Studies Review* 20 no. 3 (2018): 489–519.

Coupland, Reginald. *The Study of the British Commonwealth. An Inaugural Lecture Delivered before the University of Oxford*. Oxford: Clarendon Press, 1921.

Craven, Matthew. 'Statehood, Self-determination, and Recognition,' in Malcolm D. Evans (ed.) *International Law*. Oxford: Oxford: Oxford University Press, 2010, 203–251.

Crawford, James. *The Creation of States in International Law*. Oxford: Oxford University Press, 2007.

Croxton, Derek. 'The Peace of Westphalia of 1648 and the Origins of Sovereignty.' *The International History Review* 21 no. 3 (1999): 569–591.

Croxton, Derek. *Westphalia: The Last Christian Peace*. Houndmills, Basingstoke: Palgrave MacMillan, 2013.

Crutzen, Paul J. 'Geology of Mankind.' *Nature* 415 p. 23 (2002): 17–18.

Crutzen, Paul J. and Eugene F. Stoermer. 'The 'Anthropocene.' *IGBP* Newsletter 41, (Royal Swedish Academy of Sciences, Stockholm, 2000), 17–18.

Dahm, Bernhard. *Sukarno and the Struggle for Indonesian Independence*. Ithaca: Cornell University Press, 1969.

Dandelet, Thomas James. *The Renaissance of Empire in Early Modern Europe*. Cambridge: Cambridge University Press, 2014.

Davenant, Charles. *An Essay upon Universal Monarchy: Written in the year 1701 soon after Lewis the Fourteenth had settled his grandson Philip de Bourbon upon the throne of Spain*. London: James, John and Paul Knapton, 1734.

Defoe, Daniel. *The Interests of the Several Princes and States of Europe consider'd, with respect to the succession of the crown of Spain, and the titles of the several pretenders thereto examin'd*. London, 1698.

Delanty, Gerard and Aurea Mota. 'Governing the Anthropocene: Agency, Governance, Knowledge.' *European Journal of Social Theory* 20 no. 1 (2017): 9–38.

Deutsch, Karl W. *Nationalism and Social Communication: An Inquiry into the Foundations of Nationality*. Cambridge, MA: MIT Press, 1966.

Devetak, Richard. 'Law of Nations as Reason of State: Diplomacy and the Balance of Power in Vattel's Law of Nations.' *Parergon* 28 no. 2 (2011): 105–128.

Devetak, Richard. 'The Fear of Universal Monarchy': Balance of Power as an Ordering Practice of Liberty.' *Proceedings of the British Academy* 190 (2013): 121–137.

Dia, Mamadou. *The African Nations and World Solidarity*, trans. by Mercer Cook. New York: Praeger, 1961.

de Donno, Fabrizio. 'The Gandhian Mazzini: Democratic Nationalism, Self-Rule, and Non-Violence.' in Christopher A. Bayly and Eugenio F. Biagini (eds.). *Giuseppe Mazzini and the Globalization of Democratic Nationalism 1830–1920*. Oxford: Oxford University Press, 2008, 374–398.

Doyle, Michael. *Empires*. Ithaca: Cornell University Press, 1986.

Dubois, Laurent. *Avengers of the New World: The Story of the Haitian Revolution*. Cambridge, MA: Harvard University Press, 2004.

Dunn, John. 'Why We Need a Global History of Political Thought,' in Béla Kapossy (ed.) *Markets, Morals, Politics: Jealousy of Trade and the History of Political Thought*. Cambridge, MA: Harvard University Press, 2018, 285–309.

Dwyer, Philip. 'Napoleon and the Universal Monarchy.' *History* 95 no. 319 (2010): 293–307.

Eagleton, Clyde. 'Excesses of Self-determination.' *Foreign Affairs* 31 no. 4 (1953): 592–604.

Eagleton, Clyde. 'Self-determination in the United Nations.' *American Journal of International Law* 47 no. 1 (1953): 88–93.

Eckert, Andreas. 'Julius Nyerere, Tanzanian Elites, and the Project of African Socialism,' in Jost Dülffer and Marc Frey (eds.) *Elites and Decolonization in the Twentieth Century*. Houndsmills: Palgrave Macmillan, 2011, 216–240.

Egyptian Delegation, Collection of Official Correspondence from November 11, 1918 to July 14, 1919. Paris, 1919.

Egyptian Delegation, The Egyptian National Claims. A Memorandum Presented to the Peace Conference by the Egyptian Delegation Charged with the Defence of Egyptian Independence. Paris, 1919.

Eisenstadt, Shmul N. *The Political Systems of Empires*. New York: The Free Press, 1963.

Elden, Stuart. *The Birth of Territory*. Chicago: University of Chicago Press, 2013.

Elliott, John H. 'A Europe of Composite Monarchies.' *Past & Present* 137 (1992): 48–71.

Emerson, Rupert. *From Empire to Nation: The Rise to Self-Assertion of Asian and African Peoples*. Cambridge, MA: Harvard University Press, 1960.

Epstein, Charlotte. *Birth of the State: The Place of the Body in Crafting Modern Politics*. Oxford: Oxford University Press, 2021.

Eslava, Luis, Michael Fakhri, and Vasuki Nesiah (eds.) *Bandung, Global History, and International Law: Critical Pasts and Pending Futures*. Cambridge: Cambridge University Press, 2017.

Eslava, Luis, Michael Fakhri, and Vasuki Nesiah. 'The Spirit of Bandung,' in Luis Eslava, Michael Fakhri, and Vasuki Nesiah (eds.) *Bandung, Global History, and International Law: Critical Pasts and Pending Futures*. Cambridge: Cambridge University Press, 2017, 3–32.

Evans, Neil. "A World Empire, Sea Girt': The British Empire, State, and Nations, 1780–1914,' in Stefan Berger and Alexei Miller (eds.) *Nationalizing Empires*. Budapest: Central European University Press, 2015, 31–97.

Fabry, Mikulas. *Recognizing States: International Society and the Establishment of New States since 1776*. Oxford: Oxford University Press, 2010.

Fagan, Madeleine. 'Security in the Anthropocene: Environment, Ecology, Escape.' *European Journal of International Relations* 23 no. 2 (2017): 292–314.

Fanon, Frantz. *The Wretched of the Earth*. trans. by Constance Farrington. New York: Grove Weidenfeld, 1963.

Farr, James. 'Francis Lieber and the Interpretation of American Political Science.' *Journal of Politics* 52 no. 4 (1990): 1027–1049.

Fasolt, Constantin. *The Limits of History*. Chicago: University of Chicago Press, 2004.

Fawcett, Louise. 'Between West and Non-West: Latin American Contributions to International Thought.' *International History Review* 34 no. 4 (2012): 679–704.

Fejzula, Merve. 'The Cosmopolitan Historiography of Twentieth-Century Federalism.' *Historical Journal* 64 no. 2 (2021): 477–500.

Fernández-Santamaría, José A. *The State, War and Peace: Spanish Political Thought in the Renaissance 1516–1559*. Cambridge: Cambridge University Press, 1977.

Ferrand, Julie and Arnaud Orain, 'Abbé de Mably on Commerce, Luxury, and Classical Republicanism.' *Journal of the History of Economic Thought* 39 no. 2 (2017): 199–221.

Fiore, Pasquale. *Nouveau Droit International Public Suivant des Besoins de la Civilization Moderne*, Vols. I-II. trans. by Charles Antoine. Paris: A. Durand et Pedone-Lauriel, 1885.

Fiore, Pasquale. *International Law Codified and its Legal Sanction; or, The Legal Organization of the Society of States*. New York: Baker, Voorhis, & Co, 1918.

Fisch, Jörg. *The Right of Self-determination of Peoples: The Domestication of an Illusion*. Cambridge: Cambridge University Press, 2015.

Fitzmaurice, Andrew. *Sovereignty, Property and Empire, 1500–2000*. Cambridge: Cambridge University Press, 2014.

Fletcher, Andrew. 'A Discourse Concerning the Affairs of Spain,' in Andrew Fletcher (ed.) *Political Works*. Cambridge: Cambridge University Press, 1997, 84–117.

Fitzmaurice, Andrew. 'The Problem of Eurocentrism in the Thought of Francisco de Vitoria,' in José Maria Beneyto and Justo Corti Varela (eds.) *At the Origins of Modernity: Francisco de Vitoria and the Discovery of International Law*. Cham: Springer, 2017, 77–93.

Forsyth, Murray. 'The Old European States-System: Gentz versus Hauterive.' *The Historical Journal* 23 no. 3 (1980): 521–538.

Fontana, Biancamaria. 'The Napoleonic Empire and the Europe of Nations,' in Anthony Pagden (ed.) *The Idea of Europe: From Antiquity to the European Union*. Cambridge: Cambridge University Press, 2002, 116–128.

Foucault, Michel. 'Nietzsche, Genealogy, History,' in David Bouchard (ed.) *Language, Counter-Memory, Practice: Selected Essays and Interviews*. Ithaca: Cornell University Press, 139–164.

Franklin, Julian H. *Jean Bodin and the Rise of Absolutist Theory*. Cambridge: Cambridge University Press, 1973.

Fraser, Cary. 'Decolonization and the Cold War,' in Richard H. Immerman and Petra Goedde (eds.) *The Oxford Handbook of the Cold War*. Oxford: Oxford University Press, 2013, 469–485.

Gaffield, Julia (ed.) *The Haitian Declaration of Independence: Creation, Context, and Legacy*. Charlottesville: University of Virginia Press, 2016.

Gallagher, John and Ronald Robinson. 'The Imperialism of Free Trade.' *Economic History Review* 6 no. 1 (1953): 1–15.

Gaston, Sean. *The Concept of the World from Kant to Derrida*. London: Rowman & Littlefield, 2013.

Geggus, David. 'The Caribbean in the Age of Revolution,' in Armitage, David and Sanjay Subrahmanyam (eds.) *The Age of Revolutions in Global Context, c. 1760–1840*. Basingstoke: Palgrave Macmillan, 2009, 59–82.

van Gelderen, Martin. 'From Domingo de Soto to Hugo Grotius: Theories of Monarchy and Civil Power in Spanish and Dutch Political thought, 1555–1609,' in Graham Darby (ed.) *Origins and Development of the Dutch Revolt*. Abingdon: Routledge, 2001, 151–170.

van Gelderen, Martin. 'Universal Monarchy, the Rights of War and Peace and the Balance of Power. Europe's Quest for Civil Order,' in Hans-Åke Persson and Bo Stråth (eds.) *Reflections on Europe. Defining a Political Order in Time and Space*. Brussels: Peter Lang, 2007, 49–72.

Gellner, Ernest. *Nations and Nationalism*. Ithaca: Cornell University Press, 1983.

von Gentz, Friedrich. *On the State of Europe Before and After the French Revolution*. London: J. Hatchard, 1802.

von Gentz, Friedrich. *Fragments upon the Balance of Power in Europe*. London: M. Peltier, 1806.

Gerwarth, Robert and Erez Manela. 'The Great War as a Global War: Imperial Conflict and the Reconfiguration of World Order, 1911–1923.' *Diplomatic History* 38 no. 4 (2014): 786–800.

Getachew, Adom. *Worldmaking after Empire: The Rise and Fall of Self-determination*. Princeton: Princeton University Press, 2019.

Getachew, Adom. 'The State's Imperial Shadows.' *Ethics & International Affairs* 35 no. 4 (2021): 503–513.

Gandhi, Mohandas K. *Hind Swaraj or Indian Home Rule*. Ahmedabad: Navajivan Press, 1938.

Geertz, Clifford. 'The Integrative Revolution: Primordial Sentiments and Civil Politics in the New States,' in Clifford Geertz (ed.) *Old Societies and New States: The Quest for Modernity in Asia and Africa*. New York: The Free Press, 1963, 105–157.

Ghervas, Stella. *Conquering Peace: From the Enlightenment to the European Union*. Cambridge, MA: Harvard University Press, 2021.

Gibbon, Edward. *The Decline and Fall of the Roman Empire*. New York: Modern Library, sa.

Gilman, Nils. *Mandarins of the Future: Modernization Theory in Cold War America*. Baltimore: Johns Hopkins University Press, 2003.

Glanville, Luke. 'The Myth of "traditional" Sovereignty.' *International Studies Quarterly* 57 no. 1 (2013): 79–90.

Glanville, Luke. *Sovereignty and the Responsibility to Protect: A New History*. Chicago: University of Chicago Press, 2013.

Glanville, Luke. 'Responsibility to Perfect: Vattel's Conception of Duties beyond Borders.' *International Studies Quarterly* 61 no. 2 (2017): 385–395.

Go, Julian. *Patterns of Empire: The British and American Empires, 1688 to the Present*. Cambridge: Cambridge University Press, 2011.

Go, Julian. 'Fanon's Postcolonial Cosmopolitanism.' *European Journal of Social Theory* 16 no. 2 (2013): 208–225.

Golove, David M. and Daniel J. Hulsebosch. 'Civilized Nation: The Early American Constitution, the Law of Nations, and the Pursuit of International Recognition.' *New York University Law Review* 85 (2010): 932–1066.

Gong, Gerrit W. *The Standard of Civilization in International Society*. Oxford: Oxford University Press, 1984.

Goswami, Manu. 'Rethinking the Modular Nation Form: Toward a Sociohistorical Conception of Nationalism.' *Comparative Studies in Society and History* 44 no. 4 (2002): 770–799.

Goswami, Manu. 'Imaginary Futures and Colonial Internationalisms.' *American Historical Review* 117 no. 5 (2012): 1461–1485.

Greenblatt, Stephen. *Marvelous Possessions: The Wonder of the New World*. Chicago: University of Chicago Press, 1991.

Greenfeld, Liah. *Nationalism: Five Roads to Modernity*. Cambridge, MA: Harvard University Press, 1992.

Gross, Leo 'The Peace of Westphalia, 1648–1948.' *American Journal of International Law* 42 no. 1 (1948): 20–41.

Grotius, Hugo. *De Iure Belli ac Pacis Libri Tres*, edited by Richard Tuck. Indianapolis: Liberty Fund, 2005.

de Guevara, Antonio. *The Diall of Princes: Compiled by the reuerende father in God, Don Anthony of Gueuara, Bysshop of Guadix*. trans. by Thomas North. London, 1557.

Guilhot, Nicolas. 'Imperial Realism: Post-War IR Theory and Decolonization.' *The International History Review* 36 no. 4 (2014): 698–720.

Haakonssen, Knud. 'Hugo Grotius and the History of Political Thought.' *Political Theory* 13 no. 2 (1985): 239–265.

Haddock, Bruce. 'State and Nation in Mazzini's Political Thought.' *History of Political Thought* 20 no. 2 (1999): 313–336.

Haddour, Azzedine. 'Remembering Sartre,' in Jean-Paul Sartre (ed.) *Colonialism and Neocolonialism*. London & New York: Routledge, 2006, 1–16.

Haldén, Peter. 'A Non-Sovereign Modernity: Attempts to Engineer Stability in the Balkans 1820–90.' *Review of International Studies* 39 no. 2 (2013): 337–359.

Haldén, Peter. *Stability without Statehood: Lessons from Europe's History before the Sovereign State*. Basingstoke: Palgrave MacMillan, 2011.

Hall, John A. 'Taking Megalomanias Seriously: Rough Notes.' *Thesis Eleven* 139 no. 1 (2017): 30–45.

Hall, Rodney Bruce. *National Collective Identity: Social Constructs and International Systems*. New York: Columbia University Press, 1999.

Hardt, Michael and Antonio Negri. *Empire*. Cambridge, MA: Harvard University Press, 2000.

Harrington, Cameron. 'The Ends of the World: International Relations and the Anthropocene.' *Millennium* 44 no. 3 (2016): 478–498.

Harris, C. C. and Julius Nyerere. 'Tanganyika Today.' *International Affairs* 36 no. 1 (1960): 35–47.

Hatta, Mohammed. *Portrait of a Patriot: Selected Writings of Mohammed Hatta*. The Hague: Mouton, 1972.

d'Hauterive Comte, Alexandre Maurice Blanc de Lanautte. *State of the French Republic at the End of the Year VIII*. trans. by Lewis Goldsmith. London: J. S. Jordon, 1801.

Havercroft, Jonathan. *Captives of Sovereignty*. Cambridge: Cambridge University Press, 2011.

Hazareesingh, Sudhir. *Saint-Napoleon. Celebrations of Sovereignty in Nineteenth Century France*. Cambridge, MA: Harvard University Press, 2004.

Headley, John M. 'The Emperor and His Chancellor: Disputes over Empire, Administration and Pope (1519–1529),' in *Carlos V y la quiebra del humanismo político en Europa (1530–1558)*. Madrid: Sociedad Estatal para la Comemoración de los Centenarios de Felipe II y Carlos V, 2001, 21–35.

Headley, John M. *The Emperor and His Chancellor: A Study of the Imperial Chancellery under Gattinara*. Cambridge: Cambridge University Press, 1983.

Headley, John M. *Tommaso Campanella and the Transformation of the World*. Princeton: Princeton University Press, 1997.

Headley, John M. 'The Habsburg World Empire and the Revival of Ghibellinism,' in David Armitage (ed.) *Theories of Empire 1450–1800*. Farnham: Ashgate, 1998, 45–79.

Heater, Derek. *National Self-Determination: Woodrow Wilson and His Legacy*. London: Macmillan, 1994.

Hegel, Georg Wilhelm Friedrich. *Elements of the Philosophy of Right*. Cambridge: Cambridge University Press, 1991.

Hegel, Georg Wilhelm Friedrich. *The Philosophy of History*. trans. by J. Sibree. Kitchener: Batoche Books, 2001.

Heidegger, Martin. 'The Origin of the Work of Art,' in Martin Heidegger and David Farrell Krell (eds.) *Basic Writings*. New York: Harper Collins, 1993, 139–212.

Heiskanen, Jaakko. 'Spectra of Sovereignty: Nationalism and International Relations,' *International Political Sociology* 13 no. 3 (2019): 315–332.

Heiskanen, Jaakko. *The Ethnos of the Earth: Nationalism, Ethnicity, and International Order*. Dissertation, POLIS, University of Cambridge, 2020.

Herz, John. 'Rise and Demise of the Territorial State.' *World Politics* 9 no. 4 (1957): 473–493.

Herzog, Tamar. 'Communities Becoming a Nation: Spain and Spanish America in the Wake of Modernity (and thereafter).' *Citizenship Studies* 11 no. 2 (2007): 151–172.

Herzog, Tamar. *Defining Nations: Immigrants and Citizens in Early Modern Spain and Spanish America*. New Haven: Yale University Press, 2008.

Hill, Christopher L. 'Conceptual Universalization in the Transnational Nineteenth Century,' in Samuel Moyn and Andrew Sartori (eds.) *Global Intellectual History*. New York: Columbia University Press, 2013, 134–158.

Hinsley, Francis Harry. *Power and the Pursuit of Peace: Theory and Practice in the History of Relations between States*. Cambridge: Cambridge University Press, 1967.

Hinsley, Francis Harry. *Nationalism and the International System*. London: Hodder and Stoughton, 1973.

Hirschi, Caspar. *The Origins of Nationalism: An Alternative History from Ancient Rome to Early Modern Germany*. Cambridge: Cambridge University Press, 2012.

Hobbes, Thomas. *Leviathan*, edited by Richard Tuck. Cambridge: Cambridge University Press, 1991.

Hobson, John M. *The Eurocentric Conception of World Politics*. Cambridge: Cambridge University Press, 2012.

Hobson, John M. 'The Twin Self-delusions of IR: Why "hierarchy" and not "anarchy" is the Core Concept of IR.' *Millennium* 42 no. 3 (2014): 557–575.

Hobson, John M. and Jason C. Sharman. 'The Enduring Place of Hierarchy in World Politics: Tracing the Social Logics of Hierarchy and Political Change.' *European Journal of International Relations* 11 no. 1 (2005): 63–98.

Hoffman, Stanley. 'Hedley Bull and His Contribution to International Relations.' *International Affairs* 62 no. 2 (1986): 179–195.

Holland, Ben. 'The Moral Person of the State: Emer de Vattel and the Foundations of International Legal Order.' *History of European Ideas* 37 no. 4 (2011): 438–445.

Holland, Ben. *The Moral Person of the State: Pufendorf, Sovereignty and Composite Polities*. Cambridge: Cambridge University Press, 2017.

Hom, Stephanie Malia. 'On the Origins of Making Italy: Massimo D'Azeglio and 'fatta l'Italia, bisogna fare gli italiani'.' *Italian Culture* 31 no. 1 (2013): 1–16.

Hont, István. 'The Rich Country – Poor Country Debate in the Scottish Classical Political Economy,' in István Hont and Michael Ignatieff (eds.) *Wealth & Virtue: The Shaping of Political Economy in the Scottish Enlightenment*. Cambridge: Cambridge University Press, 1983, 271–315.

Hont, István. 'The Permanent Crisis of a Divided Mankind: "Contemporary crisis of the nation state" in Historical Perspective.' *Political Studies* 42 no. 1 (1994): 166–231.

Hont, István. *Jealousy of Trade: International Competition and the Nation State in Historical Perspective*. Cambridge, MA: Harvard University Press, 2005.

Hunter, Ian. 'Vattel's Law of Nations: Diplomatic Casuistry for the Protestant Nation.' *Grotiana* 31 no. 1 (2010): 108–140.

Hörnqvist, Michael. *Machiavelli and Empire*. Cambridge: Cambridge University Press, 2008.

Hörnqvist, Michael. 'Machiavelli's Three Desires: Florentine Republicans on Liberty, Empire, and Justice,' in Sankar Muthu (ed.) *Empire and Modern Political Thought*. Cambridge: Cambridge University Press, 7–29.

Iggers, Georg G. *The German Conception of History: The National Tradition of Historical Thought from Herder to the Present*. Middletown: Wesleyan University Press, 1968.

Imbruglia, Girolamo. 'Civilisation and Colonisation: Enlightenment Theories in the Debate between Diderot and Raynal.' *History of European Ideas* 41 no. 7 (2015): 858–882.

Isabella, Maurizio. 'Mazzini's Internationalism in Context: From the Cosmopolitan Patriotism of the Italian Carbonari to Mazzini's Europe of the Nations,' in Christopher A. Bayly and Eugenio F. Biagini (eds.) *Giuseppe Mazzini and the Globalization of Democratic Nationalism 1830–1920*. Oxford: Oxford University Press, 2008, 37–58.

Isabella, Maurizio. 'The Political Thought of a New Constitutional Monarchy: Piedmont after 1848,' in Douglas Moggach and Gareth Stedman Jones (eds.) *The 1848 Revolutions and European Political Thought*. Cambridge: Cambridge University Press, 2018, 383–404.

Jacob, Christian. *The Sovereign Map. Theoretical Approaches in Cartography Throughout History*. Chicago: University of Chicago Press, 2006.

Jahn, Beate. 'Kant, Mill, and Illiberal Legacies in International Affairs.' *International Organization* 59 no. 1 (2005): 177–207.

Jakšić, Ivan. *Selected Writings of Andrés Bello*. Oxford: Oxford University Press, 1997.

Jakšić, Ivan. *Andrés Bello: Scholarship and nation-building in nineteenth-century Latin America*. Cambridge: Cambridge University Press, 2006.

Jansen, Jan C. and Jürgen Osterhammel. *Decolonization: A Short History*. Princeton: Princeton University Press, 2017.

Jaume, Lucien. 'Citizen and State under the French Revolution,' in Quentin Skinner and Bo Stråth (eds.) *States and Citizens: History, Theory, Prospects*. Cambridge: Cambridge University Press, 2003, 131–144.

Jennings, W. Ivor. *The Approach to Self-government*. Cambridge: Cambridge University Press, 1956.

Jones, Branwen Gruffydd. 'Race, Culture and Liberation: African Anticolonial Thought and Practice in the Time of Decolonisation.' *The International History Review* 42 no. 6 (2020): 1238–1256.

Jones, H. S. 'The Idea of the National in Victorian Political Thought.' *European Journal of Political Theory* 5 no. 1 (2006): 12–21.

Jouannet, Emmanuelle. 'The Disappearance of the Concept of Empire. Or, the Beginning of the End of Empires in Europe from the 18th century.' Presentation at the Conference 'A Just Empire? Rome's Legal Legacy and the Justification of War and Empire in International Law.' Commemorative Conference on Alberico Gentili (1552–1608). New York University School of Law, 13–15 March 2008.

von Justi, Johann Heinrich Gottlob. *Historische und Juristische Schriften*, Vol. 1. Frankfurt & Leipzig: Garbe, 1760.

Kapila, Shruti. *Violent Fraternity: Indian Political Thought in the Global Age*. Princeton: Princeton University Press, 2021.

Kedourie, Elie. *Nationalism*. Oxford: Blackwell, 1993.

Keene, Edward. *Beyond the Anarchical Society: Grotius, Colonialism and Order in World Politics*. Cambridge: Cambridge University Press, 2002.

Keitner, Chimène I. 'National Self-Determination in Historical Perspective: The Legacy of the French Revolution for Today's Debates.' *International Studies Review* 2 no. 3 (2000): 3–26.

Kelly, Duncan. 'Popular Sovereignty as State Theory in the Nineteenth Century,' in Richard Bourke and Quentin Skinner (eds.) *Popular Sovereignty in Historical Perspective*. Cambridge: Cambridge University Press, 2016, 270–296.

Kelly, Duncan. 'The Goal of that Pure and Noble Yearning' Friedrich Meinecke's Visions of 1848,' in Douglas Moggach and Gareth Stedman Jones (eds.) *The 1848 Revolutions and European Political Thought*. Cambridge: Cambridge University Press, 2018, 293–321.

Kelly, Duncan. *Politics and the Anthropocene*. Cambridge: Polity Press, 2019.

King, Preston T. *The Ideology of Order: A Comparative Analysis of Jean Bodin and Thomas Hobbes*. London: Allen & Unwin, 1974.

Koebner, Richard. *Empire*. Cambridge: Cambridge University Press, 1966.

Koenigsberger, Helmut Georg. 'Dominium Regale or Dominium Politicum Et Regale: Monarchies and Parliaments in Early Modern Europe,' in Helmut G. Koenigsberger (ed.) *Politicians and Virtuosi: Essays on Early Modern History*. London: Hambledon Press, 1986, 1–26.

Koenigsberger, Helmut Georg. 'Composite States, Representative Institutions and the American Revolution.' *Historical Research* 62 no. 148 (1989): 135–153.

Kohn, Hans. 'Treitschke: National Prophet.' *The Review of Politics* 7 no. 4 (1945): 418–440.

Kohn, Hans. *The Idea of Nationalism: A Study in Its Origins and Background*. New Brunswick: Transaction Books, 2008.

Komlosy, Andrea. 'Imperial Cohesion, Nation-Building, and Regional Integration in the Habsburg Monarchy,' in Stefan Berger and Alexei Miller (eds.) *Nationalizing Empires*. Budapest: Central European University Press, 2015, 369–428.

Korean Delegation, Claim of the Korean People and Nation for Liberation from Japan and for the Reconstitution of Korea as an Independent State. Memorandum, Paris, April 1919.

Koselleck, Reinhart. 'Historical Criteria of the Modern Concept of Revolution,' in Reinhart Koselleck (ed.) *Futures Past: On the Semantics of Historical Time*. Cambridge, MA: MIT Press, 1985, 39–54.

Koskenniemi, Martti. *The Gentle Civilizer of Nations: The Rise and Fall of International Law 1870–1960*. Cambridge: Cambridge University Press, 2001.

Koskenniemi, Martti. 'Empire and International Law: The Real Spanish Contribution.' *University of Toronto Law Journal* 61 no. 1 (2011): 1–36.

Koskenniemi, Martti. 'Race, Hierarchy and International Law: Lorimer's Legal Science.' *European Journal of International Law* 27 no. 2 (2016): 415–429.

Koskenniemi, Martti. *To the Uttermost Parts of the Earth: Legal Imagination and International Power 1300–1870*. Cambridge: Cambridge University Press, 2021.

Krasner, Stephen D. 'Westphalia and All That,' in Judith Goldstein and Robert O. Keohane (eds.) *Ideas and Foreign Policy*. Ithaca: Cornell University Press, 1993, 235–264.

Kreijen, Gerard and Robert Y. Jennings. *State Failure, Sovereignty and Effectiveness: Legal Lessons from the Decolonization of Sub-Saharan Africa*. Leiden: Brill Nijhoff, 2004.

Kripp, Jacob. 'The Creative Advance Must Be Defended: Miscegenation, Metaphysics, and Race War in Jan Smuts's Vision of the League of Nations.' *American Political Science Review* 116 no. 3 (2022): 940–953.

Kristensen, Peter Marcus. 'Subject Matters: Imperialism and the Constitution of International Relations.' *Review of International Studies* (2022): 1–23. https://doi.org/10.1017/S0260210522000420

Kumar, Krishan. 'Nation-States as Empires, Empires as Nation-States: Two Principles, One Practice?' *Theory and Society* 39, no. 2 (2010): 119–143.

Kumar, Krishan. *Visions of Empire: How Five Imperial Regimes Shaped the World*. Princeton: Princeton University Press, 2017.

Kumar, Krishan. *Empires: A Historical and Political Sociology*. Oxford: Polity Press, 2021.

Körner, Axel. 'Beyond Nation States: New Perspectives on the Habsburg Empire.' *European History Quarterly* 48 no. 3 (2018): 516–533.

Lake, David A. *Hierarchy in International Relations*. Ithaca: Cornell University Press, 2011.

Lantigua, David M. *Infidels and Empires in a New World Order: Early Modern Spanish Contributions to International Legal Thought*. Cambridge: Cambridge University Press, 2020.

de Las Casas, Bartolomé. *Brevísima Relación de la Destrucción de las Indias*. Medellin: Imprenta Universidad de Antioquia, 2011.

Latour, Bruno. 'Onus Orbis Terrarum: About a Possible Shift in the Definition of Sovereignty.' *Millennium* 44 no. 3 (2016): 305–320.

Latour, Bruno. *Down to Earth: Politics in the New Climactic Regime*. Cambridge: Polity Press, 2018.

Lazier, Benjamin. 'Earthrise; or, the Globalization of the World Picture.' *American Historical Review* 116 no. 3 (2011): 602–630.

Learoyd, Arthur. 'Configurations of Semi-Sovereignty during the Long Nineteenth Century,' in Jens Bartelson, Martin Hall and Jan Teorell (eds.) *De-Centering State Making: Comparative and International Perspectives*. Cheltenham: Edward Elgar, 2018, 155–174.

Lemaignen, Robert, Léopold Sédar Senghor, and Prince Sisowath Youtévong. *La Communauté Impériale Française*. Paris: Éditions Alsatia, 1945.

Lenin, Vladimir Ilyich. *The Right of Nations to Self-Determination*. Moscow: Foreign Languages Publishing House, 1947.

Lestringant, Frank. *Mapping the Renaissance World: The Geographical Imagination in the Age of Discovery*. Cambridge: Polity Press, 1994.

Lieber, Francis. *Fragments of Political Science on Nationalism and Inter-Nationalism*. New York: Scribner, 1868.

Lieven, Dominic. 'Dilemmas of Empire 1850–1918: Power, Territory, Identity.' *Journal of Contemporary History* 34 no. 2 (1999): 163–200.

Lipset, Seymour Martin. 'Some Social Requisites of Democracy: Economic Development and Political Legitimacy.' *American Political Science Review* 53 no. 1 (1959): 69–105.

von Lisola, Franz. *The Buckler of State and Justice against the Design Manifestly Discovered of the Universal Monarchy, under the Vain Pretext of the Queen of France, Her Pretensions Translated Out of French*. London: James Flesher for Richard Royson, 1667.

Long, David and Brian C. Schmidt (eds.) *Imperialism and Internationalism in the Discipline of International Relations*. Albany: SUNY Press, 2005.

Long, David and Brian C. Schmidt. 'Introduction,' in David Long and Brian C. Schmidt (eds.) *Imperialism and Internationalism in the Discipline of International Relations*. Albany: SUNY Press, 2005, 1–11.

Lorimer, James. *The Institutes of the Law of Nations: A Treatise of the Jural Relations of Separate Political Communities*. Edinburgh: William Blackwell and Sons, 1883.

Loveman, Brian. 'U.S. Foreign Policy toward Latin America in the 19th Century,' in *Oxford Research Encyclopedia of Latin American History*, edited by William Beezley. Oxford: Oxford University Press, 2016.

Lupher, David A. *Romans in a New World: Classical Models in Sixteenth-Century Spanish America*. Ann Arbor: University of Michigan Press, 2006.

Lynch, Allen. 'Woodrow Wilson and the Principle of "National Self-Determination": A Reconsideration.' *Review of International Studies* 28 no. 2 (2002): 419–436.

MacDonald, Paul K. 'Embedded Authority: A Relational Network Approach to Hierarchy in World Politics.' *Review of International Studies* 44 no.1 (2018): 128–150.

Mackintosh, James. Substance of the speech in the House of Commons, June 15, 1824. On presenting a petition from the merchants of London for the recognition of the independent states established in the countries of America formerly subject to Spain. London: Longman, Hurst, Rees, Orme, Brown and Green, 1824.

MacMillan, Ken. *Sovereignty and Possession in the English New World: The Legal Foundations of Empire, 1576–1640*. Cambridge: Cambridge University Press, 2006.

MacQueen, Norrie. *The Decolonization of Portuguese Africa: Metropolitan Revolution and the Dissolution of Empire*. London: Longmans, 1997.

MacQueen, Norrie. 'Belated Decolonization and UN Politics against the Backdrop of the Cold War.' *Journal of Cold War Studies* 8 no. 4 (2006): 29–56.

Majumdar, Rochona. 'Postcolonial History,' in Marek Tamm and Peter Burke (eds.), *Debating New Approaches to History*. London: Bloomsbury, 2019, 49–64.

Malešević, Siniša. *Grounded Nationalisms: A Sociological Analysis*. Cambridge: Cambridge University Press, 2019.

Mamdani, Mahmood. *Neither Settler nor Native: The Making and Unmaking of Permanent Majorities*. Cambridge, MA: Harvard University Press, 2020.

Mandelbaum, Moran M. 'The Fantasy of Congruency: The Abbé Sieyès and the 'nation-state' problématique revisited.' *Philosophy & Social Criticism* 42 no. 3 (2016): 246–266.

Mandelbaum, Moran. *The Nation/State Fantasy: A Psychoanalytical Genealogy of Nationalism*. Houndsmills: Palgrave MacMillan, 2020.

de Mariana, Juan. *The General History of Spain*. London: Richard Sare & Thomas Bennet, 1699.

Markovitz, Claude. 'Cosmopolitanism and Imperialism in Nineteenth-Century British India.' *Humanity: An International Journal of Human Rights, Humanitarianism, and Development* 1 no. 1 (2021): 47–58.

Mazower, Mark. *No Enchanted Palace: The End of Empire and the Ideological Origins of the United Nations*. Princeton: Princeton University Press, 2009.

Mbembe, Achille. *Out of the Dark Night: Essays on Decolonization*. New York: Columbia University Press, 2021.

McConaughey, Meghan, Paul Musgrave, and Daniel H. Nexon. 'Beyond Anarchy: Logics of Political Organization, Hierarchy, and International Structure.' *International Theory* 10 no. 2 (2018): 181–218.

Maier, Charles S. *Once Within Borders: Territories of Power, Wealth and Belonging since 1500*. Cambridge, MA: Harvard University Press, 2016.

Malaspina, Elisabetta Fiocchi. 'Teaching International Law during the Italian Unification: A New Discipline for a New State.' *Miscellena Historico-Iuridica* 13 no. 1. (2014): 143–158.

Malcolm, Noel. 'The Crescent and the City of the Sun: Islam and the Renaissance Utopia of Tommaso Campanella.' Proceedings of the British Academy. Vol. 125. Oxford: Oxford University Press, 2004, 71–67.

Mamiani della Rovere, Terenzio Count. *Rights of Nations, or The New Law of European States Applied to the Affairs of Italy*. trans. by Roger Acton. London: W. Jeffs, 1860.

Mancini, Pasquale Stanislao. *Della nazionalita' come fondamento del diritto delle genti. Prelezione al corso di diritto internazionale e marittimo pronunziata nella Regia Universita' di Torino*. Torino: Giappachelli, 1994.

Manela, Erez. 'Asia in the Global 1919: Reimagining Territory, Identity, and Solidarity.' *The Journal of Asian Studies* 78 no. 2 (2019): 409–416.

Manela, Erez. 'Imagining Woodrow Wilson in Asia: Dreams of East-West Harmony and the Revolt against Empire in 1919.' *American Historical Review* 111 no. 5 (2006): 1327–1351.

Manela, Erez. *The Wilsonian Moment: Self-determination and the International Origins of Anticolonial Nationalism*. Oxford: Oxford University Press, 2007.

Manela, Erez. 'International Society as a Historical Subject.' *Diplomatic History* 44 no. 2 (2020): 184–209.

Mansfield, Harvey C. 'On the Impersonality of the Modern State: A Comment on Machiavelli's Use of Stato.' *American Political Science Review* 77 no. 4 (1983): 849–857.

Mantena, Karuna. 'On Gandhi's Critique of the State: Sources, Contexts, Conjunctures.' *Modern Intellectual History* 9 no. 3 (2012): 535–563.

Mantena, Karuna. 'Popular Sovereignty and Anticolonialism,' in Richard Bourke and Quentin Skinner (eds.) *Popular Sovereignty in Historical Perspective*. Cambridge: Cambridge University Press, 2016, 297–319.

von Martens, Georg Friedrich. *A Compendium of the Law of Nations Founded on the Treatises and Customs of the Modern Nations of Europe*. trans. by William Cobbett. London: Cobbett and Morgan, 1802.

Mathisen, Ralph W. 'Peregrini, Barbari, and Cives Romani: Concepts of Citizenship and the Legal Identity of Barbarians in the Later Roman Empire.' *American Historical Review* 111 no. 4 (2006): 1011–1040.

Mattern, Janice Bially and Ayşe Zarakol. 'Hierarchies in World Politics.' *International Organization* 70 no. 3 (2016): 623–654.

Mayall, James. *Nationalism and International Society*. Cambridge: Cambridge University Press, 1990.

Meinecke, Friedrich. *Cosmopolitanism and the National State*. trans. by Robert B. Kimber. Princeton: Princeton University Press, 1970.

Metha, Pratap Bhanu. 'Liberalism, Nation, and Empire,' in Sankar Muthu (ed.) *Empire in Modern Political Thought*. Cambridge: Cambridge University Press, 2012, 232–260.

Metz, Karl H. 'The Politics of Conflict: Heinrich von Treitschke and the Idea of 'Realpolitik'.' *History of Political Thought* 3 no. 2 (1982): 269–284.

Mexia, Pedro. *The Imperiall Historie: or the liues of the emperours, from Iulius Cæsar, the first founder of the Roman monarchy*. London: Mathevv Lovvnes, 1623.

Michelet, Jules. *The People*. trans. by C. Cocks. London: Longman, Brown, Green, and Longmans, 1846.

Mill, John Stuart. *Considerations on Representative Government*. New York: Henry Holt & Co, 1873.

Mill, John Stuart. *The Collected Works of John Stuart Mill*. Volume XXI, edited by John M. Robson. Toronto: University of Toronto Press, London: Routledge and Kegan Paul, 1984.

Miller, John Donald Bruce. 'The Commonwealth and World Order: The Zimmern Vision and after.' *Journal of Imperial and Commonwealth History* 8 no. 1 (1979): 159–174.

Mitchell, Audra. 'Is IR Going Extinct?' *European Journal of International Relations* 23 no. 1 (2017): 3–25.

de Montesquieu, Charles-Louis Secondat. 'Réflexions sur la Monarchie Universelle,' in *Œuvres Completes*, Tome II, Édition de Roger Caillois. Paris: Pléiade, 1951, 19–38.

Morefield, Jeanne. *Covenants without Swords: Liberal Idealism and the Spirit of Empire*. Princeton: Princeton University Press, 2005.

Morefield, Jeanne. *Empires without Imperialism: Anglo-American Decline and the Politics of Deflection*. Oxford: Oxford University Press, 2014.

Morgenthau, Hans J. *Politics among Nations: The Struggle for Peace and Power*. New York: Knopf, 1948/1960.

Moyn, Samuel and Andrew Sartori. 'Approaches to Global Intellectual History,' in Samuel Moyn and Andrew Sartori (eds.) *Global Intellectual History*. New York: Columbia University Press, 2013, 3–30.

Mukerjee, Radhakamal. *Democracies of the East: A Study in Comparative Politics*. London: P. S. King & Son, 1923.

Muldoon, James. *Empire and Order, 800–1800*. New York: St. Martin's Press, 1999.

Mulich, Jeppe. 'Empire and Violence: Continuity in the Age of Revolution,' in Tarak Barkawi and George Lawson (eds.) *The International Origins of Social and Political Theory*. Bingley: Emerald Publishing, 2017, 181–204.

Muschik, Eva-Maria. 'Managing the World: The United Nations, Decolonization, and the Strange Triumph of State Sovereignty in the 1950s and 1960s.' *Journal of Global History* 13 no. 1 (2018): 121–144.

Muthu, Sankar. *Enlightenment Against Empire*. Princeton: Princeton University Press, 2003.

Muthu, Sankar. 'Conquest, Commerce, and Cosmopolitanism in Enlightenment Political Thought,' in Sankar Muthu (ed.) *Empire and Modern Political Thought*. Cambridge: Cambridge University Press, 2012, 199–231.

Muthu, Sankar. 'Introduction,' in Sankar Muthu (ed.) *Empire in Modern Political Thought*. Cambridge: Cambridge University Press, 2012, 1–6.

Nakhimovsky, Isaac. 'Vattel's Theory of the International Order: Commerce and the Balance of Power in the Law of Nations.' *History of European Ideas* 33 no. 2 (2007): 157–173.

Nakhimovsky, Isaac. *The Closed Commercial State: Perpetual Peace and Commercial Society from Rousseau to Fichte*. Princeton: Princeton University Press, 2011.

Nakhimovsky, Isaac. 'The "Ignominious Fall of the European Commonwealth": Gentz, Hauterive, and the Armed Neutrality of 1800,' in Koen Stapelbroek (ed.) *Trade and War: The Neutrality of Commerce in the Inter-State System, Helsinki Collegium. Studies across Disciplines in the Humanities and Social Sciences*, Vol. 10. 2011, 212–228.

Nandy, Ashis. *The Intimate Enemy: Loss and Recovery of Self under Colonialism*. Oxford: Oxford University Press, 1989.

Nandy, Ashis. 'History's Forgotten Doubles.' *History and Theory* 34 no. 2 (1995): 44–66.

Nedal, Dani K. and Daniel H. Nexon, 'Anarchy and Authority: International Structure, the Balance of Power, and Hierarchy.' *Journal of Global Security Studies* 4 no. 2 (2019): 169–189.

Nehru, Jawaharlal. 'Inter-Asian Relations.' *India Quarterly* 2 no. 4 (1946): 323–327.

Nehru, Jawaharlal. Selected Speeches Vol. 1, September 1946–May 1949. Publications Division. Ministry of Information and Broadcasting, Government of India, 1949.

Nehru, Jawaharlal. *The Discovery of India*. New Delhi: Oxford University Press, 1989.

Nexon, Daniel H. *The Struggle for Power in Early Modern Europe: Religious Conflict, Dynastic Empires, and International Change*. Princeton: Princeton University Press, 2009.

Nexon, Daniel H. and Iver B. Neumann. 'Hegemonic-order Theory: A Field-theoretic Account.' *European Journal of International Relations* 24 no. 3 (2018): 662–686.

Nietzsche, Friedrich. *Twilight of the Idols*. trans. by Richard Polt. Indianapolis: Hackett, 1997.

Nkrumah, Kwame. *Neo-Colonialism: The Last Stage of Imperialism*. London: Panaf, 1970.

Nora, Pierre. 'Michelet, ou l'Hysterie Identitaire.' *L'Esprit Créateur* 46 no. 3 (2006): 6–14.

Núñez Faraco, Humberto R. 'The Entanglements of Freedom: Simón Bolívar's Jamaica Letter and Its Socio-political Context, (1810–1819).' *Global Intellectual History* 3 no. 1 (2018): 71–91.

Nyerere, Julius. 'A United States of Africa.' *Journal of Modern Africa Studies* 1 no. 1, 1963, 1–6.

Nyerere, Julius. 'Freedom and Unity.' *Transition* 14 (1964) 40–45.

Nyerere, Julius. *Freedom and Unity: Uhuru na Umoja; a selection from writings and speeches, 1952–65*. Dar es Salaam: Oxford University Press, 1967.

Obregón, Liliana. 'Between Civilisation and Barbarism: Creole Interventions in International Law.' *Third World Quarterly* 27 no. 5 (2006): 815–832.

Obregón, Liliana. 'Completing Civilization: Creole Consciousness and International Law in Nineteenth Century Latin America,' in Anne Orford (ed.) *International Law and Its Others*. Cambridge: Cambridge University Press, 2006, 247–264.

Obregón, Liliana. 'The Civilized and the Uncivilized,' in Anne Peters and Bardo Fassbender (eds) *The Oxford Handbook of the History of Public International Law*. Oxford: Oxford University Press, 2012, 917–939.

Obregón Tarazona, Liliana. 'Writing International Legal History: An Overview.' *Monde(s)* 7 no. 1 (2015): 95–112.

Ochoa Espejo, Paulina. *On Borders: Territories, Legitimacy, and the Rights of Place*. Oxford: Oxford University Press, 2020.

Ohji, Kenta. 'Civilisation et Naissance de l'Histoire Mondiale Dans l'Historie des Deux Indes de Raynal.' *Revue de Synthèse* 129 no. 1 (2008): 57–83.

Oliver, Kelly. *Earth & World: Philosophy after the Apollo Missions*. New York: Columbia University Press, 2015.

Onuf, Peter S. and Nicholas Greenwood Onuf. *Federal Union, Modern World: The Law of Nations in an Age of Revolutions, 1776–1814*. Madison: Madison House, 1993.

Oppenheim, Lassa. *International Law: A Treatise*. London & New York: Longmans, Green & Co, 1905.

Osiander, Andreas 'Sovereignty, International Relations, and the Westphalian Myth.' *International Organization* 55 no. 2 (2001): 251–228.

Osterhammel, Jürgen. *The Transformation of the World: A Global History of the Nineteenth Century*. Princeton: Princeton University Press, 2014.

Paddock, Troy R. E. 'Rethinking Friedrich Meinecke's Historicism.' *Rethinking History* 10 no. 1 (2006): 95–108.

Pagden, Anthony. *The Fall of Natural Man: The American Indian and the Origins of Comparative Ethnology*. Cambridge University Press, 1986.

Pagden, Anthony. 'Dispossessing the Barbarian: The Language of Spanish Thomism and the Debate over the Property Rights of the American Indians.' in Anthony Pagden (ed.) *The Languages of Political Theory in Early-Modern Europe*. Cambridge: Cambridge University Press, 1987, 79–98.

Pagden, Anthony. 'Instruments of Empire: Tommaso Campanella and the Universal Monarchy of Spain,' in Anthony Pagden (ed.) *Spanish Imperialism and the Political Imagination*. New Haven: Yale University Press, 1990, 37–64.

Pagden, Anthony. *European Encounters with the New World: From Renaissance to Romanticism*. New Haven: Yale University Press, 1993.

Pagden, Anthony. *Lords of All the World. Ideologies of Empire in Spain, Britain and France c.1500–c.1800*. New Haven: Yale University Press, 1995.

Pagden, Anthony. 'Fellow Citizens and Imperial Subjects: Conquest and Sovereignty in Europe's Overseas Empires.' *History & Theory* 44 no. 4 (2005): 28–46.

Pagden, Anthony. *Burdens of Empire: 1539 to the present*. Cambridge: Cambridge University Press, 2015.

Paine, Thomas. *Common Sense*. Girard, KA.: Haldeman-Julius, sa.

Paine, Thomas. *Letter addressed to the Abbé Raynal on the Affairs of North America, in which the mistakes in the Abbé's account of the revolution of America are corrected and cleared up*. Boston, MA.: Benjamin Edes & Sons, 1782.

Panizza, Diego. 'Alberico Gentili's *De armis Romanis*: The Roman Model of the Just Empire,' in Benedict Kingsbury and Benjamin Straumann (eds.) *The Roman Foundations of the Law of Nations: Alberico Gentili and the Justice of Empire*. Oxford: Oxford University Press, 2010, 53–84.

Pappé, H. O. 'Mill and Tocqueville.' *Journal of the History of Ideas* 25, no. 2 (1964): 217–234.

Paquette, Gabriel. 'The Intellectual Context of British Diplomatic Recognition of the South American Republics, c. 1800–1830.' *Journal of Transatlantic Studies* 2 no. 1 (2004): 75–95.

Paquette, Gabriel. 'The Dissolution of the Spanish Atlantic Monarchy.' *The Historical Journal* 52, no. 1 (2009): 175–212.

Paquette, Gabriel. *The European Seaborne Empires: From the Thirty Years War to the Age of Revolutions*. New Haven: Yale University Press, 2019.

Parekh, Bhikhu. 'Nehru and the National Philosophy of India.' *Economic and Political Weekly* 26 no 1/2 (1991): 35–48.

Pattberg, Philipp and Oscar Widerberg. 'Theorising Global Environmental Governance: Key Findings and Future Questions.' *Millennium* 43 no. 2 (2015): 684–705.

Pedersen, Susan. *The Guardians: The League of Nations and the Crisis of Empire*. Oxford: Oxford University Press, 2015.

Peltonen, Markku. 'Politics and Science: Francis Bacon and the True Greatness of States.' *Historical Journal* 35, no. 2 (1992): 279–305.

Pettit, Philip. *Republicanism: A Theory of Freedom and Government*. Oxford: Oxford University Press, 1997.

Petty, William. *Political Arithmetick: or A discourse concerning the value of lands, people, buildings ... As the same relates to every country in general, but more particularly to the territories of His Majesty of Great Britain, and his neighbours of Holland, Zealand, and France*. London: R. Clavel, 1690.

Pflanze, Otto. 'Nationalism in Europe, 1848–1871.' *The Review of Politics* 28 no. 2 (1966): 129–143.

Phạm, Quỳnh N and Robbie Shilliam. (eds.) *Meanings of Bandung: Postcolonial Orders and Decolonial Visions*. London: Rowman & Littlefield, 2016.

Phạm, Quỳnh N. and Robbie Shilliam. 'Reviving Bandung,' in Quỳnh N. Phạm and Robbie Shilliam (eds.) *Meanings of Bandung: Postcolonial Orders and Decolonial Visions*. London: Rowman & Littlefield, 2016, 3–20.

Phillips, Andrew. *War, Religion and Empire: The Transformation of International Orders*. Cambridge: Cambridge University Press, 2010.

Phillips, Andrew and Jason C. Sharman. *International Order in Diversity: War, Trade and Rule in the Indian Ocean*. Cambridge: Cambridge University Press, 2015.

Philpott, Daniel. *Revolutions in Sovereignty*. Princeton: Princeton University Press, 2001.

Pincus, Steven. 'The English Debate over Universal Monarchy,' in John Robertson. (ed.) *A Union for Empire: Political thought and the British Union of 1707*. Cambridge: Cambridge University Press, 1995, 37–62.

Pincus, Steven. 'The Making of a Great Power? Universal Monarchy, Political Economy, and the Transformation of English Political Culture.' *European Legacy* 5 no. 4 (2000): 531–545.

Pincus, Steven. 'Addison's Empire: Whig Conceptions of Empire in the Early 18th Century.' *Parliamentary History* 31 no. 1 (2012): 99–117.

Pitts, Jennifer. *A Turn to Empire: The Rise of Imperial Liberalism in Britain and France*. Princeton: Princeton University Press, 2005.

Pitts, Jennifer. 'Political Theory of Empire and Imperialism.' *Annual Review of Political Science* 13 (2010): 211–235.

Pitts, Jennifer. 'Empire and Legal Universalisms in the Eighteenth Century.' *American Historical Review* 117 no. 1 (2012): 92–121.

Pitts, Jennifer. *Boundaries of the International: Law and Empire*. Cambridge, MA: Harvard University Press, 2018.

Plamenatz, John. *On Alien Rule and Self Government*. London: Longmans, 1960.

Platt, Charles Malcom. 'A Triad of Political Conceptions: State, Sovereign, Government.' *Political Science Quarterly* 10 no. 2 (1895): 292–323.

Pocock, J. G. A. *Barbarism and Religion III. The First Decline and Fall.* Cambridge: Cambridge University Press, 2003.

Pocock, J. G. A. *Barbarism and Religion IV. Barbarians, Savages and Empires*. Cambridge: Cambridge University Press, 2005.

Pocock, J. G. A. 'Commerce, Credit, and Sovereignty: The Nation-State as Historical Critique,' in Béla Kapossy. (ed.) *Markets, Morals, Politics: Jealousy of Trade and the History of Political Thought*. Cambridge, MA.: Harvard University Press, 2018), 265–284.

Pollock, Sheldon. *The Language of the Gods in the World of Men: Sanskrit, Culture, and Power in Premodern India*. Berkeley: University of California Press, 2006.

Pons, Alain. 'De la 'nature commune des nations' au Peuple romantique. Note sur Vico et Michelet.' *Romantisme* 5 no. 9 (1975): 39–49.

Price, Roger. *The French Second Empire: An Anatomy of Political Power*. Cambridge: Cambridge University Press, 2001.

Prott, Volker. *The Politics of Self-Determination. Remaking Territories and National Identities in Europe, 1917–1923*. Oxford: Oxford University Press, 2016.

Prozorov, Sergei. *Ontology and World Politics: Void Universalism I*. London & New York: Routledge, 2013.

Pye, Lucian W. 'Introduction: Political Culture and Political Development,' in Lucian W. Pye and Sidney Verba (eds.) *Political Culture and Political Development*. Princeton, NJ: Princeton University Press, 1965, 3–26.

Pye, Lucian W. and Sidney Verba (eds.) *Political Culture and Political Development*. Princeton, NJ: Princeton University Press, 1965.

Rai, Lala Lajpat. *Self-Determination for India*. New York: India Home Rule League of America, 1919.

von Ranke, Leopold. '*The Great Powers*,' in Theodore H. von Laue (ed.) *Leopold Ranke: The Formative Years*. Princeton: Princeton University Press, 1950, 181–218.

Raynal, Abbé Guillaume-Thomas-François. *A Philosophical and Political History of the Settlements and Trade of the Europeans in the East and West Indies.* trans. by J. O. Justamond. London: W. Strahan and T. Cadell, 1783.

Recchia, Stefano and Nadia Urbinati. (eds.) *A Cosmopolitanism of Nations. Giuseppe Mazzini's Writings on Democracy, Nation Building, and International Relations.* Princeton: Princeton University Press, 2009.

Renan, Ernest. 'What is a Nation?' in Geoff Eley and Ronald Grigor Suny (eds.) *Becoming National: A Reader.* Oxord: Oxford University Press, 1996, 42–55.

Richardson, John. *The Language of Empire: Rome and the Idea of Empire from the Third Century BC to the Second Century AD.* Cambridge: Cambridge University Press, 2008.

Richardson, John. 'The Meaning of Imperium in the Last Century BC and the First AD,' in Benedict Kingsbury and Benjamin Straumann. (eds.) *The Roman Foundations of the Law of Nations: Alberico Gentili and the Justice of Empire.* Oxford: Oxford University Press, 2010, 21–29.

Robertson, John. 'Empire and Union: Two Concepts of the Early Modern European Political Order,' in John Robertson (ed.) *A Union for Empire. Political Thought and the British Union of 1707.* Cambridge: Cambridge University Press, 1995, 3–36.

Robertson, John. 'Gibbon's Roman Empire as a Universal Monarchy: The Decline and Fall and the Imperial Idea in Early Modern Europe', in Rosamond McKitterick and Roland Quinault (eds.) *Edward Gibbon and Empire.* Cambridge: Cambridge University Press, 1997, 247–270.

Robertson, John. *The Case for the Enlightenment. Scotland and Naples 1680–1760.* Cambridge: Cambridge University Press, 2005.

Robertson, William. *The History of the Reign of the Emperor Charles V, with a view of the Progress of Society in Europe, from the Subversion of the Roman Empire to the Beginning of the Sixteenth Century*, Vols. I & II. London: Routledge, 1857.

Rodriguez, Jaime E. *The Independence of Spanish America.* Cambridge: Cambridge University Press, 1998.

Rostow, Walt W. *Politics and the Stages of Growth.* Cambridge: Cambridge University Press, 1971.

Rothschild, Emma. 'Language and Empire, c. 1800.' *Historical Research* 78 no. 200 (2005): 208–229.

Rowley, David G. 'Giuseppe Mazzini and the Democratic Logic of Nationalism.' *Nations and Nationalism* 18 no. 1 (2012): 39–56.

Rubinelli, Lucia. *Constituent Power: A History.* Cambridge: Cambridge University Press, 2020.

Sabato, Hilda. 'On Political Citizenship in Nineteenth-Century Latin America.' *The American Historical Review* 106 no. 4 (2001): 1290–1315.

Sabato, Hilda. *Republics of the New World. The Revolutionary Political Experiment in 19th-Century Latin America.* Princeton: Princeton University Press, 2018.

Said, Edward W. *Orientalism.* New York: Pantheon Books, 1978.

Saramago, José. *The Elephant's Journey.* London: Vintage Books, 2010.

Sartre, Jean-Paul. 'Introduction,' in Albert Memmi (ed.) *The Colonizer and the Colonized.* Boston: Beacon Press, 1967, xxi–xxxi.

Scarfi, Juan Pablo. 'In the Name of the Americas: The Pan-American redefinition of the Monroe doctrine and the emerging language of American international law in the Western Hemisphere, 1898–1933.' *Diplomatic History* 40 no. 2 (2016): 189–218.

Schofield, Philip. (ed.) *Colonies, Commerce, and Constitutional Law: Rid Yourselves of Ultramaria and Other Writings on Spain and Spanish America.* Oxford: Clarendon Press, 1995.

Selby, Jan. 'Edward W. Said: Truth, Justice and Nationalism.' *Interventions: International Journal of Postcolonial Studies* 8 no. 1 (2006): 40–55.

Seville, Isidore of. *De Natura Rerum.* trans. by Calvin B. Kendall and Faith Wallis. Liverpool: Liverpool University Press, 2016.

Schmidt, Sebastian, 'To Order the Minds of Scholars: The discourse of the Peace of Westphalia in international relations literature.' *International Studies Quarterly* 55 no. 3 (2011): 601–623.

Schröder, Peter. 'The Concepts of Universal Monarchy and Balance of Power in the First Half of the Seventeenth Century – A Case Study,' in Martti Koskenniemi, Walter Rech, and Manuel Jiménez Fonseca (eds.) *International Law and Empire: Historical Explorations.* Oxford: Oxford University Press, 2017, 83–100.

Schulz, Carsten-Andreas. 'Civilisation, Barbarism and the Making of Latin America's Place in 19th-century International Society.' *Millennium* 42 no. 3 (2014): 837–859.

Schulz, Carsten-Andreas. 'Territorial Sovereignty and the End of Intercultural Diplomacy along the "Southern frontier".' *European Journal of International Relations* 25 no. 3 (2019): 878–903.

Senghor, Léopold Sédar and Kenneth Kirkwood. 'Negritude and African Socialism,' in Pieter Hendrik Coetzee and Abraham Pieter Jacob Roux (eds.) *The African Philosophy Reader.* London: Routledge, 1998, 438–448.

Seton-Watson, Hugh. *Nations and States: An Enquiry into the Origins of Nations and the Politics of Nationalism.* London: Taylor & Francis, 1977.

Sewell, William H. *A Rhetoric of Bourgeois Revolution: The Abbé Sieyès and "What Is the Third Estate?".* Durham, NC: Duke University Press, 1994.

Sharman, Jason C. *Empires of the Weak: The Real Story of European Expansion and the Creation of the New World Order*. Princeton: Princeton University Press, 2019.

Sharman, Jason C. and Andrew Phillips, *Outsourcing Empire: How Company-States Made the Modern World*. Princeton: Princeton University Press, 2020.

Sheehan, James J. 'The Problem of Sovereignty in European History.' *The American Historical Review* 111 no.1 (2006): 1–15.

Shilliam, Robbie. *Decolonizing Politics*. Cambridge: Polity Press, 2021.

Shils, Edward. 'On the Comparative Study of New States,' in Clifford Geertz (ed.) *Old Societies and New States: The Quest for Modernity in Asia and Africa*. New York: The Free Press, 1963, 1–26.

Shimazu, Naoko. 'Diplomacy as Theatre: Staging the Bandung Conference of 1955.' *Modern Asian Studies* 48 no. 1 2014: 225–252.

Simangan, Dahlia. 'Where Is the Anthropocene? IR in a New Geological Epoch.' *International Affairs* 96 no.1 (2020): 211–224.

Singh Metha, Uday. 'Edmund Burke on Empire, Self-Understanding, and Sympathy,' in Sankar Muthu (ed.) *Empire in Modern Political Thought*. Cambridge: Cambridge University Press, 2012, 155–183.

Singh Mehta, Uday. *Liberalism and Empire. A Study in Nineteenth-Century British Liberal Thought*. Chicago: University of Chicago Press, 1999.

Skinner, Quentin. *Foundations of Modern Political Thought*, Vol II: The Reformation. Cambridge: Cambridge University Press, 1978.

Skinner, Quentin. *Liberty Before Liberalism*. Cambridge: Cambridge University Press, 1998.

Skinner, Quentin. 'The State,' in Terence Ball, James Farr, and Russell T. Hanson (eds.), *Political Innovation and Conceptual Change*. Cambridge: Cambridge University Press, 1989, 90–131.

Skinner, Quentin. 'A Genealogy of the Modern State.' *Proceedings of the British Academy* 162 (2009): 325–370.

Skinner, Quentin. 'The Sovereign State: A Genealogy,' in Hent Kalmo and Quentin Skinner (eds.) *Sovereignty in Fragments. The Past, Present, and Future of a Contested Concept*. Cambridge: Cambridge University Press, 2010, 26–46.

Sieyès, Comte Emmanuel Joseph. *What Is the Third Estate?* trans. by M. Blondel and edited by S. E. Finer. London: Pall Mall Press, 1964.

Simon, Joshua. *The Ideology of Creole Revolution. Imperialism and Independence in American and Latin American Political Thought*. Cambridge: Cambridge University Press, 2017.

Sloterdijk, Peter. *Globes: Spheres II*. trans. by Wieland Hoban. Cambridge, MA: MIT Press 2014.

Smith, Adam. *An Inquiry Into the Nature and Causes of the Wealth of Nations*, edited by Edwin Cannan, Vol. 2. London: Methuen, 1904.

Spanu, Maja. 'The Hierarchical Society: The Politics of Self-determination and the Constitution of New States after 1919.' *European Journal of International Relations* 26 no. 2 (2020): 372–396.

Spruyt, Hendrik. 'The End of Empire and the Extension of the Westphalian System: The Normative Basis of the Modern State Order.' *International Studies Review* 2 no. 2 (2000): 65–92.

Spruyt, Hendrik. *The World Imagined: Collective Beliefs and Political Order in the Sinocentric, Islamic and Southeast Asian International Societies*. Cambridge: Cambridge University Press, 2020.

von Steck, Johann Christian Wilhelm. 'Versuch von Erkennung der Unabhängikeit einer Nation, und eienes Staates', in Johann Christian Wilhelm Steck, Versuche über Verschiedene Materien politischen und rechtlicher Kenntnisse. Berlin, 1783, 49–56.

Stern, Philip J. *The Company-State: Corporate Sovereignty and the Early Modern Foundations of the British Empire in India*. Oxford: Oxford University Press, 2011.

Stone, Alison. 'Hegel and Colonialism.' *Hegel Bulletin* 41 no. 2 (2017): 247–270.

Strohmeyer, Arno. 'Ideas of Peace in Early Modern Models of International Order: Universal Monarchy and Balance of Power in Comparison,' in Jost Dülffer and Robert Frank. (eds.) *Peace, War and Gender from Antiquity to the Present. Cross-cultural Perspectives*. Essen: Klartext Verlag, 2009, 65–80.

Subrahmanyam, Sanjay. 'A Tale of Three Empires: Mughals, Ottomans, and Habsburgs in a Comparative Context.' *Common Knowledge* 12 no. 1 (2006): 66–92.

Suganami, Hidemi. 'A Note on the Origin of the Word "International".' *Review of International Studies* 4 no. 3 (1978): 226–232.

Sukarno. Opening Address to the Bandung Conference, April 18, 1955. Jakarta: Ministry of Foreign Affairs, 1955.

Sukarno. 'Nationalism, Islam, and Marxism.' trans. by Karel H. Warouw and Peter D. Weldon. Ithaca, Modern Indonesia Project, Cornell University, 1970.

Sultan, Nazmul S. 'Self-Rule and the Problem of Peoplehood in Colonial India.' *American Political Science Review* 114 no. 1 (2020): 81–94.

Sultan, Nazmul S. 'Between the Many and the One: Anticolonial Federalism and Popular Sovereignty.' *Political Theory* 50 no. 2 (2022): 247–274.

Summers, James. *Peoples and International Law*. Leiden: Brill, 2013.

Suri, Jeremi. 'The Cold War, Decolonization, and Global Social Awakenings: Historical intersections.' *Cold War History* 6 no. 3 (2006): 353–363.

Tagore, Rabindranath. *Nationalism*. London: Macmillan, 1917.

Tan, See Seng and Amitav Acharya. (eds.) Bandung Revisited: The legacy of the 1955 Asian-African conference for international order. Singapore: National University Press, 2008.

Teschke, Benno. *The Myth of 1648: Class, Geopolitics, and the Making of Modern International Relations*. London: Verso, 2003.

Thakur, Vineet. 'An Asian Drama: The Asian Relations Conference, 1947.' *The International History Review* 41 no. 3 (2019): 673–695.

Thom, Martin. *Republics, Nations and Tribes*. London: Verso: 1995.

Thomas, Martin and Andrew S. Thompson, 'Rethinking Decolonization: A New Research Agenda for the Twenty-first Century,' in Martin Thomas and Andrew S. Thompson (eds.) *The Oxford Handbook of the Ends of Empire*. Oxford: Oxford University Press, 2019, 1–26.

Thompson, Martyn P. 'Ideas of Europe during the French Revolution and Napoleonic Wars.' *Journal of the History of Ideas* 55 no. 1 (1994): 37–58.

Throntveit, Trygve. 'The Fable of the Fourteen Points: Woodrow Wilson and National self-determination.' *Diplomatic History* 35 no. 3 (2011): 445–481.

Tilly, Charles. 'States and Nationalism in Europe 1492–1992.' *Theory and Society* 23 no. 1 (1994): 131–146.

Tocqueville, Alexis de. *Writings on Empire and Slavery*, edited by Jennifer Pitts. Baltimore: Johns Hopkins University Press, 2001.

Todorov, Tzvetan. *The Conquest of America: The Question of the Other*. New York: Harper & Row, 1984.

de Torres, José Camilo. *Representacion del Cabildo de Bogota Capital del Nuevo Reino de Granada a la Suprema Junta Central de Espana, 1809*. Bogota: N. Lora, 1832.

Touré, Ahmed Sékou. 'The Republic of Guinea,' Address at Chatham House, 13 November 1959, *International Affairs* 36 no. 2 (1960): 168–173.

Touré, Ahmed Sékou. *Expérience Guinéenne et Unité Africaine*. Paris: Présence Africaine, 1961.

Touré, Ahmed Sékou. *Afrika and Imperialism*. Newark, NJ.: Jihad Publishing, 1973.

Tourinho, Marcos. 'The Co-Constitution of Order,' *International Organization* 75 no. 2 (2021): 258–281.

von Treitschke, Heinrich. *Politics*, Vols. 1–2. trans. by Blanche Dugdale and Torben de Bille. New York: Macmillan, 1916.

Tully, James. 'The Unfreedom of the Moderns in Comparison to Their Ideals of Constitutional Democracy.' *The Modern Law Review* 65, no. 2 (2002): 204–228.

Tully, James. 'Modern Constitutional Democracy and Imperialism.' *Osgoode Hall Law Journal* 46 no. 3 (2008): 461–493.

Ullmann, Walter. 'This Realm of England Is an Empire.' *The Journal of Ecclesiastical History* 30 no. 2 (1979): 175–203.

Umar, Ahmad Rizky Mardhatillah. 'Rethinking the Legacies of Bandung Conference: Global Decolonization and the Making of Modern International Order.' *Asian Politics & Policy* 11 no. 3 (2019): 461–478.

United Nations, Declaration on the Granting of Independence to Colonial Countries and Peoples, 1960.

United Nations, International Covenant on Civil and Political Rights, 1966.

United Nations, International Covenant on Economic, Social and Cultural Rights, 1966.

Urbinati, Nadia. 'The Legacy of Kant: Giuseppe Mazzini's Cosmopolitanism of Nations,' in Chistopher A. Bayly and Eugenio F. Biagini (eds.), *Giuseppe Mazzini and the Globalization of Democratic Nationalism 1830–1920*. Oxford: Oxford University Press, 2008, 11–36.

Valdez, Inés. *Transnational Cosmopolitanism: Kant, Du Bois, and Justice as a Political Craft*. Cambridge: Cambridge University Press, 2019.

Valdez, Inés. 'Cosmopolitanism without National Consciousness is not Radical: Creolizing Gordon's Fanon through Du Bois.' *Philosophy and Global Affairs*, 2021.

Varouxakis, Georgios. '"Patriotism", "Cosmopolitanism" and "Humanity" in Victorian Political Thought.' *European Journal of Political Theory* 5 vo. 1 (2006): 100–118.

Varouxakis, Georgios. '1848 and British Political Thought on 'The Principle of Nationality,' in Douglas Moggach and Gareth Stedman Jones (eds.) *The 1848 Revolutions and European Political Thought*. Cambridge: Cambridge University Press, 2018, 140–161.

de Vattel, Emer. *The Law of Nations, Or, Principles of the Law of Nature, Applied to the Conduct and Affairs of Nations and Sovereigns, with Three Early Essays on the Origin and Nature of Natural Law and on Luxury*, edited and with an introduction by Béla Kapossy and Richard Whatmore. Indianapolis: Liberty Fund, 2008.

Verba, Sidney. 'Comparative Political Culture,' in Lucian W. Pye and Sidney Verba (eds.) *Political Culture and Political Development*. Princeton, NJ: Princeton University Press, 1965, 512–560.

Vick, Brian E. *The Congress of Vienna: Power and Politics after Napoleon*. Cambridge, MA.: Harvard University Press, 2014.

Vincent, Andrew. *Nationalism and Particularity*. Cambridge: Cambridge University Press, 2002.

Viola, Lora Anne. *The Closure of the International System: How Institutions Create Political Equalities and Hierarchies*. Cambridge: Cambridge University Press, 2020.

Vitalis, Robert. 'The Noble American Science of Imperial Relations and Its Laws of Race Development.' *Comparative Studies in Society and History* 52 no. 4 (2010): 909–938.

Vitalis, Robert. 'The Midnight Ride of Kwame Nkrumah and Other Fables of Bandung (Ban-doong).' *Humanity: An International Journal of Human Rights, Humanitarianism, and Development* 4 no. 2 (2013): 261–288.

Vitalis, Robert. *White World Order, Black Power Politics*. Ithaca: Cornell University Press, 2016.

de Vitoria, Francisco. 'de Indis.' in Jeremy Lawrance and Anthony Pagden (eds.) *Vitoria: Political Writings*. Cambridge: Cambridge University Press, 1991.

Vives, Juan. *On Education*. trans. by Foster Watson. Cambridge: Cambridge University Press, 1913.

Walker, Lydia. 'Decolonization in the 1960s: On Legitimate and Illegitimate Nationalist Claims-making.' *Past & Present* 242 no. 1 (2019): 227–264.

Walker, R. B. J. *After the Globe, before the World*. London & New York: Routledge, 2010.

Waltz, Kenneth N. *Theory of International Politics*. Reading: Addison-Wesley, 1979.

Wambaugh, Sarah. *The Doctrine of National Self-determination: A Study of the Theory and Practice of Plebiscites with a Collection of Official Documents*, Vol. 1. New York: Oxford University Press, 1919.

Watson, Adam. 'New States in the Americas,' in Hedley Bull and Adam Watson (eds.) *The Expansion of International Society*. Oxford: Clarendon Press, 1984.

Weitz, Eric D. 'From the Vienna to the Paris System: International Politics and the Entangled Histories of Human Rights, Forced Deportations, and Civilizing Missions.' *The American Historical Review* 113 no. 5 (2008): 1313–1343.

Weitz, Eric D. 'Self-Determination: How a German Enlightenment Idea became the Slogan of National Liberation and a Human Right.' *The American Historical Review* 120 no. 2 (2015): 462–496.

Westad, Odd Arne. *The Global Cold War: Third World Interventions and the Making of Our Times*. Cambridge: Cambridge University Press, 2005.

Westlake, John. *International Law, Vol. 1: Peace*. Cambridge: Cambridge University Press, 1910.

Weststeijn, Arthur. 'Provincializing Grotius: International Law and Empire in a Seventeenth-Century Malay Mirror,' in Martti Koskenniemi, Walter Rech, and Manuel Jiménez Fonseca. (eds.) *International Law and Empire: Historical Explorations*. Oxford: Oxford University Press, 2017, 21–38.

Whatmore, Richard. *Against War and Empire: Geneva, Britain, and France in the Eighteenth Century*. New Haven: Yale University Press, 2012.

Whatmore, Richard. 'Liberty, War and Empire: Overcoming the Rich State-poor State Problem 1789–1815,' in Béla Kapossy, Isaac Nakhimovsky and Richard Whatmore (eds.) *Commerce and Peace in the Enlightenment*. Cambridge: Cambridge University Press, 2017, 216–243.

Whatmore, Richard and Knud Haakonssen. 'Global Possibilities in Intellectual History: A Note on Practice.' *Global Intellectual History* 2 no. 1 (2017): 18–29.

Wheaton, Henry. *Elements of International Law*. Boston: Little, Brown & Co., 1866.

Whelan, Frederick G. 'Robertson, Hume, and the Balance of Power.' *Hume Studies* 21 no. 2 (1995): 315–332.

Wight, Martin. 'International Legitimacy.' *International Relations* 4 no. 1 (1972): 1–28.

Wilder, Gary. *Freedom Time: Négritude, Decolonization, and the Future of the World*. Durham, NC.: Duke University Press, 2015.

Wilson, Eric. 'The VOC, Corporate Sovereignty and the Republican Subtext of *De iure praedae*,' in Hans W. Blom (ed.) *Property, Piracy and Punishment: Hugo Grotius on War and Booty in De iure praedae – Concepts and Contexts*. Leiden: Brill, 2009: 310–340.

Wilson, Woodrow. *The Bases of Durable Peace as Voiced by President Wilson*. Chicago: The Union League Club of Chicago, 1918.

Wittgenstein, Ludwig. *Philosophical Investigations*. trans. by G. E. M. Anscombe. Oxford: Basil Blackwell, 1958.

Wokler, Robert. 'Contextualizing Hegel's Phenomenology of the French Revolution and the Terror.' *Political Theory* 26 no. 1 (1998): 33–55.

Wokler, Robert. 'The Enlightenment and the French Revolutionary Birth Pangs of Modernity.' in Björn Wittrock, Johan Heilbron and Lars Magnusson (eds.) *The Rise of the Social Sciences and the Formation of Modernity*. Dordrecht: Springer, 1998, 35–76.

Wright, Quincy. 'Some Thoughts about Recognition.' *American Journal of International Law* 44 no. 3 (1950): 548–559.

Wright, Quincy. 'Recognition and Self-Determination.' *Proceedings of the American Society of International Law at Its Annual Meeting* 48 (1954): 23–37.

Yack, Bernard. 'Popular Sovereignty and Nationalism.' *Political Theory* 29 no. 4 (2001): 517–536.

Yack, Bernard. *Nationalism and the Moral Psychology of Community*. Chicago: University of Chicago Press, 2012.

Yamada, Norihito. 'George Canning and the Spanish Question, September 1822 to March 1823.' *The Historical Journal* 52 no. 2 (2009): 343–362.

Yates, Frances A. *Astraea: The Imperial Theme in the Sixteen Century*. London: Routledge & Kegan Paul, 1975.

Zarakol, Ayşe. *After Defeat: How the East Learned to Live with the West*. Cambridge: Cambridge University Press, 2010.

Zarakol, Ayşe. *Before the West: The Rise and Fall of Eastern World Orders*. Cambridge: Cambridge University Press, 2022.

Zarakol, Ayşe (ed.) *Hierarchies in World Politics*. Cambridge: Cambridge University Press, 2017.

Zernatto, Guido and Alfonso G. Mistretta. 'Nation: The History of a Word.' *The Review of Politics* 6 no. 3 (1944): 351–366.

Zimmerman, Andrew. 'Race and World Politics: Germany in the Age of Imperialism, 1878–1914.' *The Oxford Handbook of Modern German History*. Oxford: Oxford University Press, 2011, 359–376.

Zimmern, Alfred. *Nationality and Government, and Other Wartime Essays*. London Chatto & Windus, 1918.

Zimmern, Alfred. *The Third British Empire*. London: Humphrey Milford, 1926.

Zimmern, Alfred. *Prospects of Democracy and Other Essays*. London: Chatto & Windus, 1929.

Index

Printed in the USA
CPSIA information can be obtained
at www.ICGtesting.com
CBHW071444180524
8768CB00007B/319